The Division of Rationalized Labor

The Division of
Rationalized Labor

MICHELLE JACKSON

HARVARD UNIVERSITY PRESS
Cambridge, Massachusetts
London, England
2025

EU GPSR Authorised Representative
LOGOS EUROPE 9 rue Nicolas Poussin, 17000, LA ROCHELLE, France
E-mail: Contact@logoseurope.eu

Cataloging-in-Publication Data is available from the Library of Congress

9780674296220 (cloth)
9780674302167 (epub)
9780674302174 (pdf)

For David B. Grusky

CONTENTS

The Division of Rationalized Labor

The Great
Fragmentation?

C leaning the wire, drawing the wire, straightening the wire. Cutting the heads, softing the heads, heading the shanks. 9.06 seconds per pin. 480,000 pins per day. Eighteen separate tasks. Ten specialized workers.

So Adam Smith demonstrated the power of the division of labor. No single worker could perform the eighteen tasks with sufficient skill or speed to match the output of specialized workers.[1] For every person skilled in drawing the wire, there is to be found a person skilled in cutting the heads, and for every person skilled in cutting the heads, there is to be found a person skilled in heading the shanks. The logic of the division of labor inexorably pushes toward a narrowing of job tasks, increased output, and economic growth. It is a logic that shapes our economy and society, providing the foundation for economic exchange, social integration, and social progress.

But the division of labor plays a curious role in contemporary sociological research. It is everywhere and nowhere. It is at once recognized as a fundamental and powerful force, and ignored in most explanations of social phenomena. It is one of the key concepts of social science, and yet we have no good measure of it. While some components of the specialization process—including automation, deskilling, and alienation—are carefully measured and extensively discussed, we do not know whether the division of labor occurs more quickly at some points in time than at others, or if it is more pronounced in some places than in others.[2] We do not know if occupations today are more specialized than in the past, or if workers are undertaking fewer tasks relative to their forebears. And in contrast to the other social forces highlighted in early social scientific work—such as capital accumulation, commodification, or economic growth—the division of labor is rarely highlighted in discussions of important social problems.

In this book, I look the division of labor squarely in the eye. I argue that our standard assumptions about how the division of labor marches forward over time are not well founded. I show that changes in our science and society have led to occupations, firms, and even industries being burdened with an ever-wider range of tasks. The ongoing rationalization of society—as revealed in the growing emphasis on science, regulation, and bureaucratic organization—comes together with changes in scientific reasoning to broaden occupational purviews: to get the job done, an ever-wider range of "complications" must now be taken into account. Even as specialization pressures have been brought to bear on all manner of occupations, the effect of these changes has been to dramatically expand the range of tasks that are seen as central to different types of work, fundamentally reshaping the nature of labor in late-industrial societies.

THE DIVISION OF LABOR

Classical theories of the division of labor can be traced back to one simple proposition: specialization brings productive advantages. This is a proposition that appears in almost all of the classical treatments of specialization, and once it is accepted, a number of important implications follow.

First, the range of tasks undertaken by individual workers is likely to become narrower over time. Pin factories in which work is divided among specialized workers will produce more than pin factories in which workers take on a broader range of tasks, with the result that those in the business of producing pins are likely to alter their production processes to allow workers to become more specialized as time goes on. Smith argues that there are several productive advantages associated with more-specialized workers. Most obviously, specializing in a given task means that a worker is likely to become more proficient in performing that task; performing the same task repeatedly builds the skills required to perform the task well. Specializing also saves the time required to switch tasks. Cleaning the wire requires different tools than drawing the wire and cutting the heads, and the tasks might need to be performed in different locations. A single person switching between tasks is therefore likely to be less productive than multiple people maintaining focus on individual tasks. And specialization makes possible the use of labor-saving machines: a device that replaces the whole process of manufacture is complicated to design and produce, but a device that replaces a single task is more viable. All three factors push in the direction of increasing task specialization at the level of the individual worker.

To Smith's highlighted advantages of specialization, we may add another, first identified by Charles Babbage (1833), who argued that the most important productive advantage of specialization is that it makes it possible for the employer to purchase only as much labor of a given type as is required to produce the product. As Babbage writes (1864: 436), "By dividing the work to be executed into different processes, each requiring different degrees of skill, or of force, the master manufacturer can purchase exactly that precise quantity of both which is necessary for each process. Whereas if the whole work were executed by one workman, that person must possess sufficient skill to perform the most difficult, and sufficient strength to execute the most laborious, of those operations into which the art is divided." This insight is particularly valuable, as it highlights the extent to which specialization is intimately connected to the degradation of work and a decline in worker power (e.g., see Marx 1867). The quote also suggests that specialization allows workers with different skill profiles to be parceled off into different specialized occupations, a feature that becomes increasingly important as the labor market transitions from manufacturing to services.[3] This process will, once again, produce increasing task specialization at the worker level.

Second, *occupations* are likely to become more specialized over time. As individual workers specialize in performing tasks, so do all workers within a given field, and occupational boundaries shift. The occupation of "pin maker" no longer properly captures the work carried out by a given set of workers, and it is replaced by a larger set of more narrow occupations, such as "pin wire cleaner" and "pin head shanker." Occupations across the occupational structure continue to divide, such that the tasks of the original occupations are distributed across a larger number of more specialized occupations. Specialized training regimens emerge alongside the new occupations, increasing the productivity of workers within the occupations and firming up the new occupational boundaries. Other forms of recognition—such as licensing, professional societies, and specialized academic fields—may develop, further solidifying the boundaries until the next round of specialization commences.

Third, the capacity for work to offer meaning to workers declines as special-ization increases. This is a direct consequence of workers taking on a narrower range of tasks. Specialization brings increased efficiency and higher produc-tivity, but it also reduces the connection between a worker and the end product of their labor, resulting in alienation. In the first volume of *Das Kapital*, for example, Karl Marx draws on David Urquhart to describe the "dark side" of the division of labor, writing, "To subdivide a man is to execute him, if he deserves the sentence, to assassinate him if he does not. . . . The subdivision of labour is the assassination of a people" (1867: chap. 15, sec. 5). In Marx's analysis, the division of labor makes possible the extraction of surplus value: when the labor to produce a given product is divided across many workers, no worker has a clear claim over the end product, and the profit on that product is instead claimed by the owner of the enterprise. For Marx, the increasing division of labor degrades the experience of work and facilitates worker exploitation.

A similarly pessimistic tone is adopted by Max Weber, in his discussion of the iron cage at the end of *The Protestant Ethic and the Spirit of Capi-talism* (1905: 124). In considering the possible end point of rationalized capitalism, Weber writes, "No one knows who will live in this cage in the future, or whether at the end of this tremendous development entirely new prophets will arise, or there will be a great rebirth of old ideas and ideals, or, if neither, mechanized petrification, embellished with a sort of convul-sive self-importance. For the 'last man' of this cultural development, it might well be truly said: 'Specialist without spirit, sensualist without heart; this nullity imagines that it has attained a level of humanity never before achieved.'" Weber's vision of "specialists without spirit" draws on similar themes to Marx, acknowledging that excessive specialization implies some loss of humanity for those trapped in the highly differentiated system.[4]

One consequence of a narrowing in the range of tasks that workers undertake, then, is a loss of humanity. But there may be other, more posi-tive, consequences—namely, we may become more reliant on others to pro-vide for our needs (Durkheim 1893).[5] These relations of dependence arise precisely because specialization renders individuals incapable of flourishing without cooperation with others. As functions are pulled out of the family and taken over by specialized institutions—such as schools, hospitals, and law enforcement—individuals become more reliant on society to develop and live to full capacity. For Durkheim, the solidarity-increasing benefits of specialization are even more important for society than the productivity benefits are. Individuals are pulled closer to one another and to society as a whole by virtue of their position in the division of labor.

As this brief review indicates, the classical theories of the division of labor have in common a rather straightforward prediction about the likely trajectory of specialization in modern industrialized societies. In short, we should expect more specialization rather than less. Individual workers will undertake a narrower range of tasks, and occupational boundaries will shrink around that narrower range. The narrowing of worker tasks and occupations is a clear prediction of classical theories, and the theorized consequences of specialization for workers and societies only underscore these predictions.

THE ACCRETION OF LABOR

Today, there is no person specialized in drawing the wire. No person specialized in cutting the heads, or softing the heads, or heading the shanks. Today, pins are in large part produced by machines rather than people, and the increase in productivity relative to the eighteenth century is profound.[6] The classical theorists of the division of labor would not have been surprised to hear these facts: one important advantage of specialization—from the employer's perspective—is that tasks can be automated and the demand for labor is thereby reduced.

But at least some of the classical theorists might have been surprised to discover the job tasks of the present-day pin makers. Take, for example, the person ultimately responsible for drawing the wire, who would today be classified within the "Extruding and Drawing Machine Setters, Operators, and Tenders, Metal and Plastic," occupation. The Occupational Information Network (O*NET) program, which documents the work activities and skill requirements of occupations, lists sixteen key work tasks associated with the wiredrawing occupation (O*NET 2024). These tasks include those that Adam Smith would have had little problem recognizing, such as "adjust controls to draw or press metal into specified shapes and diameters" or "operate shearing mechanisms to cut rods to specified lengths." Other tasks, such as "maintain an inventory of materials," "test physical properties of products with testing devices," and "troubleshoot, maintain, and make minor repairs to equipment" might have appeared more puzzling to the classical eye. The theorists might have quietly wondered why there was such a high degree of functional complexity in twenty-first-century wiredrawing and why so many tasks seemingly distant from the narrow act of drawing the wire were now central to the performance of this occupation.

If our classical theorist were to take a break from contemplating wire-drawing and sit down to read the *New York Times,* they might be confronted with other puzzling facts. In an article published on February 5, 2023, Ezra Klein quoted at length from a construction worker, who was reflecting on changes in his work over the past fifty years:

> The safety features on jobs when I started in the industry were not even noticeable. Safety on a job today is incredibly different. You don't walk across a beam, you walk around on a pathway marked for you to stay safe so you don't fall off the side of the building. By the time I retired, one thing that took place every day, on every job site, was a mandatory 15 minutes of calisthenics before you start your workday. That's totally nonproductive, but it led to fewer work site injuries during the day. . . . The level of reporting that you have to send to the government, to the insurance companies, to the owner, to show you're meeting all the requirements on the job site, all of that has increased. And so the number of people you need to produce that has increased.

The loss of productivity noted by the worker and the introduction of job tasks that are seemingly unrelated to the narrow job of construction (e.g., "safety," "calisthenics," and "reporting") are quite at odds with the classical predictions. Construction workers do not appear to be undertaking a smaller number of highly specialized tasks, and concerns about declining productivity in the construction sector are prominent (see Goolsbee and Syverson 2023; see also Klein and Thompson 2025: chap. 2).

Pin making and construction are far from exceptional. Across the occupational structure, workers are taking on an increasingly wide variety of tasks. In some cases, this functional complexity is the focus of approbation. In recent years, the Defund the Police movement has drawn attention to the diversity of tasks that police officers are expected to undertake. The abolitionist campaigner Joshua P. Hill, for example, wrote on Twitter:

> So today I learned the NYPD has a bee keeping division. They also have that video game truck now. And a few submarines. And robot dogs . . . Like this is so absurd. Why are we doing our city bee keeping through

the violent people with guns department? . . . Why are we sending kids to play video games with the violent people with guns who take DNA samples? Why would mental health checks be done by violent people with guns? Why would homeless services be done by violent people with guns? (2021)

Other commentary focuses on the difficulties that workers face when dealing with high levels of task diversity. The *Washington Post* noted during the COVID-19 pandemic:

As public libraries . . . have been pressed into service as coronavirus test distribution sites, librarians have become the latest front-line workers of the pandemic. . . . "The library has always been a community center, a place where the public can get something they wouldn't have otherwise, like free Internet," [a] D.C. children's librarian said . . . "it feels like we've become too good at our jobs." It becomes, "Oh, the library can handle it." We're getting more and more tasks and responsibilities that just feel overwhelming. (Weil 2022)

Even accounting for the human tendency to overestimate how special our present is relative to the past, the commentators are consistent in documenting the high functional complexity of contemporary occupations.

Many occupations are in fact becoming *more* complex over time. In Figure 1-1, I show an analysis of data drawn from O*NET. The O*NET database records the tasks required to perform over one thousand occupations, as reported by job incumbents, analysts and experts, job postings, and professional associations (O*NET 2024).[7] In the figure, I plot the average number of tasks undertaken in occupations falling in each of the major occupational groups. The solid lines rest on rigorously standardized comparisons—in which we can be confident that changes in task burdens are real rather than artifacts of changing classificatory procedures—whereas the dotted lines should be interpreted more cautiously because they may be more vulnerable to methodological inconsistencies.

Across the occupational structure, we see an increase in the number of tasks listed as integral to job performance. In every occupational group, the number of tasks increases over recent decades, with the overall average number of tasks per occupation increasing from just under thirteen to almost

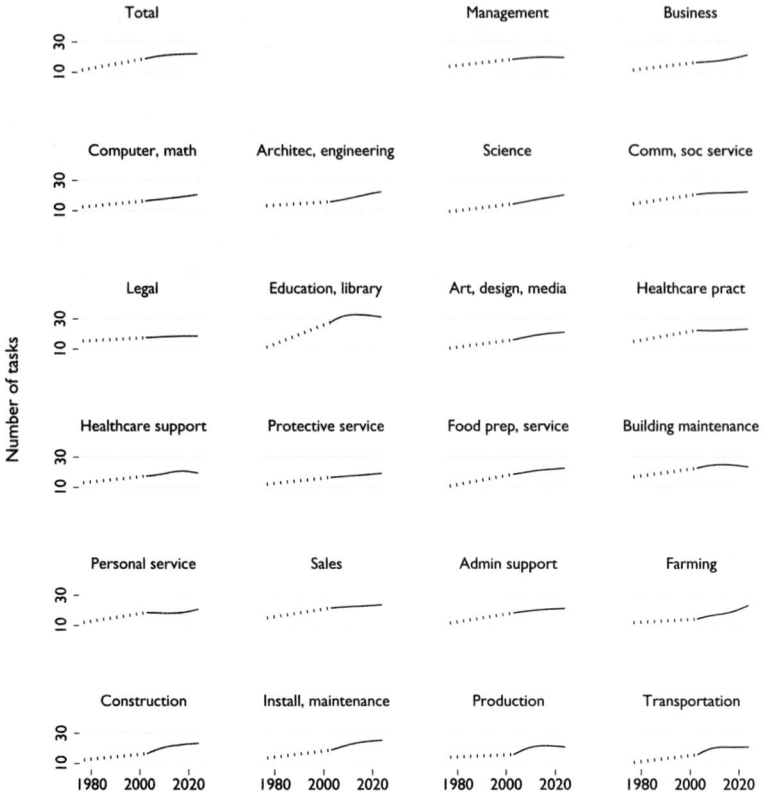

Fig. 1-1 Total number of tasks listed for occupations over time, arranged by major occupational groups.

DATA SOURCE: O*NET.

NOTE: The dotted line (1977–2003) calls out the O*NET "transitional databases," which capture the transition from the older classification of occupations to the O*NET system. Although all of the tasks included for occupations in 1977 were translated to the O*NET system, it is impossible to rule out that the observed over-time changes reflect in part the changes made to the task-coding procedure. From 2003 onward, all occupations were classified using the O*NET system, and changes in task burdens are therefore not attributable to coding changes.

twenty-two. In the group encompassing education and library occupations, where the takeoff is particularly extreme, these additional work tasks for middle school teachers included "observe and evaluate students' performance, behavior, social development, and physical health"; "guide and counsel students with adjustment or academic problems, or special academic interests"; and "provide disabled students with assistive devices, supportive technology, and assistance accessing facilities" (O*NET 2024: code 25-2022).

Even among occupations in which many fewer tasks are required, such as those in the food preparation and service sector, we see substantial task accretion. For example, bartenders are now required to "attempt to limit problems and liability related to customers' excessive drinking by taking steps such as persuading customers to stop drinking, or ordering taxis or other transportation for intoxicated patrons," while fast-food cooks are required to "maintain sanitation, health, and safety standards in work areas" (codes 35-3011 and 35-2011).

Contemporary occupations, then, exhibit a surprisingly high degree of functional complexity relative to classical predictions, and occupations have also increased in complexity over recent decades. The contemporary worker experience appears to diverge quite substantially from the specialized simplification predicted by the classical theories.

Economy and Society

Increasing functional complexity is not limited to workers and occupations. Many organizations and industries are similarly attending to a wide variety of concerns that previously would have been considered beyond their purview. The medical industry, charged as it is with protecting the health of individuals, has shown increasing interest in "nonmedical" interventions. A blog post published by the American Hospital Association's Center for Health Care Innovation (Bhatt 2019) celebrated the "exciting" work that some hospitals and health systems were undertaking to improve the health of socioeconomically disadvantaged patients:

> Denver Health, a safety-net hospital that cares for a large number of people who are not insured or under-insured, is working to convert a closed building on its campus into affordable housing. This growing trend not only better serves the health of patients and families, but also supports value-based care by reducing the demand for emergency room access. Hospitals investing in real estate may be surprising at first, but its implications for improved patient care are compelling. . . . Patients lacking stable housing are far more likely to suffer from such conditions as asthma, low weight, developmental delays and an increased lifetime risk of depression. They also are far more likely to overuse ED services, significantly driving up costs for care providers. So investing in housing is a win-win for vulnerable patients and the hospitals and health systems that care for them.

Some health care systems have installed kitchens to provide culinary classes for patients at risk of poor nutrition and associated conditions (Crawford 2023), while others provide job readiness and financial readiness programs (NYC Health+Hospitals 2018).

Similar expansions of industrial purviews are observed in the educational sector. We are accustomed to schools providing free lunch for children from poor backgrounds, but increasingly schools are providing other basic services, such as laundry facilities and toiletries for students and their families (Grose 2022). Many four-year colleges provide comparable help for poorer students, alongside programs to help students with mental health and substance abuse problems or students struggling with sexual or gender-based violence. And the interest in providing a diverse set of programs and services is not limited to the health and education industries. General Motors (2025), for example, advertises, "From day one, we look out for our employees' well-being at work and at home, so they can focus on realizing their ambitions. This is why we are proud to offer a benefits package ranging from health insurance, dental insurance, vision insurance, disability benefits, tuition assistance, adoption assistance, a Family Care Assistance Plan, plus more! This package is designed to help you achieve your best physical, emotional, and financial well-being possible." Among the twenty-six "teams" that make up General Motors, the majority are dedicated to tasks that are seemingly outside the narrow business of manufacturing cars. Human resources, medical, security, and workplace safety teams sit alongside teams dedicated to manufacturing, production and skilled trades, and purchasing and supply chain.

Once again, we can use statistical data to cast light on changes in functional complexity within industries over time. In Figure 1-2, I show changes in the occupational diversity of industries between 1880 and the present day, as captured in Census data.[8] Occupational diversity is measured using the Blau Index, which may be interpreted here as the probability that two workers picked at random from a given industry belong to different major occupational groups.[9] Insofar as industrial purviews have expanded, we would expect to see increases in the Blau Index over time.

From the late nineteenth century onward, the Blau Index has risen across all industries, indicating that industries are becoming increasingly occupationally diverse over time. Industries that were once dominated by a small number of occupational groups—such as agriculture, forestry and fishing, and manufacturing—increasingly require a broader range of occupations to produce their outputs. But all industries are now less likely to be dominated by a small set of major occupational groups. In the construction industry, for example, 90 percent of workers in 1900 were employed in construction and extraction occupations, a number that had declined to just over 30 percent by 2021. In the nondurable goods manufacturing industry,

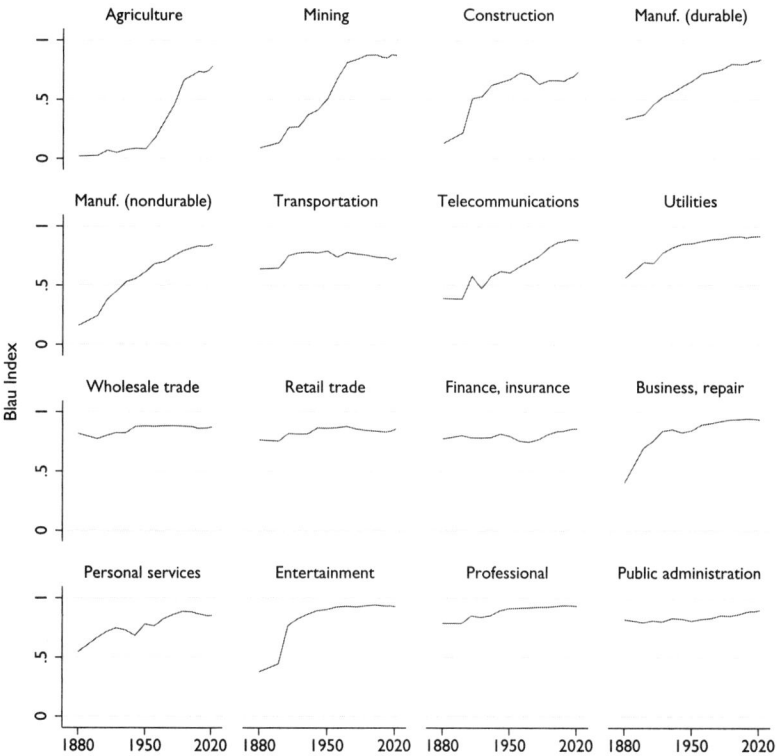

Fig. 1-2 Blau Index by industry groups.

DATA SOURCE: IPUMS USA.

NOTE: The (normalized) Blau Index was calculated on the basis of major occupational groups. As occupational coding systems change over time, I compute the index using both OCC1950 and OCC1990 classifications and then take the average.

around 90 percent of workers in 1900 worked in production occupations, while only around 40 percent work in such occupations in the present day. Even at finer degrees of measurement, similar patterns are found. For example, within the professional and related services industry, we might zoom in to examine the educational services industry, which at the turn of the twentieth century was dominated by occupations in the education and library major group. Between 1900 and the present day, the proportion of education and library occupations has declined by half, from 84 percent to 40 percent of all occupations within the educational services industry. Across both broader and finer industry groups, occupational concentration is falling.[10]

The narratives and statistical analysis are consistent in showing a broadening of the types of occupations involved in producing industry outputs. Today, all industries require a broad range of workers to produce their outputs, and across the board, the high occupational concentration of the 1880s has fallen away.

The Paradox of Specialization

In the coming chapters, I present evidence that we are far from living in a Smithian nation of simplified specialists. As we trace the development of occupations and industries over the past 150 years, we see that there has been a steady accumulation of tasks and that occupational and industrial purviews have expanded to embrace higher degrees of functional complexity. I argue that these expansions of occupational and industrial purviews are instances of a very general phenomenon that I label "the paradox of specialization." One important implication of this paradox is that workers today are required to take on more tasks than in the past and are increasingly *un*specialized with respect to the content of their work.

The paradox of specialization arises because the modern occupation is a rationalized occupation: one in which workers aim to maximize occupational outputs via well-defined and predictable procedures. Rather than work processes being determined by rules of thumb, or traditional practices passed down through generations, tasks within rationalized occupations are adopted because they maximize the outputs being pursued. Rationalized occupations are also specialized occupations: from Adam Smith (1776) onward, most scholars have united around the view that productivity is enhanced when specialists rather than generalists are charged with producing given outputs.

To ensure that both the quantity and quality of output is maximized within the rationalized occupation, scientific findings guide practices and procedures. As a result, changes in science are consequential for the types of tasks undertaken by workers. Over the past two centuries, three changes have occurred that are of particular importance. First, there is simply more scientific knowledge being produced now than at any point in history. Now, for every output, a body of scientific knowledge exists that makes it possible for workers to tailor activities to maximize productivity. But in addition to increases in the *amount* of scientific knowledge, there have also been changes in the *nature* of scientific knowledge. An increasing scientific interest in identifying sets of probabilistic causal mechanisms has made it possible to identify multiple causes for any occupational outcome. In disciplines such as medical science, this shift opened the door to including sociological mechanisms alongside biological mechanisms in explanations of disease. The development of probabilistic models also allowed for prediction, which—in cases where bad outcomes needed to be avoided—raised the possibility of taking preventive action. It became possible not just to treat phenomena such as crime, low test scores, or poor health but to *predict* and *prevent* these phenomena.

Changes in science come together with the rationalized occupation to produce quite an unexpected result. Science identifies new approaches to improving output, to increasing productivity. But when science discovers more about a given problem, that knowledge is assumed to be within the purview of the occupation that already specializes in the problem (e.g., see Abbott 1988). The rationalized occupation is obliged to take on a wider range of job tasks if that wider range will more effectively produce the outputs that the occupation specializes in. Thus, as we learn more about how to prevent certain types of disease, we see physicians increasingly offering preventive services as well as treatments after the disease has emerged. As we learn more about how to support children's learning, we see schools offering psychological and social supports as well as the narrow teaching designed to deliver a curriculum. As we learn more about how to support *workers,* we see managers adding job tasks designed to promote worker health and well-being. For any given output, science has increasingly identified a much more expansive range of worker inputs that are required to maximize productivity.

This is the paradox of specialization: occupations and industries specialize in a given social problem, but by virtue of specializing, those occupations and industries become responsible for a much broader range of tasks once the science indicates that the problems are more complicated than previously imagined. The paradox explains how specialization can develop at the societal level, while at the same time individual workers become less specialized. This is a story of a quite fundamental change in how the division of labor develops when societies become highly rationalized. Whereas classical theorists assumed that specialized occupations would be responsible for an ever-narrower range of tasks, I show that the forces of science and rationalization in fact work to complicate tasks and responsibilities. The new division of labor is characterized by an unprecedented expansion of tasks within each occupation. The purpose of this book is to come to terms with the expansion and what it implies for our economy and society.

THE MEASUREMENT OF LABOR

In this book, I show evidence that the paradox of specialization is shaping functional differentiation across a large number of contemporary occupations and industries. I present analyses of historical, archival, and statistical data to examine changes in job tasks and scientific output over the past circa 150 years, a period sometimes described as the "long twentieth century."[11] The historical analyses exploit a range of primary and secondary data sources, described in detail in each chapter and the Appendix. The primary sources include resources produced for city managers, job task analyses, federal government reports and documents, first-person accounts of work, organizational reports, and scientific publications. In some cases, the primary sources were located in physical archives; in others, the material was available in libraries and online archives. The statistical analyses are largely conducted on publicly available data, although some of the data required substantial processing in preparation for statistical analysis. To facilitate replication of the findings, all code is available in my OSF directory (see Jackson 2025), along with copies of all the datasets I am permitted to share.

In the following chapters, I examine the development of the paradox of specialization over the past 150 years in the United States. I begin in

Chapter 2 by outlining the broad changes in the key forces producing the paradox: rationalization and scientific development. I describe the emergence of the rationalized occupation and review the changes in science that showed workers how much more could be accomplished if the science were to be followed. I then present four case studies of industries and their dominant rationalized occupations (Chapters 3–6), focusing on the industries of medicine, law enforcement, education, and manufacturing. In each chapter, I trace the development of rationalization and scientific knowledge over the past 150 years and describe how and when the paradox of specialization arises. I use information on job tasks and work practices to link changes in rationalization and scientific knowledge to changes in the functional complexity of occupations.

Although I find evidence of the paradox across all four case studies, the speed, timing, and extent of its development differ across industries and across occupations within industries. In the medical industry, for example, the paradox arises early because medical occupations are well attuned to scientific developments, and the science of medicine expands rapidly across the whole period considered here. In other industries, such as manufacturing, there are in contrast periods in which task burdens are eased. In fact, the paradox of specialization arises for frontline manufacturing workers only in the mid-twentieth century, when the new science of human relations points to tasks that must be incorporated within work processes to maximize output. But there are many commonalities across the case studies too. In addition to the paradox arising in all industries, another common feature is that when the science of prediction and prevention develops, the functional complexity of occupations increases. In all of the industries considered, a diverse range of new job tasks is added to occupations for the purpose of preventing negative outcomes. Manufacturing workers take increasing precautions to protect against machine injury, while police officers show increasing interest in community intervention to prevent crime. The science of prediction and prevention expands the boundaries of all occupations, firming up the paradox of specialization across the cases considered here.

Looking forward, the paradox of specialization is likely to be an increasingly important feature of occupations over the coming decades. In Chapter 7, I conclude by discussing the likely consequences of the paradox of specialization for workers, occupations, industries, and society.

CHAPTER TWO

The Formidable Thicket

It requires good judgment and long practice to estimate the proper size to cut garments from goods of different texture, some goods being elastic, while others are stiff and hard, and will not give in making motions with the arms. The elastic goods will have to be cut close to or inside the measures; hard, stiff goods must be cut larger than the measure; very stiff goods we usually cut two sizes larger in widths, or the garments will look and feel too small . . . Practice only will give the student the idea as to how much difference to make for the different kinds of material. No very definite instructions can be given on this head; therefore we must leave it with the student, for by practice only can the difficulty be overcome.

William Larder, *Thirty Years at the Cutting-Board* (1882: 5)

In 1882, William Larder published his book on pattern cutting. He had worked at pattern cutting for thirty years and had developed a system of rules for cutting that he wished to publish to help those entering the trade. Larder's book illustrates the inconsistent rationalization of work in the late nineteenth century. To be sure, the book contains patterns, the purpose of which is to standardize the cuts that tailors make for given body sizes and fits. But the book also highlights the importance of traditional practices and rules of thumb passed down across generations of workers. No very definite instructions can be given. Larder even emphasizes that his rule "is the product of thirty years' experience and continued practice" (1882: 3).

In this chapter, I examine the changes in work since William Larder's time. I explain how the features of work and society that we take for granted today differ from the features that he took for granted in the late nineteenth century. I describe the key forces producing change in work and occupations over the past 150 years and explain how the combination of these forces operates to increase the range of tasks required of workers, thereby producing a paradox of specialization.

A SYSTEM OF RULES

Why are so many occupations in late industrial societies characterized by high degrees of functional complexity? I argue that growing complexity is a direct consequence of several important changes to economies and societies over the past 150 years, summarized in Table 2-1.

The first set of changes comes under the umbrella of rationalization, a long-standing historical process in which rational principles infuse social institutions, and action is increasingly guided by well-established and

Table 2-1 Forces that contribute to the paradox of specialization

TYPE	DESCRIPTION	EXAMPLE OF CHANGE IN WORK PRACTICES
Rationalization		
Scientization of work	Scientific evidence increasingly guides occupational practices	Childcare workers are increasingly required to study the science of early education and development to gain accreditation
Rationalization of work processes	New tasks and work processes that will better realize the occupation's ends are adopted	Factory workers implement new safety procedures to reduce injuries and consequent slowdowns in production
Rationalization of wider society	Governments increasingly regulate work processes to "internalize" societal externalities	Building contractors are required to abide by an increasing number of environmental regulations (e.g., ensuring lead abatement, filing environmental impact reports)
Scientific development		
Expansion of scientific output	Dramatic growth in the number of scientists and the amount of science produced	The new sciences of retail and personnel management now shape the job tasks of retail salespersons
Growing model complexity	Multiple mechanisms introduced to explain outcomes, supporting the establishment of ever more complicated work processes	Teachers begin to intervene in social lives of students (e.g., parental abuse, housing conditions) because of growing scientific evidence on social causes of poor performance
Evidence-based prediction	Growth of probabilistic models that make it possible to predict outcomes; bad outcomes can increasingly be prevented	General practice physicians increasingly intervene to prevent disease (e.g., screening procedures, routine blood pressure measurement, smoking cessation, obesity treatments)

universally applied rules (Kalberg 1980: 1158–1159; see also Weber 1905, 1978; Beniger 2009; Espeland and Sauder 2016; Berman 2022; Almelhem et al. 2023; Fourcade and Healy 2024; Pugh 2024). Several aspects of rationalization are important in understanding why the paradox of specialization arises. First, within rationalized occupations, occupational actors aim to maximize outputs by applying relevant scientific evidence. Over time, science becomes increasingly important in shaping job tasks. Second, there is a thoroughgoing rationalization of work processes, so rules of thumb are gradually replaced by standardized work processes designed to most efficiently realize the occupation's outputs. Specialization in reaching these ends is highly prized. And third, society as a whole is increasingly rationalized, as is perhaps most clearly expressed in the willingness of governments to intervene in economic activities for the benefit of society as a whole. Where work processes have externalities—including pollution, injury, or disease—for societies, governments can impose rules and regulations to force firms and workers to build mitigation into their work processes.

The second set of changes pertains to changes in science. In a rationalized society, changes in science are of fundamental importance because these changes filter through to work processes via occupational actors, firms, and governments. Simple changes in the raw amount of science are of course important, insofar as new scientific knowledge is available to guide workers undertaking both new and established work tasks. But science has also changed in character. As I discuss in more detail below, the probabilistic revolution brought about growing model complexity and the development of causal models that made (relatively accurate) prediction possible. These changes in the type of scientific output led to the introduction of new types of work tasks.

It is rationalization and scientific development together that deliver the paradox of specialization. Rationalization demands that occupations increasingly attend to the science relevant to occupational outputs, and the growth and complication of science mean that there is now much more scientific work that must be attended to than in the past. In the remainder of this chapter, I describe these changes in detail and reveal how the modern rationalized occupation was born.

THE RATIONALIZED OCCUPATION

A rationalized occupation is an occupation in which workers aim to maximize occupational outputs via well-defined and predictable procedures.

As I described above (see Table 2-1), the force of rationalization has three important expressions: the scientization of work, the rationalization of work processes, and the rationalization of wider society.

Because the rise of science and rationalization is typically taken for granted, the magnitude of the change is not always fully appreciated. It is therefore useful to begin by reminding ourselves of just how profound this change has been. After documenting the rise of these forces, I discuss the implications for occupational tasks. One way to capture growing rationalization is by measuring the visibility of rationalization-related concepts in prominent texts. In Figure 2-1, I present results from an analysis of the text of presidential executive orders, congressional legislation, Supreme Court orders, and the *New York Times*. The figure shows the proportion of text mentioning the terms "science," "standard," "specialize," and "duty" between 1880 and the present day.[1] The first three terms capture aspects of rationalization, and we see a strong increase in their use throughout the twentieth century: in all text types, references to science, standards, and specialization have at least doubled during this period.

The increasing prominence of science in the documents is likely a consequence both of the dramatic increase of scientific output over the period and of the growing cultural power of science. An examination of the context in which these words are used is revealing in this respect. Harry S. Truman, for example, frequently used science-related terms in his executive orders, but in almost all cases, these terms were employed as adjectives modifying "data," "research," or "fields." When Barack Obama invoked science, the adjective was also attached to "guidelines," "policy," and "decision-making." This pattern shows how scientization was bound up with other aspects of rationalization, such as standardization. References to standards increase over the century, largely because science established benchmarks that could then be the basis of standards and other policies. By the end of the twentieth century, science was conceived of not just as a well-established field of human endeavor but additionally as a tool that should be integrated into any rational decision-making process.

In Figure 2-1, we also see the increasing importance of specialization from 1880 to the present day. References to terms related to specialization (including "specialize," "specialists," and "specialization") increase substantially over time, across all three branches of government and in the *New York Times*. Individuals mentioned in the documents are more likely than

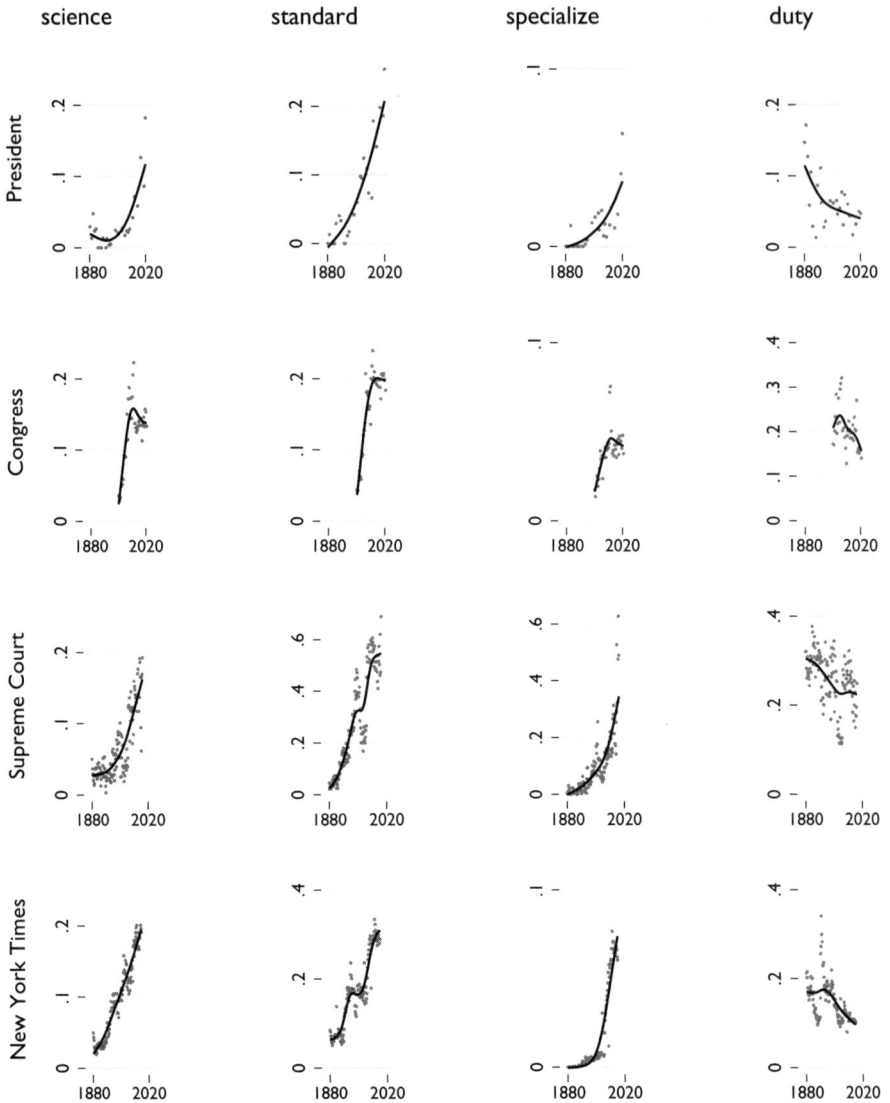

Fig. 2-1 Analysis of text drawn from executive orders, congressional legislation, Supreme Court orders, and the *New York Times*; proportion of text including term.

NOTE: Scales differ across figures. In the executive orders analysis, the measure is the proportion of all executive orders mentioning the word; each dot represents a president. In the congressional legislation analysis, the measure is the number of times the term appeared divided by the number of occurrences of the word "the"; each dot represents a congressional term. In the Supreme Court analysis, the measure is the number of times the term appeared, again divided by the number of occurrences of the word "the"; each dot represents a year. In the *New York Times* analysis, the measure is the number of times the term appeared divided by the number of occurrences of the word "day"; each dot represents a year. See Appendix for further details of the analysis.

they were in the past to be described as "specialists" with relevant expertise in the issues at hand, and equipment such as tools or clothing is increasingly described as "specialized."

The growing prominence of specialization in the texts is again not surprising, given the increasing prominence of specialization in the economy and society over this period. In most discussions of the division of labor, the productivity advantages of specialization are understood to be so great that over the long run, factories, firms, and other organizations that fail to introduce specialization will simply disappear. Émile Durkheim, for example, drawing from evolutionary theory, argues that the advantages of specialization impose a powerful selective pressure, such that more specialized organisms are more likely to survive than less specialized organisms (Durkheim 1893; see Rueschemeyer 1982 for a detailed discussion of this point; see Rueffler, Hermisson, and Wagner 2012 for a recent biological model of specialization).[2] Thus specialization should be anticipated in *every* social institution. Whether we focus on the survival of firms under capitalism or the survival of biological organisms in a given environment, more specialization is preferred because it offers advantages relative to less specialization. Even if organizations might initially discover the benefits of specialization by chance, as the benefits become clear, other organizations are likely to embrace the practice so that there is a convergence on the optimal level of specialization.[3]

These productivity-maximizing effects also give specialization substantial *cultural* power, and we are likely to see a convergence on specialization simply because people believe that specialization enhances productivity. It is for this reason that the logic of specialization can, in fact, be understood as but one aspect of the wider cultural force of rationalization. In many cases, a cultural commitment to specialization is likely to increase the payoff of specialization, such that it then *becomes* productivity maximizing. "Specialists" are so frequently described as "experts" that we are accustomed to conflating specialization with social status or competence. This is easy to see in the field of medicine, where complicated and life-threatening issues are quickly taken over by physicians labeled as "specialists," but it is also evident elsewhere in the occupational structure, when parents seek out specialist teachers for their children or consumers seek out a specialty patisserie. Audiences may similarly start to question the legitimacy of a single occupation holding on to a range of tasks that is seen to be too broad;

Defund the Police, for example, is a social movement fueled by such a legitimacy challenge.[4] There are, of course, many cases in which specialists provide better services or products than nonspecialists (e.g., see Smetana et al. 2007), but there is also much evidence that specialists are desired even when generalists would provide a service or product of equivalent quality (e.g., see Lewis et al. 2000). It is the power of the logic of specialization that pushes in the direction of ever-greater specialization, even in the absence of a benefit to productivity.

Finally, and for contrast, examine the references to the word "duty," a term that is strongly associated with custom and values. Over the same period in which words relating to science, standards, and specialization increase in prominence, references to duty decline substantially. In these patterns, we see the declining power of tradition and the corresponding increase in appeals to science and rationalized practice.

Ends and Means

The foregoing makes it clear that, over the past 150 years, the forces of science and rationalization were very much in play. The next step is to consider how those forces came together to complicate the tasks of workers.

Occupations are nothing but institutionalized tools for securing a given end. In this context, rationalization matters because the incumbents of an occupation come to understand that work practices must be complicated if they are to secure an end efficiently. Increasing rationalization is the backdrop for the emergence of the rationalized occupation. Although rationalization has many expressions, as we have seen, one very general characteristic is that there is an ongoing search for the best procedures to maximize the outputs being pursued. Appeals to science, standards, and specialization increase precisely because these practices are associated with positive outcomes.[5] In the occupational context, rationalization implies that occupational actors similarly aim to pursue procedures that maximize occupational outputs. For a rationalized occupation to exist, then, the output of the occupation must be clear and unambiguous, the output must be pursued rigorously and deliberately, and occupational boundaries must form around the pursuit of that output.

Focusing on output in defining the rationalized occupation marks a break with the standard way of conceptualizing occupations within the social science literature. An alternative approach to defining occupational groups is to focus on the job tasks undertaken within an occupation; here, occupational boundaries encompass workers performing similar job tasks (e.g., see Weber 1978; Kalleberg 2011; Martin-Caughey 2021).[6] Under this approach, a teacher would be defined with respect to the tasks of "instructing children," "managing the classroom," and "attending to the socioemotional needs of children" rather than with respect to the output of "well-educated children." The "bundle of tasks" conception dominates contemporary social science work on occupations and the division of labor because much of this work focuses on the automation of job tasks and the subsequent effects on the long-term survival of certain occupations (e.g., see Autor, Levy, and Murnane 2003; Acemoglu and Autor 2011; Levy and Murnane 2012; Gil-Hernández, Vidal, and Torrejón Perez 2023; Acemoglu and Johnson 2023; Acemoglu, Kong, and Restrepo 2024).[7] Research on the sociology of occupations has highlighted the degree to which particular bundles of tasks are associated with high wages and other labor market rewards, with implications for overall levels of socioeconomic inequality (Liu and Grusky 2013; D. Nelson, Wilmers, and Zhang 2024; see also Firpo, Fortin, and Lemieux 2011).[8]

But there are good theoretical and methodological reasons for focusing on output when conceptualizing occupations, particularly in a highly rationalized society. And defining occupations with respect to their output is hardly unprecedented: when Durkheim described the system of occupations, he emphasized the importance of outputs, writing, "Individuals are . . . grouped . . . according to the particular nature of the social activity to which they consecrate themselves. . . . It is no longer real or fictitious consanguinity which marks the place of each one, but the function which he fills" (1893: 182).[9] Theoretically, the rationalized occupation is rooted in a model of rational action; under this conceptualization, workers orient themselves toward a particular end (output) and use a range of means (job tasks) to achieve that end. The job tasks of an occupation are therefore determined by the output that is pursued, and the output must take priority in determining occupational boundaries. Alongside rationalized occupations, we should expect to see rationalized firms and rationalized industries; again, these entities are characterized by the deliberate pursuit of well-defined outputs. As we will see in the case study chapters, there is evidence that actors give a great deal of thought as to how the outputs of the occupation (and industry) can best be pursued and whether or not new tasks need to be embraced to achieve occupational outputs. Methodologically, defining occupations with respect to the tasks contained within them causes obvious problems for those interested in the division of labor: if the aim is to understand how tasks accumulate within occupations or divide across workers, the occupation cannot be principally defined by the tasks that it encompasses. Within a rationalized occupation, job tasks are free to change over time, just as long as the same output is being pursued.

Defining occupations with respect to output allows us to separate two different types of specialization that are often conflated. First, we can identify specialization at the occupational level, in which occupational groups divide to produce outputs that are ever more specialized. We saw this type of specialization, for example, when the physician occupation was divided into specialist physician occupations: by separating pediatric practice from the general physician occupation, practitioners could specialize in producing the output of child health rather than in producing health in people of all ages. Second, we can identify specialization at the worker level, which exists when there is a reduction in the number of tasks that a worker is expected to perform and the functional complexity of an occupation (or job) is thereby reduced.

Based on classical theories, the two types of specialization would be expected to be complements: if occupational specialization occurs, the number of tasks required of workers should decline. After occupational specialization, for example, pediatricians would no longer be required to perform all of the tasks associated with adult patients. However, there are two important caveats. The first is that occupational specialization is likely, in and of itself, to introduce new job tasks. In many cases, occupational specialization makes it necessary to coordinate with others to produce outputs, and the task of coordination must be taken on by workers. Modern health care is plagued by the difficulties of coordinating specialized care, such that resources must be expended to overcome the coordination problems that specialization itself has introduced. The second is that what happens to worker tasks at the moment of occupational specialization is a quite different question from what happens to worker tasks within specialized occupations over the longer term. If our interest is in understanding long-term trends, it is certainly possible to observe a trend toward specialization at the occupational level alongside a trend toward increased functional complexity at the worker level. The thesis of this book is that we are seeing precisely this combination of trends. That is, because theorists have typically failed to distinguish between specialization at the occupational level and functional complexity at the worker level, a fundamental complicating development at the worker level has been quite missed by conventional theory. It has been assumed—wrongly—that trends moved in lockstep across these two levels.

Drawing the Boundaries

It might be thought that some occupations operate outside the purview of science and can safely ignore whatever science might be saying about how best to secure the occupation's ends. All occupations feature a shared understanding (i.e., "culture") of ends and the best way to realize those ends. Are there some occupations that resist the paradox of specialization by rejecting science (and all of its complicating effects)?

One useful place to begin is by considering the professions, which have traditionally embraced science. We find in the work of Andrew Abbott, for example, a model of the division of professional labor in which professions compete with one another for control over job tasks. Which profession wins out is a function both of the objective features of given tasks and of the strength of the competing claims to jurisdiction over those tasks. The strength of a jurisdictional claim rests on the extent to which a profession can derive claims to diagnose problems, make inferences about problems, and treat problems from the abstract principles constituting the profession's knowledge system (Abbott 1988: chap. 3; see also Hughes 1958: chap. 6). This work thus highlights the importance of abstract knowledge systems to professional occupations.

But it is not just professional occupations that attend to science. As the rationalized occupation emerges, there is an increasing propensity for *all* occupations to draw on science to bolster their claim for tasks, whether or not each occupation has previously been attached to a well-established abstract body of knowledge.[10] An important consequence of the tremendous growth of scientific knowledge over the past century is that almost all occupations can now point to a body of science that is relevant to job tasks or output, and every field of human endeavor can reasonably claim to be associated with at least one field of scientific research.

In the following chapters, I examine the degree of rationalization of a set of occupations in detail and show that appeals to scientific concepts and research increased over the past 150 years. But a straightforward and revealing example of the increasing propensity to claim scientific foundations can be found in the case of barber licensing regulations. In one of the central texts of neoliberalism, *Capitalism and Freedom,* Milton Friedman mocked barber licensing laws as "ludicrous" and called them a "serious infringement on the freedom of individuals to pursue activities of their own choice" (2002). Friedman quotes liberally from a book by Walter Gellhorn, which strongly criticizes the growth of occupational licensing in the United States. Gellhorn approvingly describes the striking down of a Maryland law that "yielded to the barbers' importunities that they be raised to the level of a learned profession" (1956: 121). He continues, "The court was depressed rather than impressed by a legislative command that neophyte barbers must receive formal instruction in the 'scientific fundamentals for barbering'" (1956: 121–122, quoted in Friedman 2002: 142).

Whether Gellhorn and Friedman approved or not, the Maryland law was not atypical in its appeal to scientific reasoning. Consider, for example, barber licensing laws in Minnesota, the first state to introduce such legislation (Timmons and Thornton 2010). The first barber licensing legislation was passed in 1897 (H.F. 21, 186 §8), and it stated that a barber should be "possessed of the requisite skill in said trade to properly perform all the duties thereof, including his ability in the preparation of the tools, shaving, hair-cutting and all the duties and services incident thereto, and [be] possessed of sufficient knowledge concerning the common diseases of the face and skin to avoid the aggravation and spreading thereof in the practice of said trade." In the present day, the equivalent licensing legislation (Minnesota Statute 154.07 §1) reads, "Instruction must include the following subjects: scientific fundamentals for barbering; hygiene; practical study of the hair, skin, muscles, and nerves; structure of the head, face, and neck; elementary chemistry relating to sterilization and antiseptics; diseases of the skin, hair, and glands; massaging and manipulating the muscles of the face and neck; hair cutting; shaving; trimming the beard; bleaching, tinting and dyeing the hair; and the chemical straightening of hair." As the comparison of these statutes makes clear, the barber occupation, through the licensing legislation, was to an increasing extent making appeals to science. Much of the "scientific" language included in the statute was in fact introduced in 1927 (Minnesota Statute 5846 §7), and the appeal to science is by now well established.[11] Even without a professionalized body of knowledge, the occupation could be defined in relation to scientific principles.

The diffusion of scientific appeals across the occupational structure makes it possible for occupations far beyond the professions to legitimize claims for new job tasks. If the science points to new job tasks that will allow an occupation to pursue outputs more effectively, the rationalized occupation has an interest in taking on those tasks. The growth of the rationalized occupation lays the foundation for a new division of labor, a new distribution of tasks.

THE INNER SPIRIT

Rationalized occupations are strongly affected by changes in science. To understand why these changes have been so consequential for the division of labor, it is necessary to understand three important developments in scientific knowledge that have taken place over the past two centuries: first, the substantial increase in total scientific output; second, changes in the type of scientific knowledge produced; and third, the growing capacity for accurate prediction. Of the changes in scientific output that have occurred over the centuries, it is increases in the volume of knowledge that have been highlighted by researchers working on functional differentiation. But as I describe over the coming chapters, changes in the type of scientific knowledge produced were also important, because they pointed to new approaches to solving problems and producing output, and these new approaches were associated with new job tasks.

The Power of Truth

In June 1962, Derek J. de Solla Price, a historian of science, delivered a series of lectures on the transition from "Little Science" to "Big Science."[12] The lecture series focused on the tremendous growth in total scientific output that each generation experiences anew. He writes, "Science has always been modern; it has always been exploding into the population, always on the brink of its expansive revolution. Scientists have always felt themselves to be awash in a sea of scientific literature that augments in each decade as much as in all times before" (D. Price 1963: 15). Price argued that the growth of scientific output followed a logistic curve, such that rapid growth is to be expected up until the moment that scientific knowledge starts to become saturated. To those experiencing the steeper regions of the logistic curve, growth in scientific knowledge would be experienced as exponential.[13] It is for this reason that contemporary generations perceive an enormous recent growth in scientific knowledge, just as generations before us were similarly struck by the rapid accumulation of knowledge in their own time.

The classical theorists in fact saw the growth of scientific knowledge to be the primary impetus pushing forward the division of labor. Charles Babbage writes, for example, "The arts and manufactures of the country are intimately connected with the progress of the severer sciences . . . as we advance in the career of improvement, every step requires . . . that this connexion should be rendered more intimate" (1833: 379). And Gary S. Becker and Kevin M. Murphy state that "much of the growth in specialization over time has been due to an extraordinary growth in knowledge" (1992: 1145). As knowledge grows and science opens up new possibilities for innovation, new job tasks are introduced. As these job tasks are taken on by existing workers, the pressure to specialize grows, and new occupations emerge to take responsibility for the tasks. The specialization-enhancing effects of the growth of science therefore occur only because the expansion of knowledge sets into motion a process that is resolved through the imperative to maximize output at the individual worker, occupation, and firm levels.[14]

Technological change is similarly assumed to lead to increased specialization at the worker, occupation, and firm levels. New technological developments—or, as Adam Smith described it, the "invention of a great number of machines" (1776: book 1, chap. 1)—make it possible for some job tasks to be moved from workers to machines, with the effect that functional complexity at the worker level is reduced. The invention of the calculator, for example, simplified those jobs that previously required workers to undertake complex manual calculations. Technological developments might also encourage specialization because they facilitate the coordination of tasks across multiple workers (Becker and Murphy 1992). Communication tools, such as the telephone, make it possible for tasks to be split across individuals working in separate locations and reduce the costs of dividing tasks across workers. Although the use of machines necessitates an extension of worker tasks to include interaction with the machines (e.g., see Chase 1929; Sabel 1982; Levy and Murnane 2012; Acemoglu and Johnson 2023), the total number of tasks is reduced. In some cases, it will be possible to replace several workers undertaking a complex set of tasks with a single worker using a machine and substantially increase productivity.

Thus, although the general increase in scientific and technological output is well understood to have had profound consequences for the division of labor, the standard theories predict that the growth of science will lead to an *increase* in task specialization for workers. Conversely, in the coming chapters, I show that increases in scientific knowledge in fact bring about the paradox of specialization at the worker level, even if specialization at the occupation level is encouraged. This is because, in a rationalized occupation, the greater the volume of science that is relevant to an output, the greater the volume of science that must be taken into account for occupational outputs to be delivered effectively.

Form and Content

Alongside the expansion of scientific knowledge, the content of science was also transformed. From the dawn of the nineteenth century onward, there is evidence of a revolution in scientific thought, commonly known as the *probabilistic revolution* (Kruger, Daston, and Heidelberger 1987).[15] The probabilistic revolution changed how scientists across a broad range of disciplines understood the nature of chance, the interpretation of error, and the concept of causation. These conceptual shifts then had consequences for the type of scientific work undertaken across the disciplines, the potential for prediction, and the extent to which cross-disciplinary communication was possible. The revolution was therefore fundamental to the development of a worldview that recognizes the interconnectedness of social phenomena and the need to take that interconnectedness into account when pursuing an occupation's mission. Because the probabilistic revolution was so fundamental in determining the trajectory of the division of labor over the past 150 years, I here provide an overview of its key features.

In the simplest terms, the probabilistic revolution refers to that period of time in which the mathematical theory of probability came to be increasingly accepted and applied across the natural and social sciences (Kruger, Daston, and Heidelberger 1987: 1; see also Stigler 1986). It is generally dated to the period 1800–1930, but its effects still reverberate today. Mathematical theories of probability—championed by those such as Pierre-Simon Laplace and Adolphe Quetelet—provided scientists with new frameworks for understanding variation, chance, error, and uncertainty. In particular, probabilism provided an alternative to deterministic reasoning, which dominated the sciences at the beginning of the nineteenth century. For the probabilist, variation is an expected outcome of a causal process, and a causal explanation is possible insofar as a cause raises the probability of a given outcome (see Wise 1987 for a detailed discussion; see also Goldthorpe 2001).

The growing influence of probabilistic thinking in the nineteenth century had important implications for scientific understandings of normality and abnormality. At the beginning of the nineteenth century, normality could be defined by its opposition to the abnormal, or unnatural, state. In medicine, where this opposition was most evident, abnormal pathology was the focus of concern, and the natural state was described in contrast to the abnormal state characterizing diseased organs. By the end of the nineteenth century, normality became the focus, where "normal" represented a standard from which deviations could be judged (Warner 1986).[16] Medical science may have been at the leading edge of this conceptual shift, but the transformation in scientific understandings of normality was well underway by the end of the century (see Hacking 1990: chap. 19).[17] The concept of normality would become increasingly important in industries such as education and health care, as well as manufacturing, as the twentieth century progressed.[18]

The establishment of norms and standards was significantly aided by the explosion of quantitative data over this period. By the end of the nineteenth century, data on the vital statistics of populations—including births, deaths, and immigration—were collected on a routine basis. A US Census had been in place since 1790, but it was not until 1840 that attempts were made to extend data-collection efforts to measure aspects of the population that would be of most interest to politicians and policymakers (Wright 1900).[19] Private sector investments in data collection and quantification were just as notable. The insurance industry, interested as it was in making profit from indemnifying customers in the event of a loss, was particularly focused on the collection and analysis of data. During the nineteenth century, this industry was transformed by probabilistic thinking, and in turn, it transformed the public's understanding of risk and the mitigation of risk (Daston 1987; see also Beck 1992; Bouk 2015; Rothstein 2003).[20] The growth of statistical thinking thus went hand in hand with data collection of high enough quality to allow for scientific inference.

With high-quality data, more complex statistical analyses could be conducted. The development of multiple correlation methods by Francis Galton, Karl Pearson, and Udny Yule at the end of the nineteenth century opened up new possibilities for the analysis of quantitative data and allowed scientists to build more convincing models of the natural and social world (see Stigler 1986: chap. 10). The discipline of statistics became increasingly specialized and professionalized, but even as it pulled away, quantification and statistical reasoning became hallmarks of "science" in the other disciplines.[21] As statistics developed the tools to model complex multivariate relationships, the high degree of variability found in human populations could be captured and modeled (e.g., see Goldthorpe 2016; Xie 2013). The exposure and quantitative measurement of relationships of increasing complexity was to become a hallmark of all sciences in the twentieth century (e.g., see Weaver 1948; Hidalgo 2021).

Growing model complexity is aided by the widespread growth of probabilistic reasoning, which facilitates cross-disciplinary communication. As disciplines become ever more specialized, there is a danger that knowledge will become increasingly compartmentalized, such that scientists working in different specialized areas neither know nor understand the other's scientific field (e.g., Jacobs 2014: chap. 2). But shared methodologies and probabilistic logics make communication possible across disciplinary boundaries (e.g., see Gigerenzer et al. 1990: chap. 8).[22] New findings and theories from one discipline can be integrated into others by virtue of shared probabilistic practices, and this integration dramatically increases the amount of scientific material that might be seen as relevant to any given problem. One example of this process can be seen in medicine, where medical models of disease were gradually augmented as new scientific facts and theories emerged. Over the course of the twentieth century, the basic model was straightforwardly expanded, progressively integrating personality and behavioral causes, the social determinants of health, and later the genetic factors implicated in disease processes. The evidence called on in current conventional models of disease is drawn from multiple disciplines linked by a common logic and a common language of inference.

One of the most important consequences of the changes in the type of scientific work undertaken was that they made evidence-based prediction possible. Life insurance actuaries had been making predictions using the most meager data since the early 1800s (Hacking 1990; Bouk 2015), but the advent of regression analysis and the increasing availability of population data unleashed powerful methods for evidence-based prediction in both private and public sectors. Experimental methods and regression analysis provided a stronger foundation for prediction than had existed in the past, and the methods of causal and predictive inference were only further refined and extended over the course of the twentieth century. As Warren Weaver remarked in 1948 (543), "Science is capable of tremendous further contributions to human welfare. It can continue to go forward in its triumphant march against physical nature, learning new laws, acquiring new power of forecast and control . . . making new material things for man to use and enjoy. Science can also make further brilliant contributions to our understanding of animate nature, giving men new health and vigor, longer and more effective lives, and a wiser understanding of human behavior." As Weaver recognizes, better inference provides a sounder basis for prediction, which in turn raises the possibility of intervention. Poor outcomes can be predicted and, in many cases, prevented.

The Triumphant March

The changes in scientific output can be illustrated with a simple count of the words appearing in academic publications over the period of interest. In Figure 2-2, I show the proportion of academic publications that include a

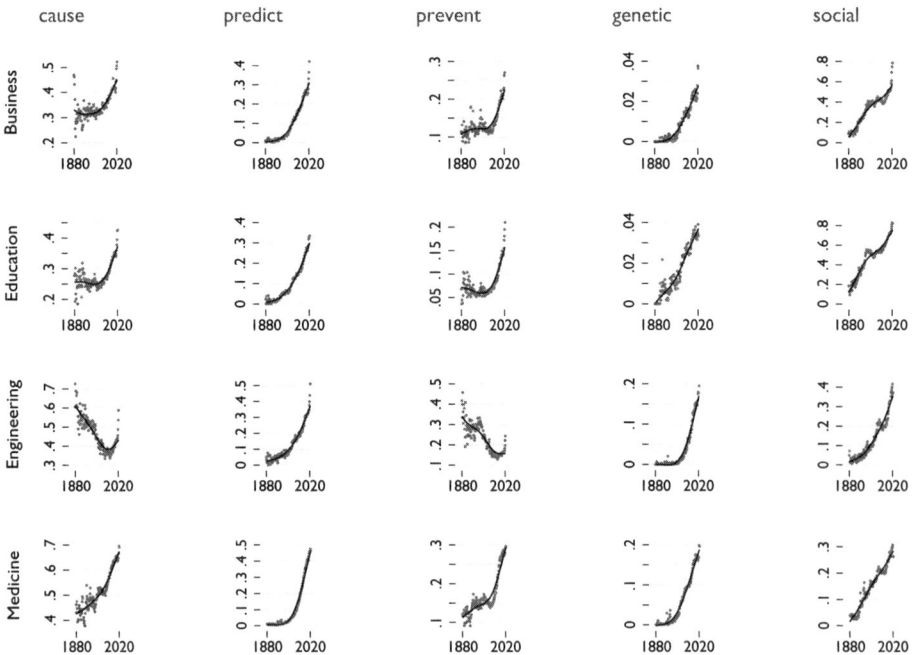

Fig. 2-2 Analysis of JSTOR text from academic publications in the fields of business, education, engineering, and medical science; proportion of publications including term.

NOTE: Scales differ across figures. See Appendix for further details of the analysis.

reference to the listed terms in the fields of business, education, engineering, and medical science.

The figure shows the probabilistic revolution sweeping through science. Focusing first on the sciences of business, education, and medicine, we see a strong increase in words related to probabilistic thinking over the period. In each of these fields, we see an increase in the use of the word "cause" and a takeoff in the words "predict" and "prevent," particularly from the mid-twentieth century onward. By the 2020s, in the region of 40–50 percent of all published articles, books, and reports made at least one mention of prediction. We also see a strong growth in mentions of both "genetic" and "social" across the scientific fields. Of particular interest is the conjunction: references to genetics increase alongside references to the social in business and education, even though both fields are relatively unconcerned with biological phenomena, while references to the social increase alongside genetics in the more biologically focused field of medicine.

Some of the same patterns are found in the field of engineering, but there are also important differences. Most notably, there is a decline in references to causes and prevention from the 1880s until the 1980s, when references start to increase again. This diverging pattern in the field of engineering appears to be due to two main factors. First, an inspection of the engineering texts that include the words "cause" and "prevent" in the late nineteenth and early twentieth century shows that these words were largely used in the context of research on machines. As research on machines became less prominent in the engineering literature, references to causes and prevention fell. Second, as I will describe in Chapter 6, the industry of engineering was rationalized relatively early, and there was much focus on the costs imposed by the high rate of machine accidents in factories in the early twentieth century. The causes of accidents and their prevention were, as a consequence, prominent in the engineering literature of the time. The tight connection between the engineering field and the problems of the manufacturing industry therefore allowed prevention to gain a foothold in the literature even before the concept of prediction became commonplace.

In sum, although the dramatic increase in scientific output in recent centuries has garnered the most attention from scholars of the division of labor, shifts in the *type* of knowledge characterizing scientific output were also significant. As science revealed new complexities of the natural and social world, it also embraced the probabilistic tools that would allow for more accurate prediction and intervention. Science increasingly made it possible to reduce risks, to intervene before "treatment" becomes necessary, and to prevent poor outcomes. These scientific developments would change our understanding of occupational boundaries and expected job tasks and determine how the new division of labor would unfold.

THE FOUNDATIONS OF COMPLEXITY

The growth of scientific knowledge and probabilistic reasoning expanded the boundaries of social problems, such that addressing these problems is now seen as requiring substantially broader interventions than were required in the past. Science has developed more detailed—and presumably better—models of human experience, albeit at the cost of greater complexity. At the same time, rationalization has pushed forward. Scientific knowledge has become indispensable to the pursuit of occupational outputs, and the logic of specialization has infused our institutions. In this section, I explain how the forces of science and specialization come together within the rationalized occupation to create the paradox of specialization, in which specialists become responsible for a much broader range of tasks.

The Generalizing Specialist

The paradox of specialization arose as the forces of rationalization and scientific development collided within occupations. Growing rationalization in occupations and the wider society pushed occupational actors to look to science for guidance on how specialized outputs should be best pursued. But as the probabilistic revolution swept through science and each output could be reconceptualized as the outcome of multiple probabilistic mechanisms with biological, economic, psychological, and social sources, the number of tasks potentially relevant to producing any given output increased.

The paradox of specialization would not arise in the absence of rationalization or if scientific development were to stagnate. Rationalization delivers the necessary conditions for the paradox to arise. First, it ensures that the products of science are understood to be relevant to occupational outputs and that maximizing output depends on looking to science for advice. Second, rationalization embeds the logic of specialization—a touchstone for the rationalized occupation. If occupational outputs are best achieved via specialization—as academics, consumers, employers, and the wider public believe—then the rationalized occupation must also be specialized with respect to output. This encourages the casting off of tasks that are unrelated to the production of occupational outputs, so police officers no longer provide medical assistance to victims of crimes or accidents, and doctors no longer manage their own ledgers and collect fees from patients. But the logic of specialization also means that when science discovers more about a given output, that knowledge is assumed to be within the purview of the occupation (or institution) that currently specializes in the output, and all associated job tasks must be embraced.[23]

The other necessary condition for the emergence of the paradox of specialization is scientific development. Although all increases in occupationally important scientific knowledge would produce the paradox, the particular form of development associated with the probabilistic revolution magnified the effect.[24] One reason the growth of probabilism within science was so consequential is that, for many occupations, the possibility of extending job tasks to preventive activities is particularly seductive. Abbott (1988) discusses prevention as an example of a "gradient" jurisdictional claim by occupations: if an occupation has control over tasks related to the treatment of a given problem, it is relatively straightforward to make a claim to the effect that the occupation should similarly have control over the prevention of that problem.[25] In general, if an occupation defines its boundaries in relation to a given problem (e.g., a pediatrician is concerned with "diseases in children") and the occupation makes claims to having scientific foundations, the prevention of the problem is as easily contained within the boundaries of the occupation as the treatment is. One interesting consequence of the rise of preventive thinking across the occupational structure is that similar job tasks might be required in quite different occupations with quite different outputs, without any feelings of competition being provoked. Insofar as child neglect is predictive of poor health and poor education, it is appropriate for both doctors *and* teachers to include among their job tasks being attuned to child neglect and its effects. As the science of prediction and prevention expands and prevention becomes increasingly feasible, the complication of occupational tasks is to be expected.

Occupational complication is only made more likely by the relatively incremental progress of science. As we consider the history of science, it is easy to be struck by discoveries and events that seem sudden and immediately transformative. But most scientific progress happens slowly, and even changes that seem fundamental in retrospect take time to diffuse. The germ theory of disease, for example, is now understood to be one of the great discoveries of medical science. But even after Louis Pasteur's experiments, the theory's basic tenets were contested, and it was unclear how the findings should be translated into medical practice (see Chapter 3). Research on the social causes of crime was being conducted over a century ago, but it took decades for law enforcement to fully integrate the science into job practices (see Chapter 4). That science is translated into occupational practice only slowly has important consequences for the division of labor. In contrast to the sudden impact on workers of the introduction of a new piece of manufacturing machinery, there is no "moment" at which a rationalized occupation is faced with deciding whether or not to adopt new job tasks. Rather, tasks are slowly integrated by practitioners who aim to "follow the science," and this slow integration makes it more likely that job tasks simply accrete.

This point can be illustrated by considering how the germ theory of disease affected occupational practices. For example, the task of delivering health care became more complicated because of germ theory, as health care practitioners were required to ensure that they did not transmit disease when providing treatment (see Chapter 3). The influence of the theory on health care is perhaps unsurprising, even if the manifold protections that we see today accreted only gradually within the health care sector. But over the long term, the germ theory of disease also complicated the tasks of a host of other occupations. For example, the theory greatly complicated the task of food manufacturing, as producers were required to build in protections against contamination, even if these protections again accreted only gradually. The job of hotel housekeeping also increased in complexity: the housekeeper had to make sure that rooms were not just thoroughly cleaned but also "disinfected." This had implications for how bathrooms were cleaned, how sheets were washed, and how air was filtered. The germ theory of disease, which is but one example of a relevant scientific innovation, slowly and gradually complicated the tasks of a large and diverse group of occupations.

People Are Not Pins

The best estimates suggest that at the time Adam Smith was writing, around three-quarters of the US labor force was engaged in farming, fishing, or mining (Lebergott 1966: tab. 2).[26] When Durkheim published the *Division of Labor,* around a third of those in the labor force were manual workers, and a third worked in agriculture (US Census Bureau 1975: tab. D, 182–232). Today, almost 80 percent of the labor force works in service sector occupations (US Bureau of Labor Statistics 2024: tab. 7).[27]

The transition from an economy based on goods to an economy based on services is widely acknowledged to have had important effects on labor market structure and the demand for skill. As automation was introduced within the car-manufacturing industry, for example, the number of front-line manufacturing workers substantially decreased, but at the same time, there was an increase in demand for higher-skilled workers to build and maintain the machines (for a nontechnical summary, see Acemoglu and Johnson 2023: chap. 7). As a consequence, many highly complex occupations, which required workers to perform a wide variety of tasks, were introduced.[28] Social scientists have documented the hollowing out of mid-level jobs and subsequent labor market polarization across a range of late industrial societies (e.g., Wright and Dwyer 2003; Autor, Katz, and Kearney 2008; Autor 2010, 2015; Kalleberg 2011; Dwyer 2013, 2023; Goos, Manning, and Salomons 2014; cf. Oesch and Piccitto 2019; Hunt and Nunn 2022).

But there is another compositional change—hidden in most discussions of the transition from "goods to services"—that has important implications for the type of science called on by the rationalized occupation: the growth of human-centered occupations. If almost all occupations can now make a claim to a scientific underpinning, occupations engaged in processing or serving humans can claim any number of scientific fields that speak to their job tasks. Human-centered occupations might reasonably claim an interest in research on human biology and physiology, human psychology and group processes, sociology and inequality, politics and economics, and more. Humans are messy products: their outcomes depend on complicated interactions among a diverse range of inputs. If a human is the focus of an occupation, the volume of scientific work that is potentially relevant to job performance and output is immense.[29] Can a doctor reasonably ignore a patient's economic situation if poverty is highly predictive of ill health and disease? Can a teacher be disinterested in processes of brain development when learning is a function of these very processes? The complexity of our current models and the diversity of disciplines that speak to human-centered outputs raise similar questions for the large majority of occupations in our labor market.

Importantly, people are not just outputs. People are also workers. Although this basic fact was appreciated well in advance of the long twentieth century, Frederick Winslow Taylor's work on "scientific management" in the early 1900s prompted substantial reflection on how worker productivity could best be encouraged (Merkle 1980: part 2). Most prominently, Elton Mayo and colleagues argued that productivity would only be maximized insofar as workers were recognized as humans. Mayo writes, for example, "The industrial worker, whether capable of it or no, does not want to develop a blackboard logic which shall guide his method of life and work. What he wants is more nearly described as, first, a method of living in social relationship with other people and, second, as part of this an economic function for and value to the group. The whole of this most important aspect of human nature we have recklessly disregarded in our 'triumphant' industrial progress" (2014: 180). The rejection of scientific management led to the development of a new science of human resource management, a science that the rationalized occupation, firm, and industry of course then had to attend to (see Bendix 1956: chap. 5; Dobbin et al. 1993; Sutton et al. 1994; Appelbaum et al. 2000). Appreciating the full humanity of the worker meant new job tasks and an increase in functional complexity. Within the rationalized firm (and wider rationalized industry), supporting worker health and well-being required the introduction of a range of different types of workers who were seemingly unrelated to the primary output of the firm. Today, we see firms devoting entire units to the mental and physical health of employees and introducing bureaucratic rules and procedures with the sole purpose of promoting worker well-being.

Similarly, the job tasks of individual workers within rationalized occupations have been influenced by the need to attend to workers as people. Workers at Stanford University, for example, received a holiday email from the BeWell unit with this advice: "As we approach the end of the year, it's important to prioritize self-care. Taking a break to concentrate on your well-being and finding ways to enhance your overall health and wellness can be a valuable investment. Not only will it benefit you, but it may also have a positive impact on your work, relationships, and other areas of life." Should workers need help in prioritizing self-care, the email—a triumph of purview-broadening, rationalized, means-ends reasoning—directs readers to classes and coaching on mindfulness, nutrition, and movement. The need to protect the health of the body and mind is thus transformed into new tasks for workers. In the same vein, the construction worker who described his "mandatory 15 minutes of calisthenics" noted that this time was "totally nonproductive" but said that "it led to fewer work site injuries during the day" (quoted in Klein 2023; see Chapter 1). In both of these cases, the recognition that output increases when we acknowledge workers as people leads to new job tasks for the rationalized occupation.[30]

Domination through Knowledge

Taylor's vision of productivity maximization was not only important because it spurred a line of research that would culminate in the development of job tasks to support workers' welfare. Scientific management, as the moniker implies, also emphasized the importance of organizational structure, largely because workers would not be capable of following the science without managerial guidance: "There is a science of handling pig iron, and . . . this science amounts to so much that the man who is suited to handle pig iron cannot possibly understand it, nor even work in accordance with the laws of this science, without the help of those who are over him" (Taylor 1911: 48). The rationalized occupation viewed through Taylor's eyes is an occupation in which workers are *organized* to attend to science, at least insofar as individual workers cannot be relied on to take notice of scientific developments themselves. This is a case in which the rationalized occupation emerges not because workers embrace science but because managers impose rationalization from the top down; this is rationalization *by fiat.*

Managerial innovations need not invoke the paradox of specialization for workers. Indeed, in the absence of complicating scientific developments, managerial structures are likely to facilitate task specialization. In bureaucracies, systematized patterns of practice provide structures that link together workers engaged in producing a given output. These patterns of practice make it possible for individual workers to take on a smaller number of the total tasks required to produce the output, because they clearly define both what the individual worker's role is and how that role fits with others in the organization. Bureaucratic rules with respect to tasks can also be used to streamline hiring processes so that those with specialized skills can be more easily matched to available positions (e.g., see Weber 1978).

There are, however, three effects of bureaucratic organization that push in the direction of increased functional complexity for workers. First, consistent with Taylor's vision of rationalization *by fiat,* if managers are required to attend to scientific developments, some part of the rationalized firm must take on those tasks that managers deem necessary to produce the output (Bendix 1956; D. Noble 1977; Sabel 1982; Piore and Sabel 1984; Baron, Dobbin, and Jennings 1986; J. Wilson 1989; Kalleberg et al. 1996; Appelbaum et al. 2000; Graeber 2019). Although deft managers might add tasks to the firm only when creating new specialized positions, it is likely that existing workers will be urged to take on at least some of the additional tasks, and thus the functional complexity of occupations will increase.

Second, bureaucratic structures amplify the effects of rationalization in the wider society: as formal rules and regulations are introduced by governmental bodies, bureaucratic structures ensure that individual workers are bound by those protocols (J. Wilson 1989; Dobbin et al. 1993; Sutton et al. 1994). Governmental bodies are, of course, themselves composed of rationalized occupations, with workers attuned to maximizing outputs by following the science.[31] Thus, regulations designed to minimize the amount of death and disability caused by work-related accidents (e.g., the Occupational Safety and Health Act of 1970) mandate a set of occupational safety and health standards that firms must satisfy.[32] Firms must ensure that these standards are met, either by adding new occupations to oversee the application of standards (e.g., occupational health and safety specialists) or by adding new tasks to existing workers (e.g., the "reporting" requirements added to the construction worker's job). Societal rationalization is therefore likely to produce increasing functional complexity at both the firm and occupation levels.

Finally, although bureaucracies help to reduce the costs of coordinating specialized workers, thereby facilitating task specialization, they also create new administrative problems and work tasks. Keeping good records, for example, is essential in modern-day medical work, where patients may be passed among multiple specialists. At the same time, physicians report being overwhelmed by administrative demands because some record-keeping tasks devolve to them. In a modern-day doctor's appointment, the physician, in a clear example of task accretion, is simultaneously negotiating recordkeeping software, delivering tests, and talking to the patient. As administrative structures become larger and ever more complex, new tasks are added to service the bureaucracy, new types of administrative workers must be found, and new types of supervisors and managers must be introduced to oversee and organize those workers.[33] All workers are likely to see increasing functional complexity as the bureaucracy adds rules and administrative structures.

From Abstractions to Data

The paradox of specialization arises as the forces of rationalization and scientific development push workers in specialized occupations to take on more and more tasks. These are cultural forces that play out over long periods of time, forces that cannot easily be quantified in a simple measure capturing the whole occupational structure. Complicating matters further, comprehensive and standardized measures of job tasks are not available over the time period that would be required to properly evaluate the theory. In the following chapters, therefore, I turn to historical case study analysis, focusing in depth on how the job tasks of a small number of industries and their dominant occupations have changed over the past 150 years.

In examining long-term changes in occupational purviews, it is important to consider both the changing job tasks of workers within these occupations and the changes within the broader industry in which the occupation sits. The effects of increasing rationalization and scientific development are felt in both occupations and industries, and examining changes in both allows for a more comprehensive account. Further, although the occupations that I consider in detail are ones that have survived in some form over the whole period, examining the broader industries in which occupations sit allows us to take account of occupations that have disappeared or emerged during the period.

The four case studies featured in this book capture variation with respect to the extent of rationalization at the end of the nineteenth century and the extent to which a body of scientific evidence existed that occupational actors might draw from. This variation is helpful in providing a foundation for causal inference, as the necessary conditions for the paradox of specialization emerge at different times in the four cases (on causal inference in qualitative case studies, see, e.g., Collier 2011; Mahoney 2012; Callis, Dunning, and Tuñón 2022). In the manufacturing industry, for example, the pace of rationalization outstrips scientific development in the first part of the period, and the paradox of specialization does not emerge until later in the twentieth century. In contrast, the medical industry was already highly

Table 2-2

			Physician (Medicine)
Science (developing–established)	Police officer (Law enforcement) Frontline worker (Manufacturing)	Teacher (Education)	
		Rationalization (low–high)	

rationalized at the beginning of the period, and a rapidly developing science delivers the paradox of specialization in short order.

In Table 2-2, I show the placement of the four industries and their dominant occupations on two dimensions that capture the degree of rationalization and scientific development at the end of the nineteenth century. In each of the case study chapters, I discuss the extent of rationalization in the occupation and industry and examine changes over time in both rationalization and the relevant science. Although there is variation across cases in the extent and expression of these changes, in the long run, all occupations and industries are expected to experience increasing rationalization and the effects of changes in scientific knowledge. There is also variation with respect to the outputs of the occupations and the extent to which these outputs pertain to people. Insofar as people are the outputs of the occupation, the effects of growing rationalization and scientific development are expected to be exaggerated, and thus the paradox of specialization will be most pronounced.

Each case study chapter also allows for a detailed discussion of an aspect of the division of labor that is particularly prominent in the industry or its dominant occupation. In Chapter 3, on the medical industry, I provide a close examination of changes in the nature of medical science over the past 150 years. In Chapter 4, on law enforcement, I consider how far policing job tasks are protected from competition from other occupations via state funding and organizational change. Chapter 5, on the education industry, considers how the proximate aims of education are contested and changed over time, reflecting both changes in society and the interests of political elites. Finally, Chapter 6, the manufacturing case study, includes a set of archival interviews with manufacturing workers from the 1940s, and these interviews allow for an in-depth examination of the experience of work within a rationalizing industry.

CHAPTER THREE

This Is Our Lane

O n November 20, 2018, the *Annals of Internal Medicine* published a paper titled "Reducing Firearm Injuries and Deaths in the United States: A Position Paper from the American College of Physicians." In the paper, the American College of Physicians (ACP) presented its updated policy position on gun violence, stating, "The medical profession has a special responsibility to speak out on prevention of firearm-related injuries and deaths" and "the available data support the need for a multifaceted and comprehensive approach to reducing firearm violence" (Butkus et al. 2018: 705, 707). In response, the National Rifle Association turned to Twitter, writing, "Someone should tell self-important anti-gun doctors to stay in their lane" (NRA 2018). Physicians across the United States started to share their experiences of treating the victims of gun violence, accompanying their tweets with the hashtag #thisisourlane. One high-profile response came from forensic pathologist Judy Melinek, who tweeted, "Do you have any idea how many bullets I pull out of corpses weekly? This isn't just my lane. It's my fucking highway" (2018).

Both the ACP's position paper and the response raise important questions about the division of labor. Why would an association of physicians need to have a position on the prevention of gun violence? Why would the NRA imagine that it was self-evident that medical professionals had no jurisdiction on these issues? And why would physicians react so forcefully to the suggestion that gun violence was not an area in which physicians held expertise?

In this chapter, I examine change and stability in the medical profession's purview over the past 150 years. I show that the expansion of the science of medicine dramatically increased the purview of medical professionals. From the beginning of the period, medical professionals saw themselves as belonging to rationalized occupations, in which science determined the range of tasks necessary to perform effectively. Thus, once the science of medicine expanded, medical professionals were vulnerable to the paradox of specialization. Physicians consequently took on a broader range of tasks, even if occupational specialization within the medical industry acted to mitigate task accretion.

A SCIENTIFIC MEDICINE

We often refer to medicine as a profession, but it is more properly called an industry, and a large one at that. Over 11 percent of the US labor force works in the medical industry, and just under 6 percent of the labor force works in a health care practitioner or technician occupation. In this chapter, I focus largely (although not exclusively) on medicine's dominant occupation: the physician occupation. As of 2019, the United States had just under a million physicians.[1]

The medical industry is a natural home for the rationalized occupation, making this field an ideal case for examining the relationship between scientific growth and job tasks. In this section, I examine changes over time in the volume and scope of medical science and consider the medical profession's response to these changes.

Islands of Enlightenment

Although the probabilistic revolution was felt across all fields of scientific endeavor, the sciences underpinning medical knowledge have perhaps been the most fundamentally transformed over the past two centuries. The broad contours of change in medical science are well established. In the modern era, medical science was revolutionized, first by the germ theory of disease and then by the discovery of DNA. Technological developments revolutionized medical treatment and diagnosis. The microscope, for example, fundamentally changed our conceptions of cancer (Koblenz 2013; Arnold-Forster 2021). The invention of the stethoscope made it possible to include auscultation as a routine part of a physical examination, the X-ray made it possible to examine internal structures without the dangers of surgery, and the computer transformed recordkeeping, information retrieval, and communication. These scientific and technological developments, among many others, laid the foundation for modern medical practice.

Broad changes in medical science are well documented, but changes in the total body of medical knowledge and the extent of differentiation within that body of knowledge are less well understood. In part, this is because it is challenging to measure these changes in scientific production. How, for example, can we capture the vast increase in the amount of medical knowledge in the modern period and its distribution across different specialist areas? How can we capture changes in which fields of knowledge were understood to fall within the scope of medicine? How did the probabilistic revolution play out in this field of scientific endeavor?

To answer these questions, I turn to *Index Medicus.* In 1879, John S. Billings and Robert Fletcher published the first volume of *Index Medicus,* subtitled *A Monthly Classified Record of the Current Medical Literature of the World.* In the years prior, Billings had been engaged in a project to catalog the contents of the Library of the Surgeon-General's Office, published as the *Index-Catalogue,* but determined that it would be desirable to produce a second publication that would focus on recent publications of relevance to medical science (see Greenberg and Gallagher 2009). *Index Medicus,* then, was designed to alert readers to all of the important contemporary developments in medical literature, promising, "The practitioner will find the titles of parallels for his anomalous cases, accounts of new remedies, and the latest methods in therapeutics. The teacher will observe what is being written or taught by the masters of his art in all countries" (1879: 1).

During its first decade, it was unclear whether or not *Index Medicus* could survive; the *Index* lost money each year, and the project was pronounced close to collapse more than once (e.g., see G. Davis 1895; *JAMA* Editor 1906). Against all odds, *Index Medicus* weathered its financial difficulties and was published in hard copy until 2004, when the decision was made to terminate the printed version in favor of online-only access (National Library of Medicine 2004). Use of the printed version of the *Index* had declined after its inclusion in the 1970s in MEDLINE, which stands today as the National Library of Medicine's main bibliographic database (National Library of Medicine 2021, 2022). But just as Billings and Fletcher had hoped, the *Index Medicus* proved to be an invaluable resource for medical science, both in its printed version and in its modern incarnations. The 1913 obituary of Billings published in the *British Medical Journal* states that the *Index Medicus* and *Index-Catalogue* were "two pieces of work without which the rapid advance of medicine in the last thirty years would have been impossible" (Brunton 1913: 642). For several decades, *Index Medicus* was mentioned by name in the *Essentials of Approved Residencies and Fellowships* of the American Medical Association (AMA).[2] And after Al Gore's decision in 1997 to make MEDLINE open-access, this progeny of *Index Medicus* was described as "the US's greatest contribution to modern healthcare" (Richards 2006: 89; see also K. Smith 2022; Greenberg and Gallagher 2009).

Given that *Index Medicus* was designed to include all scientific knowledge of importance to medical practitioners, the structure and organization of the *Index* provides insight into the structure and organization of the underlying science. By analyzing these "medical time capsules" (Clarfield 1996: 1328), and comparing classifications over time, I track changes in medical science from 1879 to the present day.

Initially, content in *Index Medicus* was arranged under a series of broad subject headings (see Greenberg and Gallagher 2009 for a discussion). Each volume also contained an index of authors and an index of subjects; the latter index represents the finest degree of classification of the volume's substantive contents. The first three terms of the 1879 *Index,* for example, are "Abattoirs," "Abdomen (Abscess)," and "Abdomen (Diseases)." In 1960, the National Library of Medicine (NLM) made the decision to rationalize and combine the various systems that had been used to classify medical literature, and the Medical Subject Headings (MeSH) system was born (NLM 1960; Coletti and Bleich 2001; Lipscomb 2000). The MeSH system was first implemented in 1963 and has been frequently updated since: as of 2022, the number of subjects indexed (labeled "main headings") stood at over thirty thousand. It is straightforward to compare the main headings across years between 1960 and 2022, as the MeSH database lists the years that headings were added and NLM makes available a list of deleted headings (e.g., see Backus, Davidson, and Rada 1987). No such crosswalk is available for years before 1960. I therefore use the 2022 MeSH classification as a dictionary and code the *Index Medicus* index of subjects to the applicable main headings.[3] I complete this coding for the years 1879, 1905, and 1931.

Each subject is assigned one or more MeSH codes, which identify the main heading's place in MeSH's tree hierarchy. For example, the main heading "Addison disease" is assigned the MeSH codes $C_{19}.053.500.263$ and $C_{20}.111.163$ (formatting added). The letter indicates the broad category at the top of the tree hierarchy; here, "C" indicates that the MeSH code is classified under "Diseases." The letter is followed by two numbers, here underlined, defining the next level of hierarchy. In the case of Addison disease, the codes indicate that the disease is classified under both "Endocrine system diseases" and "Immune system diseases." The three numbers following the period, here in italics, represent subcategories within the two sets of diseases (here, "Adrenal gland diseases" and "Autoimmune diseases," respectively). The final sets of numbers offer yet more specificity within the subcategories. In the following analyses, I take all MeSH codes assigned to the main headings in a given year and examine the top three levels of hierarchy (i.e., the first six characters in the MeSH code).

In the upper panel of Figure 3-1, I show the absolute number of codes representing broad categories associated with the main headings in *Index Medicus* between 1879 and 2022; the colors indicate which MeSH broad categories the main headings are classified under. In the lower panel, I show the relative distribution of these broad category codes over time. I distinguish the five broad categories that are most prominent over the time period: chemicals and drugs, diseases, techniques and equipment, organisms, and anatomy. The other broad categories are infrequently used.

In a comparison of the classifications over the whole time period, the most striking change is the explosion in the number of distinct topics recognized. We see in the upper panel of Figure 3-1 that there has been a dramatic takeoff in the number of broad category codes: in 1879, around 6,300 were needed to classify the main headings, a number that increased to over 92,500 by 2022. The increase in the number of broad category codes was relatively modest until the mid-1960s, when the speed of growth increased, although the period of most rapid growth did not start until around 1990. The increase in the number of index terms concurs with other sources in showing a rapid growth of scientific knowledge over the past 150 years.

Turning to the differentiation of scientific knowledge and changes in the type of scientific knowledge produced, we see that a simple account of division and further subdivision of all categories of knowledge would be a poor description of the changes over time in *Index Medicus*. All areas of medical science might have expanded, but the expansion was most prominent in the category for chemicals and drugs, which witnessed an almost sixtyfold increase between 1879 and 2022. The broad category for organisms also experienced a substantial increase: in 2022, the organisms category held

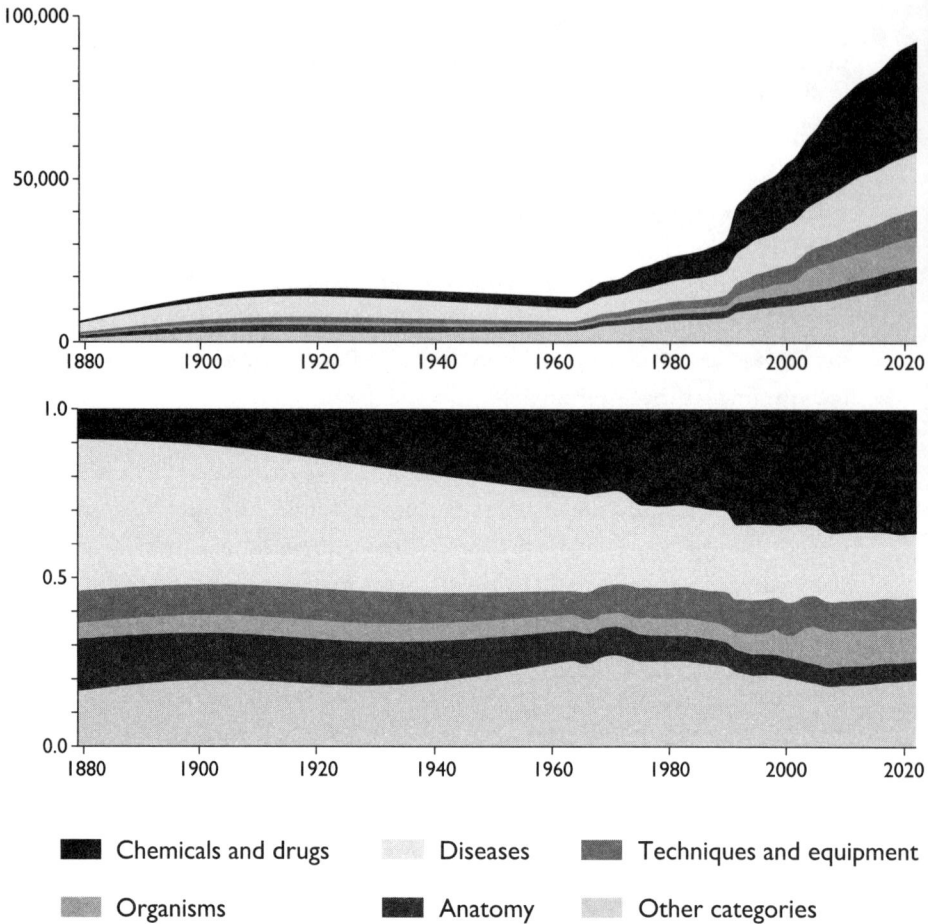

Fig. 3-1 The number of broad category codes for the main headings in *Index Medicus,* coded to 2022 MeSH classification, 1879–2022; upper panel shows absolute number of broad category codes; lower panel shows proportion of headings in each category (most frequent broad categories identified in legend, presented in top five streams in each panel).

more than thirty times the number of codes it had held in 1879. The weakest growth in the absolute number of codes is found in the diseases and anatomy categories and in the broad category for "humanities" (not highlighted in Figure 3-1).

Although the upper panel of Figure 3-1 suggests quite sudden changes in the structure of *Index Medicus,* we see in the lower panel that changes in medical science over the period are best characterized as evolutionary. There was, in fact, a relatively steady increase in the relative importance of chemicals and drugs, alongside a relatively steady decrease in the importance of diseases and anatomy. Chemicals and drugs had already taken on an increasingly prominent role in *Index Medicus* well before the takeoff in the number of main headings, with the most rapid increase in the proportion of these terms occurring between 1905 and 1931. Similarly, the declining importance of diseases and anatomy is observed across the whole of the series, not just in recent decades. Some sudden changes are seen in the smaller broad categories, such as information science, but at least some of these changes appear to be related to changing classification practices.[4] However, the more fundamental changes are those that occur gradually in the numerically larger categories, and particularly in the categories of diseases and of chemicals and drugs.

The division of medical scientific knowledge over time, therefore, is far from uniform: some categories divide and then subdivide, but in many cases the index terms—both broad and narrow—are added when new conditions, practices, and processes are discovered. To examine these changes in more detail, in Figure 3-2 I present visualizations of the structure of *Index Medicus* in 1879 and 2022, taking account of the first six characters of the MeSH codes, representing the first three levels of hierarchy within the MeSH tree. The outer gray circles represent the broad categories, the inner gray circles represent subcategories within the broad categories, and the solid circles represent finer-grained categories within the subcategories. The five broad categories called out previously are again highlighted. The changes in the broad categories over time—most notably the increase in the emphasis on chemicals and drugs, and to a lesser extent organisms, at the expense of diseases and anatomy—are of course evident in Figure 3-2. But the figure also reveals important changes at lower levels of the MeSH hierarchy.

Most prominently, we see in the solid circles the substantial increase in the number of distinctions made within the broad categories. There is considerably more detail in 2022 than in 1879, again reflecting the expansion and differentiation of scientific knowledge over the period. At the same time, there is a relatively high degree of concentration in some of the finer-grained categories in 2022—indeed, a higher degree of concentration than is found in 1879. For example, the chemicals and drugs category is much

1879

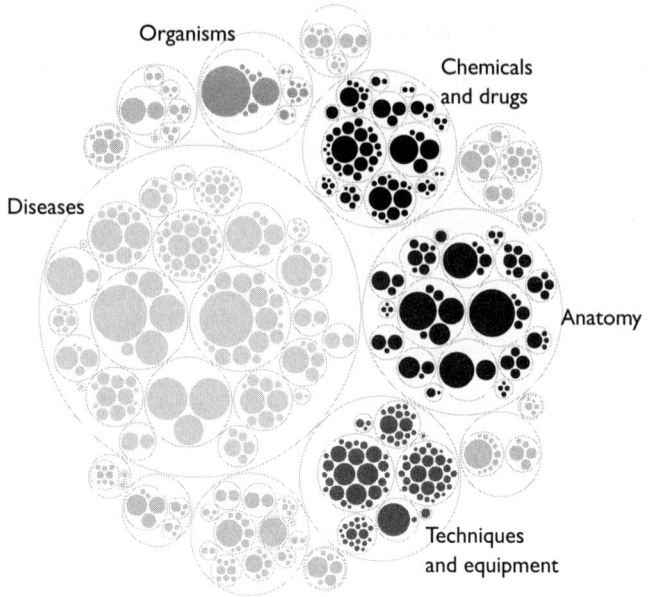

Organisms

Chemicals
and drugs

Diseases

Anatomy

Techniques
and equipment

2022

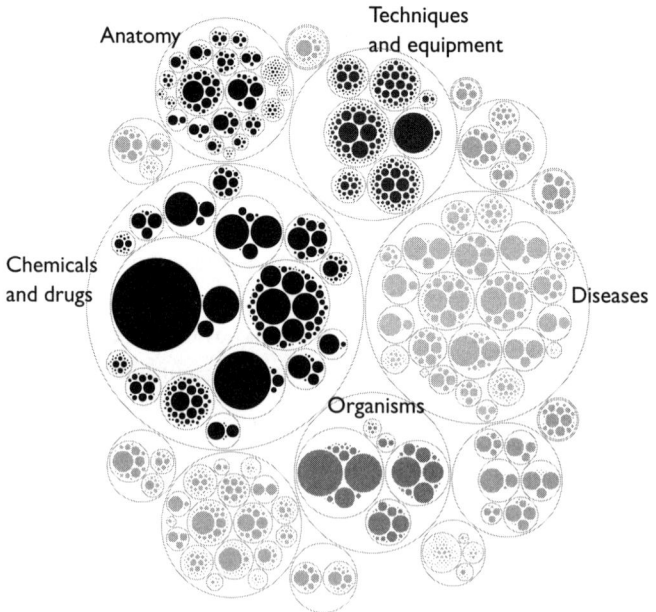

Anatomy

Techniques
and equipment

Chemicals
and drugs

Diseases

Organisms

Fig. 3-2 The distribution of main headings within broad categories in *Index Medicus,* coded to 2022 MeSH classification, 1879 and 2022.

larger in 2022 than in 1879, with many more fine-grained distinctions in the later year. Nevertheless, if two MeSH codes were to be picked at random from the entire set of codes within the chemicals and drugs category, it is *more* likely that those codes would belong to the same finer-grained category in 2022 than it was in 1879.[5] Almost 30 percent of the MeSH codes falling within the chemicals and drugs category are found in the finer-grained category of "Proteins" (D12.776), while more than 11 percent are found in "Enzymes" (D08.811). Within these fine-grained categories, we find concentration in the lower-level categories representing hydrolases and membrane proteins, both of which play important roles in drug absorption and other biological processes. Although the chemicals and drugs category offers the most extreme example of within-category concentration, in almost all broad categories, we see increased concentration in 2022 as compared to 1879.

It is also important to highlight—in line with the quantitative findings—that the earlier volumes include many examples of what would today be considered rather rare and esoteric conditions. In 1879, for example, we see a surprisingly large number of congenital abnormalities and conditions such as lycanthropy that must have been only rarely observed in the population (Guessoum et al. 2021).[6] In contrast, diseases that are among the leading causes of death in the United States, such as cancer, are less visible. Cancer was a less common cause of death in the earlier period than it is today,[7] but it was still a well-acknowledged medical problem, and key medical texts recognized both multiple varieties of cancer and multiple body parts that could be affected by cancer (e.g., see Walshe 1846). Cancers are included in the 1879 *Index Medicus* and classified under the body parts that might be affected, but the index sections for "cancer" and "tumors" are extremely brief. In this regard, it is worth noting that one of the reasons we see greater concentration in the diseases category in 2022 than in 1879 is that there is concentration in the finer-grained category "Neoplasms by Histologic Type."

The organization of research on cancer is one example of a more general pattern that is important in understanding changes over time in the structure of medical science: the decline of physiological determinism and the rise of probabilistic causal reasoning (e.g., see W. Coleman 1987). We see a clear transition over time from classification primarily based on organs and other body parts to classification primarily based on mechanism or process.

The clearest example of this is found for the category of "Abnormities," which largely captures congenital abnormalities and other neonatal conditions. In the 1879 *Index,* these abnormalities usually go unnamed and are classified simply as "abnormities" under a heading for an organ or body part. Over time, the *Index* moves to provide individual labels for these conditions, and the body part classifications fall away. Take, for example, the congenital condition of renal fusion, also known as horseshoe kidney. The condition is named in the papers cited in 1879 but is classified under "Kidney, abnormities." Today the condition is named in the MeSH subject headings, and it is classified under "Urogenital diseases," "Urogenital abnormalities," and "Congenital abnormalities." These classifications emphasize that the condition is now understood to be but one example of a set of similar processes rather than simply a feature of the kidney itself.

As is consistent with the move toward mechanisms and disease processes, an increased emphasis on causation is evident across the period. In 1879, 271 books and papers including the word "cause" as part of their title and 41 including the word "etiology" are cited by *Index Medicus.* In 1905, 377 of the books and papers cited include the word "cause," and 152 contain the word "etiology." By 1931, the number has reached 861 for "cause" and 555 for "etiology." A search of PubMed returns 20,020 uses of "cause" and 3,941 uses of "etiology" in recent titles published in the medical literature. Even accounting for the expansion in scientific terms over the period, this is evidence of a substantial increase in the interest in causation. More extreme results still are found when examining words related to prevention: there is an increase from 119 to 70,202 books and papers mentioning variants of "prevent" between 1879 and 2022.[8] In line with the changing focus of the literature, the classification systems change to include a whole range of supplementary categories capturing concepts including "causes and pathology," "etiology," and "prevention and control."[9]

In the next sections, I consider how the changes in medical science revealed through an analysis of *Index Medicus* translate into medical practice. Although it would be easy to assume that changes in the content of medical science would translate relatively straightforwardly into practice, the historical materials reveal more tension. At the same time, progress in science is clearly key to understanding changes in medical practice over the past 150 years.

The Advancing Front

The idea that a doctor was a "man of science" was firmly established well before the beginning of this period, making the physician occupation an early example of the rationalized occupation. In this section, I examine the nature of rationalization within medicine, for what it meant to be scientific was far from stable over time (Warner 1986; see also Weatherall 1996).[10] I first consider the degree to which physicians attended to science, before describing how changes in science were reflected in changing beliefs about the role of science in medical practice.

In the introduction to the AMA's first code of medical ethics, adopted in 1847 (AMA 1847: 90), John Bell writes, "The greater the inherent difficulties of medicine, as a science, and the more numerous the complications that embarrass in its practice, the more necessary is it that there should be minds of a high order and thorough cultivation, to unravel its mysteries and to deduce scientific order from apparently empirical confusion." The importance of "rational foundation" and "rational treatment" is stressed repeatedly in the earliest *Journal of the American Medical Association* (*JAMA*) papers (e.g., Eckley 1888), and the value of having approaches "put upon a more scientific basis" is also extolled (e.g., see Baker 1887: 486). Over the following decades, the commitment to science is repeatedly expressed in, for example, the institutionalized training requirements for medical practice,[11] the councils of the AMA,[12] and a wealth of books, papers, and commentaries.[13] The AMA's ethical standards have undergone many revisions since 1847, but Principle V of the current *AMA Principles of Medical Ethics* still emphasizes the connection between science and medicine, stating, "A physician shall continue to study, apply, and advance scientific knowledge" (Brotherton, Kao, and Crigger 2016). The frequent, and seemingly reflexive, invocations of science are consistent with a long-standing professional culture that takes for granted the association between scientific knowledge and medical practice.

The contrast between science-based medical practice and other types of practice is in fact important in understanding the history of occupational specialization within medicine. Initially, those who advertised themselves as "specialists" were roundly condemned by parts of the medical profession, who saw these practitioners as "quacks" who were dispensing ineffective and expensive treatment (see Weisz 2006; *JAMA* Editor 1883b). The AMA addressed the issue in the Code of Ethics (1847: 98), stating, "It is derogatory to the dignity of the profession, to resort to public advertisements or private cards or handbills, inviting the attention of individuals affected with particular diseases. . . . These are the ordinary practices of empirics, and are highly reprehensible in a regular physician." The reference to "empirics" in the Code of Ethics highlights a distinction the AMA was keen to emphasize: the distinction between the rational practitioners, who worked on the basis of science, and the empirics, who were bound to quackery and unwilling to embrace scientific principles.[14] The distinction was, of course, largely a rhetorical flourish; as John Harley Warner explains, the roots of "empiricist" as a pejorative are to be found in seventeenth-century Britain, where knowledge from experience was compared unfavorably to the rationalism of leading physicians (1986: 44). But the use of scientific commitment as an ideological cleavage does underscore the importance of the scientific identity to medical practitioners.[15]

This is not to say that medical practitioners never questioned the role of science in the profession. In the first decades of the twentieth century, a full embrace of science was viewed with suspicion by those who feared that the "art" of medicine might be lost. In part, this concern appears to have emerged in response to the dominance of the natural sciences in medical student training, particularly once that dominance was institutionalized after *The Flexner Report* (1910). Commentators expressed worries about a narrowing of the physician's traditional role in the community, a role that some feared depended on the physician being a "man of culture" as well as a "man of science." Morris Fishbein, for example, in his 1942 lecture to the Alpha Omega Alpha medical society, reviewed the case for cultural education for physicians, concluding that medical students should read widely; partake in golf, bridge, and football; and have an appreciation for art, music, drama, and travel (1942: 1245; see also Peabody 1870; *JAMA* Editor 1905b).[16] Others identified in the "art of medicine" the knowledge gained from experience, a willingness to let nature take its course, and even the unknown and unknowable effects of higher powers (e.g., Murdoch 1885; Hamilton 1887). That too close an embrace of science might leave too little room for imagination, or for humility in practice, is a long-standing theme in medical commentary (e.g., Warner 1986), and it is a theme that reappears to this day (e.g., see Swayne 2012).

Taken together, the evidence shows that throughout this period, science was a touchstone for medical practitioners; scientific discoveries offered new understandings of medical problems and thereby opened up new opportunities for medical practice. But the extent to which medical practice was influenced by changes in science went beyond the simple effects of an increase in the *amount* of science that medical practitioners needed to attend to. The historical materials show that changes in the *content* of science were also reflected in the rationalized physician occupation.

In the analysis of *Index Medicus,* we saw an increased focus on causal mechanisms in the scientific literature over the past 150 years and a dramatic increase in the number of direct references to causation. A comparison of *JAMA* papers over the period similarly reveals changes in understandings of process and mechanisms and changes in beliefs about the proper place of intervention in medical practice. A *JAMA* editorial at the dawn of the twentieth century, for example, reflected on the recent transformation of medicine brought about by the achievements of bacteriology and microscopy, noting, "The last two decades have witnessed a wonderful transformation in our conceptions of pathologic processes. . . . In the evolution of our conceptions of the causes and nature of the infectious diseases it has become clear that disease is a process. . . . Disease and health are not things, but processes" (*JAMA* Editor 1900: 96; see also Pillsbury 1904; W. Welch 1889; *JAMA* Editor 1890b; Gray 1941). Use of the terms "process" and "disease process" increases over time; the word "process," for example, is used over twice as frequently in the 1900–1909 period as in *JAMA*'s first decade, and it is used almost three times as frequently in the 1940–1949 period.[17] The focus on processes goes hand in hand with an emphasis on the micro-level mechanisms underlying disease.[18]

Over time, we see a broadening in the nature of the processes understood to be at work. Sociological and psychological mechanisms are added to biological mechanisms, interactions between individuals and the environment are hypothesized, and scientific knowledge from outside of the natural sciences is brought to bear on medical problems (e.g., see Engel 1960, 1977; McLeroy et al. 1988; Link and Phelan 1995).[19] By the 1960s and 1970s, biopsychosocial and ecological models became commonplace, and there was movement to build social science training into the medical degree. Articles in *JAMA* argue that "the time is past for armchair discussion about whether the study of human behavior has a place in medicine" (Gee 1960: 1304) and that sociology "may be more important than gross anatomy or embryology. The so-called sciences of man might indeed be more significant for the medicine of tomorrow than the sciences currently taught" (King 1970: 580; see also Engel 1979).[20] The word "sociology" does not even appear in *The Flexner Report* (1910). But as it stands today, sociology is understood to be "foundational" for the practice of medical science (Cooke et al. 2010) and is represented on the Medical College Admission Test (MCAT) alongside other behavioral sciences.[21]

Changing understandings of the causal process underlying disease are consequential for understandings of where medical professionals should intervene. As the nineteenth century drew to a close, bacteriology had turned physicians' attention to the etiology of disease and the disease process. The question then arose: What was the physician's role with respect to intervening in these and other processes? From the end of the nineteenth century to the present day, we see a transformation in the understandings of intervention that mirrored the broader changes ushered in by the probabilistic revolution. As causal processes are elucidated and the capacity to fit predictive models grows, the nature of intervention also changes. In bald terms, we see the medical profession switch focus from treatment to prevention.

The contrast can be illustrated by analyzing the discussions of medical intervention that appeared in *JAMA* through the period. In 1905, Oliver T. Osborne, the president of the American Therapeutic Society, attempted to outline and make explicit the appropriate place for intervention in medical practice. His aim in providing the illustration presented in Figure 3-3 was seemingly to remind physicians that, as important as it was to consider causal processes, more explicit attention should be paid to therapeutics, for "therapeutics involves everything of importance to the patient. All the scientific physiology, etiology, and pathology of the world is of no use to him without their final practical application through the knowledge of therapeutics" (1905: 1493). The physician's role, he argued, is to determine the

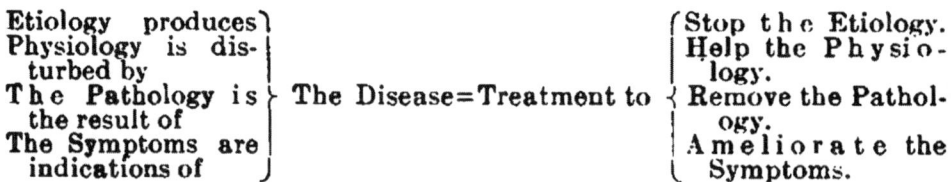

Etiology produces		Stop the Etiology.
Physiology is disturbed by		Help the Physiology.
The Pathology is the result of	The Disease = Treatment to	Remove the Pathology.
The Symptoms are indications of		Ameliorate the Symptoms.

Fig. 3-3 "The Therapeutic Art".

SOURCE: Osborne 1905: 1493.

type of treatment appropriate to the patient's circumstance. When the cause of disease is found, the aim should be to stop that cause from having deleterious effects. When the symptoms indicate the presence of a disease, the aim should be to treat the symptoms. Treatment is at all times matched to the underlying disease.

From the perspective of modern-day medicine, Osborne's illustration is as notable for what it leaves out as for what it includes. We saw in the analysis of *Index Medicus* a dramatic increase over time in references to the concept of prevention. And yet Osborne's illustration contains no explicit reference to prevention.[22] In the context of the history of the past 150 years of medicine, however, the omission of the word "prevention" from Figure 3-3 is not at all surprising. The illustration focuses on the interaction between a physician and a patient, and during this period, "prevention" was associated with intervention at the community level, particularly with respect to preventing the transmission of infectious disease. It was only later that prevention also came to be associated with individual-level interventions, such that the behavior of individuals (perhaps in consultation with their physicians) could prevent the emergence of disease.

A search for words related to prevention in the *JAMA* works from the late nineteenth century, for example, returns articles with titles such as "Yellow Fever," "Epidemic Cholera," and "Prophylaxis of Diphtheria" (*JAMA* Editor 1883c, 1883a; Buckham and Flint 1885). At this point in time, preventive medicine was essentially synonymous with public health, and one of the primary concerns of public health was the control of infectious disease. Milton Terris (1975) notes that in a description of a conference in April 1872, the secretary of the newly inaugurated American Public Health Association uses the terms "public health" and "preventive medicine" interchangeably. Epidemic control and improved sanitary conditions were key targets for public health agencies, which were squarely focused on the community-level correlates of disease. Scientific advances with respect to the germ theory of disease were understood to have laid the groundwork for more effective preventive health efforts; an 1888 article in *Science,* for example, described the attitude of medical schools toward bacteriology, explaining that the subject was of "great importance" because "the germ-theory emphasizes and makes possible a scientific study of preventive medicine" (Conn 1888: 124). Techniques for intervention to prevent disease included improved sanitation in schools and workplaces (Lamb 1891), heating and ventilation inspections (Reed 1889), and public health education (Burgess 1892).

Prevention as an individual-level intervention developed alongside increasing scientific knowledge of mechanisms and processes. It was also becoming increasingly difficult to ignore the simple fact that many of the interventions designed to improve community health—such as vaccination, tuberculosis clinics, and school health examinations—had their appreciable positive impacts by improving the health of individuals. As I describe below, the expansion of the concept of prevention to the individual level led to tension between public health practitioners and physicians (e.g., see Wood 1924; Fort 1924). As physicians took on more work that was preventive in nature and the science of individual prevention grew, the types of intervention considered to be preventive also expanded. In 1964, for example, Fred B. Rogers addressed the Section on Preventive Medicine of the AMA, arguing quite explicitly that "an opportunity to extend the horizons of preventive medicine is offered to all practitioners as our technical knowledge grows each year" (837; see also Newsholme 1927: chap. 6). Preventive care came to encompass screening for the early signs of cancers and disease (e.g., see Peters and Madden 1950), frequent and routine health examinations by both general and specialist practitioners (e.g., see Schenthal 1960), and, by the end of the century, genetic screening to identify individuals likely to succumb to disease (e.g., see Lynch, Mulcahy, and Krush 1970). The language of prevention expanded to include words such as "predict" and "risk," as research on disease mechanisms and processes made it possible to build models that would provide individualized estimates of susceptibility to any number of diseases and conditions (e.g., see Rothstein 2003; Zheng et al. 2022). For the modern hospital, curing disease is something that happens only in the event that the disease has not been predicted and prevented.

In 1933, the distinguished neurosurgeon Harvey Cushing authored a somewhat world-weary passage in *JAMA* on the growing emphasis on prevention in medicine:

> A rose by any other name is just as sweet, and there has been in common English usage for the past four hundred years what the doctor has known as prophylactic . . . meaning precautionary, medicine. And it would be a slur on the students' intelligence for a surgeon, let us say, to

point out, as he has been urged to do, that he wears rubber gloves to "prevent" infecting the patient, gives the anesthetic to "prevent" pain, removes the appendix to "prevent" peritonitis, and so on, *ad infinitum*. For his own part, he sits down and has a cup of tea to "prevent" fatigue and then to "prevent" irritation keeps away from the faculty meeting where the great importance of preventive medicine will again be pointed out to him. . . . There is only one ultimate and effectual preventive for the maladies to which flesh is heir, and that is death. (Cushing 1933: 1573)

Cushing was hardly rejecting the principle that prevention was important in medical practice; the point of his observation was rather to emphasize that the roots of prevention reached far back into the history of medicine (see Newman 1932 for a review). But the passage highlights the extent to which changes in the science of medicine came to dominate discussions about intervention in medical practice. Osborne's model of intervention within health care (Figure 3-3) had been replaced by a model in which the prevention of disease and maintenance of good health was both a plausible and desirable outcome of medical care.

FROM SADDLEBAGS TO POCKETBOOKS

As a rationalized occupation, the physician occupation is vulnerable to the paradox of specialization, whereby changes in the science of medicine lead to an accretion of job tasks. Although occupational specialization (i.e., specialization with respect to outputs) within medicine would be expected to mitigate task accretion, the substantial changes in the amount and content of scientific work would be expected to lead to increases in the functional complexity of physician occupations. In this section, I use data drawn from historical reports on the job tasks of medical professionals, information on the tools employed by physicians, time and motion studies, and nationally representative survey data for the past five decades from the National Ambulatory Medical Care Survey (NAMCS; see National Center for Health Statistics 2025) to track job tasks over time.

I examine whether there is evidence for a paradox of specialization within physician occupations. First, I describe the growth of occupational specialization within medicine over time, a growth that was explicitly described as being in response to the increasing volume of scientific work.

Next, I examine changes in the tools used by physicians, tools being a common—if indirect—measure of job tasks. Third, I describe how the move from treatment to prevention was implemented in medical practice and ask how the probabilistic revolution changed the job tasks of medical professionals. Finally, I examine how changes in the types of causal mechanisms proposed in medical science changed the nature of preventive activities undertaken by medical personnel.

Too Much Science

The section title—"From Saddlebags to Pocketbooks"—is taken from a paper published in *JAMA* in 1900. The paper describes the effects that functional differentiation had already had on the job tasks of physicians, who had lost the task of dispensing drugs to the pharmacist. The author concludes, "There are no longer saddlebags, but the duty is the same, the physician must certify in some way to the therapeutic value of the elements which go into the prescription which he writes. The responsibility is his, not the druggist's" (Whitmore 1900: 26). Reflections on the nature of functional differentiation in medicine and its effects on the day-to-day tasks of physicians are in fact rather common in the *JAMA* of the early twentieth century, not least because increasing interest in occupational specialization raised jurisdictional questions that physicians were keen to resolve in their favor (for examples of this dynamic in the nineteenth century, see Abbott 1988). But it was not only the costs of occupational specialization that were discussed. Perhaps the most appealing aspect of increasing occupational specialization, from the perspective of physicians, was the promise of being able to manage the phenomenal growth of scientific knowledge.

Medical professionals well recognized that changes in medical science had implications for the everyday job tasks of physicians: as the content of medical science expanded and the processes underlying disease were rendered less opaque, physicians understood that scientific advances would be reflected in the practice of medicine. It was also understood that the volume of new scientific knowledge was so immense that it was implausible that any one person would be able to master it all. In one of the earliest papers on specialization to appear in *JAMA*, L. Duncan Bulkley (1884: 652) remarked, "The entire field of medical knowledge has become so vast, and the advances in it so great, that it is an absolute impossibility for any one mind to perfectly grasp the former, or to follow and comprehend the latter."

This sentiment is expressed repeatedly from the dawn of the century onward, as rapid scientific production outstripped the capacity of physicians to keep up to date with best practices (e.g., see Bulkley 1889). It was also recognized that resisting occupational specialization would be quite unwise, given the large public demand for medical specialists.

The growth of occupational specialization within medicine can be illustrated by reference to Figures 3-4 and 3-5. In Figure 3-4, I show the spectacular growth of national specialist medical societies between the mid-nineteenth century—from the founding of the American Psychiatric Association—to the present day, when almost five hundred societies exist.[23] Although growth in specialist societies was initially slow, by the end of the nineteenth century, the societies were proliferating. By the turn of the twentieth century, many of today's most prominent specialist associations—including the American Public Health Association (1872), the American Dermatological Association (1876), and the American Surgical Association (1880)—were already in place. Thereafter, we see continuing and steep growth in specialist societies through to the present day, with the fastest growth occurring from the 1970s to the 1990s. The evidence from specialist societies demonstrates a takeoff in occupational specialization in medicine.

A similar story may be told with respect to graduate medical training. Specialized medical training in the United States is organized under specialist boards that offer certification in particular areas of practice. The largest and best-recognized overseer board is the American Board of Medical Specialties (ABMS), which was founded in 1933. In Figure 3-5, I show the number of different specialties (boards, specialty certificates, and subspecialty certificates) recognized by the ABMS between 1933 and 2024 (ABMS 2024).[24] Once again, we see rapid growth in the institutionalization of specialized medicine; the number of specialized boards increased from four to twenty-four over the past century, with the most recent board, the American Board of Medical Genetics and Genomics, joining the ABMS in 1991. Originally, certification under a particular board represented the highest degree of occupational specialization that it was possible to achieve, but over time, the boards started to add primary specialty and subspecialty certificates. The expansion of these specialized credentials was relatively modest until the 1970s, after which there was a substantial increase in the number of certificates offered. As of 2024, the ABMS offers certification in 137 subspecialties and 19 specialties.

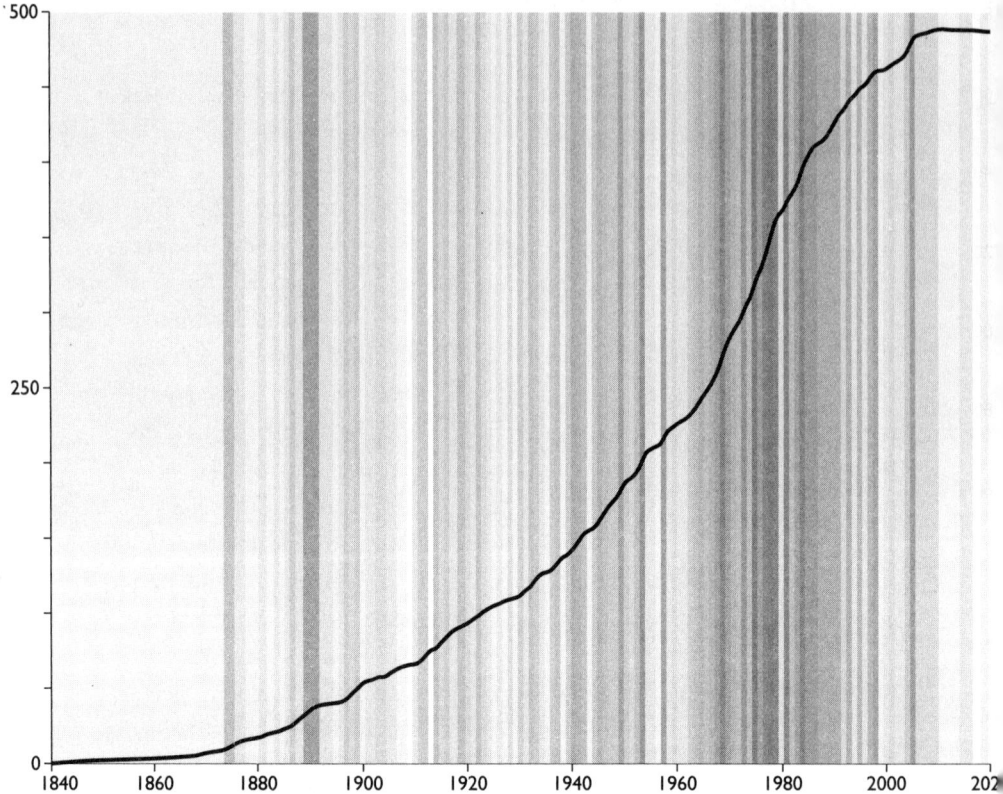

Fig. 3-4 The number of specialist medical societies, 1844–2022; shading indicates growth in number of societies each year, where darker shades indicate higher growth.

Occupational specialization allowed medical professionals to manage the dramatic growth of medical science. The force of occupational specialization pulled dispensing and laboratory work from the physician occupation and made it possible for physicians to divide up the full range of medical problems. By specializing, physicians could both satisfy the public demand for specialist physicians and develop the skills and knowledge that would allow them to deliver better patient care.

It is, however, important to emphasize that occupational specialization also had some perverse effects: as the medical industry specialized, it became ever more complex for patients and practitioners to navigate, to such an extent that the health of patients is increasingly jeopardized (see Detsky, Gauthier, and Fuchs 2012 for an overview). In turn, this has created new types of work for medical professionals, who must manage the

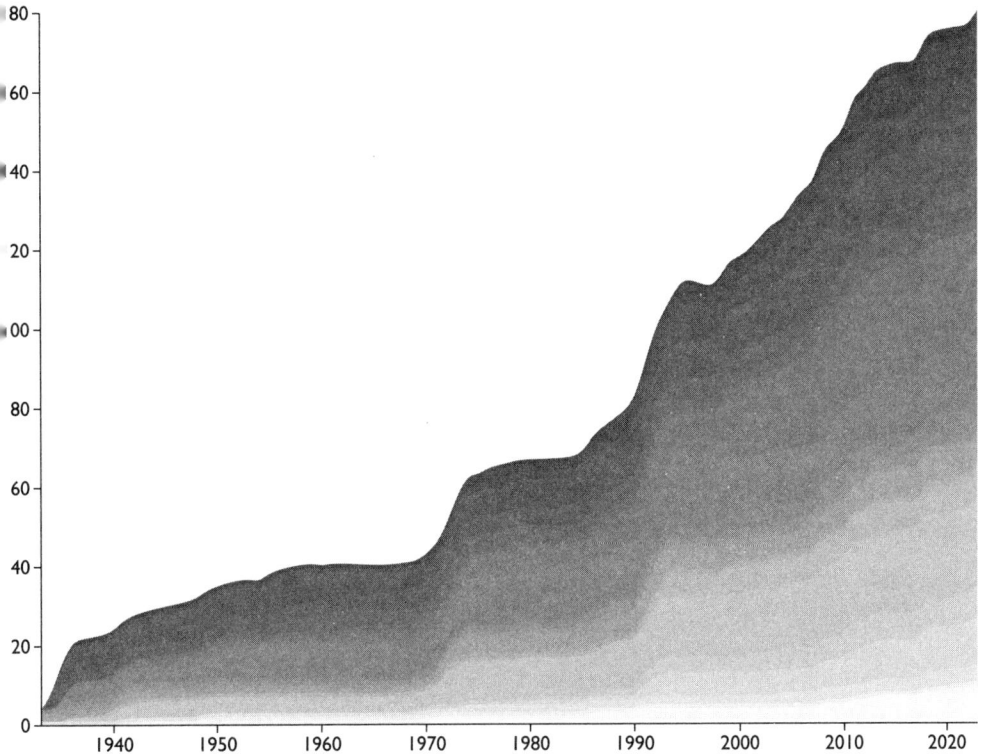

Fig. 3-5 The number of medical boards (including primary specialty and subspecialty certificates) recognized by the American Board of Medical Specialties, 1933–2024; each of the twenty-four layers represents a different medical board.

complexity introduced by occupational specialization. In 1964, for example, J. Englebert Dunphy devoted part of his address to the American College of Surgeons to his concerns about occupational specialization within medicine. He states, "All too often, especially in the case of certain cancers, the most carefully planned operation ends in prolonged illness, debilitation and death. Surgery cannot divorce itself from these responsibilities and yet it cannot meet them all alone. Team work with a competent, sympathetic and broadly educated family doctor is the only way that the surgeon will meet his responsibilities. This is the role that the general practitioner so often performs today" (Dunphy 1964: 4). As the quote suggests, primary care physicians have taken on the bulk of the responsibility for managing complexity in the contemporary medical system: primary care physicians are usually responsible for coordinating the diverse set of specialists and for helping patients to manage multimorbidity (e.g., see Alpert and Charney 1973). But occupational specialization has made it necessary for all medical personnel to work more frequently in teams (e.g., see Pew Health Professions Commission 1995; Institute of Medicine 2001; Cebul et al. 2008; P. Mitchell et al. 2012). Multidisciplinary teams represent the standard of care in many fields, and support for the team management of chronic disease was provided in the Affordable Care Act (ACA) (Kocher, Emanuel, and DeParle 2010; see also Ruhstaller et al. 2006). The growth of teamwork within medicine has increased the demand for coordination, communication, and leadership skills relative to the past, when many physicians were operating as independent practitioners. Almost all modern-day health care rests on substantial proficiency in social skills.

Nevertheless, the growth of occupational specialization within medicine both pushed some responsibilities away from physicians and toward other specialized occupations and also divided "physician outputs" across a larger number of more specialized physicians. As a consequence, the growing volume of medical science could be more successfully managed and patient care improved.

The Little Black Bag

In general, there is relatively straightforward acceptance that an advancing science of medicine will be associated with new job tasks. To be sure, grumbles about new norms of medical practice, new standards, and overwork pepper the pages of *JAMA* over the decades, but on the whole, new technologies and practices are integrated into day-to-day work. The identity of "medic as scientist" is immensely powerful in pushing medical professionals to adopt new tasks, particularly where those new tasks produce better outcomes for patients. Thus, the stethoscope became a key piece of diagnostic equipment (Dalton 1893), screening procedures were welcomed as a routine part of practice (e.g., see Peters and Madden 1950), and practice guidelines are frequently updated to reflect current standards of care (Brignardello-Petersen, Carrasco-Labra, and Guyatt 2021; J. Alexander and Cifu 2021).

The link between scientific advances and expectations with respect to the adoption of new tasks is in fact made explicit in the criteria governing medical malpractice: medical malpractice law is clear that a case of malpractice rests, to some extent, upon a failure to adhere to existing norms of medical practice (e.g., see Bal 2009). An introduction to malpractice law for physicians, published in *JAMA* in 1941, emphasizes that scientific consensus determines the boundaries of appropriate treatment: "A duty lies on the physician to conform his practice to the 'modern state of the science.' . . . Physicians are therefore under a legal duty to keep apprised of major developments and abandoned doctrines" (H. Smith 1941: 2760).[25] Thus, in the late 1800s, *JAMA* published a paper suggesting that a failure to use antiseptic during surgery could meet the test for proving medical malpractice (Eckley 1888).[26] In the late 1950s, there was a discussion of the large number of legal cases proceeding from a failure to X-ray fractures (Sandor 1957). And by 2019, physicians were advised to protect themselves against future lawsuits by considering the role that artificial intelligence played in their decision-making and procuring liability insurance that would cover the use of medical AI (W. N. Price, Gerke, and Cohen 2019).

It is clear, then, that scientific advances are expected to lead to changes in job tasks. Here, I assess the extent of change in job tasks by tracking changes in the use of tools over time. Tool use has been used in prior studies to measure functional complexity, and I here examine the contents of the physician's medical bag over the past century. The "little black bag" was a staple of the physician occupation for centuries: many physicians were required to visit patients at home and respond to emergencies, and a portable set of tools was essential (Dammery 2016).[27] Although the task of visiting patients at home has largely fallen out of the physician occupation, many physicians still maintain a medical bag for cases of emergency, and some physicians working in primary care (or general practice) still use a medical bag as part of their day-to-day activities.

In Table 3-1, I show how the contents of medical bags have changed over the past century; the lists of tools are gathered from David Dammery's "Historical Account of the Doctor's Bag" (2016), Stephen Morris's "Labour of Love" (1971), and J. Murtagh and colleagues' *Murtagh's General Practice* (2018), and I use commentaries published in the literature to help in interpreting changes in the contents.[28]

It is important to emphasize the similarity in the contents of the medical bag over time: a core set of tools has been present in the bag for the past century. Basic diagnostic tools—such as the stethoscope, aneroid sphygmomanometer, and thermometer—have been present from the 1920s to the present day. But the changes in tools over time are revealing with respect to the

Table 3-1 Contents of medical bags

1920s	1980s	2020s
Stethoscope	Stethoscope	Stethoscope
Sphygmomanometer	Aneroid sphygmomanometer	Sphygmomanometer (aneroid)
Clinical thermometer	Thermometer	Thermometer
Auriscope	Auriscope	Diagnostic set: auriscope
Ophthalmoscope	Ophthalmoscope	Diagnostic set: ophthalmoscope
Tongue depressor	Tongue spatulas	Tongue depressors
Torch	Pencil torch	Torch
Plessor (reflex hammer)	Plessor (reflex hammer)	Patellar hammer
Syringes and needles in spirit-proof case	Disposable sterile syringes and needles	Syringes 2, 5, 10 mL and needles 19, 21, 23, 25 gauge
Cotton wool in spirit	Alcohol swabs	Alcohol swabs
Rubber gloves	Disposable gloves	Examination gloves
Scalpels and other surgical instruments	Disposable scalpel	Scalpel (disposable)
Catheters	Artery forceps	Artery forceps
Chloroform and dropper bottle	Oral airway—Resuscitube or Guedel	Oral airway (e.g., Revivatube, Resuscitube, Guedel)
Assorted dressings	Scissors	Scissors
Plaster bandages	Butterfly needles	Scalp veins (butterfly) needles
Soap	Velcro tourniquet	Tourniquet
Handy Haemoglobin Chart	Paper bag (to treat hyperventilation)	Spacer (e.g., Volumatic, for asthma)
Prontosil (used in treatment of infection)	Steri-Strips	Micropore tape
Luminal tablets	Ampoule file	Pathology specimen bottles
Blue Pill and Rhubarb Compound tablets	Urine test sticks—Dextrostix and Labstix	Urine testing sticks
Microscope slides	Sample containers, swabs, transport medium	Skin swabs, throat swabs
Anthelmintics	Prescription pads	Prescription pads
Writing paper and envelopes	Notepaper and envelopes	Practice letterhead and envelopes
Fountain pen	Ballpoint pen	Pens
"Vaporole" iodine	Psychiatric recommendation forms	Recommendation forms (to psychiatric/mental hospitals)
Somnifaine	Syrup of ipecacuanha	Small needle disposal bottle
Wellcome Memorandum Book	Aspirin	Soluble aspirin (for myocardial infarction)
Glycerin and Blackcurrant pastilles	Oxazepam	Sickness/off-work certificates
Ethyl chloride spray (for local anesthesia)	Nitrazepam	X-ray, pathology referral forms

Table 3.1 *(continued)*

1920s	1980s	2020s
Trinitrin	Cotrimoxazole	Accounting and Medicare forms
Small envelopes for on-the-spot dispensing	Promethazine	Dangerous drugs record books
Nikethamide pack	Glyceryl trinitrate	Glyceryl trinitrate spray
Analgesics	Plus 17 injectable drugs	Tie-on labels for emergencies
		Laerdal pocket mask
		IV cannulas 16, 18, 20 gauge
		Quick reference cards: the doctor's bag checklist and dosage details of drugs
		Handbook of emergency medicine
		Analgesic samples
		Antibiotic samples
		Antidiarrheal agent samples
		Antiemetic samples
		Antihistamine samples
		Sedative samples
		Glyceryl trinitrate (although sublingual tablets deteriorate after opening)
		Pulse oximeter
		Continuation notes
		Sumatriptan
		Salbutamol aerosol
		Anesthetic eyedrops
		Plus 25 injectable drugs

DATA SOURCES: Dammery 2016, Morris 1971 Murtagh et al. 2018.

changing job tasks of physicians. We see, for example, the declining importance of surgery in general medical care: scalpels are still present in medical bags in 2023, but the other surgical instruments have largely disappeared; as Morris describes, "The absence of antibiotics meant that [in the 1920s] surgical instruments played a larger role" (1971: 119). Other changes in the bags point to further tasks lost. For example, glass microscope slides are included in the bag of the 1920s but have been replaced by swabs and sample containers by the 1980s. A commentary on medical bag contents from the early 1950s nicely describes the transition: "Diagnostic equipment for blood counts sounds very good, and I originally did some of my own counts. However, I soon discovered such discrepancies in my determinations, that I now trust only the work of an experienced laboratory technician" (Vorhaus and Weihe 1951: 82). Thus, while equipment to collect pathology samples is still required in the present day, its purpose is to allow physicians to safely deliver samples to the laboratory. Other equipment such as urine test sticks allows for on-the-spot diagnosis without the need for laboratory testing.

The medical bags also reveal changes in job tasks induced by the changing science of medicine. First, and most notably, the bag contains more in 2023 than it did a century earlier. The bulk of the growth comes from an increase in the number of drugs carried, an increase that echoes the changes in scientific content observed in the analysis of *Index Medicus*. In many cases, the purpose of the drugs is to stabilize the patient and ease discomfort rather than to cure, with curing being the business of other physicians after the immediate emergency has passed. Second, the inclusion of recommendation forms for psychiatric treatment by the 1980s signals the growing concern for mental health during the twentieth century. Third, the contemporary medical bag contains a large number of standardized forms designed to meet the requirements of the bureaucracy. As the medical industry as a whole has become rationalized, there has been a takeoff in bureaucratic tasks. The presence of various certificates, referral forms, and insurance forms, alongside medical record and reference items, underscores that contemporary medical practice is highly standardized and regulated. Although some administrative practices are generally considered to promote better medical care, it is important to highlight that administrative work is frequently named as a major cause of physician burnout and dissatisfaction in medicine, in large part because administrative work is perceived as "office" work rather than "doctor" work (Agarwal et al. 2020: 397; see also Young et al. 2018).

Examining the changing contents of medical bags illustrates the degree to which physician tasks have changed over the past century. The effects of occupational specialization on the tools of the general physician are clear: surgical and laboratory work is now largely undertaken by specialists, and general physicians are expected to refer patients to specialist colleagues rather than simply take on all work themselves. But developments in the science of medicine have had effects too. Some developments have reduced the functional complexity of general practice, with the discovery of antibiotics being particularly notable for its effects on emergency surgical intervention. But, on the whole, scientific developments appear to have increased the tool demands within general practice, even while the field of general practice itself became more specialized with respect to outputs. In the following section, I consider how changes in the type of science produced—as revealed in the analysis of *Index Medicus*—have affected the job tasks of physicians and other medical personnel.

From Treating the Sick to Sustaining the Well

In November 1884, Austin Flint delivered an address on therapeutics to the first annual meeting of the New York State Medical Association. He reflected on the role of the physician and the treatment of disease. During the address, he speculated, "The time will come when the physician will not be regarded as solely a therapeutist, but as a medical counselor, whose functions embrace the preservation of health and the prevention, not less than the treatment, of diseases" (Flint 1884: 598). Over a century later, Flint's prediction appears to have been unnervingly accurate. The growth of interest in prevention observed in the analysis of *Index Medicus* and the historical materials is strongly reflected in changes in medical practice. These changes are clearest with respect to the types of patients encountered, the types of disease that it is seen as feasible to prevent, and the types of procedures undertaken. Each has had implications for job tasks.

The effects of an increasing emphasis on the prevention of disease are well illustrated by the case of health care for children. At the end of the nineteenth century, there was significant and widespread concern about the comparatively high rates of infant and child mortality in the United States. Concerns are raised frequently in *JAMA* from the 1880s onward, and the act establishing the Children's Bureau in the Department of Commerce and Labor explicitly calls out infant mortality as a matter of central importance (e.g., see Stretch 1970). The high rates of mortality among young children were attributed to several important factors: high rates of communicable disease, deficient infant feeding and nutrition, and poor sanitary conditions (Buckham and Flint 1885; Greenley 1889; Pawluch 1983, 2017). During this time, leaders in the medical profession called for the diseases of children to be made a "special study" (M. Thompson 1886) and for the subject of pediatrics to be properly integrated into medical education (Rotch 1903).

Although there was an increasing interest in a medical specialization in pediatrics, the prevention of disease in children—just as the prevention of disease in adults—was initially treated primarily as a problem of public health. Those concerned about the health of children focused on interventions to tackle those factors identified as responsible for the high rates of child mortality; these interventions included the certification and subsequent pasteurization of milk (e.g., see Ostheimer 1905); the improved construction, ventilation, and heating of school buildings (e.g., see Lincoln 1891; Reed 1889, 1891; Newmayer 1913; Smiley and Gould 1941: chap. 18); improved sanitation and hygiene (e.g., see Fulton 1905; H. Moore 1923); and vaccination (e.g., see H. Moore 1923; Ulrich 1900). Notably, no single occupation was responsible for these interventions. Then, as now, public health interventions involved many parties, including politicians, to instigate legal changes; engineers and construction workers, to improve buildings; teachers and other school staff, to teach good hygiene; physicians and nurses, to treat the sick, advise local and federal government, and administer vaccines; and many, many others. The wide range of workers engaged in public health activities was generally accepted by physicians, insofar as the medical profession was understood to be the ultimate arbiter of appropriate preventive interventions. As Alice Maude Smith argued in her address to the Section on Diseases of Children of the AMA, "If preventive medicine is to assume its legitimate place among the social forces, some method of procedure must be adopted which shall place physicians in authority over these matters" (1905: 979). The role of adviser is in fact a more general obligation associated with the physician occupation; the responsibility to advise on all issues pertaining to the health or welfare of patients and communities has been stressed in many descriptions of the physician occupation throughout the past 150 years.

The quotation from Alice Maude Smith hints at a tension that was to become ever more conspicuous as preventive medicine accumulated successes and expanded into new areas of work. Public health activities, once squarely focused on community health and disease, began to encroach on activities that private physicians believed were under their jurisdiction. Free clinics provided a range of medical services, including treatment for venereal disease, Schick tests indicating susceptibility to diphtheria, and treatment for tuberculosis. Periodic health examinations of schoolchildren were also undertaken in many communities; in 1905, the New York Department of Health reported that 13,941 children were examined in metropolitan schools, and 6,294 were found to require medical attention for conditions including malnutrition, poor vision, and the aftereffects of tuberculosis infection (e.g., see *JAMA* Editor 1905a; see also Burnham 1917; Terry 1920). A detailed description of how these examinations proceeded is provided in a contemporary report by Lillian D. Wald, a nurse and key figure in the settlement house movement in New York. Wald's account discusses some of the problems that child health examinations caused in the past, most notably in September 1902, when the health department had arranged for medical inspectors to examine schoolchildren for disease. Children who were found to have signs of disease were subsequently excluded from the classroom, with the result that the "honestly administered health department was charged with demoralizing the department of education by emptying the school room" (Wald 1905: 293). As Wald points out, identifying sick children without subsequently treating them was less than ideal, and the school examination procedure was therefore reformed to include follow-up treatment for children without access to their own physicians.[29] This program, therefore, along with countless similar others, provided preventive services that had strong overlap with services previously understood to be the province of private physicians. Even more strikingly, there are examples of nonmedical personnel undertaking health examinations in some schools. During the 1918 influenza pandemic, for example, teachers were expected to observe children for signs of influenza and refer for professional examination all of those with symptoms (Stern et al. 2010; see also Newhart 1926; H. Moore 1923). These (and similar) tasks are in fact recorded as required tasks for teachers in the job task analysis presented in Table 5-1 (in Chapter 5, classified under the "Contacts with pupils" category).

It is perhaps unsurprising that medical professionals working in private practice raised concerns. Correspondence from Frank M. Wood, MD, published in *JAMA* in 1924 (861–862), offers some insight into this dynamic:

> The public health propaganda in every community is now bringing into medical practice such an army of untrained, hairbrained cultists and faddists, working in and through the public schools and free clinics, that it is up to us to meet this movement by some definite plan of action.... Free public health work now being carried on in city, state and nation is surely subversive of the best interests of the profession, and a menace to the proper practice of medicine.... Is it any more right that city, state and nation should invade the field of medicine than it would be for it to take over the business of the Standard Oil Company?

The medical profession was, of course, ultimately successful in beating down the prospect of socialized health care in the United States (Starr 2017). But the understanding that preventive techniques had individual-level as well as community-level applications was now firmly established in the minds of both medical professionals and the general public. For the general public, the possibility of preventing the appearance of disease and preserving good health underpinned a strong demand for preventive services. For medical professionals, the provision of preventive care raised the possibility of improving the welfare of patients while simultaneously securing an important ongoing role for the practitioner (e.g., see Pawluch 1983). Even as some pushed back against the preventive mindset, others saw in prevention the future of medicine, and particularly the future of pediatric and family practice. In the same year that Wood's letter was published, for example, Henry Helmholz wrote, "The practice of pediatrics will become more and more a practice of preventive medicine. Our work with the sick, by our own effort, is being taken away from us. We aim to prevent disease which formerly we were called on to treat; thus our work has changed, but not disappeared" (1924: 485).

The transition within pediatrics is well illustrated by a comparison of different editions of *The Compleat Pediatrician*, a guide to pediatrics designed to be carried by pediatricians and available as an easy reference.[30] In the first edition, published in 1934, the preface describes the book's purpose as follows:

> It is hoped that this book may be of assistance in training students and practitioners of pediatrics to arrive logically at a diagnosis by emphasizing the fact that symptoms are clues, which may be caused by several diseases, all but one of which must be eliminated by further study of the patient's other symptoms, and often by the use of laboratory methods, before the correct diagnosis can be made. (Davison 1934)

By the fourth edition, published in 1944, the text has changed to the following:

> This book is an effort to emphasize the twofold nature of pediatrics: (a) the recognition of normal children and the necessity of keeping them normal, based on a knowledge of growth, development and prevention, and (b) the recognition of sick children, their diseases and what to do for them. (Davison 1944)

And by edition seven, published in 1957, the preface states:

> This book is an effort to emphasize the threefold aim of pediatrics: (a) the appraisal of normal children and the necessity of keeping them normal, based on a knowledge of growth, development and disease prevention. Pediatrics is now chiefly child care, from conception through adolescence. (b) The recognition of ill children, their diseases, and what to do for them. (c) Now that so many conditions are prevented or quickly cured it is most important to consider each child, not as a site of a disease, but as an individual with emotional and other problems which require advice and family counsel. (Davison and Levinthal 1957)

We see in the prefaces, then, a shift over time in the understanding of pediatrics in line with the changes in science. As the preventive mindset diffused, the purview of pediatrics increased around the broader range of tasks required to produce the desired outcome.

One of the main consequences of taking on more preventive work was that medical personnel spent an increasing amount of time with patients who were, to all intents and purposes, quite well. The adoption of the routine physical examination by pediatricians and other physicians was perhaps the clearest sign that individualized preventive medicine would eventually come to dominate the practice of medicine. Routine health examinations had first been proposed in the nineteenth century as a preventive measure, but they were not endorsed by the AMA until 1922 (Haven Emerson 1923).[31] From then on, the examination of well patients became a mainstay of preventive work in pediatrics and general practice.

It is possible to examine the growing embrace of the routine health examination in pediatric practice by comparing studies of the number of well patients seen by pediatricians over time. In 1934, C. Anderson Aldrich published a paper quantifying the composition of pediatric practice work. For several years, Aldrich kept notes on which patients were seen and for which conditions. Using these data, we can calculate that Aldrich spent around 39 percent of his time engaged in routine preventive healthcare, or "well-child" visits (Aldrich 1934: tabs. 1, 5, 6, 20). Aldrich's method was subsequently applied by many other pediatricians (see Hoekelman 1983), and in Figure 3-6 I plot all available estimates from analyses of pediatric practice data.[32] To these estimates I add estimates for pediatric visits from NAMCS, a nationally representative survey of patient visits in the United States, 1973–2016. For each survey, I calculate the proportion of patient visits to pediatricians that were for well children. Each point in Figure 3-6 is scaled to the size of the sample underlying the estimate.

The figure shows that for almost a century, preventive care has constituted a substantial proportion of the pediatrician's workload: between the 1930s and 1970s, an average of around two-fifths of patient visits were for preventive care. In the 1990s, we see a steady increase in the proportion of visits for preventive care: the NAMCS studies indicate that by the end of the period, almost half of all visits were for this purpose. The later trend can be interpreted in the context of changes in guidelines from the American Academy of Pediatrics, which in 1994 released a set of guidelines for preventive care titled *Bright Futures* (M. Green 1994). *Bright Futures* championed a "health supervision" approach to care, highlighting the importance of well-child

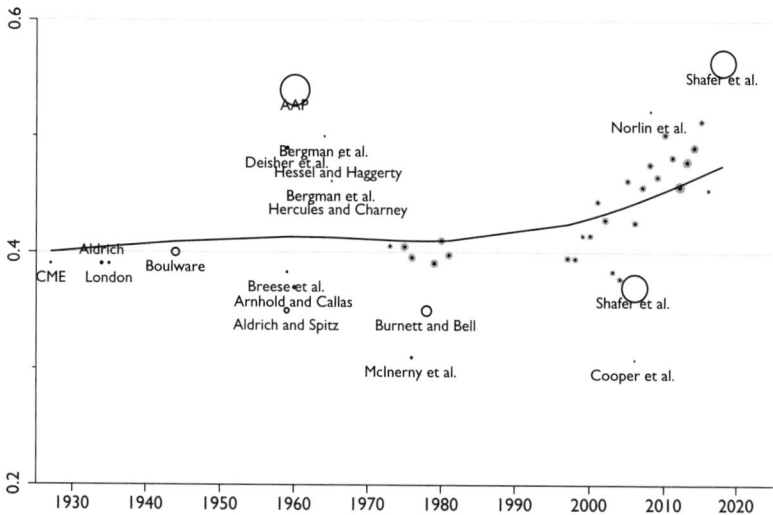

Fig. 3-6 The proportion of all patient visits to pediatricians that are for the purpose of well-child visits / preventive care; hollow circles represent estimates from the literature; solid circles represent estimates from the NAMCS; points scaled to size of samples.

DATA SOURCES: National Ambulatory Medical Care Survey (NAMCS 1973–2016; National Center for Health Statistics 2025); Aldrich 1934; Aldrich and Spitz 1960; American Academy of Pediatrics 1949; Arnhold and Callas 1966; Bergman, Dassel, and Wedgwood 1966; Bergman, Probstfield, and Wedgwood 1967; Boulware 1958; Breese, Disney, and Talpey 1966; Burnett and Bell 1978; Commission on Medical Education 1928; Cooper et al. 2006; Deisher, Derby, and Sturman 1960; Hercules et al. 1969; Hessel and Haggerty 1968; London 1937; McInerny, Roghmann, and Sutherland 1978; Norlin et al. 2011; Shafer, Hoagland, and Hsu 2021.

visits and screening tests tailored to the age of the child. The *Bright Futures* guidelines are still the bedrock of pediatric care and are updated yearly; currently the guidelines list thirty-four separate screening and preventive care tasks that pediatricians are expected to carry out at well-child visits.[33] A further boost to well-child and preventive care visits was provided by the ACA, which required (evidence-based) preventive care to be covered by private insurers, with no out-of-pocket costs. After the passage of the ACA, the proportion of well-child visits requiring out-of-pocket costs fell from 73 percent (2002–2011) to 49 percent (2011, post-ACA), and by 2018 this proportion stood at 14.5 percent (Shafer, Hoagland, and Hsu 2021).[34] These ACA-generated changes in the costs of well-child care thus solidify in law support for the preventive care recommended by pediatricians for children of all ages.

The growth of individualized preventive care and the changes in the type of prevention pursued were not just seen in pediatric practice. In Figure 3-7, I present an analysis of NAMCS, 1973–2016. The figure shows the proportion of patient visits, to three types of specialists (general/family practice, pediatrics, and surgery), that include a measure of blood pressure, diet education, at least one drug prescription, laboratory tests, or psychological counseling.[35]

Figure 3-7 shows evidence of four important trends that speak to changes in medicine with respect to job tasks and preventive care. First, we see that over time there has been a gradual expansion in the number of services provided by medical professionals during patient encounters. Fewer and fewer appointments are concluded without a listed service being provided. In general practice, the number of patient visits in which no service is provided declines from just under 5 percent in 1973 to a fraction of a percent in 2016; in surgery, there is a decline from 8 percent to 1 percent over the same period. The length of patient visits increases substantially between 1973 and 2016: primary care and pediatric visits are now ten minutes longer than in the 1970s, and surgical visits are seven minutes longer. It is important to emphasize that it is not always physicians who are responsible for providing services: even in 1960, much closer to the beginning of the individualized preventive turn, *JAMA* editorials were warning, "Nurses are questioning whether they should go on indefinitely accepting responsibility for giving more and more of the medical treatments that physicians—admittedly hard-pressed—are seeking to assign to them" (*JAMA* Editor 1960: 158). The development of new nursing roles, in particular the nurse practitioner, was an attempt to manage the increased workload of both nurses and physicians

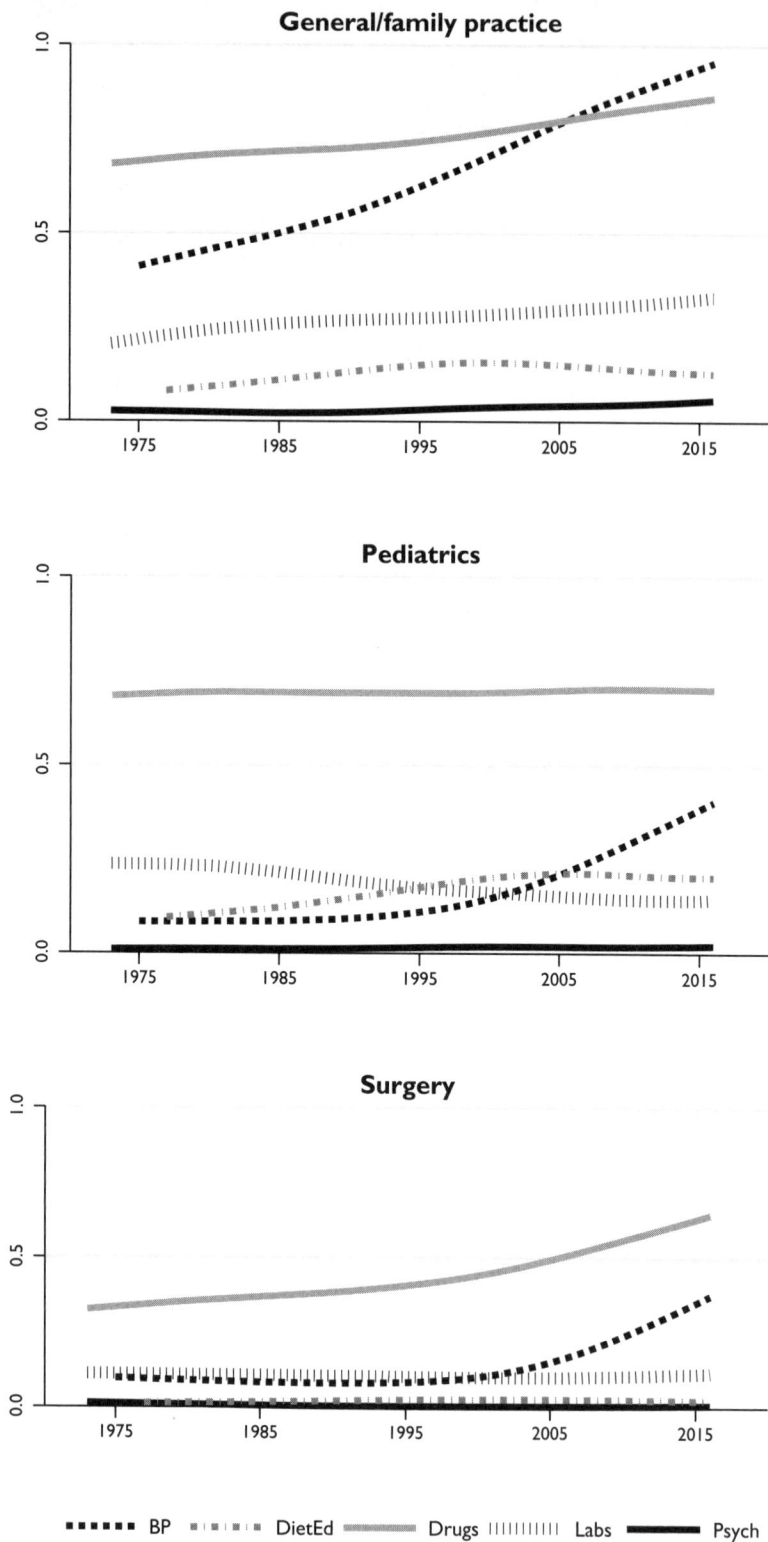

General/family practice

Pediatrics

Surgery

BP ▪▪▪▪▪▪ DietEd ▪ ▫ ▪ ▫ ▪ Drugs ▬▬▬ Labs ||||||||||| Psych ▬▬▬

Fig. 3-7 The proportion of patient visits that include the listed item, by specialty.
DATA SOURCE: NAMCS, 1973–2016.

(e.g., see Silver, Ford, and Stearly 1967; Silver, Ford, and Day 1968; Haggerty 1974; Hoekelman 1998), although the continuing growth of job tasks encouraged by the preventive mindset remained a feature of almost all patient-facing medical occupations.

The second trend evident in Figure 3-7 is an increasing focus on drug treatment in general practice and surgery. This is consistent with the trend observed in *Index Medicus* toward increasing concentration with respect to chemicals and drugs. But what is not clear from the raw trend is that drug prescription—seen by many to epitomize the doctor's role in treating disease—is increasingly becoming a preventive activity. One study comparing the use of prescription drugs between 1999 and 2012 shows that, in percentage point terms, the largest increases in prescription drug use are found for antihypertensive and antihyperlipidemic agents, commonly known as drugs that lower high blood pressure and reduce cholesterol (Kantor et al. 2015). These drugs are recommended for the prevention of stroke, myocardial infarction, and cardiovascular disease. The transition from saddlebag to pocketbook has thus been followed by another transition, from the use of drugs for treatment to the use of drugs for prevention.

The third trend revealed in the figure is a substantial growth over the past forty years in the proportion of visits in which a blood pressure measurement is taken. This trend is present across all three specialties, but it is most clear in general practice, where blood pressure is now measured in almost all patient visits, as compared to 40 percent of visits in 1975. Blood pressure measurement is recognized as one of the key preventive tools in health care today. The first set of blood pressure guidelines was published in 1977 by the Joint National Committee on Detection, Evaluation, and Treatment of High Blood Pressure (JNC), and these guidelines have been repeatedly revised in the years since then (e.g., see James et al. 2014; Kotchen 2014; Rothstein 2003: chap. 14). The evidence in Figure 3-7 suggests that the national emphasis on blood pressure management has fully permeated general practice, and its effects are also felt in pediatrics and surgery.

The fourth conclusion to be drawn from Figure 3-7 is that there has been an increase in the proportion of visits including psychological or diet counseling, particularly in general practice and pediatrics. Other forms of health education, including smoking cessation advice, substance abuse counseling, and domestic abuse screening, are also emphasized. These and similar services are frequently included in the recommended standards of care by professional organizations and medical societies (e.g., see M. Green 1994; US Preventive Services Task

Force 2014; see also Belamarich et al. 2006), but they are in some cases also required by law. California state law, for example, requires that licensed hospitals and clinics have written procedures for the use of routine screening to identify victims of domestic abuse (CA Health and Safety Code §1233.5, 2018). Screening and counseling for social problems is, in contemporary medicine, an important part of preventive care. Roger I. Lienke writes in 1970, for example, "Holistic or comprehensive evaluation of a patient as a whole biological unit in his own environment and culture is one of the basic skills of family practice" (2097). In the next section, I consider how the broadening scope of prevention— such that preventing illness required paying attention to all aspects of life, and not just the biological—is reflected in the basic job tasks of physician work.

A Second Bag of Tools

The growth of individual-level prevention was perhaps the most obvious change in medical practice induced by the growth of probabilism in the science of medicine. But as Figure 3-7 suggests, alongside changes in the amount of preventive care, there have also been changes in the content of preventive care over time. As medical science increasingly emphasized the importance of a broader range of mechanisms, and in particular the social determinants of health, preventive care expanded.

During the 1960s and 1970s, it became commonplace for the medical profession to acknowledge the effects of poverty and hunger, for example, on health (e.g., see Council on Foods and Nutrition 1970). It also became commonplace to argue that because poverty and hunger had negative effects on health, the medical profession had a legitimate interest in the mitigation of these social problems. The theoretical foundation of the *Bright Futures* report, for example, was an ecological model that conceptualized child health as the outcome of biological, psychological, and sociological factors, a model that was heavily influenced by the concept of the "new morbidity" first described in the 1960s and 1970s.[36] The "new morbidity" emphasized the broad range of problems of concern to patients and families and the broad range of causes of ill health, particularly those stemming from poor social conditions. In this context, a pediatrics for the future was imagined as "truly encompassing all of 'child health,' that is preventive, emotional, social, and educational elements, as well as the treatment of organic disease," such that the "pediatrician of the future must be prepared to move into the several new boundary areas not now considered a part of medical care" (Haggerty, Roghmann, and Pless 1975: 328; see also Haggerty 1968, 1974; Halpern 1988, 1990; Haggerty and Aligne 2005; Pawluch 1983, 2017).

The argument that the medical profession should play a role in alleviating social problems inevitably raised questions about what precisely this role should be. As interest in the social determinants of health grew, there were two main approaches to defining the medical professional's role. First, medical professionals who were privy to information in the course of providing care were advised to coordinate their work with nonmedical professionals to address the social problem. This logic underlies the following editorial published in *JAMA* in December 1970:

> Pandemics of any kind are physicians' business. . . . In the drug-abuse pandemic, the sources of the "infection" are the legions of pushers. They must be identified, revealed, and removed. Although removal is in the province exclusively of legal authorities, physicians can assist in the processes of identification and revelation. Every physician encounter with a user or abuser of drugs should include inquiry about the sources of the drugs. When sources are revealed to them, legal authorities can be expected to take appropriate action. The time has come for the medical profession to view drug pushers as infectious agents.

Other forms of coordination with nonmedical personnel included working with educational personnel to obtain better support for children with learning disabilities (González 1980) and undertaking voluntary work in the community as citizens, not as medical personnel (Detmer 1980).

In recent years, coordination with nonmedical personnel has only become a more prominent part of medical work. An example may be drawn from the case of home-visiting programs, which have gained in popularity in recent decades as a first-line approach to early childhood intervention. In 2009, the Council on Community Pediatrics within the American Academy of Pediatrics released a statement on home-visiting programs, arguing in favor of collaboration between medical and nonmedical personnel.[37] The same organization stated in 2013 (625–626) that pediatricians must have a second "bag of tools" in addition to the clinical "doctor's bag" that addresses more traditional agents of childhood disease. This second bag of tools includes skills such as being able to function in an interdisciplinary fashion and partnering with public health and child welfare entities. Once again, nongovernmental and charitable organizations played a part in pushing medical professionals to widen their purview. Alondra Nelson, for example, has described the Black Panther Party's involvement in the radical health movement. The Panthers established free clinics that operated from what Nelson labels a "social health" perspective, in which "medical care was the central but not the sole aim" (2011: loc1669; see also A. Nelson 2016; Morabia 2016).

The second approach to defining the responsibility of medical professionals with respect to social problems focused on physicians using their position to advocate on behalf of improved social policies. For example, in January 1990 the *Pulse* section of *JAMA* focused on the subject of "social advocacy" on the part of physicians.[38] Physician advocacy was tied to social problems quite explicitly. One author makes the case for social advocacy on the basis that social problems cause medical problems, writing,

> Medicine is a profession dedicated to healing and promoting the health of all people, goals not restricted to activities in the clinic, but part of a calling that gives purpose to all aspects of life. . . . Social problems profoundly affect, and even become, medical problems, but they also need to be addressed in the political arena. Even a political topic such as nuclear arms becomes medically important when political leaders are not aware of the medical consequences of their decisions. . . . All physicians have the same calling and a special obligation to promote health for all people, clinically, socially, and politically. (Pan 1990: 139)

Another author in the same issue addresses the issue of urban violence:

> Just as the medical community has drawn on its scientific expertise and cultural authority to oppose cigarette smoking and the nuclear arms race, physicians can speak out against public acceptance of violence. We need to become involved in formulating guidelines for depicting violence and sexualization in the media and advertising industries. Physicians can support increased federal regulation of handguns and other lethal weapons, as these are leading instruments of morbidity and mortality. (Uva 1990: 139)

The type of social advocacy described by these authors is still common: research finds that over 95 percent of physicians rate community participation and collective advocacy as important, and two-thirds of physicians have actively participated in such efforts (Gruen, Campbell, and Blumenthal 2006; see also Janeway et al. 2022 for a discussion). In recent years, the medical profession has been urged to take action on racial inequality, the racial wealth gap, global warming, and social welfare spending (e.g., see Peoples, Fleming, and Creary 2023; South, Venkataramani, and Dalembert 2022; McCauley et al. 2023; Bradley, Sipsma, and Taylor 2017; Macpherson and Hill 2017), and the AMA has a well-developed set of policy positions on broad social issues.

The references to nuclear arms in the previous paragraph are revealing, in that they highlight the connection between present-day advocacy efforts and the advocacy role that has long been understood to be part of the physician's role. During the Cold War, for example, *JAMA* published an opinion piece by Roger J. Bulger that argued, "Our job as physicians is to warn against the health dangers of nuclear war. . . . As physicians, our commitment to disease prevention should bring us into active involvement with this issue" (1980: 1255). Throughout the past century, physicians have been encouraged in the idea that their position affords a special status to comment on issues of public importance. To the extent to which there has been a change in the role, this change has been twofold. First, there has been a decline in how far physicians can expect to receive deference to their opinions simply because of their status as "great and learned men" within the community (N. Davis 1883; Jenkins 1949: chap. 5).[39] Second, because medicine has embraced the principle of prevention, it is possible for medical professionals to claim special expertise in relation to many issues that previously would not have been understood as medical in nature. In other words, there has been a transformation in the nature of advocacy within medicine, from status-based to expertise-based, where broad expertise-based advocacy is legitimated by an expansive understanding of the causes of health and disease.

One consequence of the broadening purview of medicine with respect to social problems was that a broader range of topics became open for discussion in the course of delivering preventive health care. Pediatricians were now expected to discuss psychosocial difficulties, educational and school-related problems, problems with family relationships, and substance abuse (e.g., see Crumley 1990; Shaywitz et al. 1990). Robert W. Deisher, Alfred J. Derby, and Melvin J. Sturman summarize the shift as follows: "Because of the dissemination of knowledge about child development, both physical and psychologic, parents increasingly are coming to the pediatrician for advice formerly given them by relatives, friends and clergy" (1960: 715). Dorothy Pawluch (2017) has argued that this new and expansive vision of pediatrics should be interpreted as an attempt by pediatricians to extend their jurisdiction after substantial falls in child mortality.[40] From the perspective of the long-term growth in interest in prevention shown in the analysis of *Index Medicus* and the historical data, this verdict must be judged as partial. Pediatricians surely wished to preserve their role in an ever-changing world, but the appeal of prevention was powerful, and as science opened up new preventive possibilities for pediatric care, the pediatricians followed.[41]

FROM TREATMENT TO PREVENTION

> We must be prepared . . . to revise the notion that physicians should heal the sick. Perhaps the physician's most productive role is as a preventer of illness, not a healer. There is, after all, no a fortiori reason why it is worthier for the physician to heal the sick than to root out and destroy the causes of sickness.

These sentences are taken from an article titled "The Need for a Medical Ideology," published in *JAMA* (Ruby and Morganroth 1970: 2097). They both reflect the changes that had already taken place in medicine over the previous century and foreshadow the changes that were to come. As it stands today, prevention is at the heart of the physician's role, and it shapes almost every aspect of the patient's experience of medicine.

Medicine is a field in which we can observe over the past 150 years the playing out of several important forces, with two in particular being of special importance. The dramatic growth of scientific knowledge is arguably more obvious in the field of medical science than in any other area of scientific endeavor. As scientific output increased, it also changed in form: causal processes were theorized and observed, mechanisms were identified, and sociological and psychological concepts were integrated to cast light on the social bases of disease. These changes in the form of scientific evidence opened the door to a fundamental shift in medical practice, from the treatment of disease to its prevention. Over the same period, the force of specialization also exerted its pressure. This force pushes toward increasing occupational specialization within medicine, which offers the possibility of managing the proliferation of scientific knowledge and providing better patient care. But occupational specialization also brings its own challenges, such that overcoming the medical system's fragmentation further complicates the delivery of medical care.

The diffusion of the preventive rationale in medicine invoked the paradox of specialization for workers by extending the range of job tasks required of medical personnel. The promise of being able to prevent illness rather than just treat it ushered in new tests, new drugs, new administrative procedures, and new areas of inquiry. Most notably, the expansion of preventive activity from the biological to the social domain has dramatically increased the purview of physicians and other personnel. Jack Geiger, one of the leaders of the community health center movement of the 1960s and 1970s, recently celebrated the ideals of that movement and argued that medicine should continue pushing to "address the social, economic, environmental, and political circumstances that determine . . . ill health. To say these things and stop there is simple rhetoric. To act on them, to give them expression in new programs and new social institutions, to make them at once a part of the experience of the oppressed and the knowledge of the health professional student, requires more. Yet it can be done" (2016: 1738). Medical professionals now have a legitimate interest in the biological, environmental, psychological, and social situation of their patients because science has established that poor health can result from any of these factors. This line of reasoning stands behind some of the recent innovations in the health care field, such as hospitals building affordable housing (e.g., see Bhatt 2019; Kuehn 2019) and providing food pantries (Greenthal et al. 2019). As it stands today, medical professionals could make a case for being interested in virtually *any* aspect of a patient's life, on the basis that preventing illness requires it.

Even while the purview of physicians has expanded under the paradox of specialization, the logic of specialization has still operated to mitigate the task accumulation produced by prevention. Occupational specialization has reduced the need for practitioners to master the whole medical literature. The growth of new positions such as nurse practitioners and physician assistants has helped to mitigate the demands on physicians, even if these new occupations are now among the least specialized in the occupational structure. Family medicine practitioners are less likely to conduct surgery now than in the past, physicians no longer dispense drugs, and medical professionals are less likely to make house calls. Furthermore, in some cases, the preventive approach simply changed the content of tasks already understood to be part of a medical professional's job. When physicians began to inquire about domestic violence during a patient visit, for example, they were not adding a wholly new task but rather changing the content of a conversation that was already personal in nature. Similarly, when the ACP spoke out against gun violence, the newness was not in the speaking out but in the preventive rationale that legitimated the interest of the ACP in gun violence.

When physicians used the hashtag #thisisourlane, they were not making a new claim for jurisdiction but making explicit a claim that had been developing over many decades, even centuries. The NRA failed to understand this. It failed to understand that while the topic of guns might have belonged to the NRA, the topic of gun violence belonged to medicine. If deaths and injuries were caused by gun violence, medical professionals had both a right and an obligation to address the issue. As our scientific knowledge increases and our predictive capacity grows, it is likely that the number of topics on which medical professionals have a right and an obligation to comment will only increase.

CHAPTER FOUR

Defund the Police

"**D**efund the Police" was the clarion call of 2020. The call had its origins in decades of community organizing and grassroots action and was amplified during the Black Lives Matter protests in the wake of George Floyd's murder. It has echoed since, in community meetings across the United States and in the outputs of the hastily convened committees charged with reimagining the police's role. Although the movement inevitably brings together individuals with diverse aims and priorities, the central focus can be summarized as follows:

> The police are meant to provide safety and security for our communities.
> But the police have always served another function in North America. The
> police have systematically inflicted violence against Black & Indigenous
> peoples across this continent.... The only solution is to defund the police,
> and to reimagine the way that we provide safety and security services for
> our society. The truth is that a close look at the activities of the police reveals
> that police are disastrously incompetent at the services they are meant to
> provide. Our communities deserve better. (Defund the Police 2020)

The Defund the Police movement is of obvious interest to scholars of race, social movements, and crime. But it should also be of interest to sociologists with an interest in how the division of labor occurs. The Defund the Police movement is notable because its express purpose is to push for increased functional differentiation. Under the current division of labor, the police are responsible for a wide range of tasks and are present in a wide variety of public and quasi-public spaces. Police officers investigate crimes and arrest suspects, provide first aid to victims of accidents and crimes, monitor traffic, patrol neighborhoods, transport prisoners, administer community programs, and do much more (O*NET 2024). Their work routinely sees them enter schools, hospitals, neighborhoods, parks, and shopping malls, and they have a legal right to enter private spaces. The central claims of the Defund the Police movement, then, are that the current division of labor is inappropriate, that the diffuseness of work tasks produces bad outcomes for all communities—and particularly bad outcomes for communities of color—and that police officers are responsible for too many tasks that should instead be carried out in other specialized occupations.

This chapter considers just how the police came to take on such a broad range of tasks. In some respects, the police occupation is an outlier relative to other occupations, in that it appears to be unusually demanding with respect to job tasks and functions. But in other respects, what has happened to the police occupation is simply one instance of the more general phenomenon common to all rationalized occupations: the paradox of specialization. At the same time that specialization pressures were brought to bear on policing, the effect of a changing science of crime was to dramatically expand the range of tasks that were seen as central to police work. Just as in the medical industry, as "prevention" came to be understood in more expansive terms, law enforcement personnel found it necessary to consider a broader range of interventions in order to pursue their occupational outputs. Police control over this broader range of job tasks was bolstered by funding, technological support, and internal occupational specialization.

THE TASKS OF LAW ENFORCEMENT

The Defund the Police movement has brought public attention to the wide range of tasks and services that the police are responsible for. Sociological and criminological scholarship has revealed that law enforcement personnel have taken on diverse roles and infiltrated multiple social institutions. Of particular interest has been the presence of police in schools and hospitals—social institutions traditionally associated with quite different functions from those of law enforcement.

Police presence in "nontraditional" settings is both routine and naturalized. The most recent estimates show, for example, that almost 80 percent of large public schools have at least one law enforcement officer present who routinely carries a firearm (Diliberti et al. 2019: tab. 12). The job tasks of police in school settings might include student counseling, teaching classes, and staff training, alongside the crime-control-oriented tasks usually associated with law enforcement activity (see Gleit 2022). Police in emergency rooms and hospitals similarly carry out a diverse range of tasks, including social control, evidence collection, and crime investigation (e.g., see Song 2021). Police presence in these spaces has been shown to put students, patients, and their family members at risk of search, interrogation, and arrest—risks that are unequally distributed, given the disproportionate presence of police in institutions serving people of color and poor people (Crenshaw, Ocen, and Nanda 2015; Goffman 2014; Lara-Millán 2014; Vitale 2021).

Police also maintain a consistent presence in communities and neighborhoods. It is here that much of the contact between the public and law enforcement personnel occurs; in 2018, around a quarter of the adult population had at least some contact with the police, and traffic stops were the modal form of contact (Harrell and Davis 2020: tabs. 1, 2). As Monica C. Bell (2020) has emphasized, forms of policing differ across different neighborhoods. In rich, white neighborhoods, police may be perceived as an amenity, given their availability and willingness to smooth interactions between residents and public safety institutions (936). In other neighborhoods, police are more likely to be engaged in hypersurveillance and patrol (see, e.g., Rios 2011; Collins, Stuart, and Janulis 2022). One form of policing that has garnered much attention in discussions of Defund the Police is so-called therapeutic policing, in which law enforcement officers take on roles more traditionally associated with social workers and "instill [poor] residents with new habits, attitudes, and dispositions" (Stuart 2016: loc. 326). Therapeutic policing can be seen as one instance of a more general phenomenon within the field of proactive policing, in which law enforcement and antipoverty strategies converge (Stuart 2016; see also Goldstein 1977; Hinton 2015, 2017; Herring 2019). Present-day understandings of community presence and patrol, thus, define a broad range of tasks as being within the proper bounds of law enforcement activity.

One reasonable question, given the claims of Defund the Police, is whether contemporary policing is truly an outlier relative to other occupations. Are activists right to raise questions about a lack of task specialization for law enforcement personnel? In Figure 4-1, I present an analysis of data drawn from the Occupational Information Network (O*NET) (O*NET 2024). I construct a measure of functional complexity using O*NET's

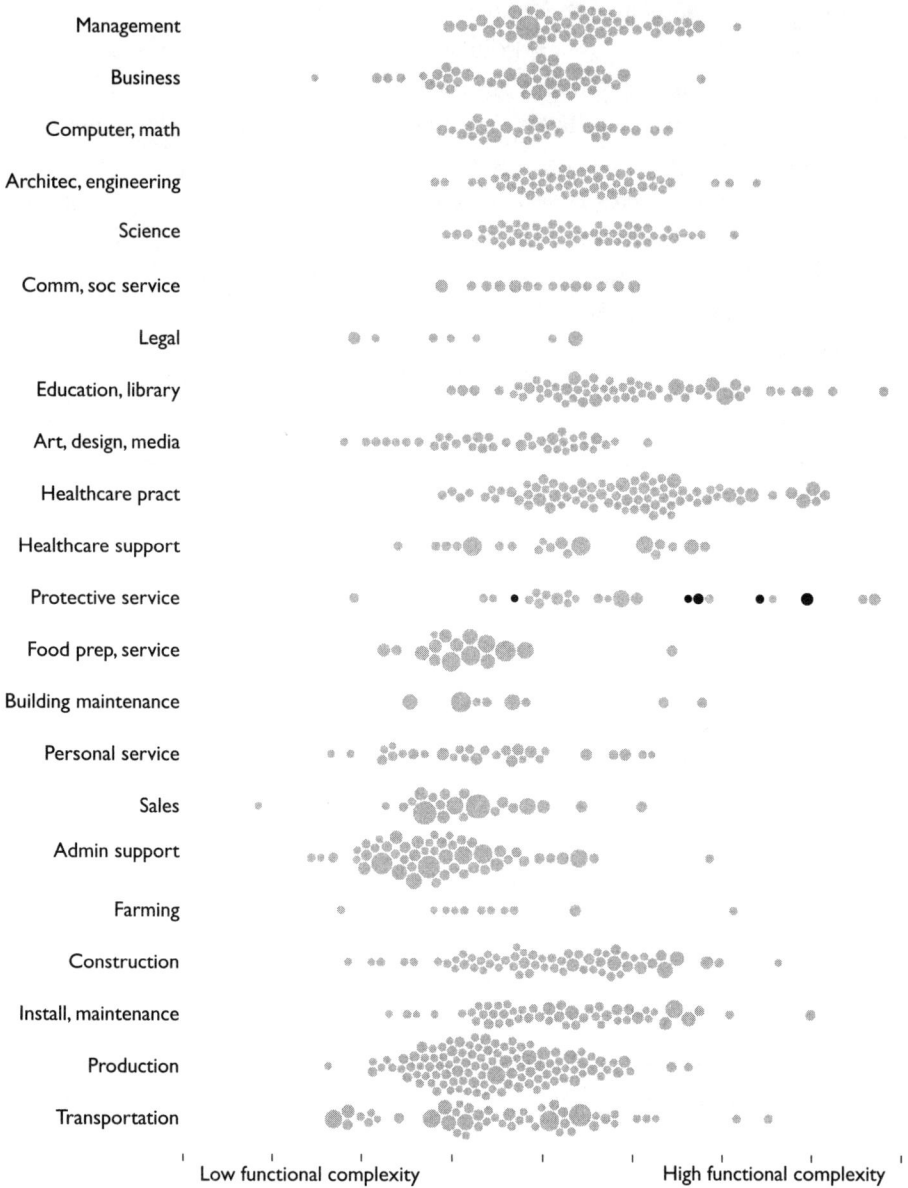

Management
Business
Computer, math
Architec, engineering
Science
Comm, soc service
Legal
Education, library
Art, design, media
Healthcare pract
Healthcare support
Protective service
Food prep, service
Building maintenance
Personal service
Sales
Admin support
Farming
Construction
Install, maintenance
Production
Transportation

Low functional complexity   High functional complexity

Fig. 4-1 Functional complexity scores for the O*NET occupations, arranged by major occupational groups, where high scores indicate highly functionally complex occupations and low scores indicate less functionally complex occupations. Policing occupations are highlighted in black.

DATA SOURCE: O*NET.

fine-grained measures of work tasks and work tools: occupations with low scores on this measure have low levels of functional complexity, and those with high scores are highly functionally complex.[1] The figure shows functional complexity scores for the contemporary occupational structure; occupations are arranged by major occupational group and scaled by the total number of employees in the occupation.

The figure reveals substantial variation in the degree of functional complexity both across and within the major occupational groups. At first glance, the placement of the occupations appears to be counterintuitive because of our tendency to assign status to "specialists." We see that many low-status occupations (e.g., workers in production and transportation) are in fact *more* specialized (i.e., less functionally complex) than many high-status occupations (e.g., health care practitioners and managers). The least functionally complex occupation in the O*NET classification is "Models," while "Career/Technical Education Teachers, Secondary School" is the most functionally complex occupation.

But as Figure 4-1 also shows, police occupations are highly complex with respect to job tasks and tool use. Although Defund the Police highlighted long-standing concerns about police activities, the degree to which the police are outliers relative to other occupations has not been established to this point. But it is clear that policing occupations *are* outliers in comparison to almost all other occupations: few occupations are more functionally complex than policing. Police officers are at the 98th percentile of the functional complexity measure, while other police occupations (i.e., "First-Line Supervisors" and "Detectives and Criminal Investigators") are found in the top 5 percent. In the Appendix, I present further analyses of the O*NET data and show that police occupations are not just outliers with respect to their degree of functional complexity; they are also outliers with respect to the degree of domination that the occupation affords and the unusually low education, experience, and training requirements. Perhaps most strikingly, law enforcement occupations are the only highly functionally complex occupations with high domination potential in which a handgun is a required tool.

SPECIALISTS IN SOCIAL CONTROL

Understanding how the police came to take on such a diverse range of tasks requires an appreciation of how two macro-level forces came together over the past century to change the boundaries of police work: the scientific push to expand the limits of the preventive state and the increasing importance of the rationalization-delivered logic of specialization in conferring legitimacy on occupations and social institutions.

To trace the development of the police occupation over time, I exploit a range of primary and secondary data sources, including resources produced for city managers, job task analyses, federal government reports and documents, first-person accounts of police and public service work, and police department annual reports. One key primary source is the *City Manager Year Book* (*CMY*, 1914–), published by the International City Managers' Association (ICMA), which was later published as the *Municipal Year Book* (*MYB*, 1934–). An important feature of the *MYB* is that the activities and functions of law enforcement workers are described every year, in similar format, across many decades.[2] The *MYB* provides an invaluable record of police functions—and contemporaneous discussions about appropriate police functions—over the past century. I combine these data sources with an in-depth study of one particular police department: the Los Angeles Police Department (LAPD). This department is one of the largest in the country and has been at the forefront of innovations in policing over the past century. I analyze data drawn from LAPD annual reports (1912–), first-person accounts of working in the LAPD, and other archival material to examine functional differentiation within a single police department. Given that federal control over the police is strictly limited, focusing on a single police department allows for an examination of the critically important local factors at play in determining police tasks.

The Preventive State

In the context of criminal justice, the "preventive state" is the label given to crime control via prevention rather than punishment (Steiker 1997; see Zedner and Ashworth 2019 for a review). The expansion of the preventive state via antiterrorism legislation after 9/11 provoked special comment, but researchers were calling attention to the increasing emphasis on crime control through prevention even in the last decade of the twentieth century. In broad terms, discussions of the preventive state and allied concepts (e.g., proactive versus reactive policing) draw comparisons between a time when police focused on catching criminals and a time when police focused on preventing crime. The period of "preventive" criminal justice is thus counterposed against earlier periods, when prevention was not a primary aim.

Although it is no doubt important to examine the institutionalization of practices associated with the preventive state, the institutionalization of preventive practices can occur only after these practices have been defined as falling within the purview of police personnel. It is crucial to understand how the abstract principle of prevention developed and laid the groundwork for the later institutional changes, as without the legitimacy derived from that abstract principle, the policing occupation would have had limited success in expanding its portfolio of functions and would have been vulnerable to losing functions to competing occupations. It is helpful to consider this abstract principle as being composed of two components. First, it is more effective to prevent crime than to "treat" it after the fact. Second, the prevention of crime requires taking an expansive view: the causes of crime are complex and structural, so preventing crime will require interventions in almost every social institution. The first of these components has always been a defining principle of police work; the second component has become more prominent over time.

That crime prevention is a long-standing feature of the policing occupation is well established; indeed, it is so long-standing a feature that Robert Peel included it in his *Instructions* and *Police Orders*.[3] The historical data confirm that crime prevention was a primary aim of the police even at the beginning of the twentieth century. The LAPD *Annual Report* of 1912, for example, states early on , "The primary object of a police department is the prevention of crime" (LAPD 1912: 4), while the *City Manager Yearbook* of 1919 (ICMA 1919: 134), states, "Efficient police work must . . . include definite preventive features, which, properly correlated, can be made to actually reduce all manner of complaints in the face of an increasing population." Similar statements can be found in the primary sources throughout the century (e.g., ICMA 1920, 1938, 1947; LAPD 1922, 1968), and today, prevention is highlighted in the LAPD's mission statement ("to reduce the incidence and fear of crime"). The aim of preventing crime is a grand constant of the policing occupation over the past century.

Given that crime prevention has always been seen as important to police work, changes in what are perceived to be the legitimate tasks of policing must come from changes in the second component of the abstract principle: that the prevention of crime requires widespread and diffuse interventions. And it is in fact here that we see significant change over time. The change comes from two sources: changes in the science of criminology and crime prevention and the emergence of new social problems that required relatively swift changes in police tasks to address.

In line with the changes wrought across the sciences by the probabilistic revolution, social scientific work on crime has been transformed over the past century (see, e.g., Laub 2004; Werth 2024 for a review). Figure 4-2 shows a word frequency analysis of JSTOR's Constellate database to illustrate some key trends in scholarship on crime in the United States. The figure confirms divergence in the two components of the preventive principle described above. Academic interest in identifying the causes of crime and preventing crime was rather stable over the century, while shifts occurred in how those aims could be satisfied. In the past, crime was prevented by "treating" the criminals, in keeping with contemporary understandings of the roots of criminal behavior. But we see that academic interest in "criminals" declined after the 1950s, while the words "social," "structure," and "predict" substantially increased in frequency. The latter changes may be understood as a manifestation of an ongoing probabilistic revolution in the field of criminology.

The historical evidence shows that the shift that occurred in academic analyses of crime over the past century was reflected in beliefs about the

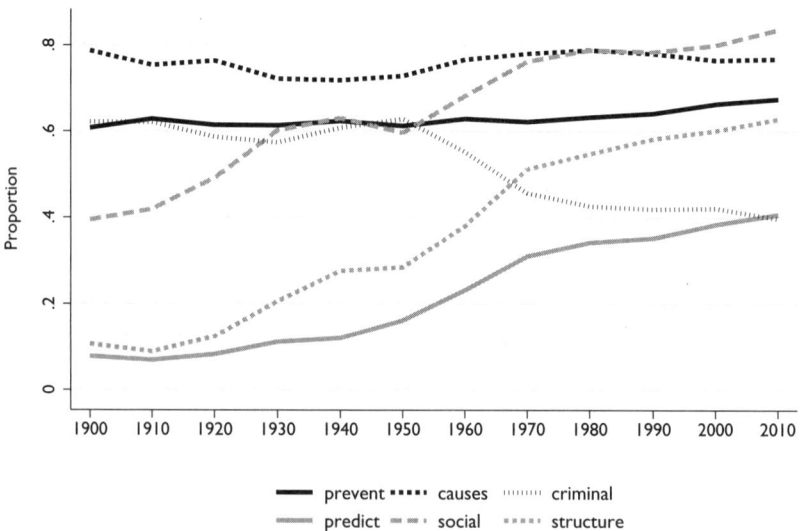

Fig. 4-2 Word frequency analysis by decade, 1900s–2010s.

DATA SOURCE: JSTOR Constellation.

appropriate tasks of policing. The conviction that crime has complex social structural causes was quickly embraced by policing experts and leaders, before it diffused as a generalized understanding of how crime might be best prevented. In the earlier years of the twentieth century, the individualistic model of crime was still invoked in conversations about policing. In the same *CMY* that discusses the importance of prevention in police work, we find the commentator distinguishing between the "real" and the "accidental" criminal, arguing that the "real criminal is defective" and that public safety departments must therefore "study the individual" to achieve reductions in crime (ICMA 1919: 135).

Individualistic approaches to preventing crime strongly limit the boundaries of "appropriate" police work because only those tasks related to catching criminals are defined as legitimate. Widening the bounds of preventive activity therefore opens up the possibility of a substantial expansion of work tasks.

The scholarly move from an individualistic to structural understanding of crime prevention started to diffuse among law enforcement and political elites in the 1920s and 1930s. The transitional period is well illustrated in the outputs of the Wickersham Commission, constituted in the Herbert Hoover administration to address the crime problem. The commission produced fourteen reports; report 13 on the causes of crime was published in two volumes, the first focusing on personality development in the criminal and the second focusing on social and ecological factors.[4] The introduction to the report states quite straightforwardly, "Criminology is remaking, the social sciences are in transition, and the foundations of behavior are in dispute. It would serve no useful purpose to put forth theories as to criminality or nonobservance of law, either generally or in America, on the basis of some one current psychology or social philosophy, with the certainty that it represents but one phase of the thought of the time and will not long hold the ground" (Wickersham 1931b: vii). By the time of the Franklin D. Roosevelt administration, it was accepted by political elites that preventing crime would require addressing a diverse set of social and structural issues, a belief no doubt amplified by anxieties about the widespread effects of the Great Depression (Pandiani 1982). Attorney General Homer Cummings was a key advocate of this approach, arguing in 1933 that crime "requires consideration of the whole structure of our social life. . . . It is a social question, with manifold ramifications touching environment, heredity, education, the home, the school and, indeed, almost every activity of life" (1933: 2; see also Cummings 1937).

The widening potential scope of preventive activity that might be undertaken by law enforcement personnel is made clear when new social problems arise. In the 1920s and 1930s, juvenile delinquency was of special concern, because of both high rates of juvenile crime and clear inadequacies in the justice system with regard to the treatment of younger people (e.g., see Rosenthal 1986, 1987). The 1930 White House Conference on Child Health and Protection included a Committee on Delinquency, for example, and on the opening day of the 1934 Attorney General's Conference on Crime, a paper on juvenile crime was presented. In the opening of the latter conference, President Roosevelt's remarks described crime as a "symptom of social disorder" and emphasized the importance of purposefully channeling "the genius of the younger generation" (Roosevelt 1934: 2). Worries about juvenile delinquency are packaged together with the philosophy of preventive early intervention, a packaging that is repeated in many of the papers presented at the 1934 conference (see, e.g., Hoffman 1934; Scudder 1934; also Vollmer 1933).

The police response to concerns about juvenile crime and delinquency may be best described as tentative. As I describe in the next section, even if prevention was clearly the preferred approach to dealing with juvenile delinquency, it was by no means clear that the police would be responsible for all, or even most, of the preventive work. There were, however, suggestions that the police *could* engage in such work. Sheldon Glueck, for example, argued at the Conference on Crime that "the value of preventive efforts with predelinquents and delinquents as part of police activity has not been sufficiently recognized" (1934: 11). Enterprising police agencies started to develop antidelinquency programs, with emphasis on prevention rather than deterrence through arrest and punishment.

The LAPD had always been at the forefront of antidelinquency efforts; the LAPD introduced a Juvenile Bureau in 1910 and founded the City Mothers Bureau in 1914. These bureaus operated under a philosophy of prevention, although they largely focused on addressing the needs of "wayward children" in order to help them reform (e.g., see LAPD 1915: 39; LAPD 1916: 22–23). In the 1930s, the LAPD expanded their antidelinquency efforts, creating a "Pre-Delinquent Detail," while the Crime Prevention Division established the LA Coordinating Councils, which brought together law enforcement officers with social agencies, schools, recreation departments, church groups, and other interested parties. The Coordinating Councils aimed to provide "constructive influences and services which [would] prevent juvenile delinquency and make the community itself a better place in which to live" (Weller 1939: 247; see Appier 2005 for a history of the Coordinating Councils; Wolcott 2005). Other crime prevention innovations included the Night Detail (introduced in 1935; see LAPD 1938: 37) and Camp Valyermo (introduced in 1936), a summer camp for underprivileged children. The LAPD *Annual Report* of 1937 described the summer camp as providing "ample opportunity for police juvenile officers to become closely associated with a large number of underprivileged children . . . creat[ing] a bond of friendship between the potential delinquent and the law enforcement officer which tends to forever protect the child from a life of crime" (30). The LAPD was no doubt an innovator, but other police departments also experimented with delinquency prevention methods and adopted innovations that had worked elsewhere. By 1935, eighty-one Coordinating Councils were operating in thirteen California counties, and similar councils could be found across the country (Vollmer 1933; ICMA 1935: 84; 1944). Specialist units focusing on juvenile crime prevention were formed in many large police departments (ICMA 1938, 1941, 1949, 1950), and across the country, departments made efforts to provide recreation and "character building" activities for young people (ICMA 1939, 1945). An example of the latter may be taken from Chicago, where the Crime Prevention Bureau proposed to "establish . . . 'play spots' throughout the city, each under the supervision of a young policeman able to teach physical education" (ICMA 1941: 439). Junior police programs also gained in popularity; in 1950, for example, Bloomington, Illinois, boasted a junior police force of nine hundred boys between the ages of ten and sixteen (ICMA 1950: 400).

The approaches to preventing juvenile delinquency in the first half of the twentieth century thus appear to have been both earnest and creative. They also entailed an expansion of police tasks into new areas that included specialized patrol activities (e.g., visiting dance halls), liaison with families and juveniles, and supervision of recreational activities. The gradual expansion of the preventive purview could also be felt in the new tasks introduced in other domains of police work (Fogelson 1977). In the postwar strike wave, for example, the police in some cities operated as mediators between union officials and management officials (ICMA 1948). When service members returned from World War II, law enforcement agencies cooperated in seizing or registering the automatic weapons that were prohibited in civilian life (ICMA 1947). The gradual expansion of preventive activities and the new understandings of what it meant to prevent crime were felt in a substantial expansion of police tasks.

The expansion of preventive work with respect to juvenile delinquency continued in the 1950s, with encouragement from the federal government. Municipal police agencies were encouraged to create specialized units to handle cases involving children and youth (ICMA 1953), and by 1954, a study conducted by the International Association of Chiefs of Police (IACP) showed that 50 percent of the sampled police agencies employed juvenile specialists (ICMA 1954; see also Kenney and Pursuit 1954). Juvenile crime once again became a source of widespread public and political concern in the 1960s, and the federal government responded by passing the Juvenile Delinquency and Youth Offenses Control Act of 1961 and founding the President's Committee on Juvenile Delinquency and Youth Crime. Once again, expansive preventive police work was emphasized. In its *Report to the President,* the committee states, "We must stress the prevention of delinquency as much as the control of delinquency. Ordinarily the consequences get more attention than the sources of the problem . . . an equal investment of resources in basic prevention activities will offer a more stable solution" (1962: 11–12). In 1965, in collaboration with the committee, the IACP released a training manual designed to help police working with juveniles, writing,

> In recent years the traditional police role has been broadened to include many aspects of social service formerly the exclusive concern of specialized social institutions such as the church, schools, and public welfare. The police today cannot be excused from applying their utmost efforts toward prevention, identification and early reversal of aberrant antisocial processes: the costly cycle of school drop-outs, unemployment, crime, and welfare dependency vitally concern all organized agencies of society including the police. (N. Watson and Walker 1965: 1)

As Elizabeth Hinton (2017) describes, Lyndon B. Johnson's administration marked a period of intense federal interest in juvenile crime and preventive activities and a move toward the substantial federal funding of local police activities (see, e.g., President's Committee on Juvenile Delinquency and Youth Crime 1964). But the emphasis on police preventive activities to control juvenile crime persisted well beyond the Johnson administration (e.g., see National Advisory Committee for Juvenile Justice and Delinquency Prevention 1980).

Just as with juvenile crime, interest in other types of preventive police work only grew during the 1960s and 1970s. This is well expressed in the LAPD *Annual Report* of 1968, which explained, "We must innovate activities which will be preventive and remedial in nature" (14). A renewed interest in preventive patrol had been evident from the 1950s onward, and "conspicuous motorized patrol" came to dominate over foot patrols by offering an efficient and cost-effective means to carry out the preventive function (e.g., ICMA 1958). New social problems were easily folded into the preventive mindset. When riots and protests provoked widespread concern, the *MYB* cautioned, "A riot doesn't simply happen. Every such incident has roots which have been nurtured within the community. . . . The police officer must recognize the growth of causation factors so the city can take preventive action" (ICMA 1966: 424). By the time that the Johnson administration identified "preventing crime" as the first objective in the sweeping report *The Challenge of Crime in a Free Society* (1967), the understanding that prevention entailed diffuse interventions in multiple social institutions was already fully established as a basic principle of policing (President's Commission on Law Enforcement and Administration of Justice 1967a).

The value of separately examining the two components of the cultural principle underlying the preventive state is twofold. First, the historical evidence shows that one component of the cultural principle has remained relatively stable over time, while the other has undergone significant change. The police occupation might always have been concerned with preventing crime, but what it meant to prevent crime underwent a substantial shift over the course of the twentieth century. Second, examining both components of the preventive cultural principle makes it clear that there was no single moment when the police occupation changed. The roots of the expansive preventive role are not to be found in a single presidential administration or a single event. Rather, the legitimacy of the police's expanded role was secured through appeals to the well-accepted cultural principle that the police were—and had always been—engaged in preventive work.

The Fundamental Duty

When social scientists discuss the division of labor, it is often in rather mechanical terms (e.g., as an "engine" of capitalism). The mechanical metaphors are distracting, however, insofar as they draw attention away from the importance of specialization as a *cultural* force. As discussed in Chapters 1–2, as rationalization progresses, specialization comes to be seen as desirable and as a mark of quality. The power of the logic of specialization as a touchstone can be seen in the statements of Defund the Police, where a key complaint is that police are undertaking work that should properly be undertaken by specialists. But its influence can also be seen within the policing occupation.

When the understanding comes that the prevention of crime will require wide-ranging efforts, it is by no means clear that the police will be responsible for these efforts. In the Wickersham Commission's *Report on Police* (1931a), concerns had already been aired about the wide scope of police tasks. Experts at the time saw the policing occupation as insufficiently specialized to meet the demands of modern society. In the introduction to the *Report on Police,* the commission notes, "There are too many duties cast upon each officer and patrolman. This is the outcome of the transition from rural or small-town policing to city communities. As the urban population increased, no diversification was made in the duties of officers or patrolmen" (7; see also Haller 1976; Fogelson 1977). The police were compared unfavorably to the post office and private businesses, which had divided up work duties and introduced coordinative management structures. The police's failure to specialize was here cast as a failure to embrace modern methods—a failure that led to inefficiency and poor performance.

It should not be surprising, therefore, that in discussions of the widening scope of preventive activity, it is assumed that nonpolice institutions, agencies, and occupations will be responsible and that the police's job is to work in collaboration with these groups. This is well expressed in Roosevelt's address to the Conference on Crime (1934: 2), when he states that solving the crime problem "can come only through expert service in marshalling the assets of home, school, church, community and other social agencies, to work in common purpose with our law enforcement agencies. We deceive ourselves when we fail to realize that it is an interrelated problem of immense difficulty." Other sources from the time show a strong focus on the family and the education system as institutions that must be mobilized in the crime prevention effort, with social welfare agencies also playing an essential auxiliary role. One example of the diffusion of responsibilities across institutions can be found in the LA Coordinating Councils discussed earlier in this chapter, in that the aim of these councils was not to take over all crime prevention duties but rather to coordinate the various specialist institutions that structure a child's life. It was not the job of the police to intervene in all of these institutions, although the police were certainly central to the group of interested parties brought together to form the councils.

Nevertheless, during this period police agencies did start to undertake a wider range of preventive activities. But the transition to more expansive preventive job tasks was met with some ambivalence by police leaders and officers, largely because these tasks were felt to be outside the purview of policing. There is evidence of police resistance in response to curfew policies, for example.

Curfew ordinances were introduced in many cities in the 1940s to curb juvenile delinquency, but some cities resisted because of the "resentment of the police at having to add a 'nursemaid's' job to their many more serious duties" (ICMA 1943). As this quote hints at, part of the resistance to taking on additional preventive responsibilities was due to an increase in the other demands being placed on police at the time. In particular, World War II pulled police officers into the armed forces, leaving many departments understaffed (e.g., see ICMA 1943; LAPD 1944). At the same time, new war-related tasks were being added to the police's charge; police were asked to guard crucial infrastructure, be on the lookout for espionage and sabotage, and enforce dimouts and blackouts (ICMA 1940, 1941, 1943). Even before the war, police administrators were keenly aware that a more expansive understanding of prevention might draw the police into activities that did not belong in the category of "police work." This is starkly expressed in the LAPD *Annual Report* of 1939, which explains that the commander of the Juvenile Welfare Division must "maintain constant surveillance over the activities of his entire personnel to obviate any tendency toward retrogression into the field of penal treatment of juvenile delinquents, or a progress into the particular field of social welfare work" (7).

One organizational response to the accretion of tasks necessitated by preventive work focused on finding new people to do these tasks rather than on broadening the understanding of which job tasks were required within the policing occupation. In the case of juvenile delinquency, policewomen were given the new assignments. In the LAPD, women were assigned to the Juvenile Bureau from early in the twentieth century, and they were seen as particularly well suited to preventive work. The 1912 *Annual Report* celebrates this innovation in policing and ties the introduction of women police

99

to success in the new preventive tasks, arguing, "A keener insight and ability to draw facts from women and children in trouble coupled with a natural, sympathetic nature, helps her to prevent crime rather than inflict punishment" (LAPD 1912: 40). The growth of women in the force alongside the expanded understanding of preventive activity encouraged the view that the future of women in the policing occupation would be tied to crime prevention (see ICMA 1946). The assignment of women officers to crime prevention duties was an innovation that continued to be advocated by police administrators through the 1950s (e.g., see ICMA 1955: 403; Kenney and Pursuit 1954).

As the preventive worldview became ever more expansive in the 1950s and 1960s, further worries about the implications for police tasks were expressed by those working in law enforcement. There was a concern both that the police were not sufficiently trained to carry out the wide range of activities newly required of them and that the activities were simply outside the realm of police work. With respect to the lack of training, there was an uptick in calls to professionalize the police, driven by worries that the policing occupation is sufficiently challenging that substantial training and credentialing is required. A special report on police professionalism in the 1967 *MYB* argues, "If a police officer is to carry out his duties intelligently and effectively, he must be a social scientist. It is necessary to get a complete man who has an understanding of his society and its people—a sense of perspective that can come only from a broad, general education" (ICMA 1967: 433; see also President's Commission on Law Enforcement and Administration of Justice 1967b).

With respect to the proper tasks of police work, just as in the earlier period, there is evidence of substantial discomfort in the 1950s and 1960s with the wide range of tasks that police personnel were expected to perform (e.g., see Parker 1954). There are suggestions that, at the very least, the police should be relieved of tasks falling well outside the crime prevention role, such as "running the dog pound," and there are proposals to introduce new police occupations, such as Community Service Officers (President's Commission on Law Enforcement and Administration of Justice 1967a: 98, 108).[5] In the aftermath of widespread social disorder and strong criticism of police tactics and police brutality in the 1960s, the police also appear to have been keen to emphasize how much was being asked of the occupation. A revealing passage is included in the LAPD's *Annual Report* of 1968: "Law enforcement is attempting to cope with problems far beyond what was ever conceived to be its area of responsibility. . . . In the beginning, the mandate to the police was relatively simple. Prevent crime and apprehend criminals. But the law of continual change has broadened this concept. It is no longer sufficient for a complacent society to pass off to the police the responsibility for ameliorating problems arising from political and social change" (6–7).

Despite the discomfort of those within the policing occupation, the task accretion associated with a broader preventive role continues. This is well illustrated in the LAPD annual reports of the 1970s and 1980s, which describe the introduction of "team policing," a patrol innovation in line with the increased emphasis on community policing and patrol that was proposed in the *Challenge of Crime in a Free Society* (1967) and Kerner Commission (1968) reports. Team policing assigned small teams of police to a particular neighborhood; the aim was to create a "small-town" police department in every neighborhood. Each police officer was expected to participate in patrol, traffic, traffic investigation, and crime investigation activities, with the intention that "groups of well-qualified generalists [would] be developed, capable of handling more problems with greater efficiency" (LAPD 1974: 13). The ultimate aspiration was that team policing would lead to police officers acquiring "a pride of ownership in their reduced piece of geography. It's their 'baby,' theirs to zealously protect from all who would challenge their capacity to do so" (LAPD 1973: 22). Initiatives like team policing were introduced across the country, as community policing was embraced by police leaders and politicians. As Hinton (2017) describes, federal funding flowed in support of community policing, while the rolling back of the state with respect to social services created community problems that the police were now first in line to solve.

The responses of police personnel to the accretion of tasks over the past century show the centrality of the logic of specialization to judgments about the appropriateness of the division of labor. As the preventive purview widens, concerns are expressed within both policing and government administration about whether it is appropriate for law enforcement personnel to take on additional tasks. It is clear that concerns about an expansive police role remain even among present-day law enforcement personnel (see Vermeer, Woods, and Jackson 2020).[6] In the recent report of the President's Commission on Law Enforcement and the Administration of Justice, produced under the first Donald Trump administration, these concerns were underlined: "Law enforcement alone is not a cure-all for criminal behavior. . . . It cannot backstop social programs that do not adequately treat the predicate conditions of crime in the first place. Tasking law enforcement officers with these duties impairs the rule of law insofar as their duties become confused and fragmented. . . . Effective law enforcement requires restoring officers to their fundamental duty of preventing and reducing crime" (2020: 35). It is worth noting that the commission's report was produced "unlawfully" by an "unrepresentative" body of commissioners who had all worked in law enforcement (e.g., see Jackman 2020), but the complaints with respect to the division of labor and inadequate task specialization are nevertheless very similar to those made by Defund the Police activists.

THE PREVENTIVE STATE MEETS SPECIALIZATION

As the foregoing indicates, cultural forces laid the groundwork for the accretion of preventive tasks within the police occupation. As the preventive purview grew wider, police tasks accreted in line with what was required to fulfill the more expansive role. At the same time, the logic of specialization was an important moderating force, at least insofar as we consider police comfort with the task accretion. In this section, I use historical job task analyses to quantify changes over the past century in the tasks that police have taken on and examine how the dual forces of prevention and specialization came together to shape police job tasks over the century.

Job task analyses aim to document all tasks that are essential to the performance of a given job (see R. Brenner and Duncan 1978 on police job analysis). Job task analyses were carried out for police officers in California in 1933, 1979, 1998, and 2016. The job tasks described in each analysis are coded to a common framework, and Figure 4-3 plots the proportion of job tasks falling within seven broad task areas over time. The figure also includes examples of job tasks that were added or eliminated between time points (see the Appendix for a discussion of the coding process; all data are available in Jackson 2025).

The job task analysis shows evidence in favor of the long-term trends discussed in the preceding sections. Of most interest is the comparison between 1933 and 1979, which the historical analysis identifies as a period of substantial change. In 1933, the police were responsible for a wide range of tasks that might be classified as community oriented, such as inspecting

1933-1979
MEET WITH SCHOOL ADMINISTRATORS TO
IDENTIFY CONCERNS
PACE VEHICLES USING SPEEDOMETER
CONSISTENT WITH TRAINING
TAKE PRECAUTIONS TO PREVENT INJURIES TO
ARRESTEES
COMPLETE PAPERWORK FOR WARRANTS

Inspects sidewalks, streets, and storm drains
Establishes fire lines at scenes of fire
Rescues domestic animals
Discovers and removes dead bodies

1979-1998
RECORD CONTACTS
PUSH DISABLED VEHICLES WITH PATROL CAR
COMMUNICATE IN LANGUAGE OTHER THAN
ENGLISH
OPERATE RADAR EQUIPMENT FOR SPEED
ENFORCEMENT

Collect bail
Fingerprint persons for noncriminal reasons
Prepare paperwork for process server

1998-2016
WORK IN CLOSE PROXIMITY WITH SPECIALTY
UNITS
ASSIST CODE COMPLIANCE WITH SCENE
SECURITY OR ENFORCEMENT
MAINTAIN SENSITIVITY IN COMMUNICATING
WITH PERSONS OF DIFFERENT CULTURAL OR
SOCIOECONOMIC BACKGROUNDS

Conduct security inspections of businesses and
dwellings
Serve subpoenas
Request that public assist in apprehension of suspects
Videotape field sobriety tests

NEW TASKS
Eliminated tasks

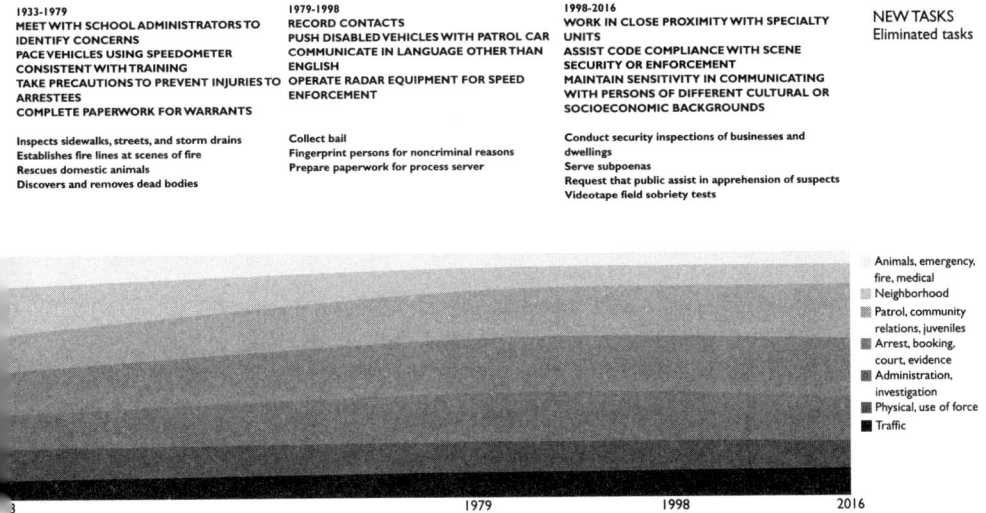

Fig. 4-3 Police job tasks.

streetlights, fire hydrants, and sidewalks; hearing general neighborhood complaints; and investigating unusual characters causing a nuisance to those living in the community. They were also responsible for a number of tasks related to medical treatment, fire extinguishing, and animal control. By 1979, many of these tasks had been eliminated. The long-run trend toward the division of labor pulled tasks that did not "fit" away from the policing occupation, and other occupations took them over. Treating victims of poison, for example, was no longer a police task in 1979; it was seen as the domain of specialized medical personnel. A more subtle example of this process can be seen in tasks related to administration and investigation, which increased between 1933 and 1979, as legal restrictions on police work (e.g., the requirement to inform suspects of Miranda rights) increased. By 2016, administrative tasks had declined in importance, and tasks that could be handled by professional administrators (e.g., writing news releases) were taken out of the police role. The push toward specialization, then, led to a hiving off of those job tasks that did not fit well with preventing or solving crime.

At the same time, we see the growing breadth of police tasks produced by a more expansive preventive purview. Tasks related to the patrol function (coded here to include community policing and juveniles) increased by around 50 percent over the whole period, a rate of increase matched only by traffic-related tasks. A qualitative analysis of how the job tasks changed over time shows shifts in how community interactions were translated into job tasks. Whereas in the past, the police were engaged in many community interactions in the course of their work, those job tasks were described in terms that we might today associate with vigilant neighbors rather than police officers; for example, the police investigated "persons who are following women," "persons who engage school children in prolonged conversation," or "delivery service not previously seen on district." These tasks were replaced with tasks more obviously tied to criminal justice system actions, such as "interview complainants, witnesses, victims, suspicious persons, and suspects to gather information" and "recognize crime series and/or crime patterns to develop investigative leads." As if to underline this point, the latter tasks are classified as "criminal investigation" tasks in the 2016 job task report, while the former tasks are classified as "miscellaneous field service duties" in 1933. As the preventive purview expands, even the community-oriented job tasks become more closely tied to the architecture and language of criminal justice.

PROTECTING THE BOUNDARIES

In this final section, I consider how task accretion in the policing occupation was legitimated and how the police were protected by the state from competition with other occupations. Although all rationalized occupations are vulnerable to accumulating job tasks as science expands, the policing occupation appears to have been particularly vulnerable in this respect: in the analysis of functional complexity across the whole occupational structure, policing occupations were shown to be outliers in comparison to almost all other occupations. I here focus on two uses of state resources that protected police tasks from interoccupational competition: coordination (via collaboration, funding, and technological and administrative investment) and organizational change. The effect—and perhaps also the intent—of these interventions was to protect the police from losing their claim over job tasks to other occupations.

When the ethos of prevention started to point to expansive interventions and community engagement, police collaboration with other community agencies and institutions came into focus. As described earlier in this chapter, initial forays into preventive activities in the field of juvenile crime control came largely via cooperation with other agencies such as the LA Coordinating Councils. In the 1930s, the cooperation and integration of specialized institutions was the order of the day, in line with the focus on allowing families, schools, and welfare organizations to play their part in reducing juvenile delinquency. But even as the police came to take on more and more preventive tasks, coordination with other institutions was emphasized by police leaders. In the late-1960s and 1970s, for example, when expansive preventive tasks were essentially normalized within the policing occupation, the LAPD annual reports describe numerous innovations in which external agencies and institutions cooperated with the police in the name of crime prevention. Cooperative projects included the Teachers' Workshop, which instructed teachers on "narcotics, juvenile procedures, and community problems" (project between Board of Education and LAPD; LAPD 1968: 20); the Law Enforcement Explorer Program, which "introduce[d] young men and women to a law enforcement career" (project between Boy Scouts of America and LAPD; LAPD 1969: 19); and the Fireman Counselor Referral Program, which matched firemen advisers to adolescent boys who had committed a first or second minor offense (project between Fire Department and LAPD; LAPD 1972: 17). Even today, many of the preventive tasks undertaken by the police are undertaken in collaboration with other institutions and agencies (Herring 2019). Although it would, in principle, be possible to initiate collaborations between these organizations and occupations outside of law enforcement, such collaborations would be extremely costly and time-consuming to organize.

Cooperation was also emphasized between police agencies and, most importantly, between federal and local crime prevention agencies. Two types of resources are particularly important in laying the groundwork for such cooperation: (1) financial and (2) technological and administrative. The increasing importance of federal and state funding for police activities is well established (e.g., see Hinton 2017; M. Alexander 2010), and the literature describes how such funding was preserved even as the state was rolled back under the influence of neoliberalism. That this fact is well known by no means diminishes its importance in accounting for why the policing occupation was able to gain, and perhaps even more importantly maintain, control over a broad range of tasks. The desirability of federal support for local law enforcement preventive activity had of course long been emphasized (e.g., see President's Committee on Juvenile Delinquency and Youth Crime 1962). But the Law Enforcement Assistance Act of 1965 opened the door to the extensive federal funding of local police activities, and just two years later, the *Challenge of Crime in a Free Society* report prioritized substantially increased federal support for states and cities (see also ICMA 1970: 470). The Omnibus Crime Control and Safe Streets Act of 1968 only further underlined the role of federal funding in the fight against crime (see Hinton 2017 for a detailed discussion of this period). From this point forward, federal and state monies were available to support many of the policing innovations introduced to tackle social problems.

As important as federal funding was in providing support for the policing occupation's wide range of tasks and responsibilities, a different (and earlier) form of cooperation was arguably even more consequential for the division of labor. The management of technological change, and the potential for such change to transform the practice of crime prevention and detection, gave police a head start in protecting their job tasks from external competition. Innovations in recordkeeping, fingerprinting, radio communications, and calls for service have been particularly valuable, in that they allow the police to benefit from efficiencies in the completion of work tasks. J. Edgar Hoover's address to the Conference on Crime (1934) focused on the gains in efficiency and job performance from cooperation between national and local agencies on recordkeeping, fingerprinting, and laboratory testing. He spoke of a "coalition against crime" and "a Library of Cooperation, an American Encyclopedia of Criminals" (5), that centralized fingerprints and records in a single "Investigative Division" accessible to all local police agencies. The aim of these innovations was to deliver efficiencies in local policing via investments at the federal level and to ensure that criminals who moved across geographic areas would not be able to avoid arrest (see Denney 2021). The result was to open the door to all manner of centralized resources, records, and technologies that only law enforcement personnel could benefit from.

For the past century, the policing occupation has also benefited from technological changes that increase the efficiency and effectiveness of law enforcement activities (e.g., see O. Wilson 1951; for a description of present-day technology exploitation in policing, see Brayne 2020; see also US Congress 2005; President's Task Force 2015). The most well-known technological development was the institution of 911 as a standardized number, which made it possible for local police agencies to pool resources and operate more efficiently.[7] But the development of technologies that linked individual police officers and patrol cars to centralized command centers was arguably more important. When the police increased their use of patrol as a means of crime prevention, two-way radios and centralized record checking allowed law enforcement to increase their influence without a corresponding increase in personnel. This is well described in the LAPD's *Annual Report* of 1968, where Mayor Samuel W. Yorty writes, "heavy man-hour consumption necessary to implement new crime control and community relations projects continue to tax our resources to their limits. . . . A major answer to the efficiency aspect of the problem lies in increased use of technological tools and in consolidation of effort with other law enforcement agencies" (LAPD 1968: 2). In 1972, the Annual Report celebrates the 1500 hours per month of flight time by police helicopters, which "amplified the Department's powers of observation, deterrence, and response" (LAPD 1972: 18). Technological innovations were particularly beneficial to the policing occupation because they not only increased efficiency within the police but, by virtue of limited access to databases and technologies, made it so other organizations and occupations could not compete. Although it is standard to refer to the state as having a monopoly over the means of legitimate violence, here we see the policing occupation benefiting from the state's monopoly on information.

An alternative form of job task protection is organizational change (Weeden 2002). Over the past century, police agencies have introduced organizational changes that promote efficiency and conform to cultural expectations that job tasks belong to specialists (Fogelson 1977). As the police occupation has taken on more and more preventive tasks, police agencies have introduced specialized units that gather together resources and expertise to tackle these new problems. This process began rather early in large police agencies such as the LAPD, and from the mid-1930s onward, the *MYB* highlights those police agencies introducing specialized juvenile units. By the 1950s, the Federal Security Agency was encouraging all police agencies to create specialized units to handle cases involving children and youth (ICMA 1953: 408). As the preventive purview widens, within-agency specialization is encouraged and supported. The LAPD explicitly links organizational changes to the division of labor and the changing meaning of prevention over time: "The individual police officer . . . has been burdened with new and unfamiliar responsibilities which have added new dimensions to police work. . . . This ever-widening spectrum of police obligation has placed the heaviest burden upon the shoulder of the Chief of Police. . . . As particular functions become more diversified, leaders with a detailed knowledge in those areas are required" (LAPD 1969: 12).

The LAPD was a leader in the development of specialized units, and specialization has become an increasingly important feature of police organization in recent decades. Figure 4-4 shows the growth of specialized units in large police agencies (with more than 150 sworn personnel) from 1987 to the present day. The data are drawn from the Law Enforcement Management and Administrative Statistics (LEMAS) surveys of state and local law enforcement agencies (United States Department of Justice 2016). All large police agencies are surveyed on a regular basis, and data collection focuses on agency expenditures, functions, training requirements, and organization.[8] I present separate figures for the smallest, middle, and largest agencies, and the LAPD is called out in the thick dashed line. We see in Figure 4-4 a substantial increase in specialized units over time, an increase that is most evident in the mid- and large-size agencies but also present in even the smaller agencies. Among the largest agencies, the number of specialized units has increased from an average of six units per agency to an average of almost twenty. In 2016, specialized preventive units included "crime prevention," "community policing," "drug education in schools," "juvenile crimes," and "repeat offenders."

Throughout, I have largely focused on speaking to the claims that Defund the Police has made with respect to the broad range of tasks undertaken by the policing occupation, as evaluating the effects of policing on Black and Indigenous people is beyond the scope of this analysis. It is important, though, to directly address the movement's claims with respect to race when considering how the policing occupation was prevented from losing tasks. Collaboration, federal funding, technological investments, and organizational changes were oriented toward solving the "problems" that politicians and public audiences cared about. Over the course of the century, the problems that rose to public and political concern were strongly influenced by race, whether via forcing events (e.g., the Watts "riots") or ideas about people of color (e.g., racial threat). Research on organizational structure in policing has described the colonial origins of policing and the influence of military models of organizational change; racial threats were met with militarized

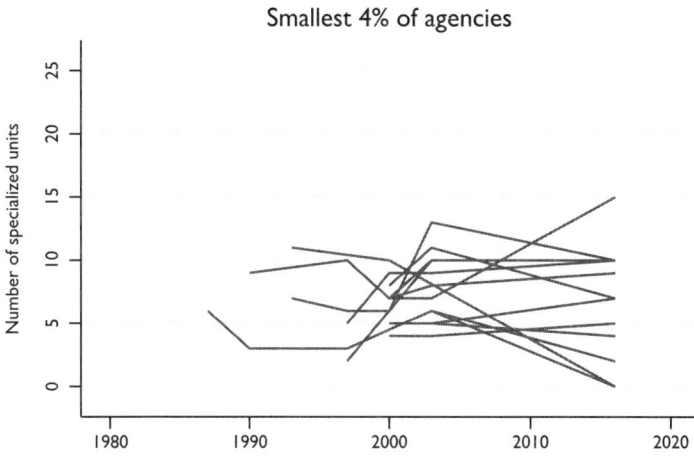

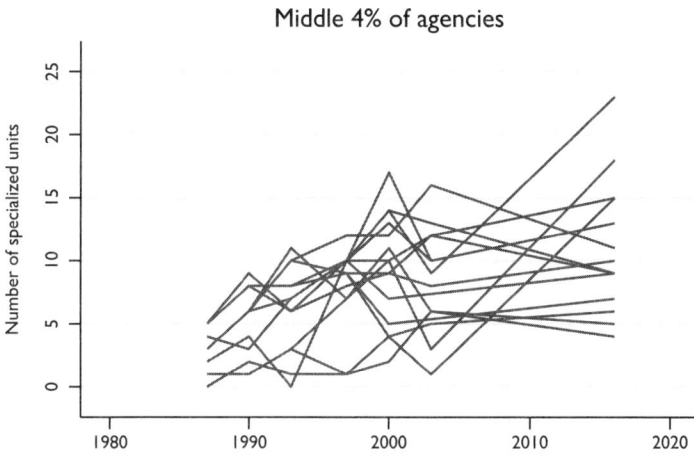

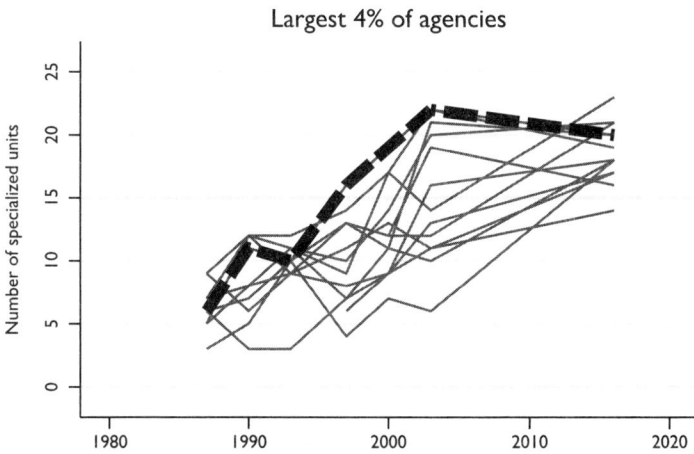

Fig. 4-4 Number of specialized units in large police agencies over time.

DATA SOURCE: LEMAS.

policing strategies that originated in colonial military methods (Go 2020). We should predict, therefore, that police job task protection will also reflect racialized practices.

Evidence for a process of racialized task protection can be found in the historical sources. The focus on juvenile delinquency in discussions of crime prevention itself reflected the racialized construction of a social problem. In the 1930s, Black, Hispanic, and immigrant youngsters were disproportionately likely to be processed by courts and were identified as being disproportionately likely to experience the "social disorganization" that produced delinquency (e.g., Wickersham 1931b).[9] The LAPD appeared to be "particularly alert" to the deviant behavior of Hispanic boys in the 1920s and 1930s (Wolcott 2001: 357), for example, and the behavior of Black youth was in focus during the midcentury (Hinton 2015). But once broad preventive duties are folded into the policing occupation, we see additional task protections emerging. A key example may be found in the Civil Rights era, when protests prompted discussions about both riot control and riot prevention (e.g., see ICMA 1966; Kerner 1968; Hinton 2017). As the purview of preventive activity widened and the Civil Rights movement produced new "problems" to be prevented, the state stepped in to provide new efficiencies in organization, cross-agency collaboration, and equipment. This was also a period in which new energy went into creating specialized units within police agencies. In 1969, the *MYB* describes the dramatic increase in "specially trained, highly mobile units to cope with civil disorders" and celebrates the SWAT team program (first developed by the LAPD) as an efficient and coordinated response to the riot problem (ICMA 1969: 319). Other agencies similarly invested in specialized units focusing on juvenile crime and crowd control during this period.

It is possible to provide a quantitative illustration of these racialized practices over the past three decades using the LEMAS data. I link the LEMAS data to Census data describing the sociodemographic composition of the communities in which police agencies are based and use a fixed effects Poisson regression to predict the number of specialized units in an agency as a function of changes in agency and local area characteristics (Cameron and Trivedi 2013). If police agencies have been simply responding to changing demands, population growth, or changing agency characteristics, we would expect to see an increase in specialized units only in response to these characteristics, consistent with a search for efficiency and claims for expertise over given work tasks. If, in contrast, police agencies have been introducing specialized units in response to changing racial demographics, this would be consistent with racialized job task protection.

The full model is presented in the Appendix; the model shows that although agency characteristics do have significant effects on the number of specialized units, there is also evidence of racialized job task protection. In Figure 4-5, I show the predicted number of specialized units as the proportion of Black, Hispanic, and immigrant people in the agency's local area varies. When, for example, the proportion of Black people in a given area increases, the police agency responds by increasing the number of specialized units. This effect is robust to an increased demand for police services (captured via calls for service), increasing population size, agency characteristics, and any time-invariant factors. Similar robust increases in the number of specialized units are found in response to growing Hispanic and immigrant populations.[10] The quantitative analyses, therefore, appear to confirm the findings from historical evidence on the push to within-agency specialization. Both types of data are consistent with police agencies engaging in racialized job task protection by making claims to expertise,

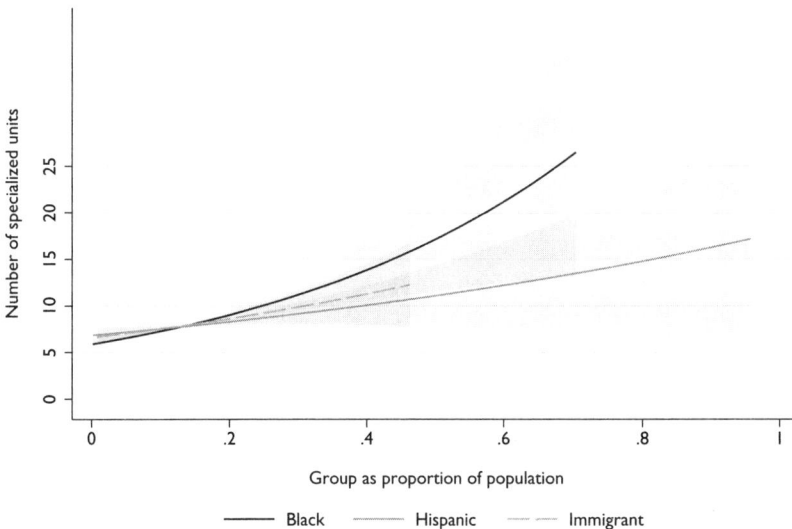

Fig. 4-5 Results of model predicting number of specialized units in large police agencies.

DATA SOURCE: LEMAS.

claims that pave the way for privileged access to federal and state resources, which in turn allow the police to dominate in the competition for preventive tasks.

THE PRINCIPAL OBJECT

Although not expressed in such terms, the Defund the Police movement is, at least in part, a movement about the appropriate level of functional differentiation in contemporary society. Sociologists have largely focused on the movement as an exemplar of collective action (e.g., Phelps, Robertson, and Powell 2021; Phelps, Ward, and Frazier 2021) or as an expected response to the negative outcomes of policing for Black and Indigenous people (e.g., Hinton 2021; Voigt et al. 2017). But for sociologists, the movement should also provoke broader questions about public expectations with respect to the division of labor, both in policing and in the wider society.

The policing occupation exhibits a high degree of functional complexity relative to other occupations in the contemporary occupational structure. But policing is simply an extreme example of the same general process that played out across all rationalized occupations: the paradox of specialization. The police had always aimed to prevent crime, but changes in science meant that the job of crime prevention looked fundamentally different at the end of the twentieth century from how it had looked at the beginning. The logic of specialization proved to be a powerful moderating force, as some tasks (e.g., certain forms of medical assistance and community services) were taken on by other occupations. But by specializing in the output of crime prevention, the policing occupation opened up a new set of tasks, one that was legitimately within the purview of a preventive body once the science indicated that prevention required expansive intervention. Having gained these job tasks, the police occupation benefited from preferential access to administrative, financial, and technological resources and from the legitimacy gained via specialization *within* police agencies. This legitimacy was achieved via a heavily racialized process, in which specialized units were introduced in response to local increases in Black, Hispanic, and immigrant people.

The analysis has implications for how we should interpret responses to the Defund the Police movement, with the reaction of Los Angeles being informative here. Los Angeles's immediate response to Defund the Police was to announce a cut of $150 million to the LAPD's operating budget

(Rector 2021a). The LAPD then announced that to manage the budget cuts, it would be necessary to focus on core parts of the LAPD's mission. As Deputy Chief Blake Chow expressed it, the LAPD would be "honing the role of officers more closely to crime prevention and response, rather than social services" (Rector 2021b). Specialized units pertaining to sexual assault, burglary, animal cruelty, robbery and homicide, commercial crimes, and traffic units were cut or reduced in size. These cuts were made to "stave off cuts to patrol and the Community Safety Partnership Bureau" (Rector 2021a). Other changes included a reduction in law enforcement personnel via hiring freezes, new policies on the use of force and crowd control, and pilot programs that included diverting calls involving suicidal people to mental health professionals.

Although some of the responses from the LAPD indicate a willingness to lose tasks to external specialists, there are hints in the above list that many of the same patterns we observe in the historical data are being repeated. As the results in this chapter indicate, the police accumulated so many job tasks because they were positioned as specialists in crime prevention. The LAPD's responses to Defund the Police entail reductions to those specialized units less closely related to crime prevention, and the protection of the patrol and community programs that are largely responsible for the substantial functional complexity that characterizes modern policing. The LAPD's *Strategic Plan* for 2021–23 emphasized "reenergized efforts of community collaboration and cultural competence" and "commitment to the expansion of community safety partnerships" (LAPD 2021: 6). Aims for the future are marked by a strong emphasis on technological solutions to efficiency and information problems. In other words, all current indications are that nothing has happened to alter the police purview with respect to crime prevention or the police's investments in the same. Insofar as crime prevention is the primary output of policing and the science of prevention continues to expand, the paradox of specialization is likely to push the police occupation in the direction of ever-greater functional complexity.

We Ask So Much

On January 25, 2024, Secretary Miguel A. Cardona wrote to all school principals and district administrators in the United States. The letter started, "Nothing could be more important than protecting the lives of children in our schools," and continued, "While recognizing that a range of strategies and actions are needed on all fronts to keep our students safe, I write to you today to emphasize a strategy where school principals and district administrators have a unique capacity to help save lives: encouraging safe firearms storage." In a prior letter to educators, sent October 30, 2023, he urged, "In the midst of this fentanyl overdose epidemic, it is important to focus on measures to prevent youth drug use and ensure that every school has naloxone and has prepared its students and faculty to use it." This followed a letter sent on September 19, 2023, in which he wrote, "As we well know, when children are healthy and well, they do better on all indicators of achievement, academic performance, attendance, grades, cognitive skills, attitudes and class behavior. . . . I am writing to ask for your collaboration . . . to help build awareness among students and families that they need to act to re-enroll in Medicaid coverage, and to help assist them in doing so."

These examples are far from cherry-picked. An inspection of the 237 key policy letters signed by the education secretary between 1999 and 2024 reveals that almost one-third focus on health or social problems; in contrast, just under 10 percent focus on test scores or other measures of performance, and around 30 percent focus on legislation or school funding.[1] It is, by now, commonplace to hear that we ask "too much" of our schools and colleges (e.g., see E. Green 2013; DeWitt 2018; see also Tyack and Cuban 1997), and concerns are raised about the welfare of educators and other school staff, who are understood to be overworked and overwhelmed (Kotlowitz 2012). And as we saw in Chapter 1 (Figure 1-1), workers in the "education and library" major occupational group have in fact experienced the most extreme takeoff over recent decades in the number of tasks required on the job. Taken together, these observations suggest that educational institutions and personnel are feeling the effects of the paradox of specialization.

In this chapter, I examine changes over time in the rationalization and functional complexity of the education industry and its dominant occupation, the teacher. I will largely focus on primary and secondary education, but many of the same patterns can be observed at the college level. To track changes at industry, firm (i.e., school), and occupation levels, I use data drawn from *Teachers College Record* (*TCR*) and the *Journal of Negro Education* (*JNE*), *United States Government Manual* descriptions of the structure and functions of the Department of Education, high school yearbooks, and teacher job task analyses. I begin by considering just what it is that the industry and its participants are attempting to work toward: the output of education.

ALL PEOPLE DO NOT AGREE

One of the most striking features of the education industry is that there is—ostensibly—little agreement among participants about what the output of the industry is. Debates about the "aims of education" have been ongoing in the academic journals and vocational literature for far longer than the past 150 years. As Aristotle recognized more than two thousand years ago, "All people do not agree in those things they would have a child taught, both with respect to their improvement in virtue and a happy life: nor is it clear whether the object of it should be to improve the reason or rectify the morals" (1888: 269). Some see the primary aim of education as training in a given body of knowledge, others see the aim as socialization into democratic citizenship, and still others emphasize the importance of practical preparation for a healthy and rewarding adult life. Nevertheless, as even the participants in these debates recognize, disagreements about the aims of education should primarily be understood as disagreements about the proximate aims required to satisfy a more amorphous and elusive end: the well-educated child. All agree, for example, that education must prepare children for participation in society and that the school is a key agent of socialization. The disagreements pertain to what is required for education to fulfill its charge. Any new proximate aim is likely to reflect a complicated mix of political, private, and public interests (e.g., see Labaree 1992, 1997), and what will be seen as essential to the output of education in one period may differ from what is seen as essential in the next.

It is important to distinguish discussions about the aims of education from discussions about the tasks that schools and teachers can be asked to take on (e.g., see J. Wilson 1989; Lipsky 2010: chap. 4). For many decades, schools and teachers have relied on public funding to support their work, and they are therefore vulnerable to being required to undertake a wide range of tasks that might be unrelated to their outputs. For example, during wars, the state might require schools to participate in training soldiers or distribute food to workers. These new tasks reflect not new visions about what schools *should* do but rather the reality that schools *can* be made responsible for performing tasks, given their position in the community. I therefore distinguish in this chapter among the proximate aims that are explicitly discussed over time, the tasks that are added to satisfy these aims, and the tasks that are added to satisfy unrelated goals.

In the remainder of this section, I trace changes over time in beliefs about the proximate aims of education and beliefs about the tasks that educational institutions can be made responsible for.

Lack of Family-Nurture

The late nineteenth century was a time of rapid expansion in public school enrollment. Official statistics show that between 1870 and 1880, the proportion of five-to-nineteen-year-olds enrolled in school increased from 0.48 to 0.58 (Snyder 1993: tab. 2). The increase in enrollment was more substantial for Black children (0.10 to 0.24) than for white children (0.54 to 0.62), a fact that the *Report of the Commissioner of Education* claimed was "partially due to the greater desire for improvement on the part of the freedmen" (1882: lxiv).[2] Growing concerns about the quality of education, social costs of ignorance, and high rates of illiteracy—particularly among Black children—had led to the establishment in 1867 of a federal Department of Education, which was tasked with collecting statistics on the state of education in the United States and sharing this information with the purpose of improving state school systems. The department was soon downgraded to an office within the Department of the Interior, but the episode reveals the level of national interest in education as both a foundational social institution and an agent of social change (for useful histories of the early Department of Education, see Lykes 1975; L. Smith 1967; on education's role in Reconstruction during the 1870s, see McAfee and McAfee 1998).

Popular images of the "little red schoolhouse" of the late nineteenth century portray an education system organized around the need to impart the three Rs: reading, writing, and arithmetic. In fact, even in the early years of the nineteenth century, it was well recognized that schools were responsible for far more than training students in a small set of basic skills. Ellwood P. Cubberley, for example, traces the development of the elementary school curriculum between the late eighteenth and early twentieth centuries (1919: 327). In the early period, the curriculum prioritized reading and study of the Bible, but spelling, writing, and arithmetic were also included.[3] By 1825, reading, spelling, arithmetic, and grammar were curricular priorities, but elementary school students were also likely to study good behavior, manners and morals, bookkeeping, geography, and sewing and knitting. And by the beginning of the long twentieth century, the priorities were reading, spelling, penmanship, arithmetic, grammar, geography, and history, with conduct, object lessons, science, drawing, music, and physical exercises making up the remainder of the curriculum.[4] Elsewhere, Cubberley characterizes these changes as representing a shift away from an "old limited curriculum for disciplinary purposes [that] could no longer meet the changed conditions of our national life." Instead, he continues, "the school was asked to concentrate its energy to some more definite purpose, to train the eye and the hand for direct and useful action, and to prepare more definitely its pupils for personal usefulness in life" (1909: 40).

As enrollments increased and most children came to expect to spend at least some time in formal education, educational and political leaders turned more decisively to consider public education's role in preparing children for adult life. In 1874, a group of "key educators" came together to release a statement in which they outlined the fundamental principles underlying a system of public education (Bureau of Education 1874).[5] The statement emphasized the position of the school as an institution of secondary socialization, sitting between the family and adult life. This position meant that schools must take on some of the work that families were traditionally responsible for, and in particular, they must take a decisive role in providing ethical guidance. Item X of the statement begins: "To compensate for lack of family-nurture, the school is obliged to lay more stress upon discipline and to make far more prominent the moral phase of education. It is obliged to train the pupil into habits of prompt obedience to his teachers and the practice of self-control in its various forms" (13). Notably, the statement includes as many items discussing discipline and ethical guidance as items discussing the "theoretical study" expected in the school (on school discipline in this period, see also J. Kennedy 1878).[6] With respect to the content of the education, the ideal curriculum would provide an appropriate foundation for an economically stable and personally rewarding adult life. Thus both the ethical and theoretical content of education operated in concert to socialize the child.

The School and Society

Although the increasing enrollment at the secondary level had focused attention on the educational elite—those who would attend high school and then college—changes in the labor market and wider society were intensifying the interest in education as a key social institution. The growing industrial sector was highlighting the importance of job-relevant training and vocational specialization of a type that the family alone could not provide. The growing urban population led to questions about how the complexity of modern life would be managed. The decades spanning the turn of the century would witness what Lawrence Cremin (1955) labeled a "revolution" in US secondary education.

As the numbers employed in manufacturing grew and commodity output increased, it was clear that the older training and apprenticeship systems would no longer provide adequate preparation for employment in the new economy (on these economic changes, see, e.g., Gallman 1960). John Dewey, writing at the end of the nineteenth century, observes,

> While our educational leaders are talking of culture, the development of personality, etc., as the end and aim of education, the great majority of those who pass under the tuition of the school regard it only as a narrowly practical tool with which to get bread and butter enough to eke out a restricted life. If we were to conceive our educational end and aim in a less exclusive way, if we were to introduce into educational processes the activities which do appeal to those whose dominant interest is to do and to make, we should find that the hold of the school upon its members would be more vital, more prolonged. (1899: 38–39)

Dewey's observations in this passage emphasize that a practical, vocationally oriented education was seen as a broadly desirable end to pursue. The "manual training" movement had encouraged the introduction of education oriented toward practical skills, first at the secondary level and later at the elementary level. Nicholas Murray Butler (1888), for example, proposed that students should spend between a quarter and a third of their time at school engaged in drawing and constructive activities (e.g., woodworking and metalworking) (see also Woodward 1887, 1890). The purpose of manual training was not to train students for any particular occupation or trade but rather to prepare students for the practice of work. In the elementary school curriculum of 1900, we see the new interest in practical education expressed through the addition of sewing, cooking, manual training, and nature work (Cubberley 1919: 327; see also Harris, Draper, and Tarbell 1895: 68).[7]

If the new economy raised questions about how children could be prepared for the world of work, changes in society raised questions about how the school should prepare younger generations to manage the challenges of modernity. The country was changing. The urban population was growing, and social life was becoming ever more complicated. Children would need to learn to form relationships with strangers, to cooperate as citizens, and to work together with others as employees in the service of industry. In short, the United States was undergoing the transition from *Gemeinschaft* to *Gesellschaft* (Tönnies 1887). Alongside these transformations, a substantial wave of immigration was bringing into the country large numbers of young adults, many of whom did not speak English (see, e.g., Carpenter 1927). As concerns were raised about the assimilation of these new immigrants and their children, some looked to the schools to manage this process (e.g., see F. V. Thompson 1920; Berrol 1969).

Education for the *Gesellschaft* required efforts to be expended on the management of social relations. The ethical training, moral guidance, and discipline of the past remained important, to be sure, but of far greater importance was preparing children for full participation in the new society. This required both direct training in civic education and moral instruction and the introduction of a style of teaching that encouraged cooperative activities among students and the nurturing of a "collective responsibility" (National Education Association 1921). Alongside academic training that would allow each student to achieve an appropriate labor market outcome, teaching for citizenship would cultivate individuals capable of handling the demands of modern society.

The "revolution," then, was the transition from a school designed for academic study to a school designed to meet the needs of wider society (Cremin 1955). In the words of the National Education Association, this revolution had established that "education in a democracy, both within and without the school, should develop in each individual the knowledge, interests, ideals, habits, and powers whereby he will find his place and use that place to shape both himself and society toward ever nobler ends" (1921: 32). As the spread of compulsory schooling laws across the states ensured that *all* children would spend at least some time in formal education, the school became well placed to conform with new visions of how education could deliver on a broad set of societal aims.

We Seek Peace—Enduring Peace

> In these times of unparalleled storm and stress, when the traditions of centuries are crumbling and the ideals of civilization are being weighed in the balance of war, the patriots of every nation are giving anxious thought to the social order that shall arise from the present chaos. Preparedness is the word that springs to every lip. . . . In its lowest terms, it means preparation for military defense against foreign aggression; in its highest reaches, it aspires to the regeneration of human nature, so that the brute in man shall forever be held in leash. However men may differ as to the means of bringing on the millennium, the fairest flower in the blood-soaked fields of the world today is the universal desire for peace on earth and good will to men.

James Earl Russell, the dean of Teachers College, understood that as the world attempted to heal the fractures of World War I, education would be called on to prevent future conflicts (1917: 1). The vision of education as a solution for social problems had thoroughly taken root in American society in the decades leading up to the war, making it quite natural for educational and political elites to turn to the schools once again as the postwar reconstruction began.

Of primary importance in the postwar reconstruction was building a social system in which there were buffers to protect from further conflict. Although in the previous decades schools had already taken on the task of training students to participate fully in their communities, the war had underlined the importance of democratic citizenship. It was imperative that children be socialized into democracy and patriotism if war was to be prevented in the future. On August 23, 1917, President Woodrow Wilson wrote to school officers to urge school personnel to "increase materially the time and attention devoted to instruction bearing directly on the problems of community and national life." In concert with the president's appeal, the Bureau of Education issued a series of leaflets, *Lessons in Community and National Life,* designed to teach students about issues of importance to the nation.[8] The leaflets covered topics from the economic (e.g., the gains to industry from using machines and "the hunger for markets"), to the sociological (e.g., the impersonality of modern life and the role of the corporation), to the practical (e.g., which foods can be substituted for wheat, meats, fats, and sugar) (US Office of Education 1917). After the war, the practical direction provided in wartime became less important than the social components of citizenship. Given the role that the United States had taken in the conflict, it was further appreciated that students would need to understand their roles in not just local but also national and international communities (e.g., see Kilpatrick 1921; T. Moore 1921).

As World War I receded from the nation's attention, another catastrophe would come to occupy the minds of educational and political leaders, raising questions again about the aims of education and the schools. As the Great Depression devastated communities across the country, the lofty aims championed after the war fell out of focus as schools were forced to reckon with high rates of unemployment and schoolchildren living in appalling poverty. One effect of high unemployment was to increase the number of students enrolled who would ordinarily have left school well before graduation (Snyder 1993). The passage of the National Industrial Recovery Act and the associated introduction of codes designed to eliminate child labor similarly increased the numbers persisting in education (Cook 1933; see also Lee 1933). An important function of the school in this period, therefore, was to act as a "custodian" for students who had little interest in academic pursuits (Mirel and Angus 1985). As Katherine M. Cook, chief of the Special Problems Division in the Office of Education, described in her discussion of how schools should manage such students, the school would need to invest in "music, home economics, vocational and educational guidance, the arts and crafts, extra-curricular activities," and emphasize the philosophy of the "common covenant" of cooperation that had been lost in the consumerism and competition of the pre-Depression period (1933: 18). Although there is evidence that in many cases schools wholly failed to make these investments (e.g., see Spaulding 1939: chap. 7; Tyack, Lowe, and Hansot 1984), there is little doubt that the political elites of the time saw education as a solution to managing the special problems of Depression-era youth.

Education was also called on as an aid to producing employable citizens. The Depression had of course led to many workers losing their jobs, and as the New Deal projects pulled thousands into relief work, it became clear that many of these workers were lacking in basic skills and training. Works Progress Administration (WPA) programs sprang up to address the deficits (e.g., see Kohn 1934). There was a double benefit: unemployed educators were put to work, and worker deficits could be remedied (Tyack, Lowe, and Hansot 1984: 129–132). These programs largely operated outside of the schools, but as the country recovered from the Depression, schools were increasingly called on to provide training oriented toward work and economic success. In contrast to the emphasis of earlier periods on vocational training directly linked to particular jobs, the focus now was on training "basic skills and habits," flexibility, and responsibility. In a revealing report from 1938, the Advisory Committee on Education writes that one important aim of education is to "prepare a young person to learn a job quickly and, if the job vanishes in the course of technological change, to shift over without serious trouble to some new type of work" (1938: 15). While being a sentiment that clearly reflects the concerns of a country emerging from an economic depression, this aim is strikingly similar to our present-day conceptions of how education should prepare students for work (e.g., see Goldin and Katz 2009).

As the nation recovered from the Depression, the threat of war in Europe was once again on the horizon. Just as had happened in the previous conflagration, the Second World War raised questions about the role of education both during the conflict and after the Allied victory (e.g., see Educational Policies Commission 1939, 1942; Gideonse 1942; Hart 1941; Zook 1942). And just as had happened in World War I, there was an interest in the education system producing adults who would be committed to the principles of cooperation and democracy.[9] In this case, though, there were three important modifications to the prior emphases. These changes are well illustrated through reference to the report of the President's Commission on Higher Education: *Higher Education for American Democracy* (1947). First, while responsible citizenship was once again emphasized, commentators focused as much on international cooperation as on cooperation in the context of a local and national community (see also Educational Policies Commission 1938: chap. 2; H. Wilson 1945). Second, inequality of opportunity was increasingly framed as a challenge to democracy. The commission (1947: 2:27) argued that educational institutions should act as pioneering agents of leadership against discrimination. Each institution should conscientiously plan and prosecute a well-organized program to reduce and, where possible, promptly to eliminate discrimination, not only by correcting its policies and practices but also by educating its students to seek the abolition of discriminatory practices in all their manifestations. And third, there was an interest in educational institutions working toward the "full, rounded, and continuing development of the person" (1:9). The recognition of humanity and the cultivation of the whole person would provide the strength of character necessary to preserve a free society.[10]

With All Deliberate Speed

The President's Commission on Higher Education had emphasized both that educational institutions should promote equality in schools and society and that students should be recognized as individuals and treated as such by schools and colleges. Although these two priorities would appear to be quite different, they were in fact assumed to represent two sides of the same coin.

As educational expansion had proceeded over the first half of the century—encouraged by compulsory schooling laws, the outlawing of child labor, and school-building programs—schools were now serving a much broader constituency than they had in the past. It could no longer be assumed, for example, that those persisting in high school were the academic elite, headed to college and then on to professional careers. Importantly, the expansion had pulled into the high schools new generations of students that were much more diverse than the generations that had come before them. By the mid-1950s, just under 90 percent of white children and over 80 percent of children of Black and other races were enrolled in school.[11] Many of these children were from more deprived backgrounds than the average student of the past. It was clear that further educational expansion, as well as the country's prosperity and security, would depend on effectively educating the students who had previously been poorly served by the education system. As Will French wrote, when contemplating the future role of the American high school,

> If a nation's policies and practices in youth education perpetuate and magnify accidents of birth it is essentially autocratic. . . . If, on the other hand, its youth education undertakes deliberately to eradicate these accidental differences, while magnifying and cultivating intrinsic personal ability and worth, the nation is inherently democratic and will raise up generations of youth who will make it more so. The comprehensive high school is one of our best means for creating social unity without crushing individuality and for developing individual diversity without cultivating social cleavages. (1955: 363)

Promoting equality of opportunity while supporting all individuals in education would require schools to take full account of the challenges faced by different students (e.g., see Brown 1950; Educational Policies Commission 1962).

The President's Commission on Higher Education had identified race as one of the key social cleavages that educators needed to address. The commission had sensibly appreciated that calls for "harmony and cooperation among peoples of differing races, customs, and opinions" were likely to be treated with some disdain if such harmony and cooperation could not be assured *within* the country (1947: 1:8; see also Bonds 1948). When the decision in *Brown v. Board of Education* was returned in May 1954, the calls for educational institutions to focus on "intergroup relations" and the socializing of students into harmonious cooperation only became louder (e.g., see G. Watson 1956; for a history of Black education pre-Brown, see Weinberg 1977: chap. 2). As school integration progressed and the Civil Rights movement made legislative gains, the school's role in reducing the effects of social divisions was emphasized.

The inequality-reducing role of education continued to be emphasized through the 1950s and 1960s, as schools grappled with what it meant to provide equal opportunity to all. Lyndon B. Johnson's Great Society reforms placed education at the heart of the approach to building a more equal society. In a message to Congress in January 1965, for example, he identified education as central to the nation's success: "Nothing matters more to the future of our country: not our military preparedness—for armed might is worthless if we lack the brain power to build a world of peace; not our productive economy—for we cannot sustain growth without trained man-power; not our democratic system of government—for freedom is fragile if citizens are ignorant." The purpose of Johnson's address was to commit to a "national goal of Full Educational Opportunity," for without equality of educational opportunity, it would be impossible for the United States to deliver on the American Dream. Accordingly, when Johnson signed the Elementary and Secondary Education Act (ESEA) into law in 1965, a central focus was to provide funding for low-income schools to improve their pro-grams, with the aim of meeting "the special educational needs of education-ally deprived children" (Public Law 89–10: §201; see Office of Education 1969 for a history of Title I).

Education was thus firmly established as a primary means of addressing key social problems, and as new problems arose, they could be straightfor-wardly folded into the broadening set of aims of education. As worries about delinquency took root in the 1960s (see Chapter 4), schools were seen as institutions that could help to address the problem. Some commentators attributed delinquency to the growing "normlessness" of the 1960s and the decline of religion and community traditions as constraints on behavior. The influential report *The Challenge of Crime in a Free Society* identified education as having a role to play in reducing delinquent behavior (Presi-dent's Commission on Law Enforcement and Administration of Justice 1967a). The commission included among its recommendations that schools should "combat racial and economic school segregation," "deal better with behavior problems," and "develop job placement services" (73–74). If the roots of delinquent behavior were to be found in experiences in the educa-tional system, the schools could play their part in reducing delinquency.

A Nation at Risk

The expansion of the aims of schooling into the solution of social problems led, on the face of it, to a straightforward backlash from defenders of the "traditional" aims of education. In a report of the Ronald Reagan–era National Commission on Excellence in Education (1983), characterized as an "open letter to the American people," this backlash was on full display. *A Nation at Risk* largely rejected the "solving social problems" vision of education that had been particularly influential over the recent decades, criticizing the "multitude of often conflicting demands we have placed on our Nation's schools and colleges. They are routinely called on to provide solutions to personal, social, and political problems that the home and other institutions either will not or cannot resolve. We must understand that these demands on our schools and colleges often exact an educational cost as well as a financial one" (6). The conception of education embraced by the report was seemingly a return to the traditional "academic" aims of education and to the pursuit of excellence (e.g., see Pulliam 1991: chap. 9). Students should leave school with a solid understanding of the "New Basics" (English, mathematics, science, social studies, and computer science), and the primary aim of education should be to prepare students for economic success.

The clear (and expressed) aim of the report was to return schools to an earlier era in which education provided the foundation for a successful career. As we have seen, this vision of education as preparation for work was, even in the very early years of compulsory schooling, hardly the dominant vision in the minds of educators or political elites. Further, as focused as the commission was on the narrow academic aims of education, the inclusion of social studies among the New Basics reveals a rather broader conception of the aims of education than is admitted to in the headline claim. The rationale for the inclusion of this subject is, of course, to train students in the key components of citizenship: to train students in the fundamentals of how the economic system works and to allow students to understand their place in the broader social structure. Even in a report that stressed a vision of education as human capital, the importance of the schools in producing responsible citizens was emphasized.

The focus on raising standards in education was to continue. The idea that the nation was "at risk" from poor educational standards became a theme of commentary on the schools, and there were increasing worries that Americans were being left behind by international competitors. An influential report from the Committee for Economic Development (1985), for example, had raised concerns about the educational and economic performance of the United States relative to competitors, in particular Japan. And when President George H. W. Bush gathered together the state governors for a two-day bipartisan summit on education, a central theme was the importance of education to economic prosperity and international competitiveness. The growth of international testing—such as the Third International Mathematics and Science Study (TIMSS) and the Program for International Student Assessment (PISA)—had revealed not only that US students were failing to "win" the international achievement competition but the United States was around the middle of the pack (US Department of Education 1996; National Center for Education Statistics 2002). The newly centered "academic standards" vision of education was therefore justified, at least in some measure, by the need to maintain economic dominance over the world market. When President Bush named his six national educational "goals" in 1990, the rationale for adopting the goals was to "keep America competitive."

It would be easy to interpret the educational goals and focus on standards as a political embrace of a narrowed set of aims for education. Indeed, *America 2000: An Education Strategy*, published by the Bush administration to outline the six national educational goals, explicitly rejected the solution of social problems as an aim of schooling. Striking a similar theme to the Reagan-era *A Nation at Risk* report, *America 2000* argued, "Schools are not and cannot be parents, police, hospitals, welfare agencies or drug treatment centers. They cannot replace the missing elements in communities and families" (Bush 1991: 10). Yet when the president introduced *America 2000*, he invited those assembled to "think about every problem, every challenge we face. The solution to each starts with education. For the sake of the future, of our children and of the nation's, we must transform America's schools" (39). His remarks also included references to schools' duty to ensure that every American would be capable of exercising the "rights and responsibilities of citizenship." And most strikingly, the sixth goal was to eliminate drugs and violence from schools.[12] Even while *America 2000* championed a narrow and "traditional" set of aims for education, it still maintained an emphasis on building well-adapted and successful citizens for the future.

President Bush's *America 2000* goals were fully institutionalized when President Bill Clinton signed the Goals 2000: Educate America Act (see US Department of Education 1996). Later in the same year, Clinton reauthorized the ESEA, known as the Improving America's Schools Act. Because the goals of the Bush era were preserved, the aims of education ostensibly remained the same. There was a strong focus on education as human capital, just as had been the case in the Bush era (M. Smith and Scoll 1995).[13] But the declaration of purpose of the amended ESEA (October 1994: §1001, a.1) opened with the following statement: "high-quality education for all individuals and a fair and equal opportunity to obtain that education are a societal good, are a moral imperative, and improve the life of every individual, because the quality of our individual lives ultimately depends on the quality of the lives of others." Once again, building a good society was central to education's role, even while the human capital aim was foregrounded.

Although the bipartisan consensus on education for economic prosperity has largely remained in place as the twenty-first century has progressed, there have—perhaps inevitably—been attempts by successive presidential administrations to tie the aims of education to a broader policy agenda. President Barack Obama, for example, embraced the power of education to promote respect and kindness, a theme that was prominent during his presidency from his inauguration address onward.[14] In his first term, President Donald Trump constituted the 1776 Commission and introduced "pro-American" teaching materials aimed toward increasing the patriotism of American students. In the report of the President's Advisory 1776 Commission, the members describe the importance of "authentic" education, which includes "moral education" and "character formation" that will enable individuals to be "self-reliant and responsible persons capable of governing themselves" (2021: 37). But these attempts should not be overstated. The primary aim of education, as expressed clearly in both the policy and rhetoric of recent decades, is economic prosperity for the individual and the wider society.

THE BORDERLAND OF DISCOVERY

As the history of the aims of education makes clear, the proximate outputs of the education system are best conceptualized as a moving target. Further, there are many examples of new tasks being added in line with the exigencies of the moment. Educators and schools could therefore be forgiven for some feeling of whiplash in keeping track of these aims and priorities. As we see in the next section, the extent to which changes in proximate outputs and tasks were filtered through to the job tasks of teachers and schools was variable, particularly in the long term. Of much greater importance in this respect were changes in the degree of rationalization of the education industry and changes in the science of education.

The Cardinal Principles

Those working in the business of education in the late nineteenth century were not short of reference material if they wished to search for advice. Even in this period, there was sufficient literature on how children should be educated that the *TCR* devoted most of its first volume (1900) to outlining the key themes and associated readings required during the college's teacher training. The list of readings for Nicholas Murray Butler's class on Principles of Education ran to nineteen pages.

One notable feature of the voluminous literature on education of this time is the number of references by authors and commentators to the "theory" or "art" of education. Even in that first volume of *TCR*, the house journal of one of the most scientifically focused institutions of education and teacher training,[15] there are forty-one mentions of the "theory" or "art" of education, versus forty mentions of "science" or "scientific."[16] Tellingly, the 1874 statement released by key educators on public education was titled "A Statement of the Theory of Education in the United States."

There are two important reasons that the terms "theory" and "art" are used in preference, or in addition, to "science" when referring to education in this period. First, disagreement over the aims of education makes it challenging to develop or accept a body of systematized knowledge oriented toward the achievement of a given outcome. Science is, at heart, a highly rationalized endeavor, and insofar as the ends of education are seen as ambiguous, it is hard to isolate the means to work toward them. In this sense, at least, it was easier for the manufacturing industry to develop scientific foundations than it was for the education industry. When training students to become teachers, the more scientifically oriented professors encouraged trainees to settle on an aim and orient themselves toward it: "It is surely not too much to demand of you that you have some definite ideal. Why, a cabinetmaker has his ideal of the completed cabinet, as he saws and cuts, planes and joints and polishes. You are engaged in forming the finest, most complex, most subtle thing known to man, *viz.* a mind; and do you propose to go on from day to day as your fancy prompts, tinkering here and tinkering there, and seeing what comes of it? Surely not" (Laurie 1892: 8). In most cases, the aim identified in such cases was incredibly broad: for example, "the realization of the Idea of Man" (Laurie 1892: 7) or "human happiness and perfection" (Bain 1879: 6). Nevertheless, it was by settling on the aim that advocates of scientific education could open the door to the rationalization of education.

The second reason for using the terms "theory" or "art" is to underscore that teaching is a practical discipline, in which educators are required to carry out the "art" (or practice) of teaching in accordance with a set of theoretical principles describing how education should be delivered. The "theory" term, then, is broad and may refer to both scientific knowledge and the knowledge derived from practical experience. But there is in the use of these terms also an insistence that the knowledge derived from experience must not be discarded in favor of "science" alone. The belief that practical experience in the classroom might offer insights that science alone could not is broadly shared among the educationalists of the time.

One reason practical experience was seen to be so important was that rules based on science were expected to be universal. There was accordingly much discussion of the conditions under which it would be possible to find universal principles of education that could apply across different contexts and periods of history (e.g., Dilthey 1888; Royce 1891a; D. Page 1885: 95). A universal pedagogy was seen as an implausible aim because of individual variability among students and contexts, meaning that the teacher's experience was the ultimate arbiter of the appropriateness of method and content. Josiah Royce, for example, writes, "Rules would here be suggested by the science at every point; yet they would never be rules that the educator could immediately apply, except with constant reference to the conditions of his own nation, age, and child. Universal these rules would be, yet never universal in so far as they were precise guides in the concrete case. Aids they would be, but never substitutes for personal insight. In short, pedagogy, as a 'science,' would be a good staff and a bad crutch" (1891a: 20).[17] The aversion to universal laws in the context of variability reflects, of course, a nonprobabilistic vision of explanation. For the probabilist, variation around a central tendency is unproblematic, and probabilistic explanation similarly allows for heterogeneity among units of analysis (Xie 2013). But at the end of the nineteenth century, such probabilistic thinking was still not widely diffused among educationalists and educational practitioners.

One science, however, was understood to be particularly relevant to the work of the educator. In the third part of his 1891 essay on education as a science, Royce writes, "The teacher . . . should furthermore be a naturalist, and the department of natural history which directly concerns him is called psychology" (1891b: 123). Christian Ufer states, "The educator . . . requires the aid of psychology; it is a science auxiliary to pedagogy" (1894: ix). And similarly, Cubberley describes psychology as the "master science" and the "guiding science of the school" (1919: 309; see also Bain 1879: 15; Harris 1891). Although there could not be uniformity in what was taught to children—because the contents would be determined by the proximate aims of education and the teacher's best judgment—there was a greater degree of uniformity in *how* children learn. Thus a scientific education could build on insights from psychologists pertaining to intelligence, child development, and learning (Dewey 1910). For those engaged in the application of psychology to the art of teaching in the late nineteenth century, the work of Johann Friedrich Herbart (building on Johann Heinrich Pestalozzi) was particularly influential (for a summary of Herbart's psychology and pedagogy, see De Garmo 1891; Ufer 1894).

The idea that the child rather than pedagogy could be the focus of an educational science would eventually come to dominate a fully rationalized education industry. But at the turn of the twentieth century, there was some frustration among the scientifically minded educationalists that teachers were unwilling to set aside their attachment to the rules of thumb developed through classroom experience. In his book on the principles and practices of teaching, James Johonnot criticizes what he labels as a "common defect" of contemporary teachers, arguing,

> The question of primary interest seems to be "How to teach the different branches," instead of "How to develop and train the faculties of the child by the use of these branches." The natural consequence of this superficial view is that teaching is too often a mere imitative art, of doubtful and varying success. Without a careful and reflective acquaintance with the constitution of the child's mind, the work of the teacher, with his geographies, arithmetics, and grammars, is scarcely less absurd than the performance of a difficult operation in surgery by one who knows all about ligatures, knives, and saws, but understands nothing of human anatomy. (Johonnot 1898: 26)

The comparison with the position of medicine arose frequently at the time. For example, Butler's syllabus for Principles of Education includes under the "Study of Education as a Science" section a heading for "analogies between a science of education and a science of medicine" (1900: 15; see also Snedden 1923). The physician's relationship to science versus the rules of thumb gained through practical experience was characterized as one that the teacher should aspire to.[18]

By the beginning of the twentieth century, the movement to more fully rationalize the education industry was well underway. The scientific management movement that was so prominent in the manufacturing industry had adherents in education too, and a flurry of work applying scientific management principles to the education industry appeared in print (e.g., Rice 1913; Vosburgh 1912; Bagley 1915; Bobbitt 1912, 1918; for a discussion, see Kliebard 2004: chap. 4). The teaching occupation was becoming increasingly professionalized, and there were attempts to standardize the type of training received by teachers (Russell 1900). The movement for scientific education emphasized the importance of standards defining the expected level of knowledge and skill that students should achieve in a range of disciplines, for it was only by the establishment of standards that there would be a "rational basis" to work toward improvement (Rice 1913: xv; Thorndike 1913: chap. 2; Ayres et al. 1918). Although there remained much emphasis on designing a rational curriculum in the scientific management of education, the focus on the subjects of education—the students—was only strengthening. Edward L. Thorndike wrote of the scientific management movement,

> Experts in education are becoming experimentalists and quantitative thinkers, and are seeking to verify or refute the established beliefs concerning the effects of educational forces upon human nature. Students of history, government, sociology, economics, ethics, and religion are becoming, or will soon become, quantitative thinkers concerning the shares of the various physical and social forces in making individual men differ in politics, crime, wealth, service, idealism, or whatever trait concerns man's welfare. (quoted in Rice 1913: xviii)

The references here to quantification and both "physical and social forces" reveal the influence of the probabilistic revolution within the science of education.

As the focus turned toward the child and multiple mechanisms were invoked to explain educational outcomes, the type of scientific evidence seen as relevant to the education industry broadened in scope. To psychology was added sociology as a discipline that should be called on to shape the practice of education (Snedden 1923). Cultural values, social control, and educational inequality were understood to be issues of importance to the education industry, and sociology could aid educators in addressing these issues. Developments in public health and medicine would also add a new dimension to the science of education. For those concerned with public health, the schools were clearly important in arresting the spread of infectious disease (e.g., through vaccination and hygiene programs). But for those concerned with education, addressing the medical problems of students also offered the opportunity to improve educational outcomes. Philip Moen Stimson writes, for example, "Health supervision of a school has two purposes; first, to facilitate the physical as well as the mental and moral development of the child, and second, to diminish to a minimum the number of days of schooling lost on account of preventable diseases" (1921: 234). Thus, insofar as physical, mental, and moral development were desirable outputs of education, improving the health of children would help to achieve them (e.g., see American Association of School Administrators 1942; Henry 1955: sec. 5; see also Ruis 2017). But even leaving these possible aims of education to one side, minimizing the days of schooling lost would certainly improve whichever other proximate outputs of the education system were prioritized.

Even as the progressive education movement emphasized the importance of science to producing the desired aims of education, there remained continuing resistance to the scientization of education. By the 1930s, the National Society for the Study of Education's Committee on Education as a Science was reflecting on the place of science within the education industry (Whipple 1938). The chair of the committee, Harold Rugg, described the work of the committee in the pages of the *TCR,* under the revealing title "After Three Decades of Scientific Method in Education" (1934). Although by this period there was far greater acceptance of the principle that scientific knowledge was relevant to the outputs of the education industry, the possibility of a "science of education" was seen to be beyond feasibility. This was in part because too many sciences were now seen to hold relevant material for the educationalist and in part because the aims of education were not (and perhaps would never be) fully settled. Education was best categorized as a "technology," to be guided by the discoveries of all of those sciences that might contribute knowledge relevant to education. The sciences identified as contributory to education were physiology, psychology, sociology, and the physical sciences (Rugg 1934: 112).

That educationalists were thinking through whether or not education could fulfill the requirements for an independent scientific discipline is an indication that the question of whether or not education *should* be rationalized was increasingly becoming moot. Two additional pieces of evidence might be brought forward in this respect. First, there are again echoes of the same debate that was present in late nineteenth-century medicine, and concerns arose that science might dominate educational practice to the detriment of other aspects. Ambrose Caliver (1933), for example, emphasizes the importance of science to the work of teachers but also emphasizes the importance of a strong moral foundation to education. Second, the focus of discussion was increasingly shifting from whether or not education might benefit from being scientific to how scientific knowledge should be used to improve educational outputs. According to Rugg, "This yearning for salvation via statistics has led to a vast neglect of the process of interpretation," and further, "Certainly we shall keep the scientific method. But increasingly in the years ahead we shall discover its place and keep it there" (1934: 122; see also Bode 1921, 1927).

As the reference to "interpretation" alludes to, one factor that was seen to be missing in a scientific education was the "human element." Educational science, with its statistics and experiments and careful measurements, was failing to pay sufficient attention to the human at the center of the educational project. To some extent, these concerns reflect a more general pattern within some of the social sciences. The growing influence of the human relations approach—so influential within the manufacturing industry—and the growing interest in attending to cultural forces and inequality were broadening the scope of the scientific knowledge seen as relevant to educational outputs (see, e.g., Henry 1960). But the concerns also reflected changes in the proximate aims of education. Just as the importance of attending to the whole child was becoming dominant in discussions of the aims of education, so the call for science to focus on the human elements of education was getting louder. L. Thomas Hopkins describes the problem as follows: "Educators must come to see that the improvement of learning is a *human problem* which must be solved through *human data* collected by *human techniques* and interpreted in a *human situation* by *human persons*" (1944: 101–102; italics in the original). This was a sentiment echoed in the *Higher Education for American Democracy* report, which called for scholars "who have a passionate concern for human betterment, for the improvement of social conditions, and of relations among men. We need men in education who can apply at the point of social action what the social scientist has discovered regarding the laws of human behavior" (President's Commission on Higher Education 1947: 91). Although this was a period in which natural science and technology were feted by public and politicians alike, the report takes pains to emphasize that if the human problems were not addressed, education would fail.

In its early incarnation, paying attention to humans meant attending to issues of emotional stability and fulfillment and understanding the child both in their home environment and in their relationships with others in the school. As the focus turned to school integration and racial inequalities in education, educationalists described the special social pressures and cultural attitudes that threatened the educational success of Black children. The psychological effects of racial inequality and discrimination were of primary concern, and the job of the educational scientist was therefore to examine the individual personality manifestations of environmental insults (e.g., see Goff 1950; A. Davis 1939). Later, scientific interest in understanding the "whole child" and the effects of inequality on educational attainment would come together in the study of cultural influences. The social science of language, aspirations, culture, and self-concept could aid educators in understanding how the learning contexts of children were shaped by those around them. Social scientists drew a direct link from circumstances of deprivation and discrimination to cultural expressions that would damage educational opportunities if not addressed (e.g., see Rousseve 1963).

If confirmation was needed that the education industry was becoming increasingly rationalized, one need look no further than the Civil Rights Act of 1964, which mandated the fielding of a survey to assess the extent and causes of educational inequality within the public schools with respect to "race, color, religion, or national origin" (§402). Popularly known as the Coleman Report, the resulting analysis would send shock waves through the educational and policymaking fields.[19] James S. Coleman demonstrated that, despite the failures of the school integration project, school resources were less important in understanding educational inequalities than were inequalities in family resources (see Karl Alexander and Morgan 2016 for a summary). This conclusion was reached on the basis of a careful statistical analysis of the survey data, an analysis that employed regression techniques to examine the relative impact of a range of relevant variables.

Of interest when considering the nature of the scientific approach employed in the report is how Coleman describes the highly quantitative research design. He writes, "Great collections of numbers such as are found in these pages—totals and averages and percentages—blur and obscure rather than sharpen and illuminate the range of variation they represent" (J. Coleman 1966: 8). Later, when introducing a set of case studies of school desegregation, he emphasizes that the studies are used, "not to indicate the overall state of affairs with regard to school desegregation in a community, but to illuminate a particular problem or solution within the school system of the community that is typical of similar situations elsewhere and hence they might be useful as a guide" (461). We see in these discussions the influence of probabilism. Central tendencies are used in the report to establish the relationships between educational inputs and outputs, but variation is acknowledged and even appreciated. The qualitative case study evidence is similarly interpreted, with the evidence casting light on "typical" cases and providing details of aspects uncaptured by the statistical results. The academic discussion and debate that followed the publication of the report focused primarily on whether or not the relationships described were well established and on how far the causal conclusions that were drawn were appropriate (H. Hill 2017).

The Coleman Report was groundbreaking in its effects on the science of education, but it also had an important effect on the degree of rationalization of the education industry. The report had introduced the concept of the achievement gap—the gap in average test score performance between members of different racial and socioeconomic groups. The potential to use test scores to both track individual performance in the educational system and measure inequality of educational opportunity provided important justification for collecting rigorous data on schools, student test performance, and sociodemographic characteristics (H. Hill 2017). The report also spurred a wealth of "production function" research on educational productivity, involving formal assessments of how far given policies paid off in improved student performance (for early reviews, see Hanushek 1986; Monk 1992). The analysis of the causal effects of given inputs on educational outputs using sophisticated quantitative techniques became well established within the science of education. More broadly, the principle that educational policy should be determined on the basis of evidence rather than rules of thumb or tradition was by now beyond question (Dickinson 2016; see Lucas 2016 for a detailed discussion of the effects of the Coleman Report on methodological work in education).

Although the Coleman Report had a constricting effect on the type of scientific knowledge that could be used to evaluate educational policy, it also emphasized the scale of the problem that education was facing if the aim was to guarantee equality of educational opportunity. The report had effectively ruled out school resources as a primary explanation of educational inequality and had rather highlighted the importance of family resources. For the education industry, this conclusion was dismal. All of the work that had been poured into "compensatory education" could be dismissed as a failure (Jensen 1967: 2). Thus, alongside the work assessing the robustness of the report's conclusions, the science of education worked to understand *why* the effect of family background was so strong and which policies might be effective in reducing inequality.

As the science of education continued to expand, there was no longer any doubt that the education industry would need to attend to it. Even if those within the industry had initially been resistant, the federal government was now operating on an explicitly rationalized basis with respect to educational policy. Standardized tests were identified as a key educational output and would be used to assess the performance of both individual students and their schools (National Commission on Excellence in Education 1983). There was growing interest in standardizing the curriculum across different schools within school districts and states, in part to meet the demands of the tests (e.g., see Au 2011).[20] A scientific approach to educational innovation was institutionalized when the No Child Left Behind legislation (§9101) established that the federal government would prioritize for funding only that research "using experimental or quasi-experimental designs in which individuals, entities, programs, or activities are assigned to different conditions and with appropriate controls to evaluate the effects of the condition of interest, with a preference for random-assignment experiments, or other designs to the extent that those designs contain within-condition or across-condition controls." Within the Department of Education, the Institute for Educational Sciences was created (see Liston, Whitcomb, and Borko 2007 for a discussion of these changes). An industry that had been debating the place of science in education at the end of the nineteenth century was, by the beginning of the twenty-first, debating whether or not industry-relevant knowledge might be obtained even in the event of nonrandom assignment to treatment.

The Curriculum and the Child

To summarize changes in the content of educational science over time, I now present an analysis of the content of two key educational journals: *Teachers College Record* (*TCR*) and the *Journal of Negro Education* (*JNE*). I use topic models to identify the main themes of the articles published in these journals and track changes in the representation of these themes in the journals over time.[21] The results for *TCR* are presented in Figure 5-1 (1900–2020), and the results for *JNE* are presented in Figure 5-2 (1930–2020).

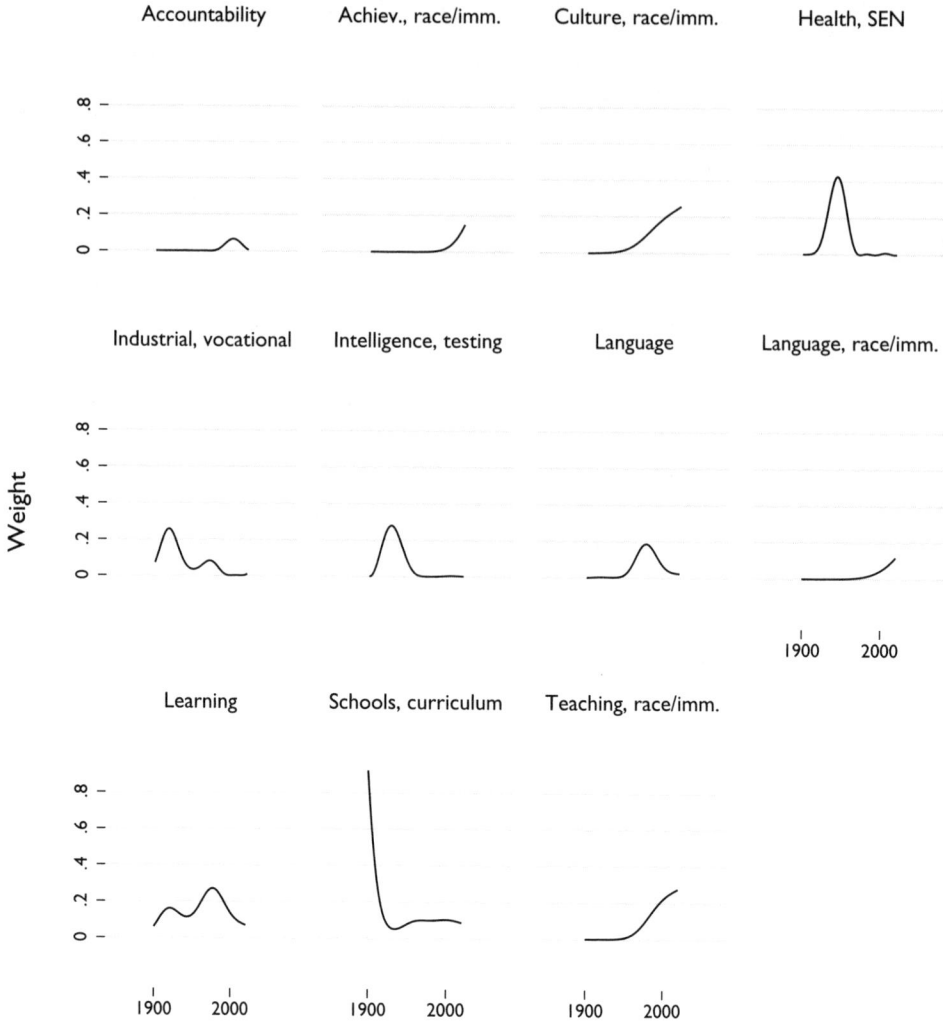

Fig. 5-1 Topic model analysis of *Teachers College Record.*

Examining first Figure 5-1, which covers the period from 1900 to 2020, the starkest finding is the substantial decline in the representation of topics pertaining to schools and the curriculum. Within these topics, words such as "syllabus," "school," "lessons," and "method" are frequently found. In the early twentieth century, these topics accounted for the bulk of the content of *TCR,* but by the 1930s, their prevalence had declined. Insofar as the practice of teaching was concerned, as the curriculum declined in visibility,

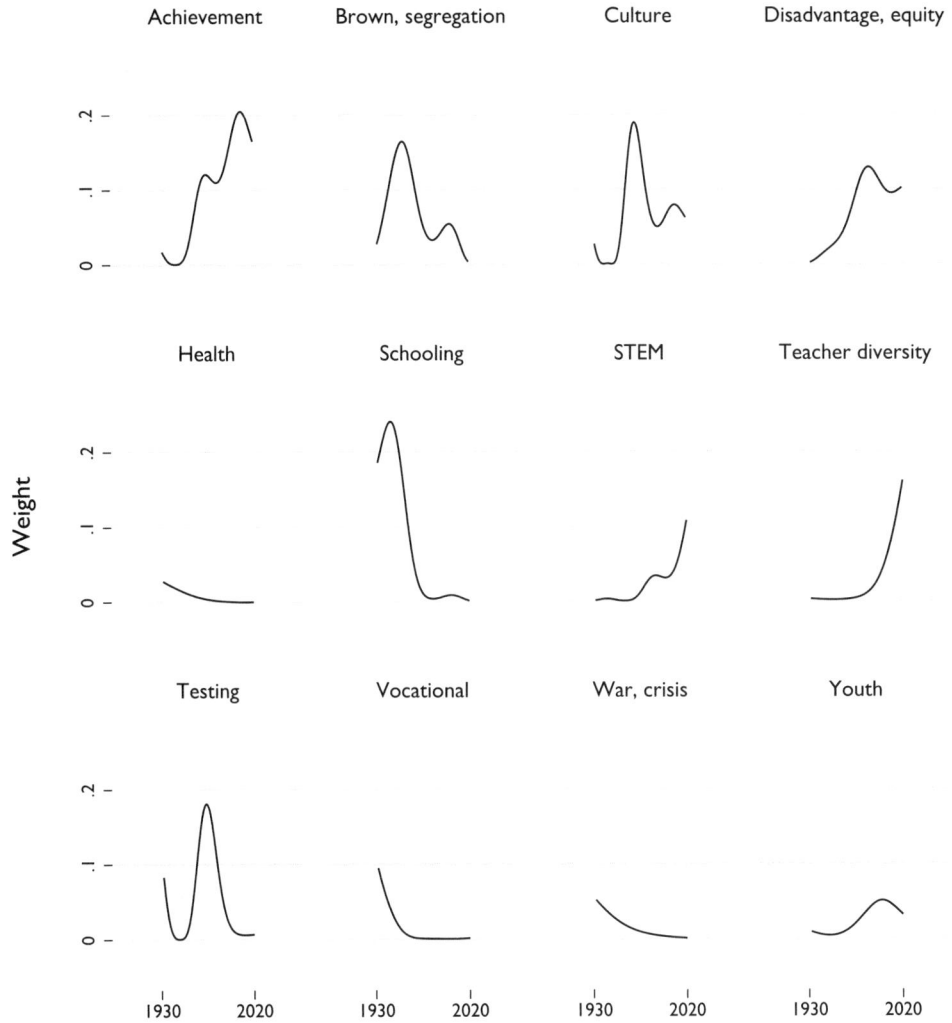

Fig. 5-2 Topic model analysis of *Journal of Negro Education.*

topics capturing words related to learning (e.g., "modes of knowing," "imagination," and "thinking") increased. But of most importance, by the second half of the century, there was a takeoff in concerns about race and immigration. The *TCR* of 2020 was as dominated by discussions of race and immigration as the *TCR* of 1900 was by discussions of schools and the curriculum. The modeling indicates distinctive clusters of words within the race and immigration themes associated with culture, language, and teaching. The move from the curriculum as the focus of the science of education to the child in their social context was complete.

Other patterns identified in the earlier historical discussions of proximate aims and the rationalization of the education industry are also evident. As discussions of the aims of education turned toward preparing students for work in the 1920s and 1930s, the educationalists were focusing on "industrial," "vocational," and "practical arts." A similar bump in themes related to intelligence and testing emerged at the same time, as educationalists considered whether or not students could be effectively matched to appropriate jobs. As good health came to be seen as important to educational outputs in the middle decades of the twentieth century, articles turned to discuss "health programs," "mental health," and "health practices." And as the *Nation at Risk* report pulled attention toward achievement tests and accountability practices, these topics increased in prevalence.

The analysis of *JNE*, presented in Figure 5-2, covers a more compressed time period than that of *TCR*. The *JNE* was founded in 1932, with the aim of encouraging and disseminating research on the education of Black people (C. H. Thompson 1932). Unlike the *TCR*, therefore, *JNE* articles throughout the period take race into account alongside other topics that are discussed. But there are strong similarities across the analyses, even if the journal's focus rules out the possibility of seeing a substantial increase in topics referring to race. As with the *TCR* analysis, we see a strong decline in the prevalence of topics related to the structure and format of schooling; in the *JNE*, these topics are captured by the "schooling" category, which includes words such as "college," "public schools," and "program." In place of these topics, we see a growth in discussions of disadvantage and equity and teacher diversity. Although these topics are different from those that emerged in the *TCR* analysis, they reflect a similar push to center the child and their social context in the science of education.

We also see, as we did with the *TCR* analysis, the science of education moving to examine new aims and themes as educationalists responded both to new events and to the rationalization of the industry. Of most importance in this respect is the scientific response to legal attempts to desegregate schools and reduce racial inequalities in education. Discussion of themes related to *Brown v. Board of Education* peak in the years after the decision, with a swift decline in the prevalence of these topics in the decades following. The small peak in recent decades is a consequence of authors taking stock of progress on the fiftieth and sixtieth anniversaries of *Brown*. Topics related to achievement increase precipitously around the Coleman Report, and the term "achievement gap" appears prominently in the results. The consequences for racial inequality of the testing and accountability era spur the growth in topics related to testing and the peak in the *Nation at Risk* era.

In both the *TCR* and *JNE* analyses, there is evidence that the changing aims of education and the growing rationalization of the education industry are reflected in discussions of the appropriate means of delivering education. In the next section, I examine how far the work of schools and teachers has changed in response to these discussions.

PRACTICABILITY AND POSSIBILITIES

The previous sections have examined changes in the proximate aims and science of education over the past 150 years. The degree to which such changes have filtered through to the work of schools and teachers is contested. In their influential book, *Tinkering toward Utopia*, David Tyack and Larry Cuban lay out "the tension between Americans' intense faith in education—almost a secular religion—and the gradualness of changes in educational practices. For over a century citizens have sought to perfect the future by debating how to improve the young through education. Actual reforms in schools have rarely matched such aspirations, however" (1997: 1). Tyack and Cuban emphasize that many aspects of schooling— patterns of instruction, age grading, and a disciplinary focus—have remained the same over time (9; see also Tyack, Lowe, and Hansot 1984: 163–169). In describing how many of the grand designs of reformers are consigned to dust, Tyack and Cuban are clearly correct: many specific policy initiatives are never implemented in schools, or they are ignored by teachers. The organization of education in the United States is highly fragmented across school districts, states, and the federal government, there is substantial variation across urban and rural school districts, and teachers have a great deal of independence in performing their roles. I will not, therefore, attempt to provide an accounting of which specific proposals were implemented in a wholesale fashion in US schools. Rather, I will look to objective information about the structure of schools and the jobs of educators to track the broad changes implemented over the past 150 years. Amid the gradualness of changes described by Tyack and Cuban, there are clear shifts in education over time that track changing expectations about what this industry should be responsible for and how education is best delivered.

There are two key routes to changing how education is delivered. First, educational institutions can take on the additional tasks that are required to better produce outputs. As "firms" within a rationalized industry, schools, colleges, and other educational institutions can take on additional tasks and assign them to existing or new staff. Second, teachers and other education workers can take on additional tasks. In the following analyses, I consider the extent to which both firms and educators are subject to the paradox of specialization, in which specialists are expected to take on a broader range of tasks.

I first consider the growing responsibilities of educational institutions. To measure the tasks that schools are responsible for, I combine the evidence from historical accounts with two additional sources of evidence. First, I examine changes in the structure of the Department of Education from the 1930s to 2010. And second, I discuss a case study of one particular school and examine changes in the structure and organization of that school over time.

The Condition and Progress of Education

One useful measure of how far changes in the aims and science of education have diffused to educational institutions is whether or not government institutions have acknowledged these changes through educational policy. In Figure 5-3, I show summary figures capturing all of the activities listed under the Department of Education (ED) in the *United States Government Manual* (e.g., Office of the Federal Register 2010).[22]

The ED was initially founded in 1867; since then, it has existed as an office or bureau within larger departments (e.g., the Department of Health, Education, and Welfare) and, most recently, as a department in its own right (1980–). From the 1930s onward, the *Government Manual* includes a list of activities for each office and department in the US government. In Figure 5-3, every listed activity for each year is represented by a circle; some activities are broken down into smaller activities, and this clustering is also represented. War activities (1945–1965) are called out in dark gray with a black rim, equal opportunity tasks are called out in solid black circles

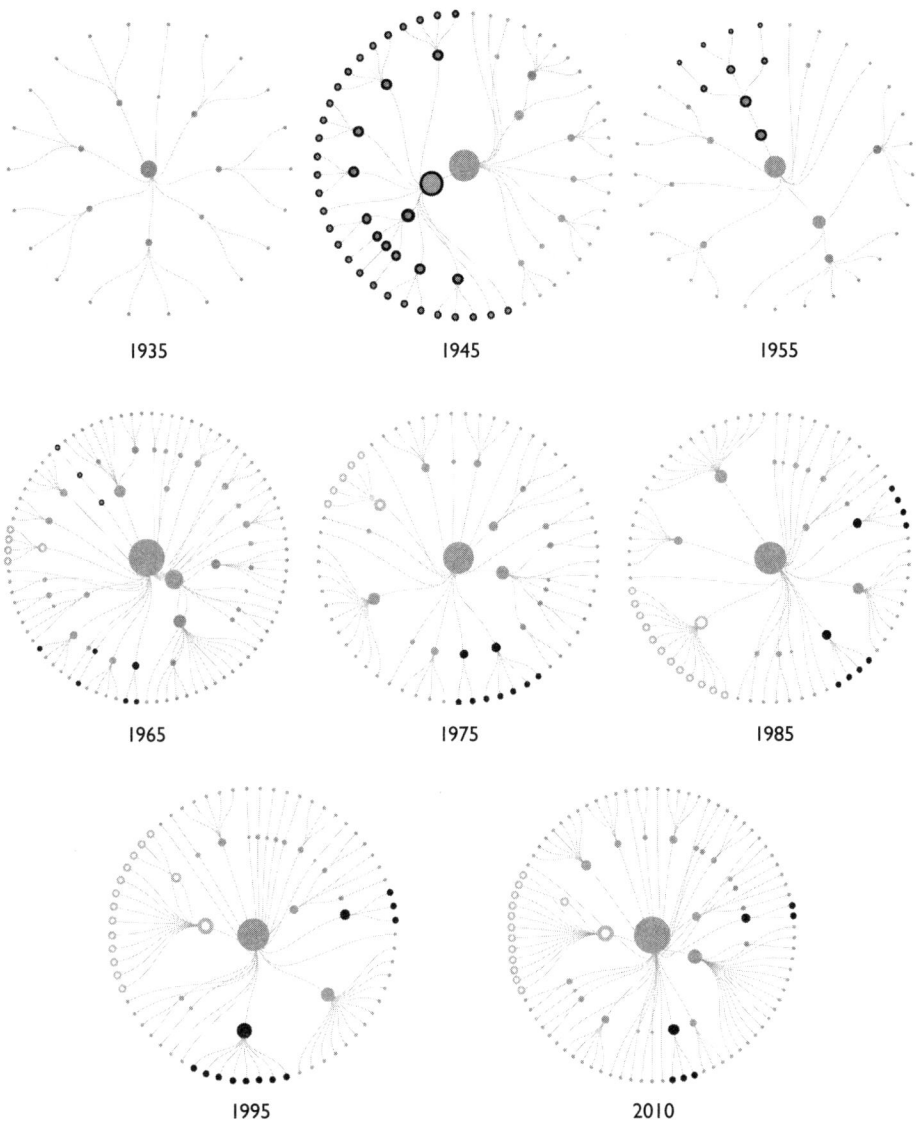

1935   1945   1955

1965   1975   1985

1995   2010

Fig. 5-3 Functions of the Department of Education, 1935–2010; war activities in dark gray circles with black rims, equal opportunity in solid black circles, special educational needs in white circles with gray rims.

(1965–), and special educational needs tasks are called out in white circles with gray rims (1965–).

The clearest result from Figure 5-3 is the dramatic growth in activities undertaken by the ED. In 1935, just thirty activities are listed, and the number increases to ninety-nine in 2010. The ED of the 1930s was narrowly focused on collecting and distributing information about education and administering a range of acts and appropriations. At the time, the ED was responsible for supervising federally aided vocational education, promoting vocational education, and compiling information and reports on this topic. In fact, almost half of the activities of the ED in 1935 involved vocational training, reflecting contemporary interest in preparing students for work.

The arrival of the Second World War dramatically increased the scope of the activities undertaken by the ED. Just under 60 percent of the activities in 1945 were classified as "war activities," including holding "driver and mechanic training programs," "produc[ing] visual aids for war training," and running cooperative programs to address "problems of utilization and disposal of surplus property." However, at least some of the new activities classified under war activities include tasks that were introduced because of broader shifts in understandings of the proximate aims and means of education. One such activity notes that the ED will "aid with programs of physical fitness and social hygiene," reflecting a well-established interest within the science of education and public health in protecting the health of students and preventing outbreaks of disease. Another states that the ED will "promote inter-American understanding and cooperation," an act that ties in with the larger patriotic and diplomatic project of the postwar period.

By the mid-1950s, the number of war activities had substantially declined, although the ED still maintained active cooperation with other agencies through the 1960s. Such activities included "distributing information related to defense" and developing "school civil defense protection programs." But some of the previous activities previously classified as "war activities" had been folded into the general activities of the department. Notably, many of the tasks included under the promotion of inter-American understanding and cooperation were now classified as "international educational relations," reflecting their centrality to the postwar vision of education as the foundation of international cooperation. These activities were further expanded in the 1960s, and they declined only from the 1970s onward; by 2010, just two activities were classified under this heading.

The activities of the ED strongly reflect the dramatic shift after the mid-century that placed the child rather than the curriculum at the center of the education industry. In Figure 5-3, the solid black circles for 1965 mark activities related to inequality of educational opportunity, and the white circles with gray rims mark activities related to special educational needs. These new activities indicate that the social and physical circumstances of students were becoming central to the interests of the education industry. The department was charged with assuring compliance with antidiscrimination legislation and offering assistance to desegregating schools, as well as coordinating programs related to the "education of the disadvantaged." With respect to special educational needs, the activities range from providing "captioned films for the deaf" to conducting studies that might be used to aid educationalists working in this field.

Activities associated with special educational needs were prominent functions of the ED from the 1960s onward. The department continued to produce and distribute educational aids, and it extended its contributions to the support of teachers working with students with special needs. Research programs, consultation services, and financial aid were added to support schools and teachers. Activities related to inequality of educational opportunity also expanded from the 1960s to 2010. The department continued in its enforcement of federal antidiscrimination legislation and expanded the range of characteristics that the assurance of equal treatment applied to (e.g., age, national origin, race, special needs, and gender). At the same time, activities that were originally introduced as "equal opportunity" initiatives were simply folded in as basic educational activities. The administration of grants for delinquent students, originally listed as an equal opportunity activity, had by 2010 been replaced with activities related to safe and drug-free schools. Preschool and after-school activities—associated in the academic literature with benefits for the socioeconomically disadvantaged—are listed as separate department responsibilities rather than as equal opportunity initiatives.[23]

Perhaps the most important general feature of the ED of the early twenty-first century was the degree to which a broad range of activities were adopted—activities that appear to reflect changes in the science of education. The department of 2010 was responsible for both advice on the "formulation of comprehensive school health education policy" and activities relating to the "health and wellbeing of students." There was support for "early intervention," "readiness skills," and English language learners.

There was a focus on the cognitive development, language, and reading skills of young children. Where the science of education has traveled, the ED has followed. More than this, many of the activities of the 2010 ED in fact relate directly to disseminating and supporting the science of education. The Institute for Education Sciences is identified in the 2010 manual as "the mechanism through which the Department supports the research activities needed to improve education policy and practice." The 2010 ED structure, then, underscores the influence of science both in the content of the education-related activities and in the extent to which science-related activities are built into the functions of the department.

Whether the accretion of ED functions will continue over the coming decades is unclear. In early 2025, President Trump indicated his intention to disband the ED, arguing that its "main functions can, and should, be returned to the States" (Executive Order No. 14242). Steps were taken to reduce the number of employees at the department, and streamline its functions (Jones and Zinshteyn 2025). But at the same time, press releases from the ED stated that the department would continue to administer "statutory programs that fall under the agency's purview, including formula funding, student loans, Pell Grants, funding for special needs students, and competitive grantmaking" (Department of Education 2025). Given that these (and other) programs were introduced to improve educational outcomes, it is likely that there will be pressure for some part of the federal or state government to take on functions that are seen as essential to maximizing educational outcomes (see Chapter 7 for further discussion of the backlash against the administrative state).[24]

Perge Modo

In September 1911, the newly constructed New Castle High School (NCHS) opened its doors to students. Located on Lincoln Avenue, the high school was around half an hour's walk from the Carnegie Steel plant located to the southwest (see Chapter 6). As the town had expanded around the growing steel industry, the existing high schools were becoming overcrowded, and it had become necessary to find a new site (Pezzuto 2017).

In this section, I trace changes in the functions of NCHS by comparing the school's yearbooks over the past century. The first edition of the yearbook—Na-Ca-Hi—was published in 1913, just two years after the construction of the new school building. The principal, Edward Sargent, introduced the yearbook as a keepsake that would "review the life of the school in its many sided activities" (NCHS 1913: 8). From 1962 onward, the yearbook was published as *Pergodian*. Each yearbook contains information about the school and its staff, the graduating class, and activities undertaken by the students.

There are many indications in the yearbooks that changes in the aims and science of education are reflected in school structures and organization. Changes in the composition of the school staff provide one basic measure of whether or not these changes are reflected in the school. In each yearbook there is a listing of school personnel and their functions, and in Figure 5-4, I show changes in the staffing of NCHS between 1915 and 2012. During this period, the school grew from 28 to 152 members of staff, and the graduating class increased from 98 to 115 (NCHS 1915, 2012).[25]

In 1915, the NCHS staff consisted of a principal and twenty-seven teachers. The teachers were distributed across ten academic and vocational departments; the commercial training department was the largest, with mathematics and English following closely behind. This was a period in which training for work and adult life was a primary aim of education, and we see this reflected both in the presence of applied and vocational teachers on the school staff and in the advice given to the graduating seniors in the yearbook. In 1918, for example, the new principal, F. L. Orth, writes, "You are graduating at an extraordinary time. An unrest pervades the world.... You should be sure of three things. First—that you are selecting a work for which you are best fitted. . . . Second—that the vocation you decide upon will be agreeable to you. . . . Third—that what you decide on doing will offer you the future you desire. . . . Keep physically fit, morally clean and mentally alert. Resolve to be useful and also to get the best things out of life" (7). Other yearbooks from this time emphasize the value of hard work, described as a "prime requisite" in a time of "keen struggle and intense competition for existence" (1919: 7), and the value of education for adult life (1921: 7). But the most striking evidence that the NCHS of the early twentieth century was oriented toward preparing students for work is found in the yearbook of 1922, where Principal Orth provides the results of "surveys" that report the returns to education in dollars and cents. Among the nine sets of results that he reports on the monetary value of education, he shares with the graduating class that "educated men and women receive good salaries. Educated men and women render efficient service. The educated

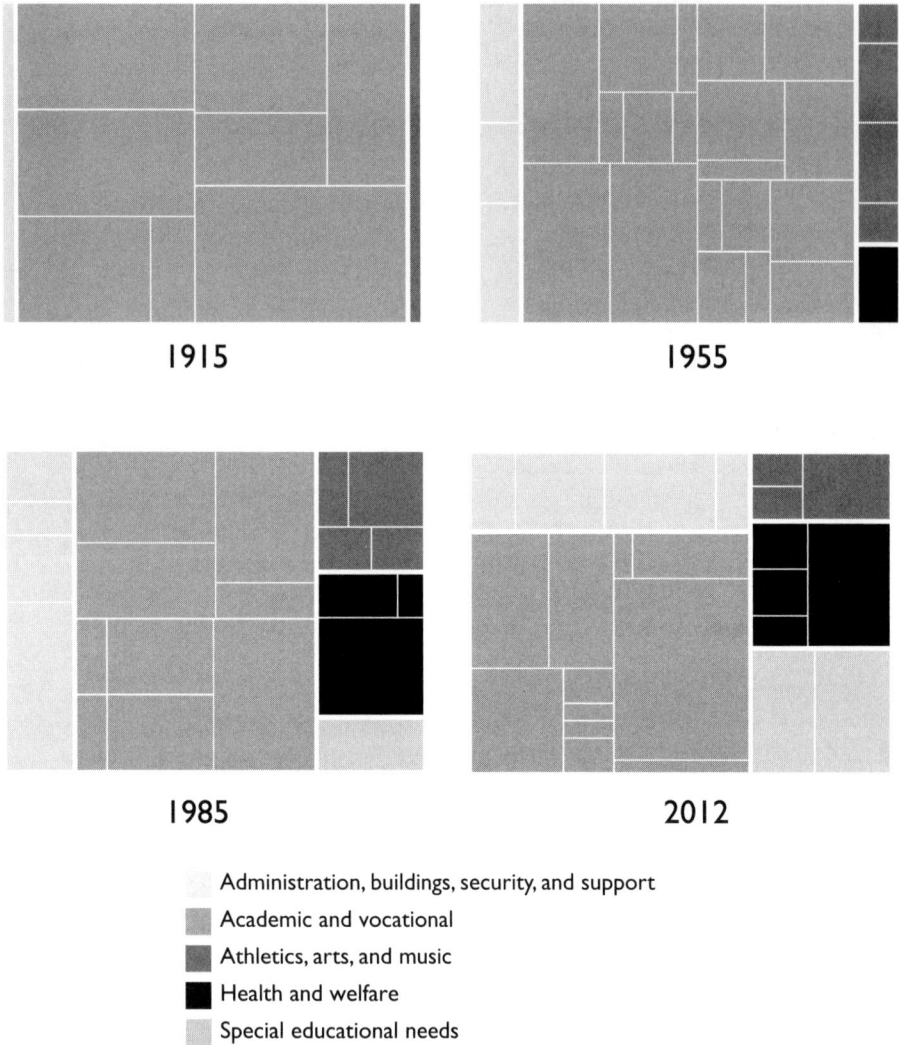

1915 1955

1985 2012

Administration, buildings, security, and support
Academic and vocational
Athletics, arts, and music
Health and welfare
Special educational needs

Fig. 5-4 New Castle High School staffing, 1915–2012.

mind is the greatest producing agency in the world." He also states that education is "the greatest factor today in combatting crime" (7) and that each day at school adds $9.02 to lifetime income.

Although the principal's missives provide some evidence that the science of public health was taken into account in the school of 1915 (e.g., "Keep physically fit"), the first evidence that this science was built into the organizational structure of NCHS is from the 1950s. Two "health" teachers are included in the roster for 1955; one of these teachers is cross-listed with "physical education." There is no record of when health teachers were first introduced to NCHS, but the more senior of the listed teachers, Austin L. Cowmeadow, first appears in the list of faculty in 1949. The field of "nutrition" is also listed, albeit as part of the "home economics" department, suggesting that the nomenclature is but a modern title for a more traditional and well-established discipline within the school. The NCHS of the 1950s also includes a guidance office, although the listed staff are teachers, who perform their roles only as secondary appointments.[26] Administrative and support staff—including clerks and librarians—also appear on the rosters of the school at this point.

During the 1940s and 1950s, there was special concern about the growing threat from war and a subsequent focus on schooling as an immunization against fascism. World War II is, understandably, ever present in the yearbooks of the early 1940s, with flags, patriotism, and mentions of "events" and a "changing world" sprinkled through the pages. The 1942 yearbook poignantly opens with the statement, "Just as our contemporaries now are doing their most to make this a free world, so we may soon be expected to promote and preserve universal peace" (8). For its part, during this period the school offered Problems of Democracy, a class that had first been introduced in the 1930s. During the war, prizes were offered to those who performed best in the class, a prize that was first offered in 1941. In the 1950s, the school listed a teacher assigned to the Problems of Democracy department, a department that is not present in any of the other time periods included in Figure 5-4.

By 1985, the organization of the school looked quite different from the preceding periods. There had been a substantial growth in positions related to health and welfare, in special educational needs, and in administrative staff. The guidance office that year reported three staff members, and a school nurse was added to the roster.[27] Through the 1960s and 1970s the growing emphasis on individual development and social issues had changed the shape of the NCHS staff. Mr. Cowmeadow, the health teacher from the 1955 yearbook, had become a teacher of "mental health" by 1965 (p. 36) and the school's "activity coordinator," with responsibilities that included planning "dances and special events," by 1967 (p. 31).[28] Faculty who focused on student mental health were added in the mid-1960s, and the yearbook of

1968 notes that the discipline "gives a background in both physical and mental health and lends a deeper understanding to our emotional make-up and its effect" (48). Other new staff positions that appeared during this time are the "home and school visitor" and the "audio-visual director" (e.g., see 1968: 46). Supporting the faculty was a growing administrative staff, with defined responsibilities in specific areas of school activities (e.g., library secretary, medical secretary, and attendance secretary).

The academic offerings of NCHS also changed during the 1960s and 1970s. The most prominent change was the introduction of a "social studies" department, which upon its invention became the largest department in the school. The 1961 yearbook describes the purpose of this department as follows: "Between man and society exist reciprocal obligations, which must be preserved impartially. An imbalance in favor of the state, for example, could result in a totalitarian government. Such political catastrophes have occurred among peoples ignorant of the specious arguments of false prophets. The social studies, however, prepare the individual to detect the subversive influences; and in so doing, preserve our national heritage" (11). Using education to build international cooperation and protect against totalitarianism is a theme with roots in the 1950s, as I described earlier in this chapter. By the late 1960s, the purpose of the department is described differently: "The social studies department including world cultures, U.S. history, P.O.D. [Problems of Democracy], and economics, teaches the theories of the basic governments of the world, the historical and cultural background for them, and the political and economical problems of the world" (1967: 33). The shift here reflects the integration of the "developing cultural understanding" and "addressing social problems" aims of education, as well as the embrace of educational science that emphasizes the importance of cultural integration for school performance (see Hertzberg 1981, chap. 5–7, for a history of social studies in this period).

By 2012, the composition of the staff had shifted further toward administration, health and welfare, and special educational needs.[29] There were multiple staff members working in special education and student support roles, and the security staff of the school had expanded. In 2024, the school district established its own police force, and the principal is quoted in the local news saying, "We thought it would be best to put more of our resources into this to ensure and give people piece of mind [sic] that they know when they sent their kids to our building, they are going to be safe" (Hartmann

2024). This focus on creating a safe environment within which children can learn is in line with broader trends toward guaranteeing safe and drug-free schools, as emphasized by the ED. Research indicates that school security staff often undertake a broader set of roles—including mentoring students and maintaining school discipline—than their official titles would suggest (e.g., see Gleit 2022).

The changes in personnel are a consequence of the shift toward a school centered on students rather than the curriculum. This change is also visible in the format of the yearbooks. In the early years, the yearbook opened with the principal's message and a listing of school faculty. From the mid-1970s onward, the faculty pictures are moved from the front of the yearbook to further back, and the yearbook instead opens with pictures of the students. There are also differences in the descriptions of the teacher role. In 1967, for example, the yearbook describes the teacher as follows: "To keep pace with the world they must . . . read, study and learn. Perhaps most important they turn from standard methods and procedures to new techniques that better themselves and the students they teach" (28). In 1995, there is a distinct shift in tone: "What makes any individual go into the teaching profession? Is it the summers off? Is it the fringe benefits? Or perhaps the satisfaction of being in charge of your own classroom? Hopefully it is because of the challenge set before them of teaching teenagers to appreciate, understand and reach their own potential" (65). In this yearbook entry we see evidence both of a decline in deference to teachers and of an unwavering belief that the student is the primary focus of the school.

One reason there has been such substantial growth in student support roles and student-centered learning is that the school serves a relatively large number of students from socioeconomically disadvantaged backgrounds. In line with trends in the science of education, there is much emphasis within the school on providing corrective interventions that will help students to achieve. The current NCHS vision statement commits to "provide a safe, respectful learning community for students that embraces diversity, promotes a high-quality academic program, and supports the development of the 'whole child.' Through use of research-based best practices, state-of-the-art resources, and relevant curricula designed to meet individual needs, the learning environment will enable students to maximize their academic potential while preparing them to be future-ready learners and resilient leaders in a global society" (NCHS 2024: 2). Free school meals are provided for all students because the school is located in a high-poverty district (see Ruis 2017 for a history of school meals). Homeless students (and their families) are guaranteed help from the school district in accessing services that will help to stabilize their situation. The Language Instruction Educational Program provides a student-centered learning environment for English language learners. Many of these programs are required by federal or state law, but they all reflect a more general interest in helping children in difficult circumstances to make the most of their educational opportunities.

NCHS is not unusual in providing such facilities for students living in disadvantaged circumstances (Gleit 2023). One recent institutional innovation is the one-stop shop, in which schools operate as community hubs to provide access to welfare services, health care, and basic amenities (e.g., see Jehl and Kirst 1993; Dryfoos 2001). These programs and organizational innovations represent a firm-level response to the requirement to support children's learning by addressing the barriers that stand in the way of success.

Goodbye, Mr. Chips

In the previous section, we saw the degree to which the education industry and individual firms (or schools) took on the additional tasks required to serve students well. In this section, I examine how the tasks of individual teachers have changed in line with the paradox of specialization.

In Table 5-1 I compare the tasks required of teachers in 1929 and 2021. The 1929 data come from the *Commonwealth Teacher Training Study,* a functional study of teaching in the 1920s that attempted to determine "what the professional practitioner does under modern conditions of practice" (Charters, Waples, and Capen 1929: xvi). The present-day data are drawn from the Pennsylvania Department of Education's *Framework for Evaluation: Classroom Teacher* (2021), which lists the evaluation criteria for teachers being assessed on their job performance—criteria against which those teaching in the NCHS of today will be evaluated.[30] By comparing the tasks required of teachers a century apart, we may examine whether changes in the proximate aims and science of education are associated with changing job tasks.

Of most interest in Table 5-1 are the tasks that have been added to and removed from the teaching occupation over the past century. Considering

Table 5-1 Teachers' tasks, 1929–2021

MAINTAINED	REMOVED	ADDED
Teach subject matter		
Plan, set up objectives		Consider appropriateness of subject for diverse students
Select and organize subject matter		Demonstrate knowledge of relationships among different fields of knowledge
Develop interests		Ensure student understanding through concepts and links to cognitive structures
Instruct		Demonstrate familiarity with wide range of effective pedagogical approaches in the discipline
Assign work		Design instruction to include multiple deliveries, using a variety of engaging learner tools and activities
Oversee student activities		Provide differentiated resources to support authentic learning, critical thinking, and student choice
Manage facilities for individual study		Ensure that students have voice and play active roles in designing and adjusting classroom routines and procedures to support their learning and personal development
Investigate and evaluate pupils' needs, abilities, and achievements		Provide materials and resources to support the learning goals and incorporate intellectual and social-emotional engagement, as appropriate
Exhibit useful teaching traits		Relate lesson content to authentic learning (real world)
Organize general and specific activities		Make extensive and imaginative use of technology
Record and report facts		
Collect data on attendance, tardiness, marks, work, personal	Collect and use data on admissions, Census, health, schedules	Administer class surveys to determine knowledge level
Search for records on attendance, tardiness, marks, work, personal	Tabulate data	
Use records and reports on admissions, attendance, tardiness, marks, work, personal, health	File data	
Keep, send, post, and receive records and reports	Mark records and reports	
	Plan records and reports	

Table 5.1 *(continued)*

MAINTAINED	REMOVED	ADDED
Supervise extracurriculars		
Supervise e.g., play, athletics, music and dramatic, graduation	Engage in informal contacts with pupils (e.g., inviting to home)	
Engage in professional and personal advancement		
Carry out activities in connection with school supplies and equipment	Carry out activities in connection with school plant (temperature, lighting, ventilation, attractiveness of school grounds)	Pursue training opportunities or nontraditional learning opportunities (e.g., professional externships) to enhance instructional knowledge and real-world content connections
Improve teaching skills		Utilize multiple sources of information to determine revisions to instructional practice (e.g., peer review)
Make professional contacts		
Manage contacts with pupils		
Set up objectives		Establish priority goals and objectives for each student
Explain school regulations		Develop learning projects based on student interest
Develop pupils' interest and attention in the performance of activities		Ensure all voices are heard, and the students formulate many questions, initiate topics, and make unsolicited contributions
Instruct students in the performance of activities		Use instructional outcomes that reference curricular frameworks, blueprints, rubrics
Inspect and evaluate behavior		Develop instructional outcomes that show evidence of student input in goal setting
Give examinations and tests, proctor exams	Give general physical exams, routine health inspections	Ensure that instructional outcomes and assessments are suitable for diverse learners and differentiated to encourage individual students to take educational risks
Excuse, dismiss, detain pupils		Provide feedback to students
Send pupils on errands, use pupil assistants		Ensure that assessments are appropriate, are differentiated, and provide opportunities for student choice

Table 5.1 *(continued)*

MAINTAINED	REMOVED	ADDED
Collect materials from pupils	Act as custodian of pupils' belongings	Encourage students to participate in designing assessments for their own work and to develop rubrics according to teacher-specified learning objectives
Induct new pupils		Establish a clear and culturally competent approach to conflict resolution
Control tardiness and absence		Foster student ownership of learning and personal development
Make announcements		Model positive responses (e.g., turn taking)
Give educational guidance		Demonstrate a high regard for student abilities
Determine desirable traits, activities, and regulations for pupils		Set clear expectations for student behavior in learning environments
Establish effective relations with pupils		Encourage students to take risks and show initiative in modifying a learning task to make it more meaningful or relevant to their needs
Provide facilities and materials		Respect personal spaces
Apply preventive measures		Use preventive measures to monitor student behavior and reinforce positive behavior
Investigate difficulties		Engage in active listening
Apply specific remedies	Supply remedies to sick pupils	Arrange learning environments for maximum accessibility and make modifications to accommodate all students
Adapt procedures to physical conditions of classroom and equipment	Clean pupils' clothing	Personalize content and language for students
Adapt procedures to individual differences		Actively seek and value individual students' cultural background
Conduct special exercises, study exercises, other activities		Determine students' social-emotional competencies
Reward and penalize		Adapt lessons for students with disabilities and varied learning styles
Exhibit effective teaching traits		Demonstrate caring and sensitivity, honoring the dignity of each member of the learning community
Schedule activities		Engage students to establish evaluation criteria for high-quality work

Table 5.1 *(continued)*

MAINTAINED	REMOVED	ADDED
Group pupils		Provide feedback to students that is specific, timely, and that comes from many sources, including other students
Provide worthwhile occupations		
Protect school community		
Maintain relations with school personnel		
Maintain relations with e.g., school board, department head, principal	Maintain relations with e.g., custodian, janitor, librarian, nurse, physician	Take a leadership role with colleagues regarding awareness of and compliance with local policies and protocols
Maintain relations with school community		
Give advice and information to parents, community	Give assistance to parents, community	Use social/digital platforms and classroom web pages for communication and sharing
Act as mediator, participate in meetings	Meet socially with parents, community	Ensure that communication with families and caregivers is frequent and sensitive to cultural traditions and equity of access, with students contributing
Develop cordial relations, cooperative spirit	Conduct business transactions	Use a variety of communications to engage families and caregivers in the instructional program
Obtain advice, assistance		Use newsletters or social media for classroom updates
Enforce child-welfare laws		
Attend to school visits		

the large number of tasks added, it is clear that the transition from curriculum-centered to student-centered teaching has had significant consequences for the tasks of teachers. Modern teachers must take into account the "whole child" when teaching, considering their socioemotional development, abilities, cultural background, socioeconomic circumstances, and learning disabilities. Teachers are expected to engage families and caregivers in their child's education and to frequently communicate and share information via social media and digital platforms.

It is the teacher's job to tailor the format and presentation of information to individual students, which may require different forms of delivery within a single classroom. And where additional accommodations are required to support a child's learning, the teacher is expected to modify and arrange the learning environment to provide those accommodations. The child-centered approach is also evident in the multiple tasks that require the teacher to facilitate the student's active role in the learning process. Teachers are required to involve students in setting learning goals, encourage them to modify learning tasks, and engage in active listening with students. Students are also to be encouraged to participate in designing assessments for their own work, and the teacher should foster a sense of ownership of learning and personal development among students.

With respect to the much smaller number of tasks that have been lost, two main types might be identified. First, we see a change in the relationship between the teacher and the community. In the past, teachers were expected to forge intimate and informal contacts with their students and with the wider community: the 1929 task list includes the requirement to nurture informal contacts with pupils by inviting them home and the requirement to build social relationships with the parents of students. These tasks have entirely dropped away, presumably because of safeguarding requirements and stronger work-life boundaries than existed in the past. Interactions among teachers, students, and their families are described in the task list of 2021 as being more instrumental, oriented toward supporting the student's learning. Second, as schools have grown larger, some tasks related to the school plant and students have been taken on by other personnel. A set of tasks related to recordkeeping, for example, is no longer in place for the present-day teacher. As professional administrators have been integrated into schools and many tasks have been taken over by computers, the requirement for teachers to file and tabulate data has fallen away. Teachers do, of course, continue to collect information from students and are frequently required to consult student records, but modern data systems have simplified these tasks. A set of tasks related to the school plant is now addressed at the level of school administration. Although teachers may attend to the physical features of their classroom (e.g., lighting and temperature), they are not ultimately responsible for the school building.[31] Similarly, teachers are no longer involved in the administration of physical examinations or routine health inspections, as these tasks have been taken on by other personnel in the school and community.

Changes in the tasks of teaching are consistent with the paradox of specialization playing out within the education industry. As the occupation becomes increasingly rationalized and the science of education expands, teachers take on new tasks that will better secure their objective of educating children. A new range of tasks related to special education and student-centered learning is added to the teacher's load, while only a few tasks are lost.

THE SUBJECT OF EDUCATION

> It is obvious at the outset that specialization in plumbing may be less disastrous socially than specialization in an area of education. What we want in the plumber is someone to fix the drain. Whether he participates in the problem of how to grow roses is of no importance. But in education it is becoming increasingly apparent that we teach not a subject but boys and girls, and the high qualifications in a small field may leave us quite unfitted to teach boys and girls unless we have an interest in and appreciation of the related problems that arise in the educative process. (J. Williams 1935: 204–205)

Over the course of the past 150 years, the education industry has become central to the experience of childhood. Almost all children will engage with the education system at some point before the age of eighteen, making the industry critical to the nation's long-term health and prosperity. The industry has consequently been a focus of public and political discussion, and there is substantial interest in maximizing educational outputs. For this reason, the education industry has, since the late nineteenth century, come to embrace the science of education. Schools now operate as rationalized firms, and the teaching occupation is now a rationalized occupation.

As the science of education and learning has developed, it has increasingly emphasized the importance of centering the child rather than the curriculum. The science emphasizes the need to focus on the way children learn rather than on the material delivered in the course of teaching. How children learn is affected by social, psychological, economic, physiological, and other factors, meaning that a large number of possible "inputs" have become of interest to teachers and the wider education industry. We have seen evidence that, as the industry absorbs this science, both schools and teachers are required to attend to a wider range of factors. In particular, special educational needs and socioeconomic and cultural factors have grown dramatically in their importance to educators.

We ask so much of our education system. We ask educators to do their best to prepare the nation's children for adulthood, and this preparation requires taking account of all those factors that might compromise the mission. But there is also a long history of the education system being mobilized to satisfy the proximate aims of governments and other powerful interest groups, further complicating the tasks of educators. Given its unique position, specializing in the production of the well-educated child, the education system has been forced to contend with both sets of complications. For when what it means to educate a child is viewed in more expansive terms, it is schools and educators that must take on the burden of doing what is asked.

CHAPTER SIX

Management and the Worker

Why, I think it is a very interesting thing, but a fellow doesn't get a chance to learn very much, but just do the same thing over and over again. You learn how to wire and solder wires, but you never learn the principles of the thing. There isn't much chance to learn as long as you have to work so steady in there like that. Those things that they have there in the boxes that you saw right across the aisle from me are something I don't know anything about, even though I would like to.

(Operating Branch M, October 16, 1929)

The manufacturing industry looms large in classical discussions of the division of labor. Pin makers, steel producers, and textile workers dominate the descriptions of changes induced by task specialization and mechanization. For this reason, perhaps, many of our theoretical expectations about how the division of labor unfolds are built on observations about how specialization plays out within this industry.

The discussion of the division of labor that has been presented to this point might appear to be similarly anchored in the labor market conditions contemporary to the current writer. Over the past century, the manufacturing industry has substantially declined: between 1910 and 2015, the proportion engaged in manufacturing declined from around a third to under a tenth of the nonfarm labor force, while there was a dramatic increase in the proportion engaged in professional services, retail, and government (Leon 2016: tab. 3). The evidence shown in prior chapters on rationalized occupations and the paradox of specialization largely pertains to occupations concentrated in nonmanufacturing industries. But these occupations and industries are precisely those most susceptible to the paradox of specialization. After all, professional occupations are defined by their attachment to well-established abstract belief systems (e.g., see Abbott 1988), and nonprofessional occupations containing large numbers of well-educated workers might similarly be at high risk of becoming rationalized occupations. Examining occupations located elsewhere in the occupational structure is therefore important. Are manufacturing occupations—sometimes assumed to be straightforwardly under the sway of the specializing tendencies of automation—subject to the same countervailing forces that have been shown in the preceding chapters to obtain elsewhere in the occupational structure?

In this chapter, I thus examine the manufacturing industry and its dominant occupations. I show that the paradox of specialization is at work in the manufacturing industry but that it has played out somewhat differently in this industry as compared to the industries and occupations considered in the prior chapters. The two forces implicated in the paradox were surely both operating in manufacturing over the past 150 years: the industry was rapidly rationalizing, while a growing scientific literature promised an increase in occupational outputs. At the same time, and as the opening quote highlights, the workers within routine manufacturing occupations acknowledged how little they understood of the science of their jobs. As this chapter shows, changes in job tasks arose because routine manufacturing occupations were rationalized *by fiat,* by engineers and managers aiming to maximize productivity. As these workers embraced the growing science and technology of manufacturing, workers further down the chain of production found their job tasks changing in line with the changing science.

I focus on three main time periods and within each time period examine the work undertaken by both frontline manufacturing workers and their immediate supervisors. Initially, in the first period, the rationalization of manufacturing work and the dominance of efficiency concerns led to a simplification of the tasks of frontline manufacturing workers but to a complication of the work of their supervisors. Despite the dominance of Smithian simplification, at least for frontline workers, in the first period, in the following two periods we see a definitive shift in favor of functional complexity. Thus, even while the manufacturing sector would seem to have special susceptibility to Smithian simplification, I show that the same paradox of specialization arises here as in the industries examined in prior chapters. But I also show that the paradox arises in the case of manufacturing not because of an increasingly complicated understanding of the occupation's output but rather because the process that produces the output comes to be understood as more complicated. Even while the manufacturing sector embraced machines, the ever-present human worker was a barrier to increasing output, and it was only by addressing the humanity of the worker through additional job tasks that success could be assured.

The manufacturing industry is one in which large amounts of archival materials describing some aspects of the content of work survive. As engineers went about rationalizing manufacturing occupations, they left detailed records of occupation, firm, and industry particulars. I use these records to describe the main trends in the manufacturing industry over the past 150 years. I draw from the archive of Frederick Winslow Taylor, the father of scientific management, and the archives of the Hawthorne Studies, Elton Mayo, and Fritz Roethlisberger, which contain detailed records of manufacturing in the late nineteenth and early to mid-twentieth century. As with all archival sources, these records are partial, and in particular, they primarily report the arrangements that engineers and managers planned or attempted to implement in a small number of firms. In using these sources, I do not propose that they represent all of the variation that existed in the manufacturing industry during the period. My aim in analyzing the archival material is to reveal the direction of travel within the industry rather than the full range of journeys taken by manufacturing firms.

I use a variety of supplemental sources to confirm this direction of travel, as well as to understand the variation in the manufacturing industry. Alongside the archival materials, I use union records, job task analyses, historical scholarship, and other written materials. To these written sources, I add the reports that manufacturing workers themselves have provided about their work over the century. I draw on interview transcripts with manufacturing workers from the Hawthorne and Mayo archives. From the Hawthorne archive, I analyze the interview transcripts of workers at the Western Electric Company in the late 1920s and 1930s. The Mayo archive contained a set of previously sealed interviews with manufacturing workers in the town of New Castle, Pennsylvania, in the early 1940s. The town was chosen for study from a short list of ten depressed towns in the United States.

It is described as a "ghost town," and the background notes further state, "Originally agricultural community, then steel town, now tin canning industry. Transformation from steel town into something else is still in progress" (Elton Mayo Papers, *New Castle Field Notes,* 1940). The interviews were conducted by George C. Homans, who was at the time a student of Mayo's at Harvard.[1] These personal accounts of factory life provide an additional source of data and allow for an assessment of how the plans of engineers and managers were translated into the day-to-day life of frontline manufacturing workers.

THE EFFICIENCY MEN

I begin with a discussion of the early twentieth century, a period of time dominated by the diffusion of machines and a commitment to efficiency, a set of forces that led to a growing simplification of manufacturing work, in line with Smithian projections. Although the growth of simplified machine production is well appreciated, it is less well appreciated that the growing simplification of machine work produced new demands for the immediate supervisors of manufacturing workers, demands that complicated their work in a host of ways. These diverging trends led to a bifurcation of manufacturing workers: routine frontline workers saw reduced functional complexity in their work, while supervisors experienced increased complexity.

Two Great Divisions

By the final decades of the nineteenth century, the story familiar to all scholars of the division of labor was well underway. Craft production had in large part given way to factory production, machines aided the production process, and increasing task specialization was expected and encouraged, as well as feared (e.g., see Fitch 1882; Wright 1884).

But all was not well. While there were periods of high economic growth during the Gilded Age, these periods were punctuated by two depressions, increasing inequality, and increasing labor unrest (see Dubofsky and McCartin 2017 for a detailed history). In considerations of how the productivity gains afforded by mechanization could be maximized, attention began to turn to the relationship between men and machines. If the Smithian vision of divided labor working alongside machines was to be realized to full effect, the manufacturing industry must become a rationalized industry.

It was already clear by this time that factory production required a more complex form of organization than traditional craft production. Carroll Davidson Wright's report to the Census Bureau on the factory system, for example, states, "A factory becomes a scientific structure, its parts harmonious, the calculations requisite for their harmony involving the highest mathematical skill" (1884: 549). At the same time, it was recognized that profound coordination problems remained in the factory system—problems that were only exacerbated by conflicts with labor. For Frederick W. Taylor, these problems could only be solved by further division of labor and increasing rationalization, and his contributions are central to understanding the push toward task simplification in frontline manufacturing jobs.

In January 1898, Taylor wrote to Robert P. Linderman, the president of the Bethlehem Iron Company, outlining some of the barriers that he saw to "systematizing" the factory floor.[2] Key among these barriers was the inequality in knowledge between frontline workers and management: while workers had full knowledge of the manufacturing process, management did not, and this arrangement increased the relative power of the workers over production. As Taylor writes,

> Certain steps must be taken which will render the management much less dependent on the individual knowledge, skill, and good will of the workmen than is generally the case in machine shops. Many of the details connected with running the machines and the management of the work in the shop which are usually left to the individual judgment of the workmen must be standardized and taken entirely out of their control.

Taylor's solution to the knowledge problem was "scientific management," a fully standardized system in which the jobs of manager and worker were both defined and delimited.

Taylor's scientific management rested on standardization, systematization, and the exhaustive division of labor. This vision was hardly innovative; Taylor sketched out a logic behind the allocation of job tasks that was essentially Smithian at heart. In a letter to Linderman sent August 8, 1898, for example, Taylor emphasized the importance of task specialization:

> A shop as large as yours and working upon a product so varied in its nature should be managed through the harmonious co-operation of a

number of men each of whom has his separate function to perform, and who is chosen for his special ability in performing that function.

Rather, Taylor's innovation was to argue in favor of the deliberate organization of specialized production, such that managers would determine the most efficient division of labor on the basis of careful measurement and planning. He underscores the importance of this point in his testimony to the House of Representatives (January 25, 1912), where he states,

> The work which under the old type of management practically all was done by the workman, under the new is divided into two great divisions, and one of these divisions is deliberately handed over to those on the management's side. . . . In short, it requires the hearty cooperation of the management at all points with the workmen, and the voluntary assumption on the part of the management of new duties which they never did before.

Both managers and workers, therefore, are assigned a specific set of tasks under scientific management. For the frontline worker, task simplification is implemented by design rather than arrived at fortuitously, via slow-moving evolutionary or selective processes. Implementing this task simplification for the worker necessitates increased functional complexity for the managers.

An illustration of the changing demands on the worker across different periods is provided in Figure 6-1, taken from a guide to personnel work published by Eugene J. Benge in 1920. The figure shows the gradual decline in the input of workers to the manufacturing process as craft systems were replaced by factory systems and traditional factory systems were then replaced by scientific management. The worker's control over production and autonomy over work was reduced until they contributed only skill and time to the manufacturing process.

Standing behind Taylor's designs was the science of production. It was clear to Taylor that if work was to be organized to optimize production, it must be organized in accordance with scientific principles. Implementing this organization entailed two precursory steps. First, it was necessary for the manager to gather together all of the information about production that the workers held. From this material could be constructed the science of production: the set of laws, principles, and facts describing the relationship between the worker and the material inputs and outputs. Thus, the

SHARE OF THE WORKER IN PRODUCTION.
Various Industrial Eras

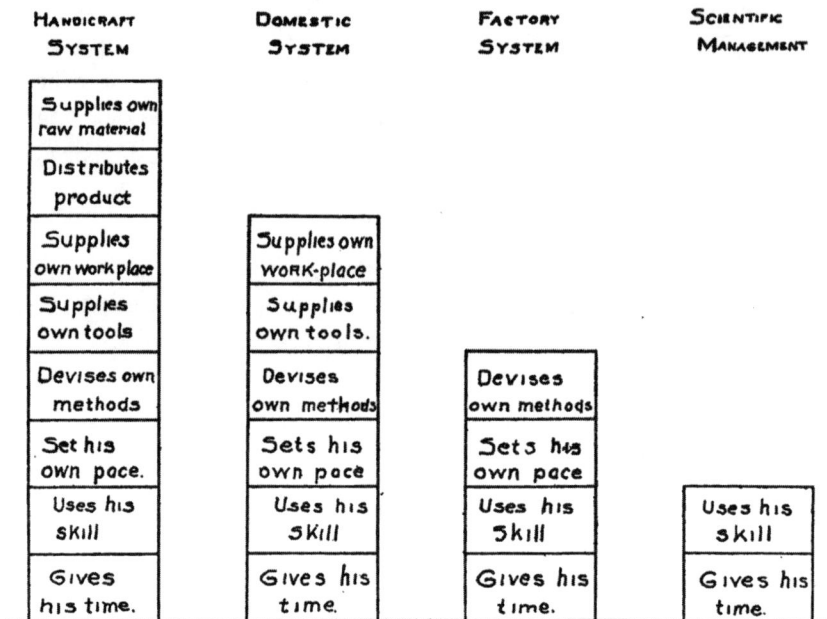

HANDICRAFT SYSTEM	DOMESTIC SYSTEM	FACTORY SYSTEM	SCIENTIFIC MANAGEMENT
Supplies own raw material			
Distributes product			
Supplies own work place	Supplies own work-place		
Supplies own tools	Supplies own tools.		
Devises own methods	Devises own methods	Devises own methods	
Set his own pace.	Sets his own pace	Sets his own pace	
Uses his skill	Uses his skill	Uses his skill	Uses his skill
Gives his time.	Gives his time.	Gives his time.	Gives his time.

Fig. 6-1 An illustration of changing demands on the worker across different periods.
SOURCE: Benge 1920: 6.

knowledge about the production process that previously took the form of workers' "rules of thumb" was formalized and recorded (e.g., see Taylor 1911: 36–37). Second, having accumulated the science of production, the manager would use that material to standardize production and design the most efficient organization of tasks and workers (see also Gilbreth 1911; Gilbreth and Gilbreth 1919, 1924; S. Thompson 1928). The managers would take on the tasks of organizing work, selecting workers, and performing quality control, while the frontline workers would specialize only in those manual tasks directly related to production. The managers, knowing how long each production task should take and which piece of machinery was needed for each task, could implement the most efficient arrangement of work and pay only for those tasks that required manual labor (see Babbage 1864).

If a science of production was required, it was unthinkable that production workers would develop such a science themselves (Taylor 1911). Taylor's vision instead placed the primary responsibility for developing the science of production with the engineers and managers, who already had expertise in other aspects of production (see also Veblen 1921; D. Noble 1977; Shenhav 2002). Nor did the science simply recreate the workers' original methods. Although gathering together the workers' rules of thumb and procedures was a necessary step toward instituting scientific management, the present-day practices were almost certainly not as efficient as they could be. By exposing the laws and designing methods and standards from first principles, the workers could produce more and better output than their haphazard efforts had previously allowed.

In Taylor's contributions, we see a strong and explicit push toward the rationalization of frontline production occupations and the wider manufacturing industry: the language of "standardization" and "systematization," alongside explicit appeals to means-ends considerations, are strong signals that rationalization was the primary aim (see Emerson 1922; Kimball 1925; Alford 1928: chap. 6; Merkle 1980: chap. 3; Shenhav 2002). This was a top-down rationalization, a rationalization *by fiat*, in which engineers and managers organized production occupations in line with scientific principles. For the frontline production occupation, this rationalization was synonymous with task specialization. For the managerial and supervisory occupations within production, rationalizing the frontline occupations meant taking on new responsibilities. Henry Towne, cited by Taylor in his testimony to Congress, underscored this point when he claimed,

> The organization of productive labor must be directed and controlled by persons having not only good executive ability, and possessing the practical familiarity of a mechanic or engineer with the goods produced and the processes employed, but having also, and equally, a practical knowledge of how to observe, record, analyze and compare essential facts in relation to wages, supplies, expense accounts, and all else that enters into or affects the economy of production and the cost of the product. There are many good mechanical engineers;—there are also many good "business men;"—but the two are rarely combined in one person. But this combination of qualities, together with at least some skill as an accountant, either in one person or more, is essential to the

successful management of industrial works, and has its highest effectiveness if united in one person. (Towne 1886: 1)

Rationalization *by fiat* thus simplified the work of those in frontline manufacturing occupations, but it pushed in the direction of increased functional complexity for the managerial workers responsible for implementing scientific management. The task simplification of frontline occupations is consistent with the standard characterization of how the division of labor developed during this period, but the parallel complication of supervisorial jobs during this period is less well appreciated.

The Rationalized Firm

Detailed records exist describing the implementation of scientific management at the companies for which Taylor operated as a consultant, and they provide important insight into the organization of work at the turn of the twentieth century. Of particular interest are the records pertaining to Bethlehem Steel Company,[3] Jones & Laughlin Steel Corporation, and Tabor Manufacturing Company, which describe company structure, the division of labor across departments and jobs, and work practices.

In Taylor's organizational plan for Bethlehem Steel, we see his vision of the rationalized firm in full splendor. As Figure 6-2 indicates, expertise, analysis, and planning were prioritized in the rationalized firm. On the right-hand side of the functional plan, we see the "experts": those with specialized knowledge pertaining to the output of Bethlehem Steel (i.e., metal products). On the left-hand side, we see the administrative units contained within the "layout unit," responsible for controlling the inputs to the production process. The tasks of this department included the analysis and planning of work, the fixing of piece rates, and the preparation of machines. The functional plan thus reveals that decisions about the organization of manufacturing and work were taken out of the hands of frontline manufacturing workers and placed in specialized units, with managers and foremen as the intermediaries.

Alongside the functional plan, Taylor provides lists of tasks for those working in the key occupations in the company. Of particular interest is the job description for supervisory occupations, which had direct responsibility for managing production on the shop floor.[4] In the plans for the installation of scientific management in Jones & Laughlin Steel Corporation, the supervisor job duties are carefully outlined, and in Table 6-1, I provide an abridged version. I have organized the tasks in Table 6-1 under broad categories indicating the type of task required of the supervisor. The list of supervisor job duties is extensive and varied, with the supervisor holding responsibility for coordination, discipline, personnel management, planning, supervision, and quality control (a similar list of duties may be found in Diemer et al. 1921).

Under Taylor's system, the supervisor occupation was not a simple one. To maximize task specialization within frontline manufacturing occupations, the supervisors were required to take on tasks such as planning and quality control, which frontline workers would have previously taken on themselves. This task specialization of frontline workers also rested on high levels of coordination across the different units of Jones & Laughlin: materials had to be in place, machines had to be in good order, and different units needed to cooperate to complete tasks. Again, the supervisors took on these roles. Taylor's rationalization of the firm thus produced increased functional complexity for the supervisors, while the frontline manufacturing occupations were reorganized, specialized, and simplified. Although the historical evidence shows that the discipline and personnel functions in particular were often ignored in practice (Daniel Nelson 1974), Taylor's supervisor job description emphasizes that tasks that were seen to be essential to the functioning of the factory were placed in the hands of supervisors.

Notably, Taylor does not even provide a detailed breakdown of the tasks of machine operatives in the factory, presumably because he assumed that the tasks of machine tending need not be explicated. As he records in a 1918 memo:

> The workman is supplied at his work station in advance with all materials, tools, drawings, instruction cards, and instructed, when necessary, in the actual work, there by avoiding all delays. . . . Such work is absolutely necessary to produce finished goods; it is evident that the machine tools are the "real producers." (Frederick Winslow Taylor Collection, *Standing Order for a Speed Boss*, November 24, 1918)

Nevertheless, Taylor did describe situations in which bonuses could be awarded, and these descriptions are helpful in understanding which tasks frontline manufacturing workers were undertaking on top of machine

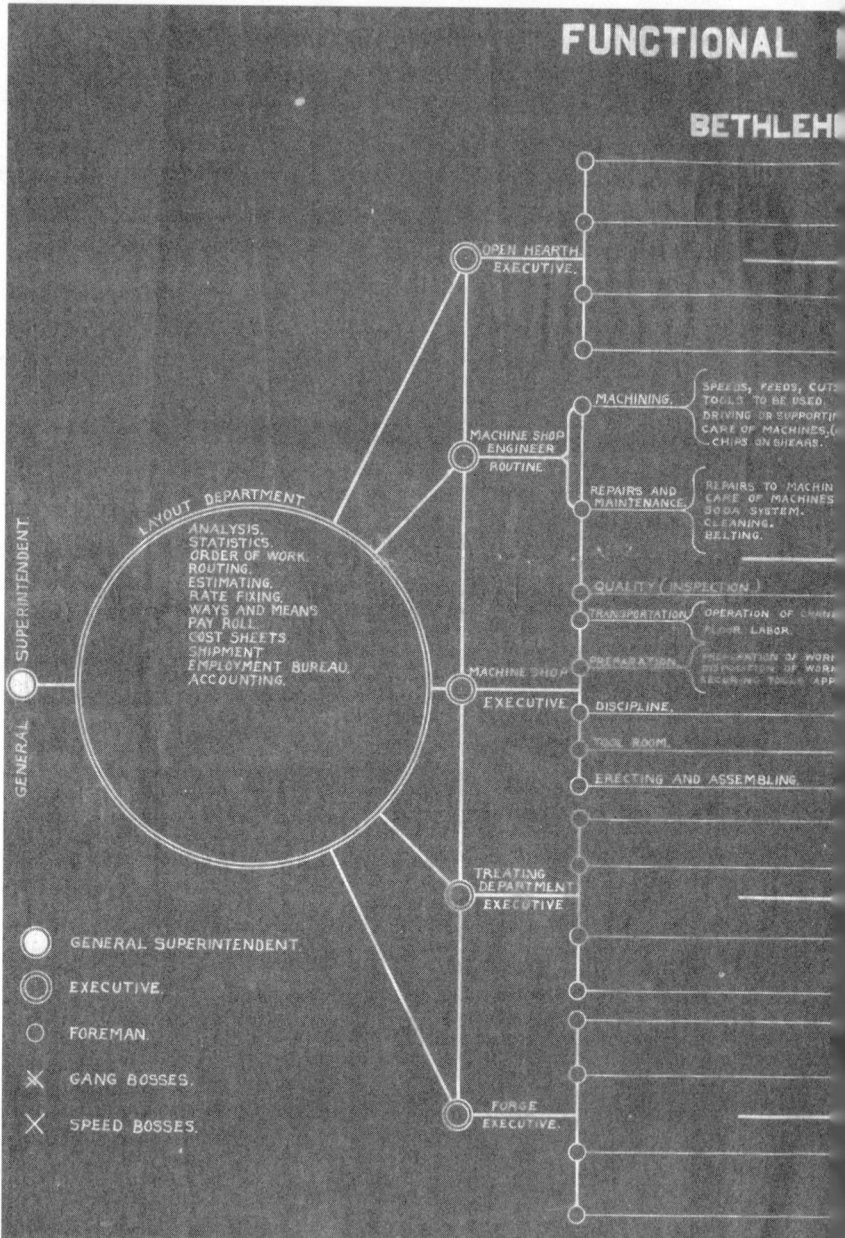

FUNCTIONAL

BETHLEH

OPEN HEARTH
EXECUTIVE.

MACHINE SHOP
ENGINEER
ROUTINE.

MACHINING.   SPEEDS, FEEDS, CUTS
              TOOLS TO BE USED.
              DRIVING OR SUPPORTIN
              CARE OF MACHINES.(
              CHIPS ON SHEARS.

REPAIRS AND   REPAIRS TO MACHIN
MAINTENANCE.   CARE OF MACHINES
               SODA SYSTEM.
               CLEANING.
               BELTING.

QUALITY (INSPECTION.)

TRANSPORTATION. OPERATION OF CRANE
                 FLOOR LABOR.

PREPARATION.   PREPARATION OF WORK
               DISPOSITION OF WORK
               SECURING TOOLS, APP

MACHINE SHOP
EXECUTIVE.   DISCIPLINE.

              TOOL ROOM.

              ERECTING AND ASSEMBLING.

TREATING
DEPARTMENT
EXECUTIVE.

FORGE
EXECUTIVE.

LAYOUT DEPARTMENT
ANALYSIS.
STATISTICS.
ORDER OF WORK.
ROUTING.
ESTIMATING.
RATE FIXING.
WAYS AND MEANS.
PAY ROLL.
COST SHEETS.
SHIPMENT.
EMPLOYMENT BUREAU.
ACCOUNTING.

GENERAL SUPERINTENDENT

⊙ GENERAL SUPERINTENDENT.

◎ EXECUTIVE.

○ FOREMAN.

✕ GANG BOSSES.

✕ SPEED BOSSES.

Fig. 6-2 Functional plan of Bethlehem Steel Company.

SOURCE: Stevens Institute of Technology, SCW Library Special Collections, Frederick Winslow Taylor Collection, 1897, box 75, fol. 2.

ORGANIZATION

COMPANY

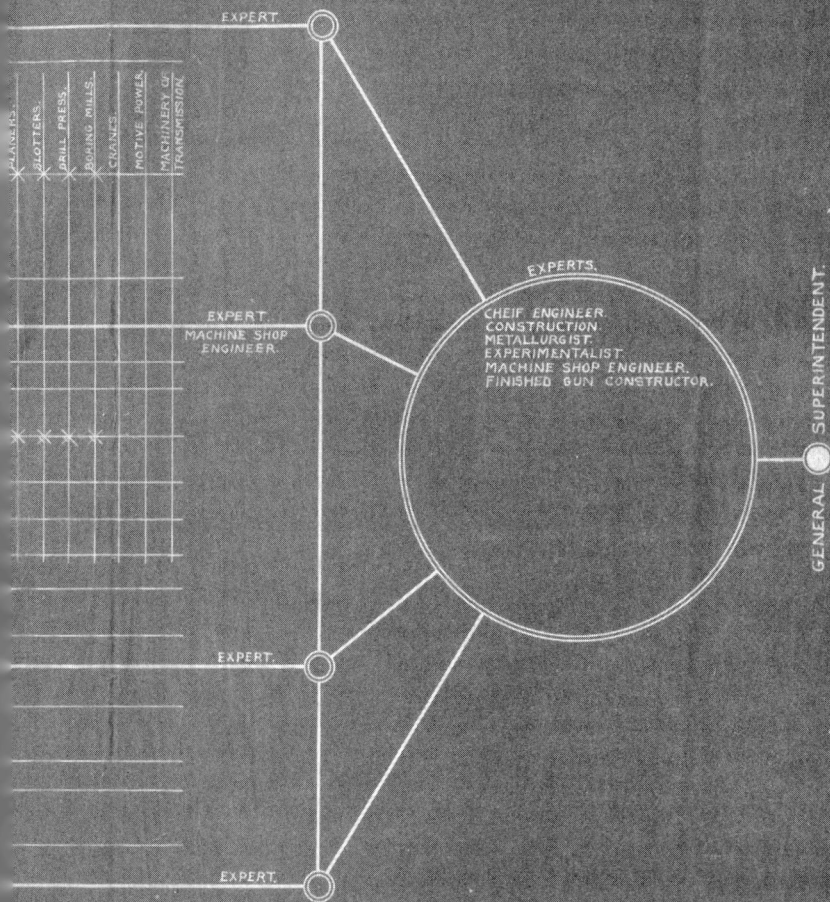

EXPERT

EXPERT.
MACHINE SHOP
ENGINEER.

EXPERTS.

CHEIF ENGINEER.
CONSTRUCTION.
METALLURGIST.
EXPERIMENTALIST.
MACHINE SHOP ENGINEER.
FINISHED GUN CONSTRUCTOR.

EXPERT.

EXPERT.

GENERAL SUPERINTENDENT.

PLANERS.
SLOTTERS.
DRILL PRESS.
BORING MILLS.
CRANES.
MOTIVE POWER.
MACHINERY OF TRANSMISSION.

Table 6-1 Duties of the general shop supervisor, Jones & Laughlin Steel Corporation

COORDINATION FUNCTION

Cooperates with the Maintenance Section in setting and maintaining standards of care and usage of all machinery and equipment

Advises Planning Division of desirable changes to take care of work, emergencies, and development of personnel

Coordinates the work of the Shop Division with the Planning Division

Insists on proper cooperation of Planning Division

DISCIPLINE FUNCTION

Is responsible for discipline of all shop sections

Is responsible for keeping all machines operating when there is work

Is responsible for orderly arrangement of the shop

Sees that Planning Department does not neglect moving of material

PERSONNEL FUNCTION

Is responsible for the training and development of the personnel in accordance with plans of training and promotion

Pays particular attention to the development of strength and executive power in all supervisors

Keeps interest in personnel with the view of prospective supervisors

Aids in the supplying of various Shop Division personnel

Takes up matters of misunderstanding and adjusts them when they are apt to cause discord

Pays particular attention to foremen and efficiency records and uses them as guides in correction of poor conditions

Makes recommendations to the superintendent to fill vacancies

Reports to the superintendent of the machine shop

Reports difficulties not readily handled between general supervisor and Planning Division heads

PLANNING FUNCTION

Is responsible for production in accordance with defined methods

Is responsible for production and best use of equipment where methods are not properly defined due to incompletion

Aids in the development of better methods

Disposes scrap materials and ensures that they are not permitted to accumulate in the shop

SUPERVISION FUNCTION

Has direct supervision of all shop sections

Is responsible for functioning of all Shop Division sections

Sees that functional supervisors carry out their duties in accordance with prescribed principles and defined duties

Sees that methods defined by the Planning Division are properly executed

Acts as acting head of both divisions in absence of superintendent

QUALITY CONTROL FUNCTION

Sees that material delivered is material desired for orders and is in proper form

Sees that all Shop Division standards of tools and equipment are properly maintained and that operators are not made to suffer for mistakes of the management

Keeps informed on various reports on production

Source: Standing Order on Supervision and Duties of the General Shop, Preparation, Methods, and Inspection Supervisors, May 1, 1924, box 92, fol. 9.

tending. Machine helpers at Tabor Manufacturing Company, for example, could earn bonuses for work on the machines that was not delayed relative to the time estimated under the piece rates and for punctuality.[5] Additionally, workmen could earn a 35 percent bonus for their weekly cleaning of the machine, just as long as the cleaning was carried out within the prescribed time limits.[6] Evidence from other job task analyses of the time indicates that care of the machine was often built into the tasks of machine workers (e.g., E. G. Allen 1916). Nevertheless, under Taylorist organization there was little opportunity for the workers in frontline manufacturing occupations to do anything but tend the machine and carry out the operations required by the supervisor.

The addition of machine-cleaning as a task for machine workers in fact reflects the influence of a broader aspect of rationalization and the changes in scientific practice that were happening at the time of Taylor's intervention. Emphasis was placed on the preparation of machines and preventive maintenance, alongside the administrative structures required to plan and organize production. In Figure 6-2, for example, we see within Bethlehem's organizational structure a machine shop charged with the care of machines and repairs or maintenance. Machine failure was—and would continue to be over the coming decades—a key threat to productivity in the manufacturing industry. Taylor recognized the threat of machine failure and argued forcefully that the prevention of breakage must be a priority. Taylor described the function of the Maintenance Department as follows:

> Its function is preventative rather than corrective, and it is of the utmost importance that this viewpoint be kept constantly in mind. . . . Under Scientific Management the Maintenance Department is operated in such a manner as to anticipate and prevent in the greatest possible degree loss in output and interruptions to manufacture as a result of machinery and equipment getting in bad condition or breaking down. (Frederick Winslow Taylor Collection, *Standing Order for Maintenance Department,* March 30, 1916)

Taylor's emphasis on preventing machine failure rather than applying corrective treatment reflects the broader trends in scientific thought associated with the probabilistic revolution. In the rationalized firm, the prevention of machine failure would increase output, reduce costs, and reduce the number of days lost to repairs.

The College Guys

Scientific management was simultaneously an enormous influence on industrialists and politicians and a failure. Few firms took up Taylor's recommendations, and even those firms that had hired Taylor as a consultant were resistant to implementing his vision in full (Daniel Nelson 1980: chap. 6).[7] But a more abstract commitment to the rationalized firm was here to stay, and Taylor's work only energized efforts to organize work and workers to maximize productivity (Merkle 1980). In the New Castle interview data we see the influence of attempts to rationalize the production industry on the experience of workers.[8]

Most strikingly, the push toward task specialization, the simplification of manufacturing work, and the use of time charts and piece rates was felt across the industry. Manufacturing workers routinely described undertaking highly specialized jobs on the factory floor, and some spent years working in the same role on the same machine. Sandy DeLaverson, for example, described his time in a New Castle factory:

> [They] make you marry the job. If you're good at one process they make you stick to it and don't advance you. Say you're at a No.1 machine and I'm at a No.2 machine. I make 40 cents, you make 55. When you quit they don't put me on the better job; they break in a new man. . . . It doesn't give you any chance to earn a trade. (March 31, 1941, car. 6, fol. 20)

By specializing in a single machine, workers became highly proficient in the skills required to work that machine, and the amount of training that the firm needed to provide was reduced.

It is not surprising that piece rates, bonuses, and other issues related to monetary rewards were frequently disparaged. The "efficiency men" had substantial power and influence over the financial fortunes of manufacturing workers, and workers characterize the factories as being "alive with engineers and men with stop watches" (October 19, 1940, car. 6, fol. 27). But there was much suspicion about the accuracy of the assigned rates and the feasibility of achieving the desired output. In talking about their jobs in the factory, the metalworkers in New Castle underlined that their work was regimented and controlled by the rates:

> One day one of those college guys was looking me over with a stopwatch. Every little while he'd look at it on his wrist. . . . I said to him, "Why aren't you satisfied? Look at my clothes, they're all wringing wet." Then Bishop comes up and talks to this guy. Next day he gave me a bigger plate, and stood there and just laughed. I put it in the roll. "Some day," I said to myself, "I'll put you in the roll." (John Dahanish, March 30, 1941, car. 6, fol. 20)

A common complaint was that the efficiency men were unreasonable in their calculations of rates and that work of high quality could not be produced under their constraints. Steel worker Steve Wheale describes the frustration of working under time charts that prescribed the time needed for each operation:

> You are expected to set up your machine and turn out a part in the allotted time. I usually don't pay any attention to it, and I'm waiting to see what happens. One operation was supposed to take 1¼ hours and I take 2½. If they raise any kick I will show them the kind of work that is done by fellows who take an hour and ¼. You can't do it properly in that time. (March 23, 1941, car. 6, fol. 21)

Wheale's complaint alludes to another dissatisfaction with the college men: that the engineers and time-study specialists did not fully understand the skill or work required to produce the firm's outputs. One of the interviewees drily notes, "When one of [the college men] was asked to operate a machine himself . . . the workmen apparently got a kick out of the fact that he couldn't do it" (Ray Bovard, November 1, 1940, car. 6, fol. 28). We see in these complaints a recognition that at least part of the frontline manufacturing worker's control over their work had been taken away and placed in the hands of management, just as Taylor had advocated.

The growth of formal administrative structures within the factory—a key indicator of growing rationalization—is also evident in the interview data. The men speak about formalized hiring processes, bureaucratic procedures, and organizational innovations. The New Castle interviewees described changes over time in hiring processes, in which the firm moved from the particularistic hiring of friends or family members of employees to formalized and centralized hiring and firing procedures. John Dennis, for example, noted,

> Back in my kid days the roller hired the men. In 1893 this stopped, but the roller still had complete control. If he didn't like a man he could turn him into the office to get his money. Later the boss told the roller what to do. (John Dennis, February 12, 1941, car. 6, fol. 24)

And Mr. Oberlitner similarly states, "the personnel man couldn't make an arbitrary choice about who was employed" (November 15, 1940, car. 6, fol. 27).[9] Those who had been involved with the factories since their teenage years saw the growth of bureaucracy clearly:

> A man who worked in a corporation tended to be "fighting shadows." A personnel man might feel that a certain thing ought to be done, but he couldn't "fight the shadow." The shadow probably had laid down certain definite rules, and the personnel man would not fight against them. (Joseph Hensley, November 15, 1940, car. 6, fol. 26)

Bureaucratic procedures had also started to infuse the factory floor, in line with some of Taylor's recommendations: systems for tool organization, inspection and quality control, and the declining importance of seniority were all remarked on by the interviewees.

MEN AND MACHINES

In the wake of Taylor's intervention, manufacturing workers in the early decades of the twentieth century were bifurcated. Frontline manufacturing operatives—including machinists, machine helpers, and the like—saw increasing task specialization in their work, as work was simplified in the cause of increasing productivity and reducing waste. In contrast, occupations with managerial or supervisorial responsibilities—including foremen, and production and planning managers—took on the responsibility of organizing production. The rationalization of the factory was in full sway, and over the coming decades, this rationalization opened the door to changes in job tasks for both branches of the manufacturing industry, leading to increasing functional complexity.

In this section, I discuss how changes in factory production in the first half of the twentieth century had consequences for the division of labor. Chief among these changes was the increasing importance of machine technology in the manufacturing sector. Task specialization and the growth in the use of machines had of course gone hand in hand in the manufacturing industry for centuries. In *The Wealth of Nations*, Adam Smith highlighted the growth of machines alongside task specialization as one of the great productivity-enhancing movements: "The invention of a great number of machines which facilitate and abridge labour . . . enable[s] one man to do the work of many" (1776: book 1, chap. 1). But between the 1910s and 1920s, the proportion of machine tenders had grown to just under 47 percent of the manufacturing labor force, such that in 1920, machine tending was the modal manufacturing occupation (Reitell 1924: 40; see also Montgomery 1979: chap. 5).

In *Men and Machines* (1929: 104), Stuart Chase provides a useful outline of the three stages of machine-aided manufacturing. He argues that machines first allow skilled workers to increase their production. Next, machines take over parts of the manufacturing process. Unskilled workers can be employed to run machines, replacing skilled workers. Finally, machines develop to the extent that the unskilled workers can be replaced by machines. At this point, skilled workers are again required to maintain and develop the machines. These automation-driven changes alter the composition of the labor market over time, such that by the end of the period the labor market may favor high-skilled workers (see Acemoglu and Johnson 2023; Acemoglu and Restrepo 2019; Acemoglu and Autor 2011; Autor, Levy, and Murnane 2003). In the early twentieth century, movement through these stages had both direct and indirect effects on job tasks. To be sure, the task specialization that Taylor had advocated was facilitated by advances in machine technology and the rise of mechanized production. But there were also counterforces, forces that were in part set in motion by some of the negative effects of technological change.

The Same Foot Press

We have seen that the logic of specialization was a powerful influence in the manufacturing industry, particularly after Taylor's intervention. But

regardless of Taylor's specific prescriptions, those organizing factory production could in fact use the logic of specialization to justify two quite different arrangements. The first is the type of specialization that Taylor proposed, in which a machine operator is tethered to a single machine and
thereby becomes an expert in running the machine (see Marx 1867: chap.
15, sec. 4). The second is a type of specialization in which the skill of machine
tending is so simplified that workers can be moved from machine to
machine without difficulty. In this case, machine tending is a similar task
regardless of the machine in question, and workers can both specialize in
the task and move across machines without loss of productivity.

There were certainly attempts to implement Taylorian specialization in
a good many factories. The secretary of the Greater New Castle Association,
Mr. Andrews, noted,

> We have no trained machinists, if you mean by "trained machinist" a
> man who has served a three-year apprenticeship and works five or six
> years in the shop. It is impossible to find such men anywhere today. . . .
> What is more important, we have a large supply of men to turn into
> trained machinists without very much trouble. (Elton Mayo Papers,
> *New Castle Interviews,* December 10, 1940, car. 6, fol. 27)

Workers in the Hawthorne studies also discussed the specialized nature of
their jobs and the parts of the work they valued. One employee reports that
their job "is interesting because it is the same thing all the time," while
another reports, "I like my job even though it is the same thing all the time.
To me this work is interesting, because I have to turn out a certain amount
of work each day, and I like to watch the output increase" (Elton Mayo
Papers, *Interviews, Substance Analysis,* July 8, 1930, box 4c, fol. 27). As these
quotes demonstrate, there were highly specialized workers who enjoyed the
fact that their jobs had been reduced to a small number of tasks, largely
devoted to serving the machine. In fact, some commentators believed that
certain types of workers might select machine-operating occupations precisely because of the highly specialized work. Women workers, for example,
might prefer narrow machine tasks, "as they are free all day to think of
anything that takes their fancy" (Vernon 1921: 84).[10]

Whether or not some workers valued highly specialized work, a rather
more common experience was that repeated work on a single machine had

the tendency to become monotonous. A worker at Hawthorne summarizes the problem well:

> To tell you the truth, the job is really monotonous because I am doing the same thing day after day and a change from one job to another once in a while would be welcome. I have been on this same foot press for the last four months and do nothing but kick all day and it surely gets very tiresome at times because after a man has been on any job for a certain length of time and gets to know all there is to know about that particular job it becomes stale and the man loses interest in it. (Elton Mayo Papers, *Interviews, Substance Analysis,* July 8, 1930, box 4b, fol. 26)

Another Hawthorne worker similarly notes, "A man is interested in his job about one day and that is when he is learning the job. The second day he knows the work and is able to turn out his rate. After that the job gets to be very monotonous" (Elton Mayo Papers, *Interviews, Substance Analysis,* July 8, 1930, box 4b, fol. 26). The monotony of machine production was a significant concern for those with an interest in industrial efficiency. A large field of research developed around the concept of "fatigue," a condition in which workers were simply unable to work to highest productivity (see, e.g., Goldmark 1912; Gilbreth and Gilbreth 1919; Spaeth 1920; Vernon 1921; Fisk 1922; Chase 1929). Monotonous work was understood to be a strong predictor of fatigue, and several authors linked Taylorian specialization to the condition. Josephine Goldmark writes, for example, "If concentration and subdivision are part of the new efficiency they are part, too, of its new strain" (1912: 59).[11]

The type of specialization that Taylor had advocated, in which frontline manufacturing workers carry out a very narrow set of tasks on the same machine, was but one version of specialization that was implemented at the time. An alternative (albeit less common) approach was to have workers run several machines, either simultaneously or successively. Insofar as machine tending was simplified and different machines required similar sets of skills, it was possible for workers both to specialize in machine tending and to work on multiple machines. John Fix, from New Castle, explains, "A machinist picks a job up and is able to do pretty nearly any old thing" (Elton Mayo Papers, *New Castle Interviews,* March 27, 1941, car. 6, fol. 21). Similarly, Ivon

Puz describes, "Machinery has been cutting down the number of men employed, particularly in the cement plant. During the depression I guess they figured they had to make money or something, and they put in new machines and made one man keep track of two or three of them" (Elton Mayo Papers, *New Castle Interviews,* April 1, 1941, car. 6, fol. 20). As the latter quote suggests, one very practical reason for implementing a version of specialization in which workers could operate multiple machines was that it provided a way for the factory to manage variations in labor supply and product demand.

Even the broader type of specialization, however, proved inadequate to the task of managing the fluctuations in labor supply and product demand that were typical of factory life in the early decades of the twentieth century. For this reason, we see in many of the factories described in the interviews a *rejection* of out-and-out specialization. One approach to managing fluctuations in labor supply was to have a small set of workers who were trained in many different skills. Several of the Hawthorne workers described their experience of "special work," a type of work in which workers were trained to perform multiple different machine jobs. One worker, for example, notes, "I am changed around from one thing to another almost every day and it is always something different and that makes it very interesting" (Elton Mayo Papers, *Interviews, Substance Analysis,* July 8, 1930, box 4b, fol. 26). A similar type of work existed in some of the steel mills; workers who were "standing turn" were expected to fill in for other workers. An alternative approach to managing labor fluctuations was to organize the factory around flexibility rather than specialization. Stephen Levitsky, of the Steel Workers Organizing Committee, describes the process at the Irvin steel mill, where, "instead of making a man indispensable, the emphasis is placed on versatility rather than specialization. So if one man goes out another can step right into his place" (Elton Mayo Papers, *New Castle Conference,* October 10, 1940). An Irvin worker elaborates:

> They have what they call a "general maintenance system" there. Whatever you are, machinist, pipefitter, or anything else, you have to do what they ask you to do. . . . In the old days a man would learn just one job, but it's different now. (Elton Mayo Papers, *New Castle Interviews,* Mr. Henderson, March 25, 1941, car. 6, fol. 21)

For managers, being able to move men around the factory was invaluable in dealing with labor shortages. Levitsky hypothesized that managers might also value flexibility because it interfered with workers forming strong relationships with coworkers, with the effect that union organizing was made more challenging.

It would be wrong to make too much of this incipient interest in flexibility; indeed, it was only in the decades that followed that an explicit push for more flexibility in work became prominent. In interview after interview, the dominant story that emerged during this period was that of manufacturing jobs that were relatively simple, relatively repetitive, and typically disliked. In sum, the rationalization of frontline manufacturing occupations during this period was largely associated with increasing task specialization for workers. Even if Taylor's quintessential highly specialized worker was rarely in place, the specialized machine operative was taking over the factory floor.

The Slaughter House

> I have two cousins who went down [to the Irvin Works] and they call it the slaughter house. One of them had his arm taken off in a machine. He was wearing a metal screen on his arm and it was caught. He would have been dragged through altogether if the fellow in the crane hadn't seen it and dropped the magnetic lift on the machine, which stopped it dead. (Elton Mayo Papers, *New Castle Interviews*, Mr. Riley, December 16, 1940, car. 6, fol. 29)

The interviews pointed to a second problem—the safety problem—that likewise foreshadowed looming changes that would ultimately complicate the job tasks of frontline manufacturing workers in precisely the way the paradox implies. It would be hard to read interviews with factory workers from the early decades of the twentieth century without being struck by just how many horrific injuries are described. The men who had worked in the steel industry would recount coworkers losing limbs or even dying on the factory floor; their descriptions of working with steel made it clear that this was a dangerous and uncomfortable working environment (see also Hard 1907). But the workers at the Hawthorne factory—a facility that produced telephone equipment for the Western

Electric Company—also described the dangers involved in working with machinery.[12]

As machines spread across the manufacturing industry, there were substantial concerns about the safety of workers. Although machines could put distance between workers and some of the most dangerous jobs in the factories, they also presented several potential dangers. First, the monotony that produced the fatigue that industrial researchers were so concerned about might also lead to carelessness in the use of machines. As concentration waned during the long hours completing repetitive tasks, accidents were likely. Machines also substantially increased the speed of production, thereby increasing the demand on the worker. As the interview quote at the start of this section suggests, if an incident occurred, there was little time to react to prevent greater injury. Finally, machines required repairs, and the repair of machines was inherently dangerous, as it was unpredictable and required workers to be in close proximity to the machines (American Engineering Council 1928: 5). Inadequate repairs produced further dangers, as one worker in Hawthorne notes:

> Some of the fellows are careless in fixing parts of their apparatus. When they get bent in, they pound it back into shape with an iron pipe, and there is a danger of being hit by steel splinters if it breaks. (Elton Mayo Papers, *Interviews, Substance Analysis,* September 15, 1930, box 4c, fol. 27)

The rate of manufacturing accidents had declined from the beginning of the twentieth century onward, but a spate of accidents in the early 1920s and the increasing severity of accidents renewed concerns that machinery posed risks to companies and workers (American Engineering Council 1928; Chase 1929).

Accidents were understood to be a severe threat to productivity. Not only did they call a halt to production, but as one Hawthorne worker highlights, "the Company [would] have to pay if the man [got] hurt" (Elton Mayo Papers, *Interviews, Substance Analysis,* September 15, 1930, box 4c, fol. 27; for a similar discussion, see Commons 1919: 61). Moreover, accidents were a possible indicator that a factory process or rule was vulnerable to failure. In a sweeping report on factory safety, published in 1928, the American Engineering Council investigated the problem of industrial accidents.

The report emphasized the danger that accidents posed to productivity and efficiency:

> A physical accident must be looked at, not as a thing in itself, but as evidence of an inability to harness and control the forces of production. When industrial forces are brought under perfect control, there will not only be a maximum of production, but the unexpected, that is, accidents, will not happen; and conversely, when accidents cease to happen it is probable that the cause may be looked for in an industrial organization so well adapted to the problem in hand that the maximum of production is being secured. (American Engineering Council 1928: 9)

The report placed the blame for accidents squarely on the shoulders of poor management:

> Industrial accidents can be controlled under modern conditions of highly efficient productivity by the same managerial skill that controls production itself. . . . Safety does not interfere with production, but, on the contrary, aids it. (American Engineering Council 1928: 23)

We see in the report recognition that industrial safety enhances productivity and that the rationalized firm is required to attend to the problem. Further, within the rationalized manufacturing firm, it is the managerial occupations that are responsible for building an environment in which accidents do not occur.

There are two important features of the American Engineering Council's discussion of safety. First, that safety is discussed with respect to means-ends calculations about productivity is a clear indication that it is rationalization—as opposed to an alternative cultural force, such as morality or personhood—that is at work. Although there were of course many morality-driven factory reformers in the early twentieth century, both in the United States and in other countries, the repeated references to output and efficiency within the manufacturing literature point to rationalization as the key driver of accident reduction.[13] Second, safety is understood to be a consequence of workplace practices, and these practices can be redesigned to reduce the rate of accidents. The responsibility for undertaking this redesign belongs to the executive.[14]

In the discussion of workplace safety practices, we see further signs of changes in industrial science associated with the probabilistic revolution. The full-throated focus on accident prevention reveals the growing interest in models of production that emphasize causal processes, prediction, and targeted intervention. The increasing focus on the prevention of accidents is in line with changes seen in other areas of practice—such as medical science—during this period, in which prevention comes to be seen as superior to treatment after the event. As it becomes clear from industrial science that accidents can be prevented via both factory design and changes in the behavior of workers, it likewise becomes clear that the rationalized firm must intervene to improve productivity.

One straightforward intervention was to develop engineering solutions for the dangers that machines posed. Insofar as mechanical fixes to the safety problem could be introduced, accidents could be reduced without any increased demand on workers; indeed, some scholars of industrial efficiency even believed that safety equipment could reduce the demand for skilled workers (e.g., American Engineering Council 1928). Thus, safety guards for machines were engineered and installed, and safety equipment such as clothing and glasses was introduced. The workers at Hawthorne were very positive in describing these changes:

> This Company is wonderful compared to the concern I worked for before I came here. . . . We did not have the safety devices we have here. This Company furnishes us with leather aprons, sleeves, gloves, and goggles. A man can't get hurt even if he tried. . . . They sure have a wonderful safety system here. If a man lives up to the Company's safety devices he will never get hurt. (Elton Mayo Papers, *Interviews, Substance Analysis,* September 15, 1930, box 4c, fol. 27)

Such reactions highlight that safety equipment might itself enhance productivity, via the mechanism of increased worker satisfaction (see also National Safety Council 1914: 275; Beyer 1917).

However, safety equipment and machine engineering could not prevent all accidents. As authors of the time noted, "Mechanical safeguarding can accomplish comparatively little. It is the 'spirit' of safety in the workmen that accomplishes most" (Commons 1919: 59). Therefore, a standard approach to improving safety in the factory was to introduce new job tasks for frontline workers and supervisors. Frank Mantinaos, of New Castle, discussed the changes that had happened in the 1930s in the steel mills. He noted, "Working conditions in the mill kept improving. . . . There were meetings every week about safety, and there was good cooperation between the foremen and the men to make good quality stuff" (Elton Mayo Papers, *New Castle Interviews,* March 20, 1941, car. 6, fol. 21). Similarly, in Hawthorne, a worker remarked, "The Company is doing very good work along the safety lines. The posters on the bulletin board remind a fellow that it does not pay to get hurt" (Elton Mayo Papers, *Interviews, Substance Analysis,* September 15, 1930, box 4c, fol. 27). Workers were expected to familiarize themselves with safety equipment, inspect and maintain machines, and cultivate a "safety-first" mindset.[15] Thus, the expanding science of industrial safety led to increased cognitive demands on manufacturing workers and to additional job tasks. During this early period, the complicating effects of such safety work do not appear to have been all that substantial, but here again there are hints of what happens when the process of production takes into account the full complexity of the human worker.

The Big Morgue

> Mike pointed to the endless ceiling with the massive machinery under it. "Look at her!" he said. "You know what we call her?—'The Big Morgue.' The few of us old hand-mill men that got something to do here ain't so bad off as the thirteen hundred or more fellows that are out starving on relief or struggling on WPA [Works Progress Administration]. When we meet on the street and get to talking we call this 'the Big Morgue,' the place where all our jobs went dead." (Ruttenberg 1939)

As we proceed through the stages of machine-aided production, the expectation is that job tasks are gradually taken away from frontline manufacturing workers. As the demands on workers are reduced, the number of workers required to produce output is reduced, and firms hire fewer workers. Much attention has been given to the loss of jobs via "technological unemployment" (Keynes 1930), on the one hand, and the growth of skilled jobs associated with designing and building machines, on the other (see especially Acemoglu, Kong, and Restrepo 2024; Acemoglu and Johnson 2023; Acemoglu and Restrepo 2019; Acemoglu and Autor 2011). Harold J.

Ruttenberg's piece on *The Big Morgue* summarized both dynamics under the heading "New Jobs—For Other Men, Elsewhere" (1939). But the experience of existing frontline manufacturing workers seeing machines added to the factory floor was different again from the experiences of these two groups of workers.

One fact that is sometimes lost in discussions of automation is that as machines are introduced, frontline manufacturing workers are thrust into a period of transition that might last for quite some time. During this period, workers may be required to clean and maintain machines, undertake inspections of products, and carry out new tasks that will in later periods be taken over by other specialized occupations (e.g., machine repairers). In Hawthorne, for example, workers describe the need to "clean [the machine] every day because when it gets dirty it won't run smooth and there is a danger of us hurting our fingers" (Elton Mayo Papers, *Interviews, Substance Analysis,* September 15, 1930, box 4c, fol. 27). Furthermore, many of the interviewees emphasize how unreliable machinery was, even after the machines were well established within the factory. Just as Taylor had described of factory production in the late nineteenth century, machines frequently failed, and frontline workers—often employed on a piece-rate basis—found it necessary to carry out repairs.

Workers at Hawthorne had many complaints about poor-quality machinery. Here, two workers describe their experiences with equipment that was not reliable:

> Some of our machines are in bad shape. We have one that is cracked in places. We have a piece of wood supporting one of the cracked parts. One of these days a man will get hurt when these cracked parts break off. (Elton Mayo papers, *Interviews, Substance Analysis,* August 13, 1930, box 4c, fol. 27)

> The equipment that I have to work with is not working the way it should. Some time ago there was an engineer here from the outside to look at it and he said he would look into it, but that was the last I ever heard from him. The machine runs wild and I have it set now so that I can get some work out of it, but if any one that don't know it fools around with it I

won't be able to use it. (Elton Mayo papers, *Interviews, Substance Analysis,* June 21, 1930, box 4c, fol. 27)

As a consequence of machine problems, frontline manufacturing workers found it necessary to undertake tasks related to maintenance and repair if they were to make their "bogey" (i.e., output quota) and remain safe on the job. The introduction of machines surely pushed toward increasing task specialization for frontline manufacturing workers, but these machine-enabling tasks mitigated the degree of specialization experienced by the workers. Thus, even during the heyday of production-line task simplification, there were several looming threats that would ultimately work to complicate manufacturing work and undermine any straightforward account of increasing task specialization.

THE HUMAN MACHINE

The introduction of more and more efficient machinery gradually reduced labor to one narrow range. In the old days there had been a number of skills, each paid at a different rate. Now, in the new continuous-strip mill, a man could be taught his work in a few weeks. There was no longer any regular ladder of promotion. The worker tended to be reduced to a dead-level mark. (Elton Mayo Papers, *New Castle Interviews,* Mr. Wilt, October 25, 1940, car. 6, fol. 28)

By the 1930s, the logic of specialization dominated most frontline manufacturing occupations. As machines continued to spread across the industry, workers found their old skills to be obsolete, and their primary role was now machine tending. The logic of specialization was largely imposed through a top-down rationalization of frontline manufacturing occupations—a rationalization *by fiat*—encouraged by the desire on behalf of factory administrators to increase output and reduce the control of labor over production. Although advances were also being made at the time in the science of production, most notably in the science of accident prevention and occupational health, changes induced by scientific development were still limited relative to the degree of task specialization in the manufacturing industry. In short, the logic of specialization was winning out.

In this section, I describe the key developments in the "human machine" period of the 1930s–1950s. During this period, the tide began to turn against task simplification, and the forces pushing in favor of complication rose. The tide turned because severe problems of industrial production remained, and these problems could not be solved through enhanced Taylorian intervention in the job tasks of workers. Continuing worries about the monotony of work, alongside the search for ever-higher productivity in the manufacturing industry, pushed toward increasing interest in alternative approaches to the organization of work. Elton Mayo summarizes the dynamic in a symposium on "national unity" held in 1945 (1945a: 48):

> New methods, new machines, new tools—physics, chemistry, engineering pursue their reckless way without regard for the historic human organization of working procedures. None can wish to limit the service of invention and innovation to mankind. But, if the historic functional groups that trained individuals simultaneously in technical skill and in human association are to be ruthlessly destroyed, it becomes our duty to examine critically the human aspect of the change, to repudiate the easy assumption that manipulative skill is the only problem for civilization.

There was a growing appreciation that the engineers had neglected an important part of the production process: the worker as a human and social animal. Taylorian rationalization of manufacturing occupations had set the stage for the influence of a new type of science: the science of human organization.

Total Mental Situation

Scientific management considered the great problems of manufacturing to be rooted in the mechanical components of the production process. To increase productivity, it was necessary to streamline job tasks, standardize production methods, and maintain the machines. These interventions, however, failed to address the productivity-reducing effects of the problems of human organization (Mayo 1935).

To some extent, the problems of human organization of most concern could be traced back to changes induced by Taylor and his cohorts (as Mayo's quote above implies.) As the logic of specialization won out in the manufacturing industry, the frontline workers once again became the weak link in the production chain. This was not because they exploited their skills and knowledge of the production process to the disadvantage of employers, as Taylor had proposed, but rather because the monotony of machine tending was more problematic than had been assumed and because the coordination of specialized workers within the factory was challenging for the managers who had taken over the organization of work. The problems faced by frontline workers are well illustrated by a set of exemplar job descriptions for shearmen's helpers published in the *Personnel Journal* in 1941. The three helper descriptions are as follows:

> 1ST HELPER. The first helper is responsible for miking the sheets for proper gauge at the front and back end of each coil sheared. He will set the gears controlling the length of the sheets at the instruction of the shearman, and inspect the top sheet of every lift for shear scratches and defects. His duties are to work with the 2nd helper in keeping the piler box ready for each lift.

> 2ND HELPER. The second helper's duties consist of piling the sheets in the piler, and setting the piler box for each new lift. He is responsible for keeping the pile straight and even.

> 3RD HELPER. It is the duty of the third helper to start the coils into the shearline, and pile scrap and waster sheets in their proper pile. He will bring the coil tickets from coils next to be sheared to the shearman, and will help the shearman set the side shear for changes in width. (Anonymous 1941)

As the job descriptions indicate, each helper is required to perform a small set of tasks. But the work required of each helper is recognized to be so narrow that the job descriptions are followed by this statement: "The duties of the helpers may be alternated to relieve monotony" (Anonymous 1941: 262). In acknowledging the need to relieve the monotony of the job, the journal is underlining the likely trade-off between the productivity-enhancing effects of task simplification, on the one hand, and the productivity-reducing effects of fatigue, on the other (see also Burtt 1929: chaps. 4–5; Harding 1931).

Just as Taylor had attacked the "rules of thumb" by which important production decisions were made in the late nineteenth century, so scientists began to attack the casualness with which the human problems of industry had been addressed.[16] Mayo and colleagues conducted a series of studies, out of which arose the clear conclusion that human problems had to be given prominence in the organization of work and that a rationalized firm would prioritize workers themselves. Although the focus on the welfare of workers marked a clear break from Taylorism—and indeed, researchers in the field of human relations were highly critical of the instrumentalism of Taylor—the principle that high productivity would result from the proposed interventions was common across the approaches. This drive may be summarized by a final thought from a steelworker from New Castle, Mr. Henderson, who remarks, "I think I'm worth just as much to the company as their machinery, and they take care of that" (Elton Mayo Papers, *New Castle Interviews,* March 25, 1941, car. 6, fol. 21).

Another commonality with Taylorism was the role that the management structure of the organization was expected to play in ensuring the welfare of frontline manufacturing workers. Once again, the foremen, supervisors, and managers would be responsible for implementing the new "worker welfare" approach. This is well illustrated by Figure 6-3, published in 1937 in a guide for job supervisors working at Western Electric. The figure lays out the supervisor's role relative to the company, and the principles that guide supervisorial work. In its structure, the figure is a celebration of rationalization: the installation service—the label given to the output of the factory—is depicted at the top, and this output rests on various "phases" of administration. The supervisor is responsible for these phases of administration, which include supervision, teamplay, training, planning, observation, and verification.[17] A key change in supervisorial responsibility between Taylorian and human relations approaches is captured in the pillar labeled "teamplay." It is here that we see the focus on cooperation among workers and the "worker welfare" concept being elevated to a central role in the management of the factory floor.

The guide for supervisors, alongside other materials prepared for supervisorial training, emphasizes that the human relations approach marks an important break with prior administrative practices. Rather than focusing exclusively on the "technical" aspects of production, the modern supervisor

Fig. 6-3 Depiction of the role of administration at Western Electric Company.

SOURCE: Installation Administrator's References, Western Electric Company, November 1, 1937, Fritz J. Roethlisberger papers, car. 10, fol. 4.

was expected to understand the needs of individual workers and to know how to coordinate those workers to operate as a well-functioning team. Elton Mayo summarizes this shift in a piece titled "How to Achieve Maximum Efficiency in Labor Utilization," prepared in 1942 with the aim of increasing production for the war effort:

> Attainment of high job efficiency requires maximum use of labor saving devices, adoption of most modern and productive shop practices such as materials lay-out, scheduling, and prevention of lost time through provision of adequate safety devices. Attainment of high man efficiency requires that, first, his physical condition is maintained at an optimum level through proper food, ventilation, light, sanitation, and safety measures, and secondly, that his psychological well being is maintained or stimulated to achieve maximum individual effort through incentives, appeals, etc. (Elton Mayo Papers)

As Mayo's piece makes clear, the shift in thinking was not a rejection of technical efficiency. Rather, the human relations approach aimed to *add* a set of concerns about "man efficiency" that would put the worker and the technical aspects on equal footing.

The addition of "man efficiency" concerns to the science of production laid the groundwork for the paradox of specialization to once again come into play. After the interventions of Taylor and his cohorts, the manufacturing industry was largely rationalized. Firms were oriented toward maximizing output via predictable and standardized procedures, job tasks were assigned to workers in line with principles of efficiency and specialization, and factory administrators were tasked with organizing production on the basis of rational principles. When the science of production expanded, the rationalized firm was required to build in new tasks and new proximate objectives to achieve these broader aims.

The paradox of specialization is evident in the tasks listed in the Western Electric guide for job supervisors. In Table 6-2, we see the six phases of administration (shown in Figure 6-3) alongside their "common factors," or components, and associated tasks. The number of tasks listed for each common factor is included in parentheses, and examples of tasks are provided for each common factor.[18] A comparison of Tables 6-1 and 6-2, laying out the responsibilities of supervisors in the Taylor and human relations

Table 6-2 Responsibilities of the supervisor, Western Electric Company

SUPERVISION: "ONE'S OWN DIRECT CONTACT WITH THE PROJECT AT HAND"

Judgment (39): "Hold huddles," "Be mindful of spirit of teamplay," "Consult others"

Knowledge (30): "Seek facts by investigation," "Make the necessary verifications of completed work," "Study systematically"

Courage (29): "A sincerity of purpose," "Be confident in the team," "Exercise fairness"

TEAMPLAY: "PROMOTES THE INDIVIDUAL'S INTEREST IN THE GROUP'S ACTIVITY, SECURES HIS ACTIVE COOPERATION IN THE SOLVING OF PROBLEMS, AND WELDS INDIVIDUAL ACTIVITY INTO SUCCESSFUL GROUP ACCOMPLISHMENT"

Imparting (36): "Interest in the other fellow's problems," "Comparison by example," "Fatherly interest"

Obtaining (47): "Harmony on the job," "Trade knowledge," "Better team men"

Retaining (18): "Comment the good of a man's work," "Rotate man's work," "Maintain discipline"

TRAINING: "THE ORGANIZED EFFORT TO ENLARGE THE CAPABILITIES OF THOSE UNDER OUR SUPERVISION"

Interest (60): "Recognize good work by commendation and reward," "Add responsibilities," "Stimulate his pride in his accomplishments"

Methods (17): "Promote practice of self-checking," "Reading with an objective," "List our teaching points in sequence"

Relations (42): "Lessens labor turnover," "Lessens accidents," "Increases the individual's capacity for service"

PLANNING: "FORESEES A BALANCED AND ORDERLY SEQUENCE OF OPERATIONS FROM APPREHENDING FACTS AS THEY EXIST OR BECOME EVIDENT, BALANCING CURRENT PERFORMANCE AGAINST THAT ANTICIPATED"

Completeness (23): "Obtain, analyze, and evaluate all available information," "Use foresight," "Consider ideas developed in huddles"

Relation (8): "Make a verification plan," "Plan your training," "Plan the manload"

OBSERVATION: "FROM DIRECT DISCUSSION WITH AN INDIVIDUAL, DISCLOSES WHAT IS LACKING IN THE MENTAL PREPARATION FOR THE PARTICULAR OPERATION HE HAS IN MIND"

Intent (11): "Determine the cause of lack of interest," "Improvement of the individual," "Improvement of quality"

Approach (53): "Know methods and requirements," "Show appreciation of his efforts," "Demonstrate where necessary"

VERIFICATION: "FROM DIRECT CONTACT WITH WORK DONE, DETERMINES ITS CONFORMITY TO PREDETERMINED STANDARDS"

Knowledge (21): "Handbook methods and requirements," "Specifications and drawings," "Intensive training in verification"

Accuracy (24): "Correct use of gauges and tools," "Proper maintenance of tools and test sets," "Understand requirements and methods"

System (10): "Plan definite progressive action to check material," "Plan definite progressive action to promote 'self-check,'" "Stimulate individual's pride in good quality job"

Source: Fritz J. Roethlisberger Papers. Installation Administrator's References, Western Electric Company, November 1, 1937, car. 10, fol. 4.

eras, respectively, highlights just how much broader the supervisor's purview was after the science of human relations had been established. Many of the broad tasks described in Taylor's supervisor job description are carried over to 1937. The supervisor has responsibility for overseeing, coordinating, and training personnel; for planning work; and for ensuring quality control. But there are two substantial changes from the previous period. First, even those phases of administration that were present in the earlier period are, in the later period, understood in more expansive terms. Quality control, for example, is conceptualized here as a system, in which workers must be trained to check their own work and to take pride in their job. The planning of production requires taking account of worker feedback alongside assigning tasks and work materials. Second, two important broad responsibilities, here labeled teamplay and observation, have been added to the supervisor's job. The supervisor is expected to have interest in the worker as a person, promote teamwork, and show appreciation of the worker and their efforts. The "worker welfare" approach of the human relations field, then, pushed toward increased functional complexity in supervisor occupations.

There are also clues about changes in other frontline manufacturing occupations in the guide for job supervisors. In their role overseeing frontline workers, supervisors are reminded to obtain a "spirit of give and take," "better team men," and "self-reliance." In training workers, they are asked to "promote health habits," "stimulate physical fitness," and encourage "home study." We see in these invocations the broadening of understandings of work-relevant attributes, and attempts to develop skills in the nontechnical aspects of work. Western Electric, like other rationalized firms, provided institutionalized support for these extracurricular activities. The Hawthorne Club, for example, organized athletics and sports events and provided entertainment and educational programming. In interviews, workers described positive feelings toward work that stemmed from the belief that the company cared for their welfare (see Roethlisberger and Dickson 1934).

In addition to encouraging their workers to develop nontechnical skills, supervisors were given explicit directions to encourage workers to push away from task specialization. As part of the supervisor's responsibility to encourage workers to give their all for the good of the team, the guide recommended that supervisors should "rotate man's work." And under the training phase, supervisors were expected to "add responsibilities" and "[provide] better all-around men as compared with specialists." Both in the broadening of the attributes and skills that are seen as relevant to work and in the direct instructions concerning task specialization, Western Electric pushed toward increasing functional complexity within both supervisor and routine frontline manufacturing occupations.

Unity and Strength for Workers

The motto of the United Steelworkers union emphasizes the importance of collectivity. Just as employers were recognizing the value of teamwork on the factory floor, so employees were finding common cause with their fellow manufacturing workers. Union membership and density dramatically increased during the 1930s and early 1940s, such that by the end of World War II, over 34 percent of nonagricultural workers belonged to a union (Freeman 1998: tab. 8A2; see also Farber et al. 2021). Union expansion was aided by passage of the National Labor Relations Act (1935) and subsequent legislation.

Unions are widely understood to have had positive effects on the wages and working conditions of union members (Farber et al. 2021; Hagedorn et al. 2016; Rosenfeld 2014). These effects have subsequently been reflected in broader changes in US society: over the twentieth century, growing union membership led to reductions in income inequality and poverty (Farber et al. 2021; Western and Rosenfeld 2011; Kalleberg, Wallace, and Althauser 1981; VanHeuvelen and Brady 2022). But of primary interest to scholars of the division of labor is the role that unions had in firming up the boundaries of manufacturing jobs and—to some degree—resisting task specialization.

As we consider the division of labor within the rationalized manufacturing occupations of the midcentury, the clash of two opposing forces is once again at the forefront. The logic of specialization pushed toward the narrowing of job tasks, seemingly aided by the increasing automation within the industry. The growing science of industry identified approaches to maximizing output, which required the introduction of new tasks for workers. But as union power strengthened, job evaluations and classifications became central to the wage negotiation process within the manufacturing industry. Insofar as wage setting was determined by the skill of a job and task specialization was prioritized by factory administrators to reduce skill requirements, unions had a strong incentive to resist the narrowing of tasks within manufacturing work.

As Stuart Chase (1929) described, as automation proceeds, machines gradually replace the tasks that skilled workers previously performed. In determining the wages of manufacturing workers, unions and employers were required to come to an agreement on the effects of automation on jobs: if skill demands were reduced by the introduction of machinery, a job could be downgraded to reflect the simplification of job tasks. In the steel industry, twelve steel companies came together to establish the Cooperative Wage Study (CWS), which aimed to "determine the wage-rate situation in the companies; determine what it should be; and determine ways and means by which to bring about ... corrections" (R. Conrad Cooper, quoted in Stieber 1959: 26).[19] After the CWS, jobs were scored to reflect their content with respect to twelve factors falling into the four broad categories of skill, responsibility, effort, and working conditions. Participating steel plants carried out evaluations to assign scores to each job, and these evaluations were the basis of subsequent wage negotiations in the steel industry.[20] When jobs changed or new jobs emerged, a further evaluation process was mandated. During this process, if disagreements emerged between the union's evaluation and the company's, an arbitration process was initiated. Estimates for the period 1947–1954 suggest that around 4 percent of all jobs in steel plants were new and around 11 percent were changed (Stieber 1959: 159).

The arrangements for determining wage rates in steel plants highlight that manufacturing industries were using standardized procedures—a rationalized approach that marked a sharp departure from traditional wage-setting procedures. Scholars have noted that job evaluation and classification procedures tended to narrow the tasks of workers, as they limited worker flexibility and movement across jobs (for a discussion, see Piore and Sabel 1984: chap. 5). But the wage-setting procedure also created an incentive for the union to push for increased functional complexity in manufacturing occupations because increased functional complexity was associated with higher pay. One effect of this incentive was purely artifactual: unions were incentivized to propose higher scores for jobs, much as the employers were incentivized to propose lower scores. Evidence from arbitration cases, in which a neutral party was expected to determine whether the union's or employer's job classification was correct, shows that the arbitrator found against the union in around two-thirds of all cases (Stieber 1959: tab. 12). The second effect, though, was likely more consequential for the job tasks of manufacturing workers. Barriers were introduced that made it more difficult for the employers to downgrade the scores of occupations. Managers could make changes to job content only insofar as those changes did not involve a change in job classification of more than one class; more substantial changes required the job to be reevaluated. In a context of increasing automation, such a restriction introduced an incentive for employers to avoid substantial changes to job content. Although the logic of specialization was powerful, the counterincentive provided by the requirement to negotiate with unions introduced a stickiness to job content and excessive functional complexity.

Regardless of the effects of the wage-setting program itself, the process of job evaluation underscores that the midcentury was a period in which automation sometimes produced increased skill requirements. As workers were expected to work with the new machines, they were required to take on new responsibilities and develop new skills. It was well understood that this stage of automation was likely to pass and that the machines would eventually run without the need for skilled workers. But the job evaluation procedure quantified the degree to which the transitional period came with increased skill demands for some workers at the front line of manufacturing.

ARCHITECTS OF THE FUTURE

As machine development continued and manufacturing firms increasingly invested in machine-based production methods, politicians, industry leaders, and workers continued to express concerns about the future of work. From the 1960s onward, the manufacturing industry would come to fully appreciate that human workers are unusually complicated factors of production. During this period, the best available evidence suggests that frontline manufacturing occupations increased in complexity.

The difficulties associated with human workers came to a head, in part, because automation was escalating. In 1964, President Lyndon B. Johnson set up a National Commission on Technology, Automation, and Economic Progress, charged with planning for a future in which automation would play an ever-larger role. The commission's subsequent report, *Technology and the American Economy,* laid out a position on automation and work that both reflected existing trends in manufacturing and established a path for the future. Of particular interest is the extent to which the report recognized the "human needs" of workers.

Perhaps the most striking passage of the report, from the perspective of the scholar of rationalization in manufacturing, is in the section on "humanizing" work. The commission recommends redesigning work in order to recognize human needs and states:

> Much of this can be justified in simple dollars-and-cents terms: industry has found that considerable savings have often been realized when job design has been reorganized to take into account the needs of the men on the job. But even when the reorganization of the work process may itself increase costs, it is the recognition of the human needs which are important. And if productivity in the past has been oriented to the increase in the amounts of goods, some of its savings in the future can be utilized to bring a greater satisfaction in work for the individual. (National Commission on Technology, Automation, and Economic Progress 1966: 89–90)

This recommendation was controversial, even within the commission: two members dissented from this analysis, writing, "Any effort to improve the work environment at the expense of overall productivity is unsound" (1966: 92).[21] And indeed, the entire report was determined to be controversial by the White House, which took steps to play down its release (D. Bell 1966; see also Lekachman 1966).

It is notable that the dissenters were engineer-businessmen, who were questioning not the idea that work could benefit from being humanized but rather the idea that this should be done at the expense of productivity. Furthermore, it was quite unnecessary to downplay the importance of productivity, as businesses would "continue to gain in effectiveness as [they] improve[d] [their] knowledge and use of technology, and especially as [they] learn[ed] to improve the management of [their] industrial organizations so as to equate ... the personal goals of [workers] with the goals of the organization itself" (National Commission on Technology, Automation, and Economic Progress 1966: 92–93). But even as rationalized firms would continue to pursue higher productivity by humanizing the worker, so would they increasingly need to contend with government interventions that aimed to protect workers and the wider society.

Enriching and Enlarging

The monotony problem in manufacturing had not gone away. The logic of specialization, working hand in hand with increasing automation, pushed in the direction of reduced functional complexity for many frontline man-ufacturing workers. Concerns about "man efficiency" and mental attitude had surely mitigated—and even reversed—the trend toward task specializa-tion, but frontline workers were still taking on a relatively narrow set of tasks. As machines became ever less demanding of worker input, there were fears that productivity would fall. There were also fears that product quality had declined and worker dissatisfaction had increased in those firms that had introduced high levels of task specialization (Argyris 1959; Blauner 1964). The most likely cause was seen to be boredom (e.g., see Conant and Kilbridge 1965; for a review, see Hulin and Blood 1968).

The social science of manufacturing, by now well developed, aimed to find a solution to the monotony problem. Often working in partnership with manufacturing firms, scientists proposed new forms of work that would be more rewarding for the workers and productivity enhancing for the firms. Given that the excessive division of labor was seen to be the source of the problems, reducing exposure to task specialization was a pri-ority. One task-specialization-reducing intervention that gained promi-nence in the early 1960s was "job enlargement." The basic principle of job enlargement was that task specialization within a frontline manufacturing job should be reduced, with specific implementations of job enlargement varying depending on the factory's output. In one of the better-known studies of job enlargement in manufacturing, Eaton H. Conant and Mau-rice D. Kilbridge (1965) reported on the introduction of a job enlargement program in a manufacturer of home laundry equipment. In this factory, the assembly-line production of equipment was replaced by "bench jobs," in which individual workers were responsible for making all parts of a subas-sembly (e.g., water pump and washer control panel). The bench jobs pro-vided greater task variety, increased worker discretion and responsibility, and increased the feeling of attachment to the final product. Conant and Kilbridge determined that bench jobs offered improvements in the quality of the final product and cost savings; the cost savings were largely due to job enlargement increasing the amount of productive time workers spent on their tasks. On the assembly line, much of the time spent was unproductive because workers needed to wait for other pieces of the assembly to be com-pleted before they could do their own work. Job enlargement cut down on the coordination costs that specialization entailed and improved the expe-rience of work for those on the front line of manufacturing.[22]

The evidence for job enlargement was far from definitive, however. Job enlargement interventions were largely studied via case studies of firms that changed their work methods rather than via controlled experiments (Lawler, Hackman, and Kaufman 1973; Hackman and Lawler 1971; Hulin and Blood 1968). Despite the purported successes, the bulk of evidence failed to support the implementation of job enlargement programs across the industry. But even as job enlargement programs were unable to gain popularity, alternative approaches to resisting task specialization in the manufacturing industry continued to be proposed. Job enrichment programs, for example, specifically focused on increasing the level of responsibility of frontline manufacturing workers, giving them some control over their job arrangements and allowing for the exercise of initiative (see, e.g., Lawler, Hackman, and Kaufman 1973; K. O. Alexander 1975; Chung and Ross 1977). While firms were experimenting with redesigning manufacturing jobs, scientists were strengthening theories on job redesign and intrinsic motivation, further underlining that the intentional broadening of job tasks could be justified on a scientific basis (Lawler 1969).

Of the many job redesign initiatives that gained prominence in the later decades of the twentieth century, the most famous is probably "flexible specialization" (Piore and Sabel 1984). Much like its predecessors, flexible specialization involved intervening in the job design process with the aim of broadening the tasks of frontline manufacturing workers. For Michael J. Piore and Charles F. Sabel, the excessive level of task specialization within the manufacturing industry was responsible for sluggish production in the United States: the lack of flexibility in production meant that businesses were slow to respond to market forces, and other countries with more flexible work arrangements were capturing market share. The solution was flexible specialization, in which frontline manufacturing workers were expected to be flexible enough to shift across jobs insofar as this was necessary. Workers would need to have a broad set of skills to make such flexibility possible.

In promoting flexible specialization, Piore and Sabel call back to many of the specialization-reducing initiatives that firms introduced over the course of the twentieth century, revealing that the tensions produced by task specialization have long been evident in the manufacturing industry. The development of alternative, more flexible work arrangements remains a feature of the science of manufacturing up to the present day (Appelbaum et al. 2000; Kalleberg 2003).

Public Law 91-596

The accident problem in manufacturing had also not gone away. Increased attention to safety on the factory floor, alongside an expansion of job tasks to encompass safety-promoting interventions, had created dramatically improved working conditions for manufacturing workers (Stout and Linn 2002). In the rationalized firm, these interventions had been justified by reference to reduced worker costs, reduced stoppage time, and improved production (e.g., see Hagglund 1981). But attention to safety was inevitably patchy across the manufacturing industries, and by the early 1960s there were worrying signs that working conditions were becoming increasingly dangerous as labor demands increased during the Vietnam War (C. Noble 1986: chap. 2). The use of the law to encourage safety in manufacturing had been a theme of workplace activism for many decades (e.g., see Eastman 1910), but as working conditions deteriorated, the calls for legal intervention grew stronger. Wildcat strikes and broader labor organizing around the safety problem increased the pressure on the federal government to act (C. Noble 1986: chap. 3; Rosner and Markowitz 2020).

Congress passed, first, the Coal Mine Health and Safety Act of 1969, followed a year later by the Occupational Safety and Health (OSH) Act of 1970. The justification given for government intervention was

> to assure so far as possible every working man and woman in the Nation safe and healthful working conditions and to preserve our human resources—(1) by encouraging employers and employees in their efforts to reduce the number of occupational safety and health hazards at their places of employment, and to stimulate employers and employees to institute new and to perfect existing programs for providing safe and healthful working conditions; (2) by providing that employers and employees have separate but dependent responsibilities and rights with respect to achieving safe and healthful working conditions. (OSH Act 1970: Congressional Findings and Purpose)

Both employers and employees, then, were required to participate in improving safety in the workplace. During this period, several further acts

were passed that had important implications for the manufacturing industry and work tasks. The National Environmental Policy Act (1969) and the
associated establishment of the Environmental Protection Agency (1970)
required firms to comply with new environmental standards, while the
Consumer Product Safety Act (1972) developed safety standards for consumer goods and required firms to attest to their compliance with these
standards (Fitzsimmons 1973; Patton and Butler 1972).

The OSH Act and others largely placed the compliance burden on
firms and regulatory agencies, but employees saw the effects of these legislative interventions on their work tasks. The most obvious effect was on
worker training: after the passage of the OSH Act, grants for training
workers were made available under the New Directions program of the
Occupational Safety and Health Administration (OSHA), and employers
instituted training programs for both existing and new employees.
Unions also invested in safety training, on the basis that workers were
best placed to observe the hazards in their workplace and to request assistance from OSHA or the union (Wegman, Boden, and Levenstein 1975;
Tobey and Revitte 1981; Luskin, Wooding, and Levenstein 1988). The OSH
Act sanctioned unannounced inspections from OSHA personnel.[23] In one
of the many texts published to aid employers in OSH Act compliance,
readers were advised that "maximum safety is attained by the combination of safe facilities and people properly trained in safe procedures"
(Anderson 1975: vii). Basic training included instruction in first aid, classroom and standard operating procedures, and safety regulations and
their enforcement.

As with prior interventions in the industry, the supervisor was first
in line to ensure that safety regulations were followed and that workers
would be safe. Although many firms employed safety specialists—
including safety engineers, safety managers, and training managers (see
Dobbin and Sutton 1998)—the supervisors were again responsible for
many of the tasks related to safety that the rationalized firm introduced.
The National Safety Council, in its *Supervisors Safety Manual* (tellingly
subtitled *Better Production without Injury and Waste from Accidents*),
writes:

> The key man in an occupational hazard control program is the first-line
> supervisor. Not only is he the direct link between top management and

the work force, but on his shoulders rests the responsibility for quality job training, development of good safety attitudes, and detection of unsafe conditions and practices. Not only must he know the techniques of human relations, but he must know the fundamentals of accident prevention. He himself must be trained if he is to review hazard control information with his workers, check personal protective equipment and safety devices and investigate accidents occurring in his area. (National Safety Council 1973: v)[24]

Similarly, the National Institute for Occupational Safety and Health (NIOSH), in its advice to firms about compliance with the OSH Act, describes the "new concept of safety as one of the inseparable parts of the supervisor's job" (1973: 686; see also Olishifski and McElroy 1970: chap. 20; Hannaford 1976).

Two important safety tasks reflected broad changes in the nature of scientific understanding that are associated with the probabilistic revolution. The first was the frame of mind that supervisors were expected to cultivate in employees, labeled "hazard identification" by those in the safety field. Workers were expected not simply to avoid accidents but to see their antecedents well before an accident became likely. As one training manual described the process,

> Projective thinking helps us to get into the habit of always observing what is happening around us in the plant and determining the worst regarding possible accidents. All supervisors have an important responsibility to anticipate and visualize what accidents might occur, what the results would be, and take action to remove the hazards. (Anderson 1975: 180–181)

In contrast to earlier versions of the "safety mindset," in which workers were expected to always remind themselves that safety was a priority, here workers were asked to consider the potential outcomes of activities and to remember that current events could set into motion a causal chain that might result in an accident. The second task was recordkeeping. Taylor's interventions had encouraged the use of records in manufacturing work, but the OSH Act and its legislative companions imposed stringent recordkeeping requirements on firms. An important reason for recordkeeping

JOB ANALYSIS Instruction Standard	DIVISION ...... Engineering DEPARTMENT ....Maintenance...... OCCUPATION ...Painter.........	JOB ANALYZED ...Painting a Chair DATE EFFECTIVE . Nov. 1. 1970......... CODE NO. EM-72

SEQUENCE OF STEPS (NOT TOO FINE OR TOO BROAD)	KEY QUALITY OR PRODUCTION FACTORS (CLEARLY TELL WHAT TO DO AND WHY)	KEY SAFETY FACTORS (CLEARLY TELL WHAT TO DO AND WHY)
1. Select work area.	1. Should be as dust-free as possible to prevent dust from sticking to painted surface while wet. This can damage finish, requiring re-work.	1. Area should be well ventilated so that toxic fumes do not accumulate, possibly causing serious illness.
2. Bring tools and supplies to work area.	2. Have all needed tools at hand before starting to avoid delay.	2. Be sure all cans of thinner, paint remover, and paint are tightly closed when not in use to minimize the dangers from fire or explosion.
3. Prepare work area.	3. Place chair on newspapers to avoid delays caused by cleaning up spills.	3. Use at least six layers of paper to absorb spilled paint remover and paint. Both of these can cause extensive damage to the floor.
4. Remove old paint from chair with paint remover.	4. Be sure all paint is removed from cracks and crevices so final finish will be uniform. Otherwise, re-sanding may be necessary to smooth out rough surfaces.	4. Follow directions on paint remover container and do not allow smoking or open flame in area to prevent fire or explosion.
5. Sand chair with sandpaper.	5. Sand all surfaces with OO sandpaper until smooth to the touch for best results. Wipe off dust. Dust left on surface will make finish rough, requiring re-sanding.	5. Gloves should be worn while sanding to prevent abrasions and splinters.
6. Apply first coat of paint.	6. Coat of paint should be light and applied with even strokes to minimize brush marks for most attractive results.	6. Follow directions on paint container. Same as #4, NO SMOKING OR OPEN FLAME.
7. Apply second coat of paint.	7. Same as #6.	7. Same as #6.
8. Clean up area and tools	8. Clean brushes thoroughly in paint thinner; then shake out thinner. Paint left in brush can ruin brush for further use if it is allowed to harden.	8. Dispose of all papers and wipe any spilled paint from floor or other surfaces. Papers left on floor can present fire or tripping hazards.
9. Store tools and supplies.	9. Brushes should be hung up by the handle to keep weight off the bristles. The weight of the brush on the bristles can deform them and ruin the brush.	9. All paint, thinner, and remover must be tightly sealed both to preserve them and to prevent escape of fumes which could cause fire or explosion.

Fig. 6-4 Job analysis safety form, for compliance with OSH Act.

SOURCE: Job analysis—Instruction Standard (Form), NIOSH 1973: 685, fig. 47-1.

was that high-quality data collection allowed OSHA to undertake analysis that could be used to predict future accidents and make workplaces even safer (e.g., see Stout and Linn 2002; OSHA 1977: chap. 3). OSHA could impose heavy fines for inadequate recordkeeping. Again, the burden of accident recording was placed on supervisors, who were on the front line and were therefore well placed to write up the accident soon after it happened (National Institute for Occupational Safety and Health 1973: 688).

An example of how the new emphasis on safety and hazard prevention shaped work tasks can be found in Figure 6-4. The figure is taken from NIOSH's guidance, which emphasizes the importance of the supervisor carrying out a full job analysis to identify potential hazards. For each work task listed in the sequence of steps, there is also a quality control or production factor for the step and a set of safety considerations and associated tasks. As can be seen in the safety considerations, each task is made substantially more complicated when safety is considered: personal protective equipment is introduced, additional tasks are needed to guarantee the safety of each step, and there is an emphasis on following written directions when potentially hazardous chemicals are in play. A more subtle change can be seen in the "hazard identification" mode of thinking that the job analysis encourages. The causal logic behind each precaution is laid out, linking the actions of the worker to the outcome and to possible safety problems at each step.

Although compliance with the OSH Act was assessed within the workplace, an interesting feature of compliance guidance and advice was the extent to which *non*workplace activities were possible safety risks (Anderson 1975: chap. 14; NIOSH 1973: chap. 2; National Safety Council 1973: chap. 4). Much as we saw in the medical field, where the proposed causes of ill health gradually expanded to include psychological and then social factors, activities outside the workplace were of interest to those identifying potential hazards. In training manuals, firms were encouraged to think about nonworkplace accidents as an additional threat to productivity, justifying the firm's interest in improving nonoccupational safety. Poster displays and training courses on safe driving, accidents in the home, and fire prevention were all seen as appropriate interventions for the safety-conscious firm. Such interventions would reduce nonoccupational accidents, reduce absenteeism, and feed into higher levels of productivity for the firm.

As observers of contemporary US politics will appreciate, the OSH Act and others are a frequent target of ire for Republican politicians, who express worries about excessive regulation (see C. Noble 1986; Michaels 2008; Michaels and Barab 2020; on the current challenges faced by OSHA, see Rosner and Markowitz 2020). The long-term future of health and safety regulation is likely to remain politically contentious, but in the absence of a strong welfare state, firms will continue to have productivity incentives that push in the direction of improving safety inside and outside the workplace (Dobbin and Sutton 1998; see Chapter 7 for further discussion of this point).

A PARADOX, BY FIAT

> Industry in these days is entirely given over to self-improvement. It has incorporated in itself the results of scientific discovery to such an extent that it becomes difficult in certain areas to distinguish the practical or industrial from the other type of research. (Mayo 1927: 19)

Elton Mayo was a true believer in the power of science to improve the lives of manufacturing workers. In common with many other scientists over the course of the twentieth century, he saw the relationship between industry and scientific research to be a mark of modern, rationalized production (Mayo 1930).

Mayo's conviction that the manufacturing industry should be science based was far from unique. The search for more efficient production had, throughout the twentieth century, encouraged the leaders of the manufacturing industry to turn to science. Just as we see in other specialized fields of science, the science of manufacturing expands over time and does so in ways that reflect broad trends in scientific reasoning. Taylor's focus on machine reliability and worker efficiency is augmented by the science of human relations, extending the interest of managers to the psychological and social context of workers. Investment in preventive activities similarly increases over the period.

While there are broad similarities between the manufacturing industry and the other industries considered, there are also important differences. First, unlike the industries of medicine, law enforcement, and education, the manufacturing industry experienced periods in the long twentieth century when the logic of specialization definitively won out. Frontline manufacturing workers saw their range of job tasks reduced as more efficient machines were introduced into the industry. Other changes (e.g., concerns about safety) mitigated the narrowing produced by automation, and other workers (e.g., the supervisors responsible for ensuring safety on the factory floor) saw their job tasks increase, but there was nevertheless a version of Smithian simplification in play in the early decades of the twentieth century. It was only later, when the science of human relations gained influence, that the rationalized manufacturing workers saw their job tasks increase.

Second, insofar as we see evidence of the rationalization of manufacturing occupations, the evidence is consistent with a process of rationalization *by fiat*. Task specialization was imposed on manufacturing workers, partly via the deliberate narrowing of job tasks by engineers, who saw specialization as offering the promise of higher productivity, and partly via the introduction of machinery that would capture parts of the worker's job. Similarly, it was engineers and engineer-managers who were responsible for feeding the contents of manufacturing science into the work tasks of frontline manufacturing workers.

Regardless of how the rationalization of manufacturing occupations and the wider industry was arrived at, the combination of the rationalized occupation with changes in the content of science nonetheless brought about the paradox of specialization for frontline manufacturing workers, and particularly for the supervisors on the factory floor. But a third important difference in the case of manufacturing is that the paradox came about not because the output was discovered to be more complicated than previously understood but rather because the *process* by which the output was produced was understood to be more complicated. Highly specialized workers were more prone to fatigue and produced less. Workers isolated from their coworkers were similarly unproductive. Workers who were prone to accidents were more likely to be injured or to cause lost time on the factory floor. To increase output, therefore, it was necessary to address these problems via the addition of work tasks. Whatever Taylor might have dreamed with respect to the ideal manufacturing worker, increased productivity was not to be found in the ever more specialized frontline worker who was an addendum to the machine. Instead, increased productivity was to be found when employers recognized that machines required human workers and that human workers were not machines.

CHAPTER SEVEN

The Fracturing

The field of science is unlimited; its material is endless, every group of natural phenomena, every phase of social life, every stage of past or present development is material for science. The unity of all science consists alone in its method, not in its material. . . . This extension of the material of science into regions where our great-grandfathers could see nothing at all, or where they would have declared human knowledge impossible, is one of the most remarkable features of modern progress. The universe grows ever larger as we learn to understand more of our own corner of it. (Pearson 1892: 15–17)

The universe has continued to grow larger since Karl Pearson first wrote these words in the late nineteenth century. Science has cast light on dark corners and extended into new regions of investigation. We have seen possibilities in science that our great-grandparents could not imagine. Science has produced vast bodies of knowledge, in a diverse range of fields, unified by the language of probability.

In this book, I have aimed to show how the growth of probabilistic science combined with the rationalization of society to fundamentally change the division of labor and the nature of work. There has been a widespread assumption that, over time, the work carried out in occupations will become increasingly specialized and workers will take on an ever-narrower range of tasks. This assumption has proved to be wrong. The case studies in this book have shown evidence of a quite different process operating to determine the division of labor: a paradox of specialization, in which specialists are required to take on a broader range of tasks.

THE PARADOX OF SPECIALIZATION

The paradox of specialization arises because two key forces collide to produce an unexpected result. The first force is rationalization, a thoroughgoing cultural transformation that entails the institutionalization of means-ends reasoning and the adoption of universal rules to guide behavior. The second is scientific development, and particularly the type of scientific development witnessed over the course of the ongoing probabilistic revolution.

Over the past 150 years, we have seen the emergence of what I have labeled the "rationalized occupation," in which occupational outputs are increasingly pursued in line with standardized and scientized procedures. Rationalization represents a break with tradition, habit, and rules of thumb. The rationalized occupation is also a specialized occupation because specialization in a given output tends to be optimizing.

The case study chapters revealed the emergence of the rationalized occupation, the rationalized firm, and the rationalized industry. I examined four industries and their dominant occupations and found evidence of the increasing rationalization of occupational practices in each. Some occupations rationalized early. The medical industry and its dominant occupation of physician, for example, relied on scientific evidence and standardized rules to determine job practices even at the beginning of the period considered here. Any deviations from rationalization—such as a reliance on rules of thumb or complaints that medicine was missing elements of art or humanity—were modest and inconsequential for job practices. In contrast, other industries and occupations were much less rationalized at the end of the nineteenth century. In some cases, this was because of active resistance to rationalization; in others, it was because there was simply a lack of systematized knowledge to be drawn from. Teaching, law enforcement, and especially manufacturing work were more reliant on rules of thumb and traditional job practices. In all of these occupations, there were concerted efforts over the following 150 years to rationalize the work being carried out, by introducing standards and explicit links to scientific work. In the case of teaching and law enforcement, the rationalization was relatively endogenous, being driven by actors closely involved in the occupations. But in the case of manufacturing occupations, the process was rather one of rationalization *by fiat,* as owners and managers forced rationalized practices on frontline manufacturing occupations and the wider industry.

Rationalization tightens the link between scientific outputs and occupational practices. Scientifically backed practices become institutionalized in occupational training regimes, licensing regulations, and standards for practice. Within medicine, for example, standardized training and standards of practice placed science at the heart of the physician occupation and the wider medical industry. In law enforcement, science was integrated via recommended practices and new standards, while state and federal government monies were made available in support of science-backed initiatives. Government actors were also able to directly introduce science-based practices in some industries. In the education industry, for example, the federal government determined that robust scientific evidence would be required in order to implement new policies within the sector. And governments increasingly introduced science-based legislation—for example, with respect to public health or safety policy—that would require at least some occupational practices to comport with scientific work.

As the rationalized occupation emerged, changes in science became ever more consequential for the character of work. In addition to changes in the raw quantity of science, there were changes in the *nature* of scientific work. The probabilistic revolution in scientific thought, which began in the early nineteenth century, had two important consequences for the type of science produced. First, probabilism allowed for greater model complexity. Within probabilistic models, it is possible to account for multiple mechanisms that cause an outcome and capture much more of the variation existing within human populations. The common language of probability makes it possible for results from one field of scientific work to be pulled into another, such that biological, economic, physical, psychological, and social mechanisms can be compared and jointly modeled. Second, probabilism made it possible to build more plausible causal models and to predict what might happen in the future with reasonable accuracy. The increasing popularity of causal inference techniques and algorithmic approaches to causal modeling are thus but the most recent incarnation of a much longer-term trend in scientific work. Strong predictive models further raised the possibility of prevention; in other words, it became feasible to intervene to prevent a bad outcome from occurring.

I have shown that both types of changes were present in the scientific literature of relevance to medicine, law enforcement, education, and manufacturing. In each of these broad fields of inquiry, scientific models increased in complexity over the past 150 years. All of the fields considered here saw increasing diversity with respect to the mechanisms called on in scientific work. The science of education, for example, integrated work on health, psychology, and sociology over the course of the last century. Indeed, one particularly notable change was the introduction of psychological and then sociological mechanisms to explain outcomes across a very wide range of industry-relevant fields. Medicine, which had previously focused on addressing the biological roots of disease, became attuned to the psychological and sociological causes of disease. Criminology moved from an account of the causes of crime rooted primarily in biology and abnormal psychology to an account rooted in sociology. Even the science of engineering showed increasing interest in social mechanisms, and from the mid-twentieth century onward, the engineering literature includes discussions of human relations, teamwork, and worker motivation. Although it was the science underlying human outputs that witnessed the most extreme increase in complexity over the past century, the manufacturing case study confirms that any occupational output that depended on human workers would see the influence of a broader set of scientific disciplines.

The development of the science of prevention was no less impressive. Toward the end of the nineteenth century, for example, the science of medicine was strongly oriented toward identifying appropriate treatments for disease and understanding how diseases were transmitted. Over the past 150 years, mechanistic and predictive models have become dominant, and there is a special interest in understanding both the proximate and distal causes of disease and identifying those most at risk. Similar trends toward predictive models are evident in criminology, where interest lies in identifying risk factors for crime, and in the science of education, which prioritizes the identification of factors that might interfere with learning. The development of a science of prevention has been least prominent within manufacturing, but even here, the science of safety indicates a strong interest in identifying risks before they arise.

When science expands and changes, the rationalized occupation is required to take account of an ever more complex and growing body of science relevant to its specialized output. In the course of their work, physicians were obliged to consider not just the biological causes of disease but also the patient's psychological state and social condition. Teachers and law enforcement officers similarly saw the benefits of addressing the broader causes of poor performance and deviance. Teachers embraced student-centered learning and became sensitive to the cultural and social needs of their students. Police officers increasingly engaged with communities and with young people, aiming to mitigate the social causes of crime. Within manufacturing, new work processes emphasized the human and social side of work: managers were charged with motivating employees, and frontline workers took on new tasks designed to mitigate monotony and comply with worker-focused regulations. The broadening scope of the occupations considered here was legitimated because a rationalized occupation was required to take account of new discoveries that would better secure the objectives of the occupation.

The science of prediction and prevention offered further opportunities for the paradox of specialization to emerge. As predictive models clarified the likely results of changing given inputs, workers were given a plausible route to tailor inputs to produce the outputs desired. Wholly preventive activities could also be built into the set of work tasks. Law enforcement officers could reasonably intervene in communities before crimes occurred if doing so reduced overall levels of crime. Physicians could introduce routine blood pressure measurements at every appointment if doing so meant that strokes and heart disease could be prevented in the future. If the identification of multiple mechanisms producing outputs broadened the list of possible inputs, prevention broadened the timescale over which intervening in inputs was possible and desirable. The science of prediction and prevention again pushed in the direction of broader occupational purviews and an increasing number of job tasks.

Rationalization and scientific development together deliver the increasing functional complexity that characterizes the history of many occupations over the long twentieth century. It is the paradox of specialization that accounts for the unexpected result of increasing task burdens across the occupational structure. It is the paradox of specialization that accounts for the widening array of occupations required to produce industry outputs. And it is the paradox of specialization that accounts for the long-term increase in job tasks in medicine, law enforcement, education, and manufacturing.

Time and Motion

The paradox of specialization results from the interplay of dynamic cultural forces. But it was far from inevitable that the paradox would arise.

The particular empirical findings discussed here are the result of the forces of rationalization and scientific development operating in concert. Had one or the other of these forces not been in place, the paradox would have been interrupted.

But for the changes in science, the effects of growing rationalization on job tasks would have been limited. In and of itself, growing rationalization might be expected to *simplify* job tasks; after all, the logic of specialization implies that productivity is maximized when functional complexity is reduced. We see the triumph of this logic in the manufacturing industry of the early twentieth century, when frontline manufacturing occupations were rationalized *by fiat*. In the service of increasing productivity, the functional complexity of some frontline manufacturing occupations was reduced, because task specialization was assumed to offer the greatest returns. This was a period in which the science of manufacturing was largely focused on machine development, and the logic of specialization therefore dominated. It was only later, when the science of manufacturing indicated that new tasks were required to maximize output, that the functional complexity of front-line occupations increased.

Likewise, but for the changes in rationalization, changes in science would not have had nearly as much influence on job tasks. The findings of scientific endeavors are only consequential insofar as occupational actors attend to those findings, and rationalization was the mechanism through which a tight link was established between scientific outputs and occupations. Because science is the revered source of guidance in a rationalized system, occupational practices came to be based on what the science said. When science made the prevention of bad outcomes possible, it was rationalization that meant that occupational actors would attend to this science and build prevention into the set of job tasks.

With a few key changes in history, one could imagine rationalization and science developing on quite different timescales over the past 150 years. If the emergence of the rationalized occupation had significantly predated the growth of probabilism within science, the logic of specialization might have operated to dramatically narrow the range of outputs pursued in an occupation before science opened up a range of potential new job tasks. In contrast, if the rationalized occupation had emerged more slowly, while probabilistic science developed unhindered, we might have seen stability in the task demands of occupations because what happened in science would not have been seen as relevant. Only when science *is* seen as relevant will scientific evidence be brought in to guide job practices.

The Complexity of Explanation

I have sought to identify the leading causes of the increase in functional complexity. But the world is messy, and leading causes can be no more or less than that: even leading causes are unlikely to be the *only* causes. Although I have highlighted two cultural forces—rationalization and scientific development—as being responsible for increasing functional complexity, it is essential not to lose sight of other cultural and noncultural forces that had an impact. I briefly discuss in this section some of these other forces—specifically, the accretion of new objectives, growing individualism and social hierarchy differentiation, economic interests, and demographic change.

I begin by considering the accretion of new objectives as an account that is not well explained by the paradox of specialization. There is no doubt that accretion of this sort is responsible for some of the observed increases in functional complexity. During World War II, for example, police officers were required to guard infrastructure and prevent industrial sabotage, while medical personnel developed techniques to treat battlefield injuries and the after-effects of wartime service (e.g., see Barr and Podolsky 2020). After the war, there was pressure on the education industry to reduce the chances of another war by training students in the spirit of international cooperation. In Chapter 5, on the education industry, further examples of the accretion of new objectives were provided. As education was increasingly seen as valuable preparation for work, there was interest in adding tasks that would help students find appropriate jobs. The emphasis on vocational education at the beginning of the twentieth century encouraged schools to include manual training in their offerings. Later in the twentieth century, guidance counselors were introduced to ensure a good match between students and jobs. Likewise, the political interest in international economic competitiveness toward the end of the twentieth century led to the accountability era, when standardized testing was used to evaluate schools, and teachers were therefore incentivized to "teach to the tests."

The dynamic of "ends accretion" has been comprehensively examined in bureaucracies, most notably by James Q. Wilson, who argued that government agencies accumulate "contextual goals," and that these contextual goals have "risen dramatically" over time (1989: 12). Recent discussions of the concept of "everythingism" have revived concerns that policymakers are increasingly "distracted" from their original goals, and that "every proposal, project or policy is [treated as] a means for promoting every national objective, all at the same time" (Joe Hill 2025: 6). While some of the new objectives added to occupations might be interpreted as new formulations of already existing ends (e.g., what it means to produce a well-educated child), it is clear that other objectives are added with less regard for the original aims of the occupation (e.g., some of the wartime tasks of police and fire personnel).[1] The distinction between the paradox of specialization and ends accretion hinges on whether or not a plausible case can be made that the new end is a reconceptualization or reasonable extension of the occupation's aims. If scientists straightforwardly integrate the new end into their work, and occupational actors follow the science to determine their job tasks, the paradox of specialization will still arise. But if occupations take on tasks to serve entirely new ends, the increase in functional complexity must be attributed to other factors.[2]

It also seems likely that some changes in the functional complexity of occupations are due to the influence of other cultural forces, with two forces frequently discussed in the sociological literature standing out as being potentially relevant. First, we might suspect that growing individualism will increase the demands on workers, because those in human-centered occupations are increasingly required to take on job tasks to demonstrate that the "customer" is of utmost importance. Theories of "personhood," for example, emphasize the influence of individualism in the contemporary United States; empirical studies within this theoretical tradition often point to changes in the education industry and the development of the "whole child" approach as illustrations of individualism's growing reach (e.g., Frank and Meyer 2002; Furuta 2017; Wotipka et al. 2023). The case of education is a particularly good fit for personhood theory, even if the evidence from the case study chapters would suggest that much of the occupational interest in the whole person can in fact be attributed to earlier scientific developments that described the gains to productivity that would be afforded by attending to outputs (and workers) as people.[3] But growing individualism is no doubt an additional cultural force that should be considered as a contributor to the changing task demands of human-centered occupations.

The second cultural force might be termed "social hierarchy differentiation." Although the United States once had a small and integrated elite, the society gradually developed a host of specialized elite sectors, a development that means that incumbents of some elite occupations do not as frequently play a generic elite role. In the present day, teachers are not expected to invite students into their home, and physicians are not expected to use their position as "great and learned men" to oversee local governmental bodies. The decline in traditional social hierarchies, and the subsequent differentiation into more specialized social hierarchies, has been responsible for a decline in functional complexity within occupations that would previously have afforded workers some status within the community.[4]

One essential noncultural factor to examine, of concern to all scholars of work and the division of labor, is economic interests. For our purposes, economic interests are most relevant because they affect how science developed and was adopted; what masquerades as pure science is often instead the scientization of the priorities of economic elites. This "endogeneity" account is not so much an alternative account as a recognition of the many complex and power-laden ways that scientific priorities emerge. David F. Noble (1977), for example, has described how the manufacturing industry's adoption of technology went hand in hand with the development of corporate capitalism: economic interests determined how science would be directed and adopted within the industrial sector (see also Braverman 1974). Noble's observation that science has been shaped by corporate capitalism and that corporate firms have adopted scientific technologies in line with their interests is clearly on the mark. In the case study chapters, I did not discuss in any detail how far science was influenced by the interests of capital or power, but it is surely the case that scientific progress in these fields was not independent of economic factors. In the science of education, for example, the politically determined aims of education were taken up by the educational scientists, who swiftly integrated the concerns of the politicians as the concerns of science. The science of medicine has been encouraged in its pursuit of new drugs by the corporate funding of pharmaceutical development and the priorities of insurance companies. And the degree to which scientific work is adopted within industries, firms, and occupations is likely to be similarly influenced by the interests of capital and power. The rise of artificial intelligence is an obvious case in point because no one could deny the powerful effects of corporate interests on how the science develops and ultimately affects job tasks (e.g., see Acemoglu and Johnson 2023; see also Fourcade and Healy 2024). This line of scholarship is, however, in no way at odds with the paradox. It is simply a recognition that science itself is embedded in the economy and affected by economic interests. This does not undermine the key point that—whatever lies behind the development of probabilistic science—it then has the effect of increasing functional complexity.

Another noncultural factor that lies behind the paradox is demography and the associated social change. Demographic changes have both created demand for certain types of work and revealed problems that scientists have worked to solve. One contemporary example can be found in the medical industry, as it gears up to manage the baby boomers' transition into elder care. Psychiatrists are being urged to train up in geriatric psychiatry, and there are calls to develop knowledge and infrastructure to manage the higher rates of substance abuse observed in the baby boom generation (Jeste 2000; Patterson and Jeste 1999). In the early part of the twentieth century, high rates of immigration and growing urbanization were the social changes of most concern. The education industry was charged with managing the growing number of English language learners in this period and in imbuing the social skills necessary to encourage cooperation in urban settings. The pressures of urbanization were also felt in law enforcement, which was pushed to consider the possible disequilibrating effects of the decline of small-town rural life and the population growth in the cities. Changes in the racial composition of some areas and protests around Civil Rights also led to new tasks for police officers and the wider law enforcement industry. Thus, demographic changes have both led to the development of new specialist occupations and created new tasks within existing occupations and thus complicated them. In most cases, such demographic forces also led to the development of new types of scientific knowledge (e.g., new pedagogical approaches for "diversity and inclusion" teaching), with the implication that, here again, it is mainly a matter of recognizing that science is embedded in a larger demographic setting that affects its development.

These accounts make it clear that the paradox of specialization operated within the context of all manner of demographic forces, cultural and economic forces, and idiosyncratic events (e.g., World War II). In some cases, these forces are best understood as complements to the paradox, as they operated quite independently from the laws of rationalization and scientization. In other cases, they affected how science developed, and they may therefore be seen as antecedents.

Micro, Meso, Macro

The theory and evidence presented in this book have largely been at the macro level, and the focus has been on broad patterns and trends in functional complexity in occupations, firms, and industries. I have talked in general terms about "occupational actors," without interrogating who these actors are, why they make the decisions that they do, and which micro- and meso-level processes might be of importance in helping the paradox of specialization come to fruition. But previous work on the division of labor has underscored that changes in task burdens arise through interaction among micro-, meso-, and macro-level processes (Abbott 1988). And although the central occupational actor is the worker, individual workers may in fact have little control over broader occupational purviews. Rather than workers themselves controlling the tasks they undertake, the key occupational actors are likely to be professional organizations, unions, employers, and politicians.

The extent to which an industry or occupation is controlled or funded by the state is one factor in determining which actors are involved in accepting or imposing a broadened industrial or occupational purview. In the case of the manufacturing industry, for example, the most important occupational actors at the beginning of the twentieth century were the owners and managers of factories because they had the power to impose work practices on frontline manufacturing workers. As union density increased through the midcentury, unions became important occupational actors too, and wage negotiation processes gave manufacturing unions a role in determining the functional complexity of frontline occupations. Later, as state and federal governments increasingly adopted regulations designed to reduce injury from accidents and protect worker health and well-being, they became actors capable of imposing a broadened purview on the manufacturing industry and the occupations within it. These governmental actors were not occupational actors per se, but their roles allowed them to both impose regulations that would directly affect working practices and intervene directly in workplaces to put a halt to noncompliant practices.

In contrast, even from the beginning of the period considered here, the government was a much more central occupational actor in the education industry. Funding for public schools is provided primarily by local and state governments, with the federal government also contributing a small percentage through special programs (e.g., Title I grants). This gives governmental actors enormous power to shape the tasks of the education industry and teachers. Discussions by political actors about the appropriate aims of education, and attempts to introduce new tasks to serve those aims (e.g., training in democracy), provide one example of how this power might be used. Another is the takeoff in special educational needs provisions, which, although motivated by scientific work on the "whole child," was strongly supported via federal government policy and funding. Similarly, governmental funding of the law enforcement industry has given political actors substantial control over the tasks of police officers. Federal funding, for example, underpinned some of the preventive activities taken on by police officers in the 1960s and 1970s and facilitated the coordination among local police departments and other agencies. And during the Defund the Police protests, we saw politicians align themselves either for or against the movement by proposing changes to police budgets and job tasks (see, e.g., Phelps 2024).

It should be underlined that insofar as political actors have played a role in determining the functional complexity of occupations, their motivations in intervening are frequently rationalized and science based. Health and safety regulations are likely to have increased the functional complexity of all occupations because new job tasks are required of workers to comply with the regulations. The motivation for introducing health and safety legislation was partly a desire to institutionalize human rights (e.g., see Dobbin and Sutton 1998), but the legislative design process also entailed embracing the science of accident prevention and recognizing the burden on society of dealing with the consequences of workplace injuries. In both the education and law enforcement industries, sweeping government reports integrated and disseminated state-of-the-art science and proposed evidence-based policies that subsequently filtered down to the tasks taken on by industries, firms, and occupations.

Similar processes are at work within unions and professional organizations. These organizations, which set the expectations for appropriate practices within occupations and train or credential workers, are again conduits of rationalization and new developments within probabilistic science. It is often actors within these organizations that integrate new science and standards, which then become the basis for professional or union codes of conduct. Within the medical industry, professional codes of conduct are a key means through which science is integrated into practice: physicians are only licensed insofar as their work practices accord with science-based standards, and cases of malpractice are assessed with respect to compliance with those standards. In the manufacturing industry, unions have been key actors in assuring compliance with safety standards and in pushing for healthy workplaces (Malinowski, Minkler, and Stock 2015). To be sure, unions and professional organizations advocate changes in job practices even without a science-based rationale, but they are nevertheless vectors through which changes in science can be passed on to industries, firms, and occupations.

It is possible that individual workers will, over time, exert less and less influence over their job tasks relative to other occupational actors. As rationalization continues to march forward, there will likely be more emphasis on the development of formalized occupational knowledge systems and bureaucratic structures, and workers will increasingly be monitored to ensure compliance. Workers within the traditional professions (e.g., medicine and teaching) may experience less freedom in determining how to pursue their outputs and be more vulnerable to electronic monitoring designed to evaluate compliance with the most efficient job practices (for discussions of the effects of algorithmic rationalization, see Fourcade and Healy 2024; Lei and Kim 2024; Pugh 2024). In occupations outside of the traditional professions, rationalization will continue to be imposed on workers (by fiat), with compliance with desired practices again assessed via monitoring. We might predict a future in which each and every occupation is associated with a specific body of scientific knowledge that is built into bureaucracies and systems of practice. Although we are accustomed to assuming that there is a sharp division between professional and nonprofessional occupations, rationalization has already flattened out differences across occupational groups, and it is likely to continue to chip away at those differences that remain.

The paradox of specialization results from occupational purviews being widened because of changes in science, but one issue that the case study chapters opened up is the importance of "job task protection" activities. The policing occupation, for example, has benefited from administrative, financial, technological, and organizational changes that place significant burdens on occupations that might wish to compete for tasks. The research shows that nonprofit organizations and schools are successful at the task of crime prevention (Sharkey, Torrats-Espinosa, and Takyar 2017; Deming 2011), but these organizations are constrained in competing for "crime prevention" funding, given the difficulty in tying their activities to crime reduction in the eyes of the public and politicians. When combined with the state's monopoly over the means of violence, the state's ability to marshal other types of resources provides the police occupation with a uniquely high level of protection from competition. Within manufacturing, unions have similarly acted to protect job tasks, by carefully defining the tasks required in given occupations and preventing employers from deskilling occupations without extensive negotiation with the union. Organizational and bureaucratic changes represent a relatively opaque form of job task protection, but it is a form that may act as a restraining force on the division of labor. These mechanisms again highlight the importance of attending to the micro- and meso-level processes through which occupational purviews are negotiated and tasks are protected from potential competitors (see Abbott 1988).[5]

LIFE IN THE CAGE

I have characterized the development of industries and occupations over the past 150 years as being determined by the interplay of two forces: rationalization and the development of probabilistic science. In all four of the case studies presented here, I have found evidence for a paradox of specialization, in which specialists are required to take on an increasing range of tasks in order to deliver on occupational outputs. In this final section, I consider the implications of these findings for workers, industries, and society.

Specialist without Spirit

Classical predictions of how the division of labor would unfold envisioned increasing task specialization within jobs and occupations. Because functional complexity was expected to decline over time, discussions of the possible consequences of the division of labor focused on the degradation of work and worker alienation. But the paradox of specialization implies that workers are managing an *increase* in job tasks, which raises questions about how that increase is likely to affect workers' experiences of their jobs. If older sociological and economic work were accepted, the increase in tasks might be seen as an unmitigated good. From the point of view of the worker, increases in functional complexity should protect against monotony and, at least for some workers, also increase the sense of efficacy and meaningfulness in work. It is therefore useful to ask whether workers are in fact appreciating having jobs that are increasingly expanding with new challenges and scientifically grounded tools and methods. Or is the sociologist's dream better considered a nightmare, instead reminding us to be "careful what you wish for, lest it come true?" Because we are still in the midst of this grand social experiment, it is clearly too early to tell, but it is useful to discuss two warning signs that at least give pause.

One clear consequence of the takeoff in the number of tasks required to do a job well is that workers are overburdened. While burnout is often attributed to proximate causes (e.g., the pandemic), in fact it is arguably a direct consequence of the paradox of specialization. Burnout is prominently discussed in the industries of medicine, law enforcement, and teaching, and although the discussion is less prominent in manufacturing, the manufacturing industry in fact saw the biggest surge in workers quitting in the postpandemic "great resignation" (Long 2022). In some cases, increased functional complexity might be expected to lead to more rewarding jobs because it is challenging for human workers to work for long periods on a narrow range of tasks. The manufacturing industry has, at times, deliberately increased the functional complexity of frontline manufacturing occupations via "job enlargement" programs to make the jobs more appealing to workers. But in many cases, increased functional complexity simply makes the job more challenging to perform. This means that workers are likely to work longer hours, and they are more likely to experience an imbalance between work and family life. Multiple task demands may also produce worse occupational outcomes because human brains are poor at task switching: research shows that switching tasks frequently leads to slower and more error-prone task performance (Monsell 2003). Workers who rise to the challenge of performing all tasks required of them, then, are likely to burn out quicker and might also underperform in each task completed.

It is also likely that some workers are simply not able to meet the challenge of increased functional complexity. In this case, workers are aware of the number of tasks required to do the job well, but they cannot perform them all. Teachers cannot design a curriculum, center the student in their teaching, personalize learning content for each student, keep good records, and attend to all the student problems that might hinder learning. Physicians cannot diagnose disease, administer treatment, fill out patient records, consider the full range of problems that might cause disease, and intervene to address those problems. These tasks cannot all be performed well, and some cannot be performed at all in the time available. Research on bureaucracies and street-level bureaucrats has documented in some detail the overwhelming demands placed on frontline public service workers and the various strategies that workers use to manage those demands (e.g., see Lipsky 2010: chap. 7, 9–10). One worker response to the problem of being overburdened is to engage in "role-crafting," in which workers independently redefine their jobs to reduce task demands (e.g., see Bruning and Campion 2018). When, for example, a physician insists that a problem can only be addressed by a physician within a different specialty, this may have as much to do with role-crafting as with any concerns about jurisdiction. Although one response is to role-craft the problem away, another is to blame oneself for failing to do it all.

The second warning sign of interest is the increasing awareness of "moral injury" within the medical field (Dean and Talbot 2023). The concept is well illustrated in the following quote from a physician reported by NPR: "At Austin's CD Doyle clinic for people who are homeless . . . nearly every patient has unmet needs impacting their health: a man with a foot infection from wearing wet boots—his only shoes—too long; another young man, new to Austin, hearing voices because he is out of his antipsychotic medication; others needing surgery, follow-up with a specialist, transportation. I have to steel myself against overwhelming feelings of helplessness when I'm there, wanting to assist, not knowing how" (Doggett 2023). Physicians are inevitably faced with patients whose needs cannot be addressed by the physician alone. The science of medicine makes it clear that the health of such patients will surely suffer if these needs are not addressed, but the individual physician is not in a position to provide transportation, dry boots, or a home to all the patients who might need these resources. In the case of the medical industry, this type of moral injury is often exacerbated by the demands of insurance companies and the (in)affordability of health care. But many of those in human-centered occupations will face similar issues, and workers are often tasked with dealing with the failures of the welfare state (see Lipsky 2010: chap. 6). Police officers, for example, have long complained that they are required to address problems that arise from socioeconomic conditions over which they have no direct control (e.g., LAPD 1968; see also Hinton 2017). And teachers and school administrators have also been found to spend a great deal of time and effort managing the home conditions of students who are performing poorly at school (Gleit 2023). Across human-centered occupations, workers are confronted with problems that they cannot solve, in the full knowledge that failing to solve these problems will compromise the output that the occupation produces. This is a different kind of misery than the classical theorists predicted for specialized workers, but it is a misery all the same. Science has provided an understanding of the social causes of disease but not the tools with which to address those causes successfully. If physicians are allowed to prescribe an antidepressant but not a house to their homeless patient, it is hardly of use to the physician to know, via predictive science, that a house is what they really need.

If these downstream effects prove to be as debilitating as some have surmised, it is possible that measured labor productivity growth will decline. There are two ways in which this might happen. In the extreme version of productivity decline, the tools for getting the job done are grossly inadequate to the task, and workers are so demoralized that their total output declines. The physician, for example, does not even do a good job of prescribing antidepressants because they know that they should be doing so much more and are thoroughly demoralized as a result. The less extreme version predicts a decline in measured productivity but not a decline in the more overarching concept of societal health. Under this version, the modern physician does have at least some tools at their disposal that allow them to treat upstream causes, and they do a better job of helping patients as a result. Because they are focused on finding a house for their homeless client, they prescribe fewer antidepressants, and measured productivity thus declines. Even this outcome might be broadly

desirable. Better outputs are captured relatively poorly in standard productivity measures, and measures are also weak in capturing some of the
positive externalities produced by the rationalized occupation. Paul
Krugman (2023), for example, recently responded to concerns about
declining productivity in the construction sector (see Chapter 1) by
arguing that increased environmental, health, and safety regulation may
have reduced measured productivity growth but that present-day and
future generations are better served by cleaner air and a low rate of accidents (see Coyle 2025 for a detailed discussion of alternative measures of
economic progress).

The burnout effect also makes it difficult for people to rely on others.
Émile Durkheim (1893) stressed that a well-functioning division of labor
produces bonds of dependence among people: to survive in a modern
society, it is necessary to rely on others to produce goods and services that
one cannot produce oneself. Insofar as workers are overwhelmed and
unable to perform effectively, it may be more difficult to rely on others, and
an individual's trust in the wider society might be betrayed. One hypoth-
esis about why the years after the pandemic have been so stressful is that a
dynamic of this type has been in play (on stress, see American Psychological Association 2023). The pandemic imposed additional tasks on
workers and made existing tasks more challenging to perform, with the
effect that service quality declined and customer frustration rose (Hambley and Springle 2023). Not being able to rely on those around us may
have increased stress and reduced our feeling of closeness to our community, with potentially long-term consequences for social trust and collective attachment.

A related problem arises insofar as many different occupations are
addressing the same problems and performing very similar tasks. As it
stands, for example, both doctors and teachers must pay attention to the
home environment because both health and educational attainment will be
affected if there are problems in the home. In such circumstances, both the
doctor and the teacher might work hard to improve the home environment,
which raises the possibility of the effort being wasted by both parties. If, for
example, a social worker could have intervened to improve the home environment, the jobs of both the doctor and the teacher would have been made
easier. Once again, being let down by others is likely to affect levels of social
trust and cooperation. The paradox of specialization exaggerates this

general problem of coordination with other occupations, for it is far easier to tolerate poor-quality work when that work does not have consequences for one's own output.

How, then, could these potential negative outcomes be avoided? One plausible path forward entails institutionalizing the incipient "social responses" that are already in play and that prove to have a strong evidentiary foundation (e.g., see Jackson 2020). If, for example, a person who is unhoused has a doctor's appointment, we could imagine an alternative world in which the doctor can in fact refer them to on-site housing in which they can stay until social services builds a comprehensive plan for them. This is hardly far-fetched: the total cost of building such housing is no higher than the cost of equipping hospitals with a bank of cutting-edge machinery, while the per-unit cost of providing a client with an apartment within such a development would be far less than that of many surgeries. In some hospitals such on-site housing developments already exist (Bhatt 2019). The same types of well-validated practices may gradually come to be implemented in other occupations. The employer may come to have a full range of preventive tactics to support worker welfare, including financial-training services, friendship circles, and well-developed career ladders that allow for mobility. The "environmental impact statement" for construction workers could be streamlined into a minor inconvenience or converted into regularized payments that happen on the natural (e.g., carbon pricing) rather than stalling out the project. It is hard at this point to envision the exact protocols on which we will settle in each industry, but the forces for rationalization and probabilistic science are likely strong enough to ensure that the voices pushing us to find a way will gradually and slowly prevail.

Whatever the precise protocols happen to be, it is indisputable that this vision entails a daunting coordination problem. If the revolution plays out roughly as suggested here, we will have a complicated thicket of overlapping occupational practices, a world in which, for example, social services are delivered not just by social service organizations but also by manufacturing firms, hospitals, and schools. The resulting complication in the division of labor will need to be addressed. Although one could imagine that each company will develop a thousand-page bureaucratic referral handbook that describes the in-house and outsourced services, it is likely that we will ultimately have to find alternative methods of resolving the growing complexity in the division of labor. The problem is likely to be particularly challenging to address in a society as decentralized as the contemporary United States. Artificial intelligence offers a possible solution in this respect: if each firm trains AI models on their internal practices, it will be relatively straightforward to develop new practices that meet the coordinative challenge. If a doctor, for example, finds that their patient is suffering from a combination of drug abuse, homelessness, and unemployment, they will be able to secure an AI-based prescription that delivers the in-house medical treatment (e.g., antidepressants or addiction treatment protocol), the in-house housing treatment (e.g., a unit in the hospital's own housing development), and the subsequent referral to the core service providers (e.g., job training or financial training). This simple technical solution can be straightforwardly applied to a variety of industries, thus solving a coordinative problem that might otherwise seem overwhelming.

Sensualist without Heart

The paradox of specialization arises because, within a rationalized occupation, workers are obliged to attend to all of the science relevant to occupational outcomes. As I described above, the paradox has had consequences for the nature of work in late industrial societies, as workers attempt to manage the growing functional complexity of occupations and industries. But there has also been growing skepticism of the very idea of a rationalized occupation. Indeed, there is increasing evidence of a straightforward backlash against the rationalization of occupations, industries, and the wider society.

This type of backlash can be found in a document published by Marc Andreessen in 2023, the *Techno-Optimist Manifesto*. In a section titled "The Enemy," Andreessen identifies a set of ideas and institutions that are standing in the way of progress:

> Our present society has been subjected to a mass demoralization campaign for six decades—against technology and against life—under varying names like "existential risk," "sustainability," "ESG," "Sustainable Development Goals," "social responsibility," "stakeholder capitalism," "Precautionary Principle," "trust and safety," "tech ethics," "risk management," "de-growth," "the limits of growth."

> Our enemy is the ivory tower, the know-it-all credentialed expert world-view, indulging in abstract theories, luxury beliefs, social engineering, disconnected from the real world, delusional, unelected, and unaccountable—playing God with everyone else's lives, with total insulation from the consequences. (Andreessen 2023)

Whether or not Andreessen's proposed solution of technology-driven growth and free markets will deliver on the ambitions of the manifesto is of less importance than the faults he identifies in our current systems. The manifesto straightforwardly rejects many aspects of rationalization and the scientization of contemporary work. Similar themes are found in the speeches of prominent right-wing politicians and in the Republican Party platform and associated documents. Criticisms focus on three aspects in particular: the diminished role of the family, the extent of bureaucracy and regulation, and the politicization of science.

The rise of institutions that replace some of the functions of the family have loomed especially large in these discussions. The development of specialized institutions for education, health care, and law enforcement have meant that the family no longer has primary responsibility for educating children, providing health care, or protecting life and property. The removal of these functions from the family, however, has reduced the control that family members have over the provision of these functions, particularly in the context of increasing rationalization. Within a rationalized occupation, the pursuit of outputs is guided by science, efficiency, and standards, and individual family preferences about how outputs should be secured are less likely to be honored. Further, because workers within rationalized occupations are expected to attend to a broad range of inputs, these workers are more likely to take an interest in aspects of life that would, in the past, have been solely the family's business. Teachers, for example, might be forced to reckon with aspects of a child's personal identity and culture to provide an effective education.

Part of the right-wing backlash to rationalization is a clear response to the diminished role of the family: not only have outputs been taken over by specialized institutions but, additionally, the family has little control over how those outputs are pursued. The Republican Party platform (2016 and 2020) thus includes the lines "Parents have a right to direct their children's education, care, and upbringing" and "We support the right of parents to determine the proper medical treatment and therapy for their minor children" (2016: 34, 37). There is also emphasis on what teachers and physicians should be prohibited from doing in the absence of parental knowledge or consent. Although there is of course room, within our current system, for the family to be involved in decisions pertaining to outputs, the future of the rationalized occupation is indeed one in which families would be expected to have ever less control over the means through which occupational outputs are produced and workers would be expected to have ever more interest in aspects of life previously reserved for the family.

Another aspect of backlash pertains to the rationalization of the wider society, and particularly the rise of the administrative state. As the United States has become increasingly rationalized and the bureaucracy of the state has grown, we have seen a growth in regulations aimed toward building societal externalities into occupational and industrial practices. As previously described, health and safety legislation reduced the amount that the state would need to spend on accident victims, but it increased the functional complexity of many occupations. Some of the new job tasks introduced across the occupational structure are related to preventive or risk management activities that the state has mandated employers to introduce. At the same time, the welfare state has expanded significantly, and government spending on individual income transfers (e.g., Medicare, housing subsidies, and food stamps) has substantially increased over the past century.[6] As a consequence, the modern United States has been described as "essentially a huge insurance company with an army" (Krugman 2010).[7]

It would be naive to assume that every dollar of government funding was well spent or that federal bureaucracies are always well functioning. But at least some of the right-wing discourse on bureaucracy and regulation appears to be a straightforward backlash against societal rationalization and the expanded purview that science imposes on the rationalized occupation. Democratic politicians are criticized for not taking into account the economic costs of increased regulation or the extent to which regulation removes choice from individuals and families.[8] The Republican Party platform, for example, states that environmental problems should not be addressed through "top-down, command-and-control regulations that stifle economic growth and cost thousands of jobs" (2016: 22), and at the start of President Trump's second term, executive orders calling for reductions in the "federal bureaucracy" were issued as a means to "reduce inflation, and promote American freedom and innovation" (Executive Order No. 13957). A reduction in the administrative state would entail a reduction in federal spending, the removal of regulation, and a reduced necessity for occupations to mitigate societal-level externalities.

If one backlash against rationalization entails dismantling the administrative state that makes intervention feasible, another entails questioning the quality of the science on which the rationalized occupation depends. As the quote above from the *Techno-Optimist Manifesto* indicates, there is seemingly a growing frustration with scientists and a suspicion that ideological preferences are being smuggled into policy using scientific reasoning. Another of Trump's executive orders lays bare this concern, stating that "ideological dogmas have surfaced that elevate group identity above individual achievement, enforce conformity at the expense of innovative ideas, and inject politics into the heart of the scientific method" (Executive Order No. 14177).[9] There has been a decline in confidence in scientists among Republican voters, and this decline appears to have accelerated during the pandemic (Kennedy and Tyson 2023; Oreskes and Conway 2022; see also Furnas, LaPira, and Wang 2025). Scientists are also increasingly likely to align with the Democratic Party, although the evidence suggests that the scientists' move away from the Republican Party is a consequence, rather than a cause, of growing conservative distrust in science (Kaurov et al. 2022). Nevertheless, the perceived left-wing bias of science presents a challenge to the integration of scientific work within the rationalized occupation and wider society.

It is unclear how consequential the right-wing backlash against rationalization might be. Even as the Republican Party platform, executive orders, and other documents reject aspects of rationalization, there are still references to "sound science" and "science-based standards" (e.g., Republican Party 2016: 22, 17). It is possible, however, that the current backlash against rationalization might operate to suppress regulation in the coming years, thus reducing the need for some of the bureaucratic and preventive tasks currently taken on by workers. Occupations that are dependent on government funding might also find their functional complexity suppressed relative to others, as politicians take a more active role in deciding which science will be built into job tasks. However, given that much of the rationale for using science to direct job tasks is based on the principle that outputs are improved when science is taken into account, any backlash effects might, in the end, be quite limited.

The Victory and Death of Sociology

> Although the social sciences have not attained, and in the nature of
> things cannot attain, the exactness of generalization reached by the
> physical sciences, they are as indispensable to efficient individual
> conduct and social practice as technology is to machine industry; and
> reliance on them will increase as society grapples resolutely with its
> problems and potentialities. (Educational Policies Commission 1937: 62)

The foregoing quotation is taken from a report on the function of education in American democracy, published by the Educational Policies Commission in 1937. The chapter in which these words are found considers
education-relevant changes that had occurred since the founding of the
republic. The commission identified an increasingly central role for the
social sciences in "social practice," a role that has indeed become more
prominent in the period since the report's publication. In this final section
of the book, I argue—in straight-on Hegelian fashion—that sociology is an
idea that has won over the world.

Why did sociology become so central to our understanding of the world?
It is perhaps surprising, after all, that the rise of probabilistic thinking
vaulted sociology to a position of centrality in organizing production. There
are two important reasons that this is the case. First, the occupational
structure has become increasingly human centered, and sciences that aid in
the understanding of humans have become essential. Humans must be
manipulated, shaped, and understood in order to maximize outputs across
the occupational structure. Sociology aids in understanding how human
outputs can be maximized and additionally provides an opportunity for
nonhuman outputs to be maximized via intervention with human workers.
Because of its special role in speaking to humans as both inputs and outputs, sociology can be employed to improve outcomes in all occupations.
Second, probabilism meant that multiple sciences had to be drawn on to
maximize outputs, given that it invoked a multiplicity of mechanisms.
There are many occupations for which sociology could hardly be the first
science called on. The medical industry could never jettison biology, the
education industry would never forgo psychology, and manufacturing
would not abandon engineering. But sociology could be an auxiliary

science within these occupations. And because most occupations pursue human outputs and all occupations employ human workers, sociology's centrality to the rationalized occupation was assured.

Changes to society also gave sociology a more prominent role. In particular, growing concerns about racial and economic inequality and the legislative gains of the Civil Rights movement have increased demand for a science that aims to understand how inequality is produced and reproduced. It is impossible to tease out definitively whether the increasing concern about inequality across the occupational structure was due to changes in understandings of individual rights or an acknowledgment that inequality would be detrimental to occupational outcomes. But there is much evidence in the education, health, and law enforcement industries, at least, that occupational actors saw inequality as a challenge to maximizing outputs. Sociology offers the possibility of addressing the mechanisms through which inequality affects outputs, making it a science indispensable to the human-centered occupations of the contemporary United States.[10]

Sociological partisans might find reason to celebrate the discipline's central role in the contemporary occupational structure. Unless workers are replaced wholesale by machines and economies are transformed to focus once again on nonhuman outputs, sociology is likely to continue to be fundamental. Some hesitation, however, might be prudent. For sociology has proved itself so useful to such a broad range of occupations that it is in danger of being fractured across the full set of applied sciences. The last stage of this cultural development might be a sociology that is everywhere and nowhere, a sociology that has both underpinned the division of labor and been destroyed by it.

Appendix

I use multiple data sources to examine changes in work over the past 150 years. Details of specific data sources and methodological approaches are included below, and data and syntax files are available in my OSF directory (Jackson 2025). Ultimately, the validity of my conclusions will be judged by a comparison of my data, analysis, and interpretation with the data, analysis, and interpretations of other scholars. Transparency and openness are essential in allowing others to assess the robustness of my results.

The data sources and methodological approaches differ across chapters, and I describe the details of each analysis in the sections for each chapter below. First, I consider data and methodological issues common to many or all chapters.

CHALLENGES TO COMPARISON OVER TIME

One issue common to all chapters is the difficulty of accurate comparison over long periods of time. Studies that examine changes (or stability) over long periods are vulnerable to several types of bias. Three types of bias are of special concern: selection bias, a lack of variation, and presentism.

First, selection bias is always likely when using historical data. The data sources that exist today are but a small fraction of the sources that existed in the past and an even smaller fraction of all of the data that could have been collected in the past. Data sources that are currently accessible are potentially different from those that are not, for reasons that may be related to the subjects of study. For example, those interested in building a scientific occupation are likely to have been more eager to publish their work in journals, to push for licensing, and to keep good records. More rationalized occupations are also more likely to have been the subject of job task analyses, on which I rely heavily.

An important procedure that I adopted to address the issue of selection bias was to select the industry and its dominant occupation(s) before searching for appropriate data. Doing so meant that the ease of finding data on an industry and occupation was not a factor in determining which cases were discussed. One consequence of this decision is that I do not have precisely the same types of data for each industry and occupation. It would have been desirable, for example, to present multiple job task analyses for each dominant occupation in each industry, but these are available for only some of the occupations discussed, for only some periods of time. I therefore include analyses of other data—including tool lists, time use studies, and school yearbooks—that allow inferences to be drawn about changes in job tasks. A second procedure that I adopted was to search for multiple data sources that could speak to the job tasks undertaken within an occupation. It was also important to examine whether or not evidence from multiple sources provided similar results on changes over time. Similar results across many sources of evidence and industrial and occupational domains were helpful in establishing the major findings of the study.

A second problem, related to selection bias, is lack of variation. As all good probabilists know, variation is a feature of the world, and any analysis should aim to capture and measure variation alongside the central tendency that may be the focus of the analysis. Knowledge of the true extent of variation might undermine theories that appeared to be strong on the basis of evidence from central tendencies. But insofar as only a selection of data sources survives over time, variation is likely to be suppressed. In turn, this means that it is difficult to assess whether the central tendency reflects a relatively common experience or many workers experience something quite different. Approaches to mitigating selection bias, as described above, are likely to reduce the problem of a lack of variation, but without access to more data, there is unfortunately little to be done.

Finally, a presentist bias frequently arises in studies that trace changes over a long period of time. This bias has two components: there may be changes over time in data production, such that modern sources are more accurate than older sources, and there may be cultural changes that make it more challenging to understand the context—and therefore meaning—of materials pertaining to the past. There is little question that both types of bias are expected to operate in any study that includes historical materials. With respect to the accuracy of data, one significant advantage of drawing on data collected during the past 150 years is that even data from the beginning of the period were collected and recorded with some care. Job task and time use analyses, for example, were central to Frederick Winslow Taylor's scientific management, and data collection procedures were similar to the present-day methods. Notably, though, there are many more useful data sources in the present day than there were in the past, and social scientists of the future are likely to be better served should they wish to examine long-term changes in the nature and experience of work. With respect to minimizing presentist bias in the understanding of context, in each chapter I combined qualitative and quantitative data with the aim of examining different aspects of work, from the perspectives of different types of workers. The interview data were particularly illuminating in this respect (see Chapter 6), as they allowed for a comparison of the plans of managers with on-the-ground experiences of work. The work of historians within each of the specialist fields studied here (i.e., history of medicine, law enforcement, education, and manufacturing) was of course also immensely valuable.

APPENDIX

JOB TASK ANALYSIS

In several chapters, I present comparisons of job task analyses over time. I use job task analyses produced by managers (e.g., in manufacturing), state actors (e.g., the Pennsylvania Department of Education's *Framework for Evaluation*), and the federal government (Occupational Information Network [O*NET]). All of these job task analyses aim to capture the set of tasks performed in an occupation.

There are two main methods used when conducting job task analysis. The most common method used today is to survey a proportion of those working within a given occupation and ask how frequently a set of tasks is carried out, where the set is defined by expert analysts and higher-level administrators. The O*NET data, for example, are based on responses by sampled workers within each occupation to a questionnaire designed by experts. The questionnaire asks the worker to assess the importance of a set of tasks relevant to their occupation, with the aim of identifying those tasks that are essential. But in the past, such large-scale data collection efforts were less frequently undertaken. There were some notable exceptions (e.g., the job task analysis reported in Chapter 5, on teachers' job tasks). But in many other cases, job task analyses were more likely to be carried out at the company or even firm level. Even in this case, however, the aim of the analysis remained identifying those tasks essential to the performance of the occupation. (See M. Wilson 2014 for a history of job task analysis; see also Anonymous 1922; Benge, Burk, and Hay 1941.)

One important question for my study is whether a job task analysis truly reflects the nature of work within an occupation at a particular point in time. Three possible approaches to addressing this question might be taken.

First, we might point to the robustness of the methods used to categorize job tasks both in the past and in the present day. The procedures underlying job task analysis are remarkably robust: the method was well established, even early in the twentieth century, and there was much literature describing how the method should be carried out (see Zerga 1943 for a bibliography). Furthermore, there were significant incentives to accurately reflect job content because the optimal matching of workers to jobs relied on an accurate job analysis (American Management Association 1924; National Metal Trades Association 1938; Anonymous 1939; Atkins 1924; Bickley 1918; Roberts 1935; Rowe 1922; Uhrbrock 1922). It is nevertheless clear that job task analyses are likely to do a poor job of capturing the full range of variation in job tasks across workers within the same occupation. For example, in many of the historical materials, it was understood that workers in rural areas might often need to take on a broader range of tasks than a job task analysis might suggest. Indeed, it is still the case that, for example, physicians in rural areas might be required to perform a much broader range of tasks than physicians in urban areas. Although O*NET distinguishes between "core" and "supplemental" tasks, which might capture some of the within-occupation variation, the full range of variation is likely to be missing from a job task analysis, even if the central tendency is well represented (see Van Iddekinge, Tsacoumis, and Donsbach 2002).

Second, as sociologists, we might argue that the *institutionalization* of job tasks is of primary interest, and job task analyses are highly effective at capturing institutionalized job tasks. In essence, important decisions about the organization of work will be based not on the peculiarities of any individual worker's eclectic list of tasks but on the set of tasks that are widely understood to be integral to the job. Because job task analyses list all the tasks that are understood to be important to the job, these data, whether or not they correspond precisely with experiences of work, are valuable for scholars of the division of labor.

Third, and insofar as the institutionalization of job tasks is seen as less important than the actual tasks that workers undertake on the job, we might draw on additional data to assess how closely the job task analysis matches the experience of work. Triangulation with other data sources is helpful in assessing the accuracy of the primary data. In Chapter 6, for example, I compare job task and interview data for manufacturing workers, and in Chapter 3, I analyze data on time use among physicians. Comparison across diverse data sources makes it possible to evaluate whether or not the changes observed in job task analyses are also observed when different data and measures are employed.

1: THE GREAT FRAGMENTATION?

Figure 1-1

In Figure 1-1, I present an analysis of data drawn from O*NET. The O*NET database records the tasks required to perform over one thousand occupations, as reported by job incumbents, analysts and experts, job postings, and professional associations (O*NET 2024). These characteristics are coded into a common classification of knowledge, skills, and abilities, such that each occupation can be scored on a range of dimensions.

The figure plots the average number of tasks undertaken in occupations falling in each of the major occupational groups; in other words, for each major occupational group, for each year of data, I take the mean number of tasks across occupations within the group and plot this number. I use both "core" and "supplemental" tasks to facilitate comparison over time, because the earliest O*NET databases do not distinguish between the task categories. Comparison of the average number of core tasks over a more compressed time period (2003 onward) indicates that the general pattern of an increase in tasks is supported.

I use generalized additive models (GAMs) to smooth the results (Hastie 2017). Individual occupations are weighted according to size (measured using Bureau of Labor Statistics data from 2023; see Bureau of Labor Statistics 2023). Because the occupational composition of the major groups may change over time, I have also examined changes within particular occupations and whether or not the pattern differs across occupations that are merged (e.g., two occupations become one), newly introduced, or persistent over time. The pattern of increasing task burden is broadly similar across all of these comparisons.

For the period 1977–2003, O*NET provides what are known as "transitional databases," which mark the transition from the older classification of occupations to the O*NET system. Although all the tasks included for occupations in 1977 were translated to the O*NET system, it is impossible to rule out that the changes observed between 1977 and 2003 reflect in part the changes made to the task-coding procedure. From 2003 onward, all occupations were classified using the O*NET system, and changes in task burdens are therefore not attributable to coding changes. To distinguish these periods in the figure, I use a dotted line to indicate the transitional-databases period and a solid line for 2003 to the present day. All code is provided in Jackson (2025), and data are freely available for download from O*NET.

Figure 1-2
Figure 1-2 presents an analysis of data drawn from the Census, accessed via IPUMS (Ruggles et al. 2024). I calculate a measure of occupational diversity for each of the major industry groups.

I use the integrated occupational and industrial codes provided by IPUMS to harmonize Census data (see Ruggles et al. 2024). The samples are restricted to include only those individuals currently in the labor force. I use both the OCC1950 and OCC1990 classifications as measures of occupation, and in the analysis I calculate the Blau Index using both measures and then take the average. The Blau Index was calculated on the basis of major occupational groups and thus captures within-industry diversity with respect to those major groups. It is important to calculate with respect to major groups because calculation with respect to minor groups might simply capture changes in the occupational structure or occupational coding systems. Further, increasing minor group occupational diversity would be consistent with classical accounts of the division of labor: the subdivision of the pin-maker occupation, for example, would be reflected in increases in the Blau Index if calculated on the basis of minor groups. Calculation on the basis of major occupational groups instead makes it possible to examine changes in the basic types of occupations required to produce the output of an industry. I use the IND1950 integrated codes as a measure of industry, again aggregating to broader industrial groups.

I measure occupational diversity using the Blau Index. There are many possible measures of diversity in the literature—including the Simpson Index, the Hirschman-Herfindahl Index (HHI), and entropy. It is unfortunately the case that the same label is sometimes given to both a measure and the inverse of that measure. The Blau Index has the desirable property of being interpretable as the probability that two workers picked at random from a given industry belong to different major occupational groups (Blau 1977). I use the divcat package in Stata to compute this index (Enzmann 2015) and present the normalized index scores in Figure 1-2 (i.e., scores are constrained to fall between 0 and 1). When the Blau Index increases, greater major group occupational diversity is required to produce the outputs of the industry.

All syntax is provided in Jackson (2025), and data are freely available for download from IPUMS.

2: THE FORMIDABLE THICKET

Figure 2-1

In Figure 2-1, I present the results of content analysis of several types of text: presidential executive orders, congressional legislation, Supreme Court orders, and the *New York Times*. I use GAMs to smooth the results.

Presidential executive orders were accessed via the American Presidency Project (Woolley and Peters 2024). The document collection is based on published collections, and the executive orders from the pre-1945 period are therefore likely to be underrepresented relative to those from the later period (but note that all results are presented as relative frequencies). The terms searched for were "scien*," "standard*," "speciali*," and "duty." The figure shows the proportion of all executive orders that include the term. These calculations were carried out separately for each president.

Congressional legislation text was searched using the Congress.gov website. The terms searched for were "scien*," "standard*," "speciali*," and "duty." Legislation text is highly variable with respect to length, so to standardize the measures, I searched for the word "the" in the text and calculated the proportions in the figure by dividing the number of times the term appeared by the number of occurrences of "the." These calculations were carried out separately for each congressional term.

In the Supreme Court analysis, I examine the official orders of the court by year. The terms searched for were "scien*," "standard*," "speciali*," and "+duty -goods -'duty on' -'active duty' -'off duty.'" The "duty" term was modified because so many of the court's cases pertained to duties on goods or to military issues. I standardized the measures by comparing to occurrences of "the" in the official orders. A careful inspection of Figure 2-1 reveals that there was a decline in the mention of *all* of the terms during the period of the Warren Court. This period was unusual in that the court broke with prior and subsequent courts in its unwillingness to appeal to precedent. (See Little 1981 for a full discussion of this period in the court's history.)

Finally, I use the *New York Times* archive to examine changes over time in the terms "science," "standard," "specialize," and "duty." Word variants are automatically included in the archive search. I standardized the measures by comparing to occurrences of the word "day" (the word "the" could not be searched for). I calculated the proportions in the figure by dividing the number of times the term appeared by the number of occurrences of "day" in the text.

A Stata file containing the word counts is included in Jackson (2025), alongside the syntax used to produce the figure.

Figure 2-2

I use the Constellate database to conduct text analyses of JSTOR content. I searched academic publications in the fields of business, education, engineering, and medical science, and the figure shows the proportion of all publications in the field including the term by year. I searched for the terms "cause," "predict," "prevent," "genetic," and "social." I use GAMs to smooth the results. A Stata file containing the results is included in Jackson (2025), alongside the syntax used to produce the figure.

3: THIS IS OUR LANE

Figures 3-1 and 3-2

In Figures 3-1 and 3-2, I present an analysis of *Index Medicus* for the years 1879–2002. For 1879, 1905, and 1931, I hand coded the index terms to the 2022 MeSH classification. From 1960 onward, I use the National Library of Medicine's MeSH database to track index terms; the database lists added and deleted headings by year. In Figure 3-1, I show both the absolute and the relative distribution of the broad category codes over time. In Figures 3-1 and 3-2, I present visualizations of the content of *Index Medicus* in 1879 and 2022 at a finer level of detail than in Figure 3-1. I take account of the first six characters of the MeSH codes, representing the first three levels of hierarchy within the MeSH tree. Figures 3-1 and 3-2 were produced using the package provided by Michele Mauri and colleagues (2017). Coded data and syntax files are available in Jackson (2025).

Finally, I discuss the results of word searches of *Index Medicus* and PubMed. For 1879, 1905, and 1931, I search *Index Medicus* for the terms "cause," "etiology," and "prevent*." For the later period, I conducted a search of PubMed for the terms, restricting the search to items published between 2017 and 2022.

Figures 3-4 and 3-5

In Figure 3-4, I show the number of national specialist medical societies between the mid-nineteenth century and the present day. Names of medical societies were collated from websites and *JAMA*. Societies were removed as well as added; removals occurred both when societies were dissolved and when they merged with other societies. The figure was produced using the package provided by Mauri and colleagues (2017), and data and syntax files are available in Jackson (2025).

In Figure 3-5, I show the number of different specialties (boards, specialty certificates, and subspecialty certificates) recognized by the ABMS between 1933 and 2022 (American Board of Medical Specialties 2024). The figure was produced using the package provided by Mauri and colleagues (2017), and data and syntax files are available in Jackson (2025).

Table 3-1

Table 3-1 presents an analysis of the contents of medical bags in the 1920s, 1980s, and 2020s. The lists of tools are gathered from David Dammery's "A historical account of the doctor's bag" (2016), Stephen Morris's "A labour of love," (1971), and J. J. Murtagh and colleagues' *Murtagh's general practice* (2018).

Figures 3-6 and 3-7

Data for Figure 3-6 are taken from the National Ambulatory Medical Care Survey (NAMCS) (1973–2016; see National Center for Health Statistics 2025) and from estimates reported in the literature (Aldrich 1934; Aldrich and Spitz 1960; American Academy of Pediatrics 1949; Arnhold and Callas 1966; Bergman, Dassel, and Wedgwood 1966; Bergman, Probstfield, and Wedgwood 1967; Boulware 1958; Breese, Disney, and Talpey 1966; Burnett and Bell 1978; Commission on Medical Education

1928; Cooper et al. 2006; Deisher, Derby, and Sturman 1960; Hercules et al. 1969; Hessel and Haggerty 1968; London 1937; McInerny, Roghmann, and Sutherland 1978; Norlin et al. 2011; Shafer, Hoagland, and Hsu 2021).

In the NAMCS analysis, I use data drawn from the patient record form. For each appointment, the practitioner completed one of these forms, which collected information on patient and visit attributes. One question asked for the "major reason for this visit" and included "well adult/child exam" or "preventive care" as a response. The patient record form was unfortunately changed at several points in time, including with respect to the "major reason" question. In the early NAMCS datasets, practitioners were directed to identify *all* major reasons for the visit, but from the 1980s onward, only one reason could be chosen. The question format change appears to have had an effect on the estimates. To address this problem, I examine changes in the estimated proportion of well-child visits when the measure changed and then apply an adjustment (+.09) to the estimated proportions from 1980 onward. Note that Stephanie Cooper and colleagues (2006) use forced-choice measures similar to the later NAMCS studies, but this estimate is not adjusted, as in this case I have no time series on which to evaluate the effect of using different measures. Paul R. Shafer, Alex Hoagland, and Heather E. Hsu (2021) use data from insurance claims to evaluate the proportion of "wellness visits," and therefore these estimates represent privately insured children only.

The GAM is fitted using unweighted estimates. The scatter points are weighted to represent the size of the samples underlying the estimates; the weights for the two estimates from Shafer, Hoagland, and Hsu (2021) are capped at 1,000,000 to ensure that the points for other studies are visible (the actual sample sizes are 21,451,976 for 2006 and 19,979,162 for 2018). Harold Jacobziner and colleagues' 1963 article "How Well Are Well Children?" is excluded from this analysis because the research pertained to children examined at health stations during the New York City Well Child Conferences. Eric J. Slora and colleagues' 2006 article "Patient Visits to a National Practice-Based Research Network" is excluded because the paper resamples a group of pediatricians included in the NAMCS sample.

Data for Figure 3-7 are taken from the NAMCS (1973–2016). I focus on three specialties and examine the proportion of visits that include a range of different tests or procedures. I fit GAMs for each specialty-test/procedure combination and present figures for each specialty separately.

All syntax needed to reproduce the NAMCS analyses and Figures 3-6 and 3-7 is available in Jackson (2025), and the NAMCS data are available directly from the Centers for Disease Control and Prevention.

4: DEFUND THE POLICE

Figure 4-1
In Figure 4-1, I present an analysis of data drawn from O*NET on the skill content and task requirements of occupations (O*NET 2024).

I create a measure of functional complexity using the data on work tasks and work tools, as tasks and tools have traditionally been seen as determinants of the degree of functional complexity in an occupation (or role). The sociological literature on functional differentiation has emphasized work tasks in particular. Andrew Abbott (1988), for example, highlights the importance of attending to work tasks and to control over work tasks in understanding the division of labor. In the archaeological and anthropological literature, tool use and tool complexity provide useful measures of functional complexity for prehistoric societies (e.g., Ambrose 2001; Johnson-Frey 2004; Haines, Feinman, and Nicholas 2004), and researchers working on animal behavior also examine tool use and complexity to assess task complexity and specialization (e.g., Hunt 2000). O*NET contains fine-grained measures of work tasks and work tools for each O*NET-SOC code (see O*NET 2024 for data files and detailed descriptions of all measures).

I use two measures to capture the functional complexity of occupations. First, I construct a score based on the work tasks listed for each occupation. Incumbents of each occupation complete a questionnaire evaluating the importance of certain work tasks to their occupation; the tasks listed for each occupation are determined by specialized O*NET task developers, and incumbents are given an opportunity to add their own tasks at the end of the questionnaire (see O*NET 2021). Two scores are provided for each task for each occupation: the first indicates the degree to which a task is required to perform an occupation, while the second indicates the importance of that task to the occupation. For each task, I multiply the two scores and then take the sum of scores for all tasks. This measure may be understood as a weighted measure of the total number of distinct tasks undertaken in any occupation. The second measure is a score derived from the O*NET Content Model Work Activity measures. Occupations are scored on a common set of forty-one broad measures of work activity; the categories include "Controlling Machines and Processes," "Documenting/Recording Information," and "Assisting and Caring for Others." Incumbents are required to assess the importance of each activity to their occupation and the level of that activity required to perform their occupation. I multiply the scores for each assessment together for each of the forty-one work activities and take the sum. The two measures capture complexity in work tasks: highly functionally complex occupations will have high scores on the measures, while less functionally complex (i.e., more specialized) occupations will have low scores.

To capture functional complexity through tool use, I exploit O*NET's database on tools and technology, which lists, for each occupation, "those items necessary to carry out central functions required by an occupational incumbent's work role and responsibilities" (Dierdorff, Drewes, and Norton 2006: 4). Tools used in an occupation are assigned a United Nations Standard Products and Services Code (United Nations 2021); I use the family codes, which group together related commodity categories. For example, in the Information Technology Broadcasting and Telecommunications segment code, the family codes distinguish among five subcategories that capture different types of information technology and telecommunications. Within this segment, computers and computer accessories are classified in the same family, while telephones are classified in another. For each occupation, I simply count how many different tool families are represented. The logic behind this measure is that highly complex occupations, in which a diverse range of functions is carried out, will require a wide range of tools.

I transform the measures to z-scores and use multidimensional scaling to identify an underlying dimension of functional complexity (scaled from −4 to +4). In Figures 4-1, A-4-1 and A-4-2, occupations are plotted and scaled according to their size, using Bureau of Labor Statistics data from 2023 (US Bureau of Labor Statistics 2023). All code is provided in Jackson (2025), and data are freely available for download from O*NET and BLS. Figures 4-1, A-4-1 and A-4-2 were produced using the package provided by Mauri and colleagues (2017).

In the chapter, I refer to additional analyses using O*NET data. The O*NET database includes, for each occupation, an expert rating ("Job Zone" classification) of the level of education, experience, and training required to carry out the job effectively (Rivkin and Craven 2021). This five-category measure provides a useful indication of how much vocational preparation is required for jobs across the occupational structure.

In Figure A-4-1, I cross-classify the functional complexity measure with O*NET's measure of education, experience, and training requirements. We see a relatively strong relationship between functional complexity and the vocational preparation required for an occupation. As functional complexity decreases, the average level of education, experience, and training required decreases, in line with standard expectations. But Figure A-4-1 also reveals that police occupations are outliers not just with respect to the functional complexity of the occupation but also with respect to the level of vocational preparation required to carry out the job. Put simply, policing occupations are substantially more functionally complex than would be predicted on the basis of their moderate level of vocational preparation. The score for police officers (2.65) is well above the mean for occupations with medium vocational preparation requirements (0.16) and substantially higher even than the mean score for occupations with extensive requirements (0.65).

We can also plot the functional complexity measure against a measure of domination. I construct a measure of domination using the O*NET measures of work context, which include "Frequency of Conflict Situations," "Impact of Decisions on Co-workers or Company Results," and "Physical Proximity." I identify all variables that might plausibly capture a worker's capacity to dominate other people, and run a factor analysis to examine correlations among those variables. On the basis of this analysis, I identify a subset of variables that load strongly on a single factor that I identify as domination. I create an additive scale from these variables, where high scores indicate high potential for domination and low scores indicate low potential. In Figure A-4-2, I plot the functional complexity scores against the domination measure.

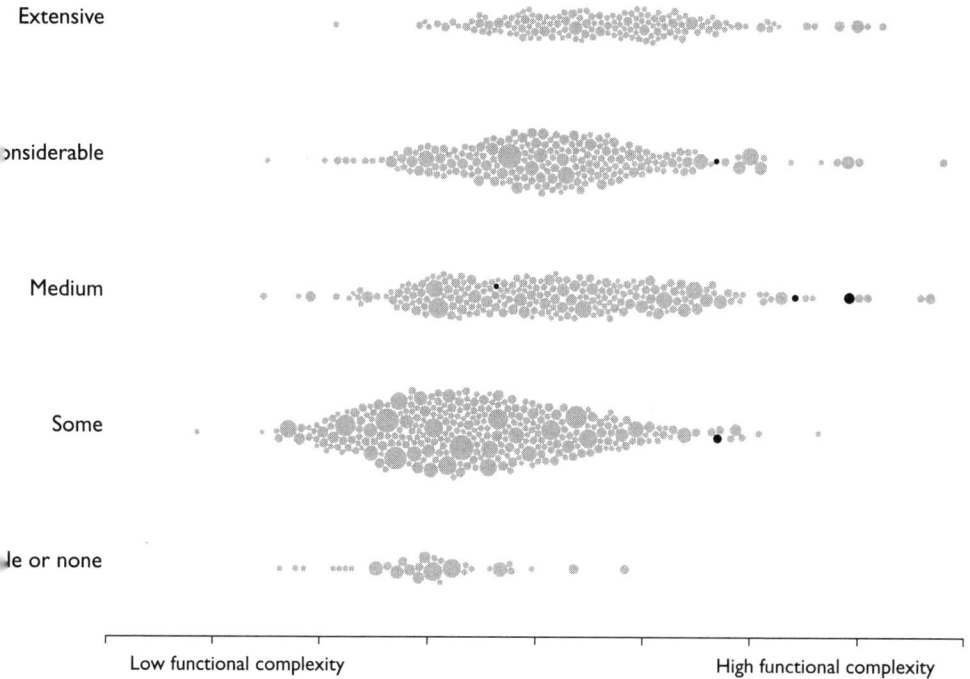

Fig. A-4-1 Functional complexity scores for the O*NET occupations, arranged by education, experience, and training requirements, where high scores indicate highly functionally complex occupations and low scores indicate less functionally complex occupations. Policing occupations are highlighted in black.

DATA SOURCE: O*NET.

As Figure A-4-2 shows, there is a modest relationship between functional complexity and domination (unweighted $r = 0.36$), indicating that more functionally complex occupations provide more opportunities for domination than less functionally complex occupations. Nevertheless, we see that police occupations are unusual in exhibiting both high functional complexity and high domination potential. The occupation "Police and Sheriff's Patrol Officers" has the highest domination score of all occupations, and all policing occupations fall in the top two percentiles of the domination measure. All other occupations falling in the top percentiles of both measures are in health care, with "Acute Care Nurses" and "Critical Care Nurses" as examples of occupations with particularly high functional complexity and domination scores. Although the measure of domination captures the extent to which job incumbents are able to control other people or impose their will, it unfortunately does not capture the number of people likely to be affected by the incumbent's behavior. A measure of domination weighted by the numbers of those subject to the domination would likely show the police as even more extreme outliers.

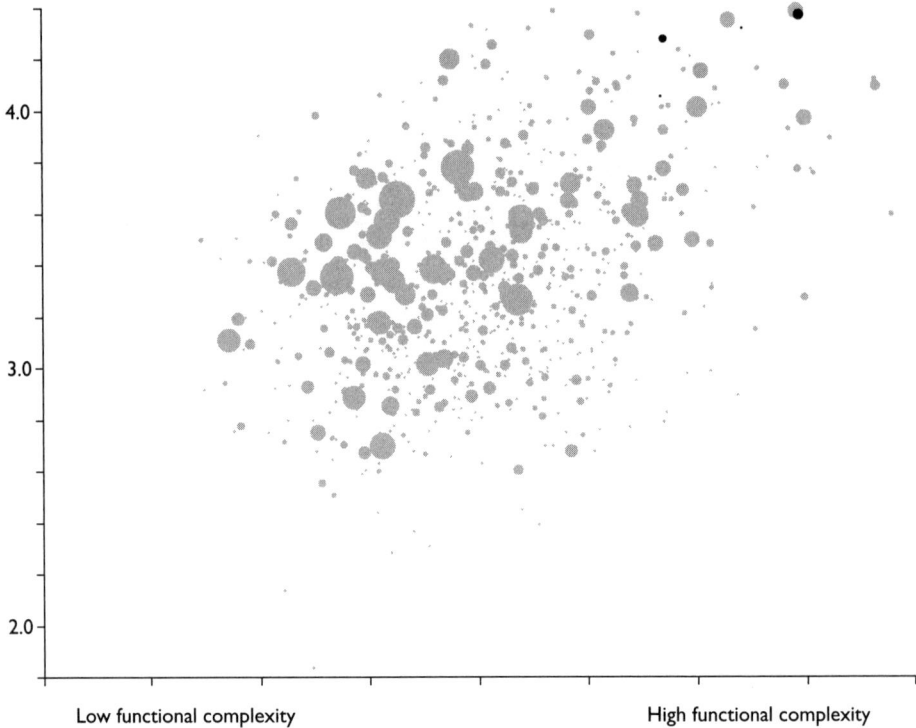

Fig. A-4-2 Functional complexity by domination scores for the O*NET occupations. Policing occupations are highlighted in black.

DATA SOURCE: O*NET.

Finally, in Table A-4-1, I show functional complexity and domination scores for occupations in which a handgun is a required tool. As expected, a large number of law enforcement occupations require the use of a gun, but Table A-4-1 emphasizes that these occupations have unusually high functional complexity and domination scores relative to other occupations in which a handgun is required.

Figure 4-2
I conducted a search of JSTOR content using the Constellate database, restricting the search to articles containing the words "crime" and "United States" and further restricting the search to articles in the fields of economics, law, political science, and social science. In Figure 4-2, I plot the proportion of all articles containing the key words by decade, between 1900 and 2019. A Stata file containing the data underlying Figure 4-2 is available in Jackson (2025).

Table A.4.1 Functional complexity and domination scores for the O*NET occupations that require a handgun

	COMPLEXITY	DOMINATION
Animal control workers	0.28	4.15
Bailiffs	0.26	3.77
Correctional officers and jailers	1.02	4.29
Criminal justice and law enforcement teachers, postsecondary	0.23	3.34
Customs and Border Protection officers	0.14	4.26
Detectives and criminal investigators	2.41	4.32
Fire inspectors and investigators	2.56	3.78
First-line supervisors of correctional officers	1.83	4.24
First-line supervisors of police and detectives	1.69	4.28
Fish and game wardens	1.67	4.06
Fishing and hunting workers	2.41	2.88
Gambling surveillance officers and gambling investigators	−0.57	3.81
Park naturalists	1.36	3.29
Police and sheriff's patrol officers	2.94	4.37
Private detectives and investigators	−0.65	3.31
Probation officers and correctional treatment specialists	0.63	4.13
Security guards	0.84	3.72
Transit and railroad police	−0.32	4.19
Transportation vehicle, equipment, and systems inspectors, except aviation	−1.89	3.58

DATA SOURCE: O*NET.

Figure 4-3

In Figure 4-3, I draw on four separate job task analyses conducted in California in 1933, 1979, 1998, and 2016. Each task listed in the job task analysis was recorded in an Excel spreadsheet, and I then coded tasks into broad task categories. The three later job task analyses were conducted by the same agency, and there were clear efforts to use a broadly similar method of classifying the job tasks, which facilitated comparison across the time periods. However, it was also clear that the list of tasks was more streamlined in some periods than in others: tasks that were listed separately in one year's task analysis were combined in another year. In the text, I focus on the relative importance of the different task types in each period, because changes in the type of work taken on by police officers are of most interest in my analysis. Focusing on relative importance also mitigates the difficulties of directly comparing the numbers of tasks across periods. To capture types of work, I initially coded the tasks to fourteen broad categories, before grouping tasks into a smaller set of categories for the purposes of presentation in Figure 4-3. An Excel file containing the coding is available in Jackson (2025).

Figures 4-4 and 4-5

Figures 4-4 and 4-5 present analyses of Law Enforcement Management and Administrative Statistics (LEMAS) data; the data contain information on a range of law enforcement agency characteristics. Surveys are completed by agencies via web or mail, and the response rate was around 80 percent in 2016 (US Department of Justice 2016). I use data from 1987, 1990, 1993, 1997, 2000, 2003, and 2016. I could not include 2007 and 2013 in the final dataset because data on calls for service are not available in these years. I use information from the LEMAS surveys on the number of sworn officers employed in the agency, the number of calls for service per year (via any source), and the number of hours of training required for new officers. Each LEMAS survey includes a measure of the number of specialized units in each agency. Large police agencies (more than 150 sworn personnel) are required to tick boxes to indicate which specialized units are present. The number of units provided in the survey differs over the years, but there are almost no cases in which agencies tick all boxes; this suggests that the size of the list is not a strong constraint.

I link the LEMAS data to Census and American Community Survey (ACS) data using Federal Information Processing Series (FIPS) county codes. Unfortunately, counties are not identified in the public access Census and ACS data, so where possible IPUMS generates county codes based on other geographic identifiers; most counties cannot be identified, so many LEMAS cases are lost in this step (see the IPUMS codebook entry for "countyfip" for more information). Because Census data are collected infrequently, for the years between Censuses I interpolate values. I include in the models measures of the proportion of Black, Hispanic, and immigrant people in each county, alongside the county's median household income and population size. All syntax is available in Jackson (2025).

In Table A-4-2, I show a selection of Poisson fixed effects models predicting the number of specialized units within each agency at each point in time (y_{it}, where i indexes individual agencies and t indexes time). I include models for the effects of individual sociodemographic characteristics before and after controlling for a broader set of county and agency characteristics. The dependent variable y_{it} is assumed to have a Poisson distribution with parameter μ_{it}, which depends on a vector of variables x_{it}, according to $\ln\mu_{it} = \delta_i + \beta x_{it}$ where δ_i is the fixed effect.

5: WE ASK SO MUCH

In the introduction to Chapter 5, I describe the proportion of letters signed by the education secretary or deputy secretary. From a list of all letters signed by these leaders, I code the main theme of the letter into the following categories: college costs, curriculum, disasters, discipline/safety, equity, funding, government, health,

Table A.4.2 Predicted number of specialized units within police agencies

	(1)	(2)	(3)	(4)	(5)	(6)
Proportion Black	4.45				3.10	2.13
	0.39				0.44	0.45
Proportion Hispanic		3.57			1.60	0.96
		0.19			0.42	0.43
Proportion immigrant			5.72		1.95	1.33
			0.26		0.56	0.56
Proportion white				−3.84		
				0.16		
Median household income ($10,000s)					0.00	0.00
					0.00	0.00
Log population size					0.17	0.01
					0.09	0.10
Proportion attended college					1.22	1.33
					0.20	0.21
Log number of sworn officers						0.34
						0.06
Log number of calls for service						−0.00
						0.00
100s hours training required for new officers						0.00
						0.00
AIC	9,843.39	9,587.35	9,464.02	9,333.57	8,765.92	8,546.07
BIC	9,849.14	9,593.10	9,469.78	9,339.33	8,800.45	8,597.87

Source: Data from LEMAS (US Department of Justice 2016) and Census (Ruggles et al. 2024).

military, performance, programs, religion, social problems, and teachers. Categories are exclusive and exhaustive. The letters were dated between January 28, 1999, and January 25, 2024, and the total number of letters coded is 237. A full list of the letters—including links to the original letter sources on the Department of Education's website—is available in Jackson (2025).

Figures 5-1 and 5-2
In Figures 5-1 and 5-2, I present the results of a topic model analysis of data drawn from *Teachers College Record* (*TCR*) and the *Journal of Negro Education* (*JNE*). I list the titles of all articles published in *TCR* between 1900 and 2020 at ten-year intervals (1900, 1910, 1920, etc.). A total of 2,476 *TCR* titles are analyzed. I list the titles of

all articles published in *JNE* for every year between 1932 and 2020, giving a total of 4,370 titles.

The topic models are fitted using latent Dirichlet allocation (LDA), an inductive technique that identifies the main themes—or topics—present in a document or set of documents (Blei, Ng, and Jordan 2003). I fit topic models for each journal separately, choosing the number of topics on the basis of standard measures of model coherence. In both cases, the coherence measures return a large number of topics, and I therefore recode into a smaller number of topics on the basis of theoretical priors and sensitivity to the subject matter. I predict the total average weight for each topic over the time period and use GAMs to smooth the results. The full syntax needed to reproduce the topic model analysis and figures is available alongside the data in Jackson (2025).

Figure 5-3
In the analysis of the functions of the Department of Education, I list all of the functions and responsibilities included under the department (or its precursors) between 1935 and 2010 and code to a common coding scheme (Office of the Federal Register 2010). I initially developed a set of categories based on the functions listed in 1935, and new categories were added as new functions appeared over the following decades. Coded data are available in Jackson (2025). Figures were produced using the package provided by Mauri and colleagues (2017).

Figure 5-4
The yearbooks for New Castle High School are available through the State Library of Pennsylvania's POWER Library. Permanent URLs for the four years included in the analysis of staffing—1915, 1955, 1985, and 2012—are included in Jackson (2025). All listed staff members were assigned to a broader category:

- Administration, administrative support, building, and security
- Academic and vocational disciplines
- Athletics, music, and arts
- Health and welfare
- Special education

Coded data are available in Jackson (2025).

Table 5-1
In the final analysis, I present a streamlined comparison of teacher job task analyses from 1929 and 2021. The 1929 data are drawn from *The Commonwealth Teacher Training Study* (Charters, Waples, and Capen 1929: 257–303; a permanent URL to a digital version is included in Jackson 2025). The 2021 data are drawn from the Pennsylvania Department of Education's *Framework for Evaluation: Classroom Teacher* (2021). Using this document, I identified which tasks from 1929 were still present in 2021 and coded new tasks where they were introduced. The marked-up *Framework*

document, plus a summary comparison of tasks between 1929 and 2021, is included in Jackson (2025).

6: MANAGEMENT AND THE WORKER

The analysis in Chapter 6 largely rests on data held in several archives. The first is the Frederick Winslow Taylor Collection, housed in the Samuel C. Williams Library's Archives and Special Collections at Stevens Institute of Technology, Hoboken, New Jersey. I also draw on several archives held by Baker Library Special Collections and Archives, Harvard Business School, Massachusetts. I consulted the Western Electric Company Hawthorne Studies Collection, Elton Mayo Papers, and the Fritz J. Roethlisberger Papers. Details of sources cited (with current box and folder numbers) are included in the text and references.

Included in the Elton Mayo Papers was a set of interview transcripts from a study undertaken by Mayo in the early 1940s. The transcripts were sealed until I requested access in 2023. The interviews were conducted with both employed and unemployed manufacturing workers in the town of New Castle, Pennsylvania, in the early 1940s. The researcher charged with leading the study (and conducting many of the interviews) was George C. Homans, who later become well known in his own right. The New Castle study was never published, and there is no explanation as to why. However, reasonable guesses may be made in light of the fact that the interviews were conducted in 1940 and 1941 and Homans was called up to the Naval Reserve in the spring of 1941. Mayo writes in *The Social Problems of an Industrial Civilization* that the New Castle study "cannot well be developed until the return of George C. Homans (Lt. Comdr. George G. Homans, U.S.N.R., on active service)" (1945: 87). Homans remained in service in the Pacific until 1953, when he returned to Harvard as a full professor (Hamblin and Kunkel 1977). By this point, Mayo had died (he died in 1949), and Homans was working on the structure and processes of small groups.

Notes

1. THE GREAT FRAGMENTATION?

1   See Adam Smith 1776, chapters 1, 2, and 3. For a useful discussion of pin factories and the data drawn upon by Smith, see Peaucelle and Guthrie 2011; see also R. Allen 2011.

2   Even in the early 1990s, when macro-level analysis of the division of labor was more popular, Andrew Abbott noted in a review of the literature on work and occupations that only around 10 percent of the research listed in *Sociological Abstracts* mentioned the division of labor. Of this research, around two-thirds focused on issues related to technology, while the other third focused on the division of labor with respect to home and work (Abbott 1993: 193). A JSTOR database search indicates that study of the "division of labor" peaked in sociology in the 1960s and 1970s, and it has been in rapid decline since the 1990s.

3   Babbage's identification of different "types" of workers with different skill profiles distinguishes him from Smith. Adam Smith sees increased productivity as arising from the advantages of task specialization: by virtue of specializing, workers become more proficient and more efficient, and automation is facilitated. But for Babbage, task specialization encourages selection on skills. Under his model, productivity is increased, in part, because of a more effective matching of workers to tasks.

4   Note that the "specialists without spirit" quotation has been attributed to Goethe, but it was, in fact, invented by Weber to echo the themes of Nietzsche's *Thus Spoke Zarathustra*. See Kent 1983 for a useful discussion.

5   Durkheim writes, "In effect, on the one hand, each one depends as much more strictly on society as labor is more divided," and "the most remarkable effect of the division of labor is not that it increases the output of functions divided, but that it renders them solidary" (1893: 131, 60–61).

6   See Pratten 1980 for a history of pin making spanning the eighteenth century to the late twentieth century.

7   See the Appendix for more information on the O*NET database.

8   Data from Ruggles et al. 2024; full details of the analysis are included in the Appendix.

9   The Blau Index was developed by the sociologist Peter Blau to measure racial/ethnic diversity within a population (see Blau 1977). The Blau Index is the

inverse of the Simpson Index, which is also known as the Hirschman-Herfindahl Index (HHI) in the economics literature.

10 There are just three finer-grained industries in which the Blau Index has fallen slightly between 1900 and 2021: warehousing and storage, hospitals, and postal service. In the case of hospitals, the fall can be accounted for by two main factors. First, there has been a substantial increase in the number of nurses over time. Second, hospitals as we understand them today are a relatively new phenomenon and were only just emerging at the beginning of the twentieth century. The composition of the hospital industry has therefore changed substantially over time: this industry comprises long-term care, community hospitals, federal hospitals, and for-profit hospitals, but the proportion of hospitals engaged in long-term care has fallen over time, while the proportion of large, for-profit institutions has increased, with implications for the type of workers needed. The dominance of physician and nursing occupations within the hospital industry (ca. 60 percent of all occupations) means that the Blau Index is primarily driven by these compositional changes.

11 The time period covered varies depending on the particular industry and occupation. Where key moments in scientific or industrial-occupational development occur outside of this time period, I extend the window to consider them.

2. THE FORMIDABLE THICKET

1 Unfortunately, a full series of congressional legislative text is only available for 1951 onward.

2 In the *Division of Labor in Society,* he writes, "The division of labor is not peculiar to the economic world; we can observe its growing influence in the most varied fields of society. The political, administrative, and judicial functions are growing more and more specialized. It is the same with the aesthetic and scientific functions. It is long since philosophy reigned as the science unique; it has been broken into a multitude of special disciplines each of which has its object, method, and thought" (Durkheim 1893: 40). In extending the concept to noneconomic fields, Durkheim is building an explicit link between social structure and the selective mechanisms at work in the natural world.

The conceptualization of the division of labor as an evolutionary process leads both Herbert Spencer and Durkheim to emphasize population size, alongside population density, as a key driver of specialization at the societal level (see Perrin 1995 for a useful discussion of the similarities and differences in Spencer's and Durkheim's accounts of the causes of the division of labor). Spencer, for example, in his *Principles of Sociology,* argues that "heterogeneity of structure is made possible only by multiplicity of units. Division of labour cannot be carried far where there are but few to divide the labour among them" (1916: 11). And in the *Division of Labor,* Durkheim writes, "The division of labor varies in direct ratio with the volume and density of societies . . . the growth and condensation of societies . . . *necessitate* a greater division of labor. It is not an instrument by which the latter is realized; it is its determining cause" (1893: 262). The mechanism by which increases in population and population density translate into increases in specialization is growth in competition (1893: 266; see also Perrin 1995: 793–795). As the pressure on available resources is increased by a growing population, competition for resources is exaggerated, and specialization arises. Through the division of labor, outputs are maximized, and direct competition for the same scarce set of resources is reduced. It is the "struggle for existence" (Durkheim 1893: 270) that accounts for the causal effect of population size and density on specialization.

3   Research in both psychology and sociology has examined how specialization emerges in small group settings. This research establishes the conditions that promote or impede specialization, and the individual- and group-level returns to specialization (e.g., Almaatouq et al. 2021; Baer and Odic 2022; Erikson and Shirado 2021).

4   As a consequence of legitimacy challenges, an occupation with control over a wide range of tasks may have to exert more and more effort to maintain control over tasks as time goes on. This effort can be straightforwardly conceptualized as occupational closure (e.g., see Weeden 2002; Wilmers 2020), in that such efforts build boundaries that protect an occupation and its incumbents from losing a claim over job tasks.

5   This is not, of course, equivalent to the claim that all scientific findings are true. Science sometimes produces poor results, and findings might not replicate. Scientists might be biased, or their work might be used in the service of economic or political interests (e.g., see Labaree 1992; D. Noble 1984). All that is required is for science to be more likely than a nonscientific approach to return positive occupational outcomes.

6   Weber writes that "the term 'occupation' will be applied to the mode of specialization, specification, and combination of the functions of an individual so far as it constitutes for him the basis of a continuous opportunity for income or earnings" (1978: 140), elsewhere discussing the "type of functions undertaken by the same person. He may combine managerial functions with those of carrying out specifications; or his work may be specialized in terms of one or the other" (118). Occupations, then, are defined with respect to the tasks contained therein and not with respect to outputs.

7   Historically, social scientists and government agencies have defined occupations according to several different criteria. In the United States, measures of occupation and industry were often combined in official statistics, but by the 1930s there was an interest in developing an occupational classification that could be used to address the key economic and social issues of the day. Alba M. Edwards, a Census Bureau statistician responsible for designing the updated classification, had argued many years earlier that "statistics of occupation . . . should show . . . not only the skill and intelligence of the worker, and his position in the industry, as employer, employee, or working on his own account, but, as a means for the study of the risk, healthfulness, and numerous other problems connected with his occupation, they should show, also, the specific services rendered, work done, or processes performed by him.

NOTES TO PAGES 23-28

Therefore, occupations should be classified with respect to the kind of work done or the character of the service rendered, rather than according to the article made or worked upon, or the place where the work was done. The worker and his work should be their basis, and not the industry and its product" (Edwards 1911: 621; see Conk 1978 for a detailed discussion of the 1870–1940 period). Today, the Census Bureau writes, "Occupation data describe the kind of work the person does on the job" (2020: 107), highlighting the basic continuity between Edwards's definition and those that followed.

8 Other work within sociology has examined the importance of occupation for income or earnings; this research emphasizes the importance of considering occupation in explanations of economic outcomes and economic inequality (e.g., see Mouw and Kalleberg 2010; Weeden et al. 2007). Another strand of research—building directly on Weberian theory—highlights the importance of occupational closure in understanding individual economic outcomes and stratification processes (see especially Parkin 1979; Weeden 2002).

9 Note that while social scientists generally define occupations with respect to their tasks, research on job quality and labor market polarization has also examined outcomes when occupations are cross-classified with industries or sectors. The rationale for including these cross-classified measures, however, is that they capture additional dimensions of jobs that might be important when evaluating worker outcomes; occupations in this literature are still conceptualized as bundles of tasks (see Dwyer 2025 for a discussion; see also Council of Economic Advisers 1997: chap. 4; Wright and Dwyer 2003; Eurofound 2021).

10 Abbott argues that the professions are set apart by their appeals to abstractions (chap. 11). He writes, "Any occupation can obtain licensure . . . or develop an ethics code. . . . But only a knowledge system governed by abstractions can redefine its problems and tasks, defend them from interlopers, and seize new problems" (1988: 8). In arguing that the rationalized occupation attends to science, I am not claiming that increasing numbers of occupations are turning into professions (although see the discussion in Chapter 7). Rather, my claim is that science has expanded so substantially that it can be used to further the production of the outputs of all occupations. As occupations become increasingly rationalized, science is drawn on by workers across the occupational structure.

11 Minnesota is not at all unusual in requiring the study of scientific material. See Timmons and Thornton 2010: 742.

12 The lectures were later published as Little Science, Big Science (D. Price 1963).

13 Logistic growth of course looks exponential to those who experience the takeoff portion of the curve and is only revealed to be logistic when the rate of growth starts to decrease (D. Price 1963: 23). Price suggested that the midpoint of the logistic curve was probably reached in the 1940s or 1950s but that this would only be confirmed when the full growth curve was revealed (31). It was Price's position that the growth curve held for both narrow and broader definitions of

"science" and that virtually any measure of scientific output would return the same result.

14 The basic model of how knowledge growth leads to specialization is elegant in its simplicity, but it necessarily smooths over some of the more complicated causal paths that are bound up in the process. One complication is that the causal path linking knowledge and specialization runs in both directions. To be sure, an increase in knowledge might promote specialization, but specialization might also lead to increases in knowledge. The productivity-maximizing benefits of specialization apply to knowledge just as they apply to the outputs of manufacturing, setting up a positive feedback loop between specialization and knowledge. Given this possibility of reverse causation, statistically isolating the macro-level causal effect of knowledge on specialization is challenging in the contemporary world and virtually impossible over a long timescale. Another complication is that the extent to which knowledge growth alters occupational practices is influenced by power and interests. Unions, for example, might resist the introduction of technology that threatens deskilling or unemployment for workers, while capitalists might impose those very technologies in the pursuit of profit (e.g., see D. Noble 1977, 1984). The interests of state actors—perhaps especially the military—are also powerful in shaping the direction of knowledge growth and technological development (e.g., see D. Noble 1984; see also Dobbin 1994).

15 There is some disagreement with respect to whether or not the probabilistic revolution fulfills the criteria for a scientific revolution. I. Bernard Cohen (1987) examines the evidence for a radical shift in understanding consistent with revolution and concludes that there is sufficient evidence that there was a revolutionary change in scientific thought, particularly insofar as we focus on the application of probabilistic thinking across the disciplines, and particularly insofar as we extend the period of consideration through the twentieth century. He prefers, however, to talk of a "probabilizing revolution," which followed the introduction of probabilistic and statistical methods to the natural and social sciences (40).

16 This transition is well illustrated by John Harley Warner's study of hospital case records from Cincinnati and Massachusetts in the mid-1800s. In the 1800s, the word "natural" was used in just under 40 percent of case records, while the word "normal" appeared in none. By the 1880s, "normal" appeared in around 60 percent of case records, completely supplanting the word "natural," which appeared in under 2 percent of case records (Warner 1986: 88).

17 Sociologists might be interested to note that Auguste Comte was a key figure in this transition and that he played a foundational role in establishing the idea of "normal" as an ideal. Comte's role is discussed in detail in Hacking 1990: chap. 19. For a detailed discussion of the role of averages and aggregates in Quetelet and Durkheim, see Desrosières 1998: chap. 3.

18 The adoption of "normal" as a standard is likely—for sociologists at least—to again bring to mind the concept of rationalization. One might reasonably ask whether or not the probabilistic revolution should simply be understood as but

another instance of rationalization. Weber did use the language of probability; for example, the concept of "life chances" (1978: 927) is fundamental to Weber's discussion of class, status and power, and Weber's outline of his sociology of action is infused with probabilistic language (e.g., "The interpretation of a sequence of events will . . . be called *causally* adequate insofar as, according to established generalizations from experience, there is a probability that it will always actually occur in the same way" (1978: 11). In making such appeals to probabilistic thinking Weber was typical of intellectuals of his time. But there is little evidence that he either identified the probabilistic revolution as a defined historical event, or saw transformations in understandings of probability as part of the rationalization process. See Swidler 1973 and particularly Kalberg 1980 for detailed discussions of the various conceptualizations of rationality and rationalization found in Weber's work. See Strand and Lizardo 2022 for a recent discussion of probabilistic thinking in Weber's work; also Lazarsfeld and Oberschall 1965, on Weber's empirical research.

19 In Martin Van Buren's Second Annual Message to Congress (December 3, 1838), he stated, "The suggestion presents itself whether the scope of the measure might not be usefully extended by causing it to embrace authentic statistical returns of the great interests specially intrusted to or necessarily affected by the legislation of Congress."

20 Life insurance risks were assessed by comparing applicant characteristics against population statistics, and over the course of the century, the life insurance industry increasingly took responsibility for collecting as well as analyzing data. For example, life insurance actuaries initially relied on existing tables of heights and weights to evaluate mortality risks, or companies constructed their own tables; by the end of the century, the Association of Life Insurance Medical Directors of America had founded a committee to develop standard height and weight tables for industry use (Czerniawski 2007).

21 Charles Camic and Yu Xie (1994), for example, document the importance that early twentieth-century American sociologists attached to statistical methods in establishing sociology as a science distinct from other competing disciplines. Franklin H. Giddings plays a key role in Camic and Xie's account. In his introductory textbook, Giddings writes, "It is as necessary that the scientific student of human society should know the essentials of statistical theory and method as that he should know the essentials of biology, psychology, and anthropology" (Giddings 1924: 208).

22 See Luhmann 2013 on the importance of communication in integrating highly differentiated systems.

23 Abbott's (1988) work cautions us to avoid simplistic assumptions about which occupations will win out over others in the competition for tasks and highlights the importance of occupations being able to legitimate their claims for control over new tasks by reference to abstract principles. But the paradox of specialization can be distinguished from a straightforward competition for new tasks: in the former situation, it is not that new tasks have been invented absent an application, such that

they now need to be distributed across occupations, but rather that the scope of the solution to a problem already controlled by an occupation has expanded. This expansion leads occupations to introduce tasks that match the ambition of their expanded scope. The battle for control over a given social problem has already been won; it is after the victory that the problem comes to be understood in more expansive terms and new job tasks accumulate.

24 The logic of specialization—in and of itself—would of course provide a strong foundation for allowing occupational actors to claim all new tasks that would seemingly better secure occupational outputs, whether or not those tasks originated in science (e.g., see Abbott 1988). However, because the rationalized occupation is particularly attuned to scientific developments, the paradox of specialization is most likely to arise within rationalized occupations when new tasks are delivered via science.

25 A "gradient" claim, for Abbott, is one in which an occupation already has responsibility for the severest forms of a given problem and can easily make claims to control "weaker" forms too. For Abbott, prevention is a weaker version of the "strong" problem that treatment addresses (1988: 100).

26 Estimates are for the year 1800, which is the first year for which reliable estimates are available. Estimates include both free and enslaved persons. Note that estimates for the UK, where Smith was writing, show a substantially lower proportion of the labor force in these occupations (ca. 35 percent) (R. Allen 2009; Shaw-Taylor 2009).

27 Sum of workers in "Management, professional, and related occupations," "Service occupations," and "Sales and office occupations." For a discussion of changes in the service sector, see Kalleberg 2011: 29–31.

28 The introduction of new technologies might of course also change task demands *within* occupations. Daron Acemoglu and David Autor (2011) provide the example of the introduction of automatic grammar and spelling checks within word processing software, which removed a task from secretarial workers, thus simplifying their jobs (see also Acemoglu, Kong, and Restrepo 2024, for a discussion of technology and changes in task demands). In the case study chapters, I discuss the effects of the introduction of new technologies in more detail.

29 Research on street-level bureaucrats has pointed to the challenges that arise because frontline government workers "cannot control the nature of the material with which they work . . . they do not have control over client's circumstances even when conditions are favorable for intervention" (Lipsky 2010: 78–79). But street-level bureaucrats comprise only part of the large group of workers concerned with human outputs (see e.g., Dwyer 2013).

30 Notably, in both of these examples, the motivation for prioritizing worker health is described in economic terms. In contrast to literature that suggests a growing emphasis on individualism and "personhood" in the postwar period (e.g., Frank and Meyer 2002), the evidence in the case study chapters is consistent with rationalized organizations attending to workers as people primarily because this

maximizes productivity. See also Berman 2022 on the growth of cost-benefit reasoning in policy development.

31 I focus here on the tasks added by governments to maximize overall societal outcomes. The accretion of new ends (i.e., not directly related to this aim) is discussed in Chapter 7.

32 The rationale for the act was described as follows: "(a) The Congress finds that personal injuries and illnesses arising out of work situations impose a substantial burden upon, and are a hindrance to, interstate commerce in terms of lost production, wage loss, medical expenses, and disability compensation payments. (b) The Congress declares it to be its purpose and policy, through the exercise of its powers to regulate commerce among the several States and with foreign nations and to provide for the general welfare, to assure so far as possible every working man and woman in the Nation safe and healthful working conditions and to preserve our human resources" 29 U.S.C. §651 (US Congress 1970).

33 There is a limit on the rate of administrative expansion: if already-large organizations continue to expand, existing managerial and administrative structures can be repurposed to adapt to new employees, reducing the need for further bureaucratic specialization (e.g., see Blau 1970).

3. THIS IS OUR LANE

1 Estimates from American Community Survey 2019. Of those in the labor force, 11.2 percent work in the medical industry, and 5.9 percent work in health care practitioner and technician occupations. Estimates obtained via IPUMS (Ruggles et al. 2024).

2 For example, "Institutions offering approved residencies and fellowships should maintain an adequate medical library . . . [that includes] the Quarterly Cumulative Index Medicus" (AMA 1950: 997).

3 Coded files are available in Jackson 2025.

4 For example, a large number of geographic codes (broad category Z) were introduced when the MeSH headings were implemented in 1963, but since that date, the number of Z codes used has remained stable.

5 The normalized Blau Index is 0.97 for 1879 and 0.90 for 2022.

6 When one reads the 1879 index with a modern sensibility, one of the most striking details is the prominence of amputation and the paucity of entries for more refined surgical techniques. Syphilis and its effects are conspicuous, and syphilophobia is recognized as an index term.

7 William Roger Williams estimates a death rate for all cancers of 60 per 100,000 (1908: 46), which may be compared to a rate of 144 per 100,000 in 2020 (Centers for Disease Control and Prevention 2022).

8 In 1905, variants of "prevent" are used in 195 titles, a number that increases to 592 titles in 1931.

9 Note that these supplementary categories (known as "Qualifiers" in the MeSH system) are not included in the quantitative analysis.

10 John Harley Warner (1986), for example, discusses the changing meanings of empiricism and rationalism during the first half of the nineteenth century and the changes in what is understood to constitute a scientific basis for practice (for a detailed discussion of statistical thinking in medicine during this period, see Cassedy 2013). By the 1880s, laboratory science was beginning to shape medical understandings of what constituted scientific knowledge (see especially Warner 1986: chap. 9).

11 *The Flexner Report* (1910: 53) explicitly states, "Medicine is part and parcel of modern science." Indeed, Flexner's report has been criticized for an overemphasis on science to the detriment of professional practice. Flexner's insistence that science must be central to medical training pushed out clinical care as a focus of medical education; this, some have argued, reduced the status of the profession and increased patient dissatisfaction (T. Duffy 2011).

12 In 1915, for example, the Constitution and By-Laws of the AMA were amended to add the *Council on Scientific Responsibility*, which comprised representatives of "the four main divisions of the Scientific Assembly: Medical Sciences, Medicine, Surgery, the Specialties" (AMA 1915: 61). As of 2022, the AMA included seven councils, one of which was the *Council on Science and Public Health*.

13 See, for example, *JAMA* Editor 1924; Gray 1941; Whitehead 1980; M. Brenner 2000.

14 The science/quackery distinction is one that recurs in editorials and academic work. A *JAMA* editorial in 1924, for example, states, "Only the quack and the faker divorce their practices from the fundamental sciences; and even these outcasts attempt to incorporate the semblance of scientific precision and nomenclature in the hocus pocus of their ministrations" (*JAMA* Editor 1924: 968).

15 See Warner 1991 for a detailed discussion of the references to "science" in the Code of Ethics, and associated controversies.

16 It is notable that *JAMA* has, since its inception, published poetry, literary quotes, and reviews of nonscientific books. Even today, *JAMA* regularly publishes poetry in its Poetry and Medicine section (e.g., Zhang 2022).

17 I control here for the number of words and pages in each period, as the format of *JAMA* changes significantly over time.

18 This might, at first glance, seem tautological, but the rationalism of early nineteenth century medicine illustrates that a processual focus can exist even in the absence of micro-level explanation (see., e.g., Warner 1986).

19 Although the movement to include social sciences among the sciences relevant to medicine built over the twentieth century, there were those much earlier in the history of medical science who saw links between the social sciences and medicine. For example, a *JAMA* editorial of 1890 includes the sentence "Medicine is a department of science which embraces and combines under one administration a large part of the provinces of biology, chemistry and sociology" (*JAMA* Editor 1890a: 869). Notably, though, the editorial was making the claim that medicine *encompassed* many of the other sciences and not that more sociological training might be required for medical professionals.

20 There were, in fact, calls to include sociology in medical training well before this period. S. W. Welch included in his chairman's address to the Section on Preventive and Industrial Medicine and Public Health (St. Louis, May 1922) the argument that "modern attempts to solve, or, at least, to reach an approximate solution of fundamental problems, have led in our own day to the development of a number of comparatively new sciences associated with the basic human needs: food, shelter, defense and propagation. They are still rudimentary in a large degree and practically unstandardized. For this reason they are likely to be lumped together in our minds under the general title of 'the social sciences,' and to receive from us scant consideration or respect. Examined closely, are not every one of these embryonic sciences which deal with the major problems of human existence fundamentally a part of medical science?" (S. Welch 1922: 342).

21 The MCAT in 1946 included a section on "Understanding Modern Society," which was designed to "test the alertness of the applicant to social issues" (Stalnaker 1950: 429). Although the test included social science content, it is well documented that scores on this part of the test were taken less seriously by medical school admission committees than scores on the science parts (e.g., Glaser [1958: 279] writes, "Particular significance is assigned to the score measuring science achievement"; see also McGaghie 2002; K. Mitchell et al. 2016). The MCAT was subsequently revised several times, and in the fifth version of the test, first administered in 2015, a section on "Psychological, Social, and Biological Foundations of Behavior" was included (Kaplan, Satterfield, and Kington 2012; Schwartzstein et al. 2013). On the history of the MCAT, see McGaghie 2002; K. Mitchell et al. 2016.

22 Prevention is mentioned once in Osborne's address, when he describes advances in medicine over past millennia, concluding, "All for what? For the advance of the prevention, treatment, and amelioration of disease, i.e., therapeutics" (1905: 1493).

23 Names of medical societies were collated from websites, and from *JAMA* from the nineteenth century onward. Societies were removed as well as added; removals occur both when societies are dissolved and when they merge with other societies. All data are available in Jackson 2025.

24 Although most specialty and subspeciality certificates persist once adopted by the ABMS, subspecialty certificates are, at times, removed.

25 Hubert Winston Smith goes on to say that a physician "may, therefore, be negligent in using an obsolete method no longer employed by the average practitioner. He might cite the court by book, page and verse authoritative statements from the middle ages that one may judge a specimen of urine by looking at it, but visual examination would not be taken in lieu of a Benedict test for sugar" (1941: 2760).

26 Quoting George E. Stubbs's address to the Surgical Section of the AMA, W. T. Eckley writes, "This is the bacteriological era in medicine. . . . So well-proven is antiseptic surgery say some, that a surgeon should be held liable at law for damages, if in the practice of surgery, where he had failed to use antisepsis his patient was not healed" (1888: 133).

27 The first description of a medical bag is found in Hippocrates, and this fact suggests that such bags have been in use for at least the past 2,400 years (Tsoucalas et al. 2011).

28 In contrast to the other sources discussed in this chapter, details of the tools included in medical bags are collated from both US and non-US sources. Although it is possible that the contents of medical bags might have differed systematically across countries, there is no evidence in the primary sources to suggest that this is the case. In fact, the invocation of the "black bag" as a metaphor in the US medical literature (e.g., Audet et al. 2004), alongside the US commentaries cited in the text, would suggest that there was much similarity in the contents of medical bags across the United States, Canada, Australia, and the United Kingdom.

29 See J. Duffy 1974 for a detailed history of public health in New York City during this period.

30 A review of the first edition of the book in the *American Journal of Diseases of Children* states, "[The author] has omitted no detail of any importance" (*AJDC* Editor 1935).

31 See Han 1997 for an outline of the history of the periodic health examination, including the role of insurance companies in calling attention to the benefits of examinations; see also Cronin 1916.

32 Note that the Commission on Medical Education calculated the proportion of well-child visits several years before Aldrich. However, the method is generally attributed to Aldrich (1934) in subsequent papers. See Appendix for further details of the papers included in Figure 3-6.

33 The evidence suggests that pediatricians fail to complete many of these tasks. Chuck Norlin and colleagues (2011) report that, on average, only 42 percent of the topics recommended by *Bright Futures* were addressed in the well-child visits that they observed. They conclude that there was "little congruence" with the age-specific recommendations of *Bright Futures* (2011: 18).

34 One might have expected the proportion of well-child visits requiring out-of-pocket costs to fall to zero upon passage of the ACA. However, the ACA allowed some plans that were in operation before the ACA to be exempt from these requirements. Other provisions relating to out-of-network providers and to visits entailing more than one type of care made it possible for patients to receive charges even in the context of the ACA (see Kirby, Davidoff, and Basu 2016 for a detailed discussion).

35 The patient record form from which these measures are constructed changes across years, so year-on-year comparisons are less helpful than the general trends revealed; for this reason, rather than showing the data points for each year, I present fitted lines from generalized additive models to display the trends.

36 The "new morbidity" has several other labels, including "new pediatrics," "ambulatory pediatrics," and "community pediatrics." For discussions, see Pawluch 1983; Halpern 1988.

37 Recommendation 5 of the Council on Community Pediatrics' statement on home-visiting programs includes the following: "There is ample reason to believe that the synergy of home visitors working with pediatric clinicians could have positive effects on child health and development. Home visitors should be considered to be a complementary collaborative partner in the provision of developmental assessment and other components of well-child services, especially for at-risk populations" (Council on Community Pediatrics 2009: 602). See also Finello, Terteryan, and Riewerts 2016.

38 *Pulse* was the medical student supplement of *JAMA*. The supplement had a student editorial staff independent from the editorial staff of *JAMA* and was designed to showcase student writing.

39 See Paul Starr (2017: chap. 1), who argues that the power, status, and authority of modern physicians is grounded in standardized education and licensing.

40 See Halpern (1990) for a critique of Pawluch's argument. Halpern argues that pediatricians were not in fact experiencing a reduction in demand during this period.

41 Pawluch further argues that pediatricians were not fully comfortable with the new tasks entailed by the more expansive purview of the specialty.

4. DEFUND THE POLICE

1 Work tasks and work tools have traditionally been seen as crucial determinants of the degree of functional complexity in an occupation (on tasks, see, e.g., Abbott 1988; on tool use, see, e.g., Ambrose 2001; Johnson-Frey 2004; Haines, Feinman, and Nicholas 2004; Hunt 2000). For further details on the measure of functional complexity, see the Appendix.

2 Each year, experts in the various aspects of city government (e.g., public health, fire administration, and personnel administration) provided short summaries of activities in each domain and reported on current controversies and issues.

3 The *Instructions* note, "It should be understood, at the outset, that the principal object to be attained is the prevention of crime" (quoted in J. Lyman 1964, which also contains a useful overview of early police philosophy).

4 See Calder 2012 for a detailed description of the Wickersham Commission and the fourteen reports.

5 A detailed discussion of the community service officer (CSO) role is beyond the scope of this analysis. But it is likely that some of the administrative tasks that the police lost over time (see Figure 4-3) were taken up by CSOs rather than professional administrators. CSOs do not, however, appear to have had an appreciable impact on the number of preventive tasks the police undertake. To some extent, this is likely due to unreliable funding for the CSO scheme, such that police agencies could not always employ CSOs.

6 Although note that some research suggests that this expansive role can also be a source of pride for police officers. Kim (2024) reports the findings of an

ethnographic study of police officers, and argues that the wide range of tasks undertaken by police officers is sometimes used to justify the use of force. When police officers receive criticism for inappropriate use of force, they may react by pointing to their "social work" tasks to resist being stereotyped as racist or oppressors.

7 Although the 911 innovation might be interpreted as an intervention relating to the reactive side of police work, it is notable that the *Challenge of Crime* report encourages further diffusion of 911 in the section on the *prevention* of crime (President's Commission on Law Enforcement and Administration of Justice 1967a: vi). However, in contrast to the general thrust of the report, the commission is here recalling an earlier time when crime prevention entailed removing offenders from society.

8 For more details on the LEMAS survey, see the Appendix.

9 In the section of the report dealing with "Social Factors in Juvenile Delinquency," the authors write, "Disorganization among the foreign immigrants is paralleled by a similar disorganization among the Negroes. . . . Unlike the immigrant, the Negro has relatively few stabilizing traditions extending back over 'hundreds of years.' Neither does he have as a background a stable community organization which has remained unchanged over a long period of time. His institutions are very new and inadequately developed. Consequently they break down completely as agencies of social control in the process of adjustment to the complex life of an urban community. This social disorganization is accompanied by a large amount of personal disorganization and demoralization among Negro adults as well as among Negro children" (Wickersham 1931b: 104–105).

10 For a model showing the effect of an increase in the white population, see Model 4 in the Appendix Table A-4-2. Note that the effect in this case goes in the opposite direction: an increase in the proportion of white people *decreases* the predicted number of specialized units.

5. WE ASK SO MUCH

1 See the Appendix for more details of the analysis.

2 Although it is more than clear that there were increases in enrollment during this period, it is possible that the rate of increase is overstated, as there are concerns that improved data collection might account for some of the increase in measured enrollment (see Snyder 1993: chap. 2).

3 A Massachusetts law from the seventeenth century provides further evidence of the curricular priorities of the pre–Civil War United States. The charmingly titled Old Deluder Satan Law of 1647 states: "It being one chief project of that old deluder, Satan, to keep men from the knowledge of the Scriptures . . . it is therefore ordered by this Court and Authoritie therof; That every Township in this Jurisdiction, after the Lord hath increased them to the number of fifty Housholders, shall then forthwith appoint one within their town to teach all such children as shall resort to him to write and read."

4 Some corroboratory evidence may be found in the *Report of the Commissioner of Education for the year 1886/87.* The report includes a program of study for a one-room district school in Indiana (1887: 180). The program lists reading, arithmetic, language, writing, grammar, geography, history, and physiology, and the phrase "intellectual and moral training" is used to describe the purpose of education.

5 The key educators included state superintendents, presidents of colleges and universities, and secretaries of state boards of education.

6 Items X–XIII deal with discipline and ethics in the school, while items XIV–XVII deal with theoretical study in the school.

7 "Nature work" entailed teaching children about the environment around them and the agricultural "objects and practices" that were part of rural life. Nature study was not introduced to teach children how to become farmers per se, but at the same time, "there is no effective living in the open country unless the mind is sensitive to the objects and phenomena of the open country; and no thoroughly good farming is possible without this same knowledge and outlook" (Bailey 1908: 15).

8 The leaflets were designed for use with students of all ages and contained separate lessons for elementary and high school students.

9 As the initial quotation from James Earl Russell hints at, preparation for democratic citizenship was but one of the elements necessary for a country prepared to fight on behalf of its ideals. The draft boards had revealed that many young men were not sufficiently prepared for military service because of poor health and illiteracy. Such revelations underlined the need for schools to focus on raising educational standards and provided further justification for focusing attention on equality of educational opportunity (e.g., see Norton 1944).

10 The focus on the "whole person" has been labeled in some sociological literature as "personhood" (e.g., Frank and Meyer 2002; Furuta 2017; Furuta, Drori, and Meyer 2024; Wotipka et al. 2023). Note, however, that personhood is largely attributed to the rise of individualism in this literature, and it is not generally coupled with the aim of equality of opportunity.

11 In 1955, 87.0 percent of white five-to-nineteen-year-olds were enrolled as compared to 82.9 percent of five-to-nineteen-year-olds of Black and other races (Snyder 1993: tab. 2).

12 The president suggests in his remarks that this goal ensures that every student will be able to learn, but the creation of drug-free schools also entailed adding drug prevention and drug education within the schools (e.g., see Office of National Drug Control Policy 1989).

13 The continuity of purpose was hardly surprising. *America 2000* was the result of a bipartisan effort, and Clinton had been closely involved, as he had been the chair of the National Governors Association at the time of the state governors' summit.

14 Obama says in his inauguration address, "For as much as government can do, and must do, it is ultimately the faith and determination of the American people upon which this nation relies. It is the kindness to take in a stranger when the

levees break, the selflessness of workers who would rather cut their hours than see a friend lose their job which sees us through our darkest hours." He strikes a similar theme in his Back to School address of September 14, 2010: "But the truth is, an education is about more than getting into a good college or getting a good job when you graduate. It's about giving each and every one of us the chance to fulfill our promise; to be the best version of ourselves we can be. And part of what that means is treating others the way we want to be treated—with kindness and respect."

15 The obituary of James Earl Russell, the dean of Teachers College from 1897 to 1927, for example, includes the phrase "he campaigned unceasingly for the scientific movement in education" (Anonymous 1945).

16 Many of these mentions are within book titles because the first volume included so much material on the readings required in Teachers College classes.

17 Royce is here paraphrasing Wilhelm Dilthey's highly influential paper on universal pedagogy, originally published in German. Highlighting the distinction between "science" and "art," Dilthey (1888) writes, "The great questions of education which currently concern the nation cannot be decided in a universally valid way for all times and peoples, but can only be dealt with on the basis of more precise professional knowledge of history and the current life of education through a kind of artistic action in which the gifts of the statesman and the pedagogue work together."

18 But note that within medicine at the time, there were concerns that an overemphasis on science meant that physicians were in danger of forgetting some of the cultural aspects of the job; see Chapter 3.

19 Notably, the report was so controversial that its release was stage-managed by the Johnson administration such that media attention was relatively limited at the time of release (see H. Hill 2017 for a discussion).

20 See Apple 1995 for a discussion of the (deskilling) effects of such innovations on the work of teachers.

21 The underlying data are the titles of all articles published in these journals. Topic models are fitted separately for each journal, and the final models are chosen according to standard fit criteria. Topics were recoded to a set of smaller broad themes, which are presented in Figures 5-1 and 5-2. See the Appendix for further details; full data and syntax are available in Jackson 2025.

22 Both the data and codes underlying Figure 5-3 are included in Jackson 2025.

23 Note that the broader conception of equalizing activities that I am describing here is not reflected in the color coding of Figure 5-3.

24 If other parts of government take on these functions, it will be more challenging to undertake an analysis of educationally relevant government activities. The analysis presented here is informative precisely because a department dedicated to education was responsible for activities designed to improve educational outcomes. Insofar as other organizations take on these activities, their functions would also need to be included in any future analysis in order to capture industry-wide interventions.

25 In 1915, another sixteen students are listed as "Commercials."

26 The need for guidance counseling for students was first discussed in the early years of the twentieth century, when there was an emphasis on schools undertaking vocational training. The *School Journal* of November 1913 contains a striking passage outlining who should be responsible for such training: "Already enough high schools have established vocational instruction to cause the appearance of a new educational difficulty. Shall the school teachers give advice as to what avocations the pupils shall pursue; or shall there be separate vocational advisers? . . . Three facts militate against the school teachers as advisers: 1. They do not know the world into which the pupils must go. 2. They are not experts in individual human psychology and cannot judge the pupils wisely. 3. Their advice, when given, arouses antagonisms and jealousies in the four quarters of the teachers' world, in the faculty, among the pupils, among the parents, and among the board members and citizens generally" (Anonymous 1913: 4). On guidance in schools, see National Society for the Study of Education 1938.

27 The school nurse is described as being responsible for "encourag[ing] the students to seek excellent personal health through regular dental and physical examinations and care. Duties of the school nurse include; administering first aid, being prepared to cope with emergencies, and assisting with such school projects as the periodical examinations of the students" (NCHS 1961: 17).

28 Mr. Cowmeadow was aged fifty-nine in 1967, and he does not appear in the school staff lists in the 1970s. For a period in the early 1970s, his wife, Barbara J. Cowmeadow, worked as an administrator in the food services department of the school (e.g., see NCHS 1972: 48). Austin L. Cowmeadow's father is one of the interviewees in the New Castle study described in Chapter 6.

29 Note that the 2012 yearbook provides less detail on the precise roles of the teaching staff and others in the school. I have researched each person listed under the teaching staff to assign a discipline, but there remains a large number of teachers for whom the roles are unknown. Similarly, the health and welfare and the special educational needs support staff are not assigned to specific roles. I have assigned half of these staff members to the "health and welfare" category and half to "special educational needs" in Figure 5-4.

30 Pennsylvania passed a law in 2020 to revise the processes used to evaluate professional educators (Act 13). The *Framework for Evaluation* was based on Charlotte Danielson's *Framework for Teachers* (e.g., Danielson 2013). Further details of the analysis are included in the Appendix.

31 Tyack and Cuban (1997) call out the improved heating, ventilation, and safety of schools as one of the great achievements of the past century, an achievement that is rarely recognized in discussions of educational reform.

6. MANAGEMENT AND THE WORKER

1 See the Appendix for more details of the interview data.

2 Both of the letters described in this section are held in the Frederick Winslow Taylor Collection (*Correspondence between Frederick Winslow Taylor and Bethlehem Steel Company*, 1898).

3 Bethlehem Steel Company was formerly known as Bethlehem Iron Company.

4 Here I examine the job description for the general shop supervisor.

5 Frederick Winslow Taylor Collection, *Memo A3T: Bonus to be paid to gang bosses, tool room attendants, etc.,* December 23, 1913. See Carter 1925 for an overview of scientific management procedures at Tabor.

6 Frederick Winslow Taylor Collection, *Memo DM1A: Duties of the gang boss,* August 25, 1919.

7 See, for example, the correspondence between Taylor and Linderman (of Bethlehem Steel), where Taylor's irritation at lack of progress is made clear. He writes to Linderman, "Your company is not paying sufficiently large salaries to keep the good men which it has, and you therefore cannot hope to attract from other Works the additional men most urgently needed to carry on the improved scheme of management which the writer is introducing. . . . Unless adequate steps are taken to correct the above trouble it is an extravagance on your part to pay the writer the wages which he is receiving, and the writer on his part cannot afford to waste his time and risk his reputation training good men at your expense" (Frederick Winslow Taylor Collection, *Recommendation no. 11,* October 5, 1899). See also Chandler 1981.

8 The interviews quoted from in this section are included in the Elton Mayo Papers (*New Castle Interviews,* 1940). Note that the interviews were conducted in the 1940s, but many interviewees use the opportunity to reflect on life in the factory over the prior decades.

9 In the same interview, Oberlitner suggests that "the systematizing of employment methods was due to the depression, when so many men wanted work that they had to do something of this sort."

10 Henry Ford was another who believed that monotony suited a certain type of worker. He claimed, "Some of our tasks are exceedingly monotonous, but then, also, many minds are monotonous—many want to earn a living without thinking, and for these men a task which demands no brains is a boon" (quoted in Chase 1929: 158–159).

11 In the introduction to Goldmark's *Fatigue and Efficiency,* Frederic S. Lee similarly observes, "The man or woman or child is still essential to the method and the machine, and while the inanimate agent demands more and more of him, his fundamental physiological powers are probably not so very different from what they were when he built the pyramids and made papyrus. He may sharpen his attention, shorten his reaction time, and develop manual skill; scientific management may step in and direct his powers more intelligently; but sooner or later his physiological limit is again reached on the new plane" (1912: v–vi).

12 See A. Page 1941 for a history of the Bell Telephone Company, which includes a chapter on Western Electric (chap. 12).

13 One particularly explicit reference to output considerations in the accident prevention movement may be found in the Manufacturer's Session of the Third

Safety Congress: "Safety-first is not a philanthropic movement on the part of employer to employee. Safety-first is a hard practicality of business extension. It is a matter of dollars and cents; and whether you know it or not, you are prompted to its support from a very selfish standpoint" (National Safety Council 1914: 269; see also Alford 1928: chap. 11; Koepke 1934).

14 One of the report's key recommendations is that, "Major industrial executives have as much responsibility to initiate accident prevention as to initiate improvement in productivity" (American Engineering Council 1928: 35).

15 See, for example, the paper of Chas. C. McChord, of the Interstate Commerce Commission, in the *Proceedings of the First Co-operative Safety Congress*: "In making safety the dominant idea in the minds of employees, by continually talking about it and pointing out methods for its attainment, an important step in the right direction is taken. It is necessary for the employee to think right before he can act right" (National Safety Council 1912: 35).

16 In a speech at a meeting of the Business Problems Group, Mayo says of scientific management, "Whereas a highly skilled account has been taken of all the material and mechanical problems of industry, there has been no account whatever in dealing with men. It has been by mere rule of thumb. You cannot make too careful an investigation of the human situation, but even when you have the evidence before you and decide on a plan of action there is still the difficulty of getting it across to the personnel" (Elton Mayo Papers, Rittenhouse Hotel, February 24, 1925).

17 The guide clarifies that while only six pillars are labeled, another twelve pillars exist.

18 Note that the number of tasks provided under each common factor is not exclusive; tasks might appear under more than one heading. However, only a relatively small number of tasks are repeated across the common factors.

19 R. Conrad Cooper was US Steel's assistant vice president for industrial relations, and in this role he negotiated with the union on job classification.

20 The wage-setting rules were established over multiple rounds of negotiation, and many adjustments were made to the original CWS proposals. See Stieber 1959 for a detailed recounting of each stage of the negotiations.

21 The dissenters were Patrick E. Haggerty, the president of Texas Instruments, and Philip Sporn, the chair of the System Development Committee, American Electric Power Company.

22 Coordination costs are also known as "balance delay" in the manufacturing context. For more detailed discussion of balance delay costs in the laundry equipment case study, see Kilbridge 1960; Conant and Kilbridge 1965.

23 For relatively mixed evidence on the effectiveness of OSHA inspections, see R. S. Smith 1979; Viscusi 1979, 1986.

24 The text of the 1973 fourth edition is substantively similar to the text of the first edition, published in 1956. This emphasizes that the attention to safety encouraged by the OSH Act built on prior work within the industry. Notably, key differences between the texts are the addition of references to the OSH Act and

guidance with respect to compliance. Also notably, both editions begin with a discussion of the monetary costs of accidents to the firm.

7. THE FRACTURING

1   The reasons for adding new objectives may differ across the public and private sectors. Within the public sector, ends might accrete because governments add new objectives without funding for additional workers, or because there are attempts to reduce government spending via workforce reductions without reducing the number of ends pursued. Within the private sector, ends might accrete so that employers can reduce the total number of personnel in an organization. If existing workers can be forced to take on additional tasks, employers might be able to reduce worker costs and thus increase profits.

2   Note that components of the paradox might still be in operation, even if new and unrelated ends are added to an occupation. If occupational actors can be convinced to pursue a new end, the logic of specialization might then operate to persuade workers that all tasks needed to pursue this end should be adopted.

3   Although a full evaluation of the effects of growing individualism is beyond the scope of this analysis, it must also be made clear that the case study evidence indicates that—contra the claims of personhood theory—concerns about workers (and customers) were present well before the post–World War II period (e.g., the influence of human relations within the manufacturing industry and the influence of psychology within medicine and education).

4   A broad definition of rationalization would, of course, see a decline in traditional social hierarchies as an indicator of increasing rationalization. Here, I am focusing on the proximate effects of declining traditionalism.

5   Note that a competition for job tasks will only be successful insofar as other occupations actually choose to compete for those tasks. In the case of law enforcement, for example, some occupational organizations expressed disquiet at the idea of taking over tasks currently controlled by the police. One of these organizations, Social Service Workers United–Chicago, wrote an open letter stating, "If all we do is replace police with social workers without eliminating these carceral aspects of social work, we will simply subject vulnerable people to cops by a different name" (Sato 2020).

6   The total government spending on "Payments for individuals" stood at 16.1 percent of gross domestic product (GDP) in 2023, or 70.7 percent of all government spending. In 1940, this category of spending represented 2.1 percent of GDP, or 21.9 percent of all government spending (US Office of Management and Budget 2023: tab. 6.1).

7   Krugman is here paraphrasing Peter R. Fisher, who made this claim sometime during 2002, when he was undersecretary of the Treasury (Thoma 2013).

8   Criticism of excessive bureaucracy and regulation is not exclusive to right-wing commentators. Voices toward the left of the political spectrum are increasingly expressing worries that current regulations stand in the way of progress.

Marc J. Dunkelman, for example, has argued that the government is "too ham-strung to serve the public good" (2025: 332). And Ezra Klein and Derek Thompson's "abundance" agenda takes aim at regulations that restrict affordable housing and investment (2025: conclusion).

9 For a description of the Trump administration's "war on science," see Mueller (2025).

10 It is not surprising, then, that sociology has been targeted in some of the right-wing complaints about contemporary science and scientists (Patel 2024; Parsons 2025).

References

Abbott, Andrew. 1988. *The system of professions: An essay on the division of expert labor.* University of Chicago Press.

Abbott, Andrew. 1993. The sociology of work and occupations. *Annual Review of Sociology* 19 (1): 187–209.

Acemoglu, Daron, and David Autor. 2011. Skills, tasks and technologies: Implications for employment and earnings. In *Handbook of labor economics*, 4, edited by David Card and Orley Ashenfelter, 1043–1171. Elsevier.

Acemoglu, Daron, and Simon Johnson. 2023. *Power and progress: Our thousand-year struggle over technology and prosperity.* Hachette Book Group.

Acemoglu, Daron, Fredric Kong, and Pascual Restrepo. 2024. Tasks at work: Comparative advantage, technology and labor demand. National Bureau of Economic Research, Paper 32872.

Acemoglu, Daron, and Pascual Restrepo. 2019. Automation and new tasks: How technology displaces and reinstates labor. *Journal of Economic Perspectives* 33 (2): 3–30.

An act to regulate the practice of barbering, the licensing of persons to carry on such practice, and to insure the better education of such practitioners in the state of Minnesota. 1897. H.F. 21, 186 § 8.

Advisory Committee on Education. 1938. *Report of the Committee: February 1938.* US Government Printing Office.

Agarwal, Sumit D., Erika Pabo, Ronen Rozenblum, and Karen M. Sherritt. 2020. Professional dissonance and burnout in primary care: A qualitative study. *JAMA Internal Medicine* 180 (3): 395–401.

AJDC Editor. 1935. The Compleat Pediatrician. *American Journal of Diseases of Children* 50, no. 3 (September): 820.

Aldrich, C. Anderson. 1934. The composition of private pediatric practice: A method for keeping adequate clinical records. *American Journal of Diseases of Children* 47 (5): 1051–1064.

Aldrich, C. Anderson, and R. H. Spitz. 1960. Survey of pediatric practice in the US. In *Careers in Pediatrics, Report of the 36th Ross Conference on Pediatric Research,* edited by R.H. Spitz, 57–74. Ross Laboratories.

Alexander, Jason T., and Adam S. Cifu. 2021. Interpreting the ACC/AHA Clinical Practice Guideline Recommendation Classification System. *JAMA* 326 (8): 761–762.

Alexander, Karl, and Stephen L. Morgan. 2016. The Coleman Report at fifty: Its legacy and implications for future research on equality of opportunity. *RSF: The Russell Sage Foundation Journal of the Social Sciences* 2 (5): 1–16.

Alexander, Kenneth O. 1975. On work and authority: Issues in job enlargement, job enrichment, worker participation and shared authority. *American Journal of Economics and Sociology* 34 (1): 43–54.

Alexander, Michelle. 2010. *The new Jim Crow: Mass incarceration in the age of colorblindness.* New Press.

Alford, Leon Pratt. 1928. *Laws of management applied to manufacturing.* Ronald.

Allen, E. G. 1916. Adopting standards to meet trade training requirements. *The ANNALS of the American Academy of Political and Social Science* 65: 205–207.

Allen, Robert C. 2009. *The British industrial revolution in global perspective.* Cambridge University Press.

Allen, Robert C. 2011. Why the Industrial Revolution was British: Commerce, induced invention, and the scientific revolution. *Economic History Review* 64 (2): 357–384.

Almaatouq, Abdullah, Mohammed Alsobay, Ming Yin, and Duncan J. Watts. 2021. Task complexity moderates group synergy. *Proceedings of the National Academy of Sciences* 118 (36): e2101062118.

Almelhem, Ali, Murat Iyigun, Austin Kennedy, and Jared Rubin. 2023. Enlightenment ideals and belief in science in the run-up to the Industrial Revolution: A textual analysis. IZA Discussion Paper 16674. http://dx.doi.org/10.2139/ssrn.4668604.

Alpert, Joel J., and Evan Charney. 1973. *The education of physicians for primary care.* US Department of Health, Education, and Welfare, Public Health Service.

Ambrose, Stanley H. 2001. Paleolithic technology and human evolution. *Science* 291 (5509): 1748–1753.

American Academy of Pediatrics. 1949. *Child health services and pediatric education.* New York: Commonwealth Fund.

American Association of School Administrators. 1942. *Health in schools—twentieth yearbook: Includes report of the executive secretary and list of members.* American Association of School Administrators.

REFERENCES

American Board of Medical Specialties. 2024. *ABMS guide to medical specialties (2024)*. Technical report. American Board of Medical Specialties.

American Engineering Council and National Bureau of Casualty and Surety Underwriters. 1928. *Safety and production: An engineering and statistical study of the relationship between industrial safety and production*. Harper.

American Management Association. 1924. *Job analysis and its use: Report of the committee*. American Management Association.

American Medical Association. 1847. *Code of medical ethics of the American Medical Association: Originally adopted at the adjourned meeting of the National Medical Convention in Philadelphia, May 1847*. American Medical Association.

American Medical Association. 1915. *House of Delegates proceedings, annual session*. American Medical Association.

American Medical Association. 1950. Proceedings of the San Francisco Session. *Journal of the American Medical Association* 143 (13): 1161–1183.

American Psychological Association. 2023. *Stress in America 2023: A nation recovering from collective trauma*. American Psychological Association.

Anderson, C. Richard. 1975. *OSHA and accident control through training*. Industrial.

Andreessen, Marc, 2023. The techno-optimist manifesto. *Andreessen Horowitz*. https://a16z.com/the-techno-optimist-manifesto/.

Anonymous. 1913. Teachers as vocational advisors. *School Journal* (November): 4.

Anonymous. 1922. Evolution of job analysis. *Monthly Labor Review* 14: 440–443.

Anonymous. 1939. How to rate workers' value: What leading companies have done to ease complaints of discrimination; Each job must be measured. *Business Week* (February): 44–45.

Anonymous. 1941. III Job descriptions. *Personnel Journal* 19 (7): 261–262.

Anonymous. 1945. Dr. Russell dead; Columbia ex-dean. *New York Times* (November 5, 1945).

Appelbaum, Eileen, Thomas Bailey, Peter Berg, and Arne L. Kalleberg. 2000. *Manufacturing advantage: Why high-performance work systems pay off*. Cornell University Press.

Appier, Janis. 2005. "We're blocking youth's path to crime": The Los Angeles Coordinating Councils during the Great Depression. *Journal of Urban History* 31 (2): 190–218.

Apple, Michael W. 1995. *Education and power*. Routledge.

Argyris, Chris. 1959. The individual and organization: An empirical test. *Administrative Science Quarterly* 4 (2): 145–167.

Aristotle. 1888. *A treatise on government: Translated from the Greek of Aristotle.* Translated by William Ellis. George Routledge and Sons.

Arnhold, Rainer G., and Evelyn R. Callas. 1966. Composition of a suburban pediatric office practice: An analysis of patient visits during one year. *Clinical Pediatrics* 5 (12): 722–727.

Arnold-Forster, Agnes. 2021. *The cancer problem: Malignancy in nineteenth-century Britain.* Oxford University Press.

Atkins, Paul M. 1924. Employee specifications. *Industrial Management* 68: 115–118.

Attorney General. 1934. *The Attorney General's Conference on Crime: Constitution Hall and Memorial Continental Hall, December 10 to December 13, 1934, Washington, D.C.; Addresses and program.* Attorney General.

Au, Wayne. 2011. Teaching under the new Taylorism: High-stakes testing and the standardization of the 21st century curriculum. *Journal of Curriculum Studies* 43 (1): 25–45.

Audet, Anne-Marie, Michelle M. Doty, Jordan Peugh, Jamil Shamasdin, Kinga Zapert, and Stephen Schoenbaum. 2004. Information technologies: When will they make it into physicians' black bags? *Medscape General Medicine* 6 (4): 2.

Autor, David H. 2010. *The polarization of job opportunities in the US labor market: Implications for employment and earnings.* Center for American Progress and The Hamilton Project.

Autor, David H. 2015. Why are there still so many jobs? The history and future of workplace automation. *Journal of Economic Perspectives* 29 (3): 3–30.

Autor, David H., Lawrence F. Katz, and Melissa S. Kearney. 2008. Trends in US wage inequality: Revising the revisionists. *The Review of Economics and Statistics* 90 (2): 300–323.

Autor, David H., Frank Levy, and Richard J. Murnane. 2003. The skill content of recent technological change: An empirical exploration. *Quarterly Journal of Economics* 118 (4): 1279–1333.

Ayres, Leonard Porter, Edward Lee Thorndike, Ernest James Ashbaugh, Eugene Alexander Nifenecker, Melvin Everett Haggerty, Frank Washington Ballou, George Melcher, Burdette Ross Buckingham, Stuart Appleton Courtis, Charles Hubbard Judd, et al. 1918. *The measurement of educational products.* Vol. 17. Public School Publishing.

Babbage, Charles. 1833. *On the economy of machinery and manufactures.* Charles Knight.

Babbage, Charles. 1864. *Passages from the life of a philosopher.* Longman, Green, Longman, Roberts & Green.

Backus, J. E., Sara Davidson, and Roy Rada. 1987. Searching for patterns in the MeSH vocabulary. *Bulletin of the Medical Library Association* 75 (3): 221.

Baer, Carolyn, and Darko Odic. 2022. Mini managers: Children strategically divide cognitive labor among collaborators, but with a self-serving bias. *Child Development* 93 (2): 437–450.

Bagley, William Chandler. 1915. *Classroom management: Its principles and technique.* Macmillan.

Bailey, Liberty Hyde. 1908. *On the training of persons to teach agriculture in the public schools.* Government Printing Office.

Bain, Alexander. 1879. *Education as a science.* D. Appleton.

Baker, Henry B. 1887. Scientific collective investigation of disease: Read in the Section on State Medicine, at the Thirty-Eighth Annual Meeting of the American Medical Association, June, 1887. *Journal of the American Medical Association* 9 (16): 486–491.

Bal, B. Sonny. 2009. An introduction to medical malpractice in the United States. *Clinical Orthopaedics and Related Research* 467 (2): 339–347.

Baron, James N., Frank R. Dobbin, and P. Devereaux Jennings. 1986. War and peace: The evolution of modern personnel administration in US industry. *American Journal of Sociology* 92 (2): 350–383.

Barr, Justin, and Scott H. Podolsky. 2020. A national medical response to crisis—the legacy of World War II. *New England Journal of Medicine* 383 (7): 613–615.

Beck, Ulrich. 1992. *Risk society: Towards a new modernity.* Translated by Mark Ritter. Sage.

Becker, Gary S., and Kevin M. Murphy. 1992. The division of labor, coordination costs, and knowledge. *Quarterly Journal of Economics* 107 (4): 1137–1160.

Belamarich, Peter F., Rachelle Gandica, Ruth E. K. Stein, and Andrew D. Racine. 2006. Drowning in a sea of advice: Pediatricians and American Academy of Pediatrics policy statements. *Pediatrics* 118 (4): e964–e978.

Bell, Daniel. 1966. Comment: Government by commission. *Public Interest* 3: 3–9.

Bell, Monica C. 2020. Located institutions: Neighborhood frames, residential preferences, and the case of policing. *American Journal of Sociology* 125 (4): 917–973.

Bendix, Richard. 1956. *Work and authority in industry: Managerial ideologies in the course of industrialization.* Wiley.

Benge, Eugene J. 1920. *Standard practice in personnel work.* H. W. Wilson.

Benge, Eugene J., Samuel L. H. Burk, and Edward N. Hay. 1941. *Manual of job evaluation procedures of job analysis and appraisal.* Harper Bros.

Beniger, James. 2009. *The control revolution: Technological and economic origins of the information society.* Harvard University Press.

Bergman, A. B., J. L. Probstfield, and R. J. Wedgwood. 1967. Performance analysis in pediatric practice: Preliminary report. *Academic Medicine* 42 (3): 249–253.

Bergman, Abraham B., Steven W. Dassel, and Ralph J. Wedgwood. 1966. Time-motion study of practicing pediatricians. *Pediatrics* 38 (2): 254–263.

Berman, Elizabeth Popp. 2022. Thinking like an economist: How efficiency replaced equality in US public policy. Princeton University Press.

Berrol, Selma. 1969. Immigrants at school: New York City, 1900–1910. *Urban Education* 4 (3): 220–230.

Beyer, David S. 1917. Accident prevention. *The ANNALS of the American Academy of Political and Social Science* 70 (1): 238–243.

Bhatt, Jay. 2019. *Hospitals offering housing: Improved patient care.* American Hospital Association, December 12, 2019. https://www.aha.org/news/healthcare innovation-thursday-blog/2019-12-12hospitals-offering-housing-improved -patient-care.

Bickley, E. H. 1918. Records that match the man to the job. *Factory* 21: 28–30.

Billings, John S., and Robert Fletcher. eds., 1879. *Index Medicus: A Monthly Classified Record of the Current Medical Literature of the World.* F. Leypoldt.

Blau, Peter M. 1970. A formal theory of differentiation in organizations. *American Sociological Review* 35 (2): 201–218.

Blau, Peter M. 1977. Inequality and heterogeneity: A primitive theory of social structure. Free Press.

Blauner, Robert. 1964. *Alienation and freedom: The factory worker and his industry.* University of Chicago Press.

Blei, David M., Andrew Y. Ng, and Michael I. Jordan. 2003. Latent Dirichlet allocation. *Journal of Machine Learning Research* 3 (January): 993–1022.

Bobbitt, John Franklin. 1912. The elimination of waste in education. *Elementary School Teacher* 12 (6): 259–271.

Bobbitt, John Franklin. 1918. *The curriculum.* Houghton Mifflin.

Bode, Boyd Henry. 1921. *Fundamentals of education.* Macmillan.

Bode, Boyd Henry. 1927. *Modern educational theories.* Vol. 508. Vintage Books, Random House.

Bonds, Alfred B. 1948. The President's Commission on Higher Education and Negro higher education. *Journal of Negro Education* 17 (3): 426–436.

Bouk, Dan. 2015. *How our days became numbered.* University of Chicago Press.

Boulware, J. R. 1958. The composition of private pediatric practice in a small community in the South of the United States: A twenty-five year survey. *Pediatrics* 22 (3): 548–558.

Bradley, E. H., H. Sipsma, and L. A. Taylor. 2017. American health care paradox— high spending on health care and poor health. *QJM: An International Journal of Medicine* 110 (2): 61–65.

Braverman, Harry. 1974. *Labor and monopoly capital: The degradation of work in the twentieth century.* Monthly Review Press.

Brayne, Sarah. 2020. *Predict and surveil: Data, discretion, and the future of policing.* Oxford University Press, USA.

Breese, B. B., F. A. Disney, and W. Talpey. 1966. The nature of a small pediatric group practice. *Pediatrics* 38 (2): 264–285.

Brenner, Michael J. 2000. The New Atlantis and the frontiers of medicine. *JAMA* 283 (17): 2296–2296.

Brenner, Robert M., and James T. Duncan. 1978. *Police job-task analysis: An overview.* Law Enforcement Assistance Administration.

Brignardello-Petersen, Romina, Alonso Carrasco-Labra, and Gordon H. Guyatt. 2021. How to interpret and use a clinical practice guideline or recommendation: Users' guides to the medical literature. *JAMA* 326 (15): 1516–1523.

Brotherton, Stephen, Audiey Kao, and B. J. Crigger. 2016. Professing the values of medicine: The modernized AMA Code of Medical Ethics. *JAMA* 316 (10): 1041–1042.

Brown, Ina Corinne. 1950. The role of education in preparing children and youth to live in a multi-racial society. *Journal of Negro Education* 19 (3): 384–387.

Bruning, Patrick F., and Michael A. Campion. 2018. A role–resource approach-avoidance model of job crafting: A multimethod integration and extension of job crafting theory. *Academy of Management Journal* 61 (2): 499–522.

Brunton, Lauder. 1913. John S. Billings, MD, formerly librarian of the Surgeon General's Office, Washington, and founder of the "Index Medicus." *British Medical Journal* (March): 642.

Buckham, T. R. 1885. Prophylaxis of diphtheria. *Journal of the American Medical Association* 5 (2): 53–54.

Bulger, Roger J. 1980. A physician considers nuclear war. *JAMA* 244 (11): 1255–1255.

Bulkley, L. Duncan. 1884. Specialties, and their relation to the medical profession. *Journal of the American Medical Association* 3 (24): 651–655.

Bulkley, L. Duncan. 1889. On the relation between the general practitioner and the consultant or specialist: Read before the American Academy of Medicine, November 13, 1888. *Journal of the American Medical Association* 12 (5): 155–158.

Bureau of Education. 1874. *A statement of the theory of education in the United States of America: As approved by many leading educators.* US Government Printing Office.

Burgess, O. O. 1892. Abstract of an address. Delivered at the opening of the twenty-second annual meeting of the Medical Society of the State of California, April, 1892. *Journal of the American Medical Association* 18 (20): 609–611.

Burnett, Robert D., and Leo S. Bell. 1978. Projecting pediatric practice patterns. *Pediatrics* 62 (4S): 625–690.

Burnham, William H. 1917. A health examination at school entrance. *Journal of the American Medical Association* 68 (12): 893–899.

Burtt, Harold Ernest. 1929. *Psychology and industrial efficiency.* Appleton.

Bush, George H. W. 1990. Address before a joint session of the congress on the state of the union (January 31, 1990).

Bush, George H. W. 1991. *America 2000: An education strategy.* US Government Printing Office.

Butkus, Renee, Robert Doherty, Sue S. Bornstein, and Health and Public Policy Committee of the American College of Physicians. 2018. Reducing firearm injuries and deaths in the United States: A position paper from the American College of Physicians. *Annals of Internal Medicine* 169 (10): 704–707.

Butler, Nicholas Murray. 1888. *The argument for manual training.* E. L. Kellogg.

Butler, Nicholas Murray. 1900. Syllabi for Teachers College courses in education: Principles of education. *Teachers College Record* 1 (4): 15–33.

Calder, James D. 2012. Between brain and state: Herbert C. Hoover, George W. Wickersham, and the commission that grounded social scientific investigations of

American crime and justice, 1929–1931 and beyond. *Marquette Law Review* 96: 1035–1108.

Caliver, Ambrose. 1933. The Negro teacher and a philosophy of Negro education. *Journal of Negro Education* 2 (4): 432–447.

Callis, Anna, Thad Dunning, and Guadalupe Tuñón. 2022. Causal inference and knowledge accumulation in historical political economy. In *The Oxford Handbook of Historical Political Economy,* edited by Jeffery A. Jenkins and Jared Rubin, 55–74. Oxford Academic.

Cameron, A. Colin, and Pravin K. Trivedi. 2013. *Regression analysis of count data.* Vol. 53. Cambridge University Press.

Camic, Charles, and Yu Xie. 1994. The statistical turn in American social science: Columbia University, 1890 to 1915. *American Sociological Review* 59 (5): 773–805.

Carpenter, Niles. 1927. *Immigrants and their children, 1920: A study based on Census statistics relative to the foreign born and the native white of foreign or mixed parentage.* Vol. 7. US Government Printing Office.

Carter, John W. 1925. The production control method of the Tabor Manufacturing Company. *The ANNALS of the American Academy of Political and Social Science* 119 (1): 92–96.

Cassedy, James H. 2013. *American medicine and statistical thinking, 1800–1860.* Harvard University Press.

Cebul, Randall D., James B. Rebitzer, Lowell J. Taylor, and Mark E. Votruba. 2008. Organizational fragmentation and care quality in the US healthcare system. *Journal of Economic Perspectives* 22 (4): 93–113.

Centers for Disease Control and Prevention. 2022. *An update on cancer deaths in the United States.* US Department of Health and Human Services, Centers for Disease Control and Prevention, Division of Cancer Prevention and Control.

Chandler, Alfred D., Jr. 1981. The American system and modern management. In *Yankee enterprise: The rise of the American system of manufactures,* edited by Otto Mayr and Robert C. Post, 153–170. Smithsonian Institution Press.

Charters, W. W., Douglas Waples, and Samuel P. Capen. 1929. *The Commonwealth teacher training study.* University of Chicago Press.

Chase, Stuart. 1929. *Men and machines.* MacMillan.

Chung, Kae H., and Monica F. Ross. 1977. Differences in motivational properties between job enlargement and job enrichment. *Academy of Management Review* 2 (1): 113–122.

Clarfield, A. Mark. 1996. Finding pleasure and history in the Index Medicus. *CMAJ: Canadian Medical Association Journal* 155 (9): 1327.

Cohen, I. Bernard. 1987. Scientific revolutions, revolutions in science, and a probabilistic revolution 1800–1930. In *The probabilistic revolution*, vol. 1, *Ideas in history,* edited by Lorenz Kruger, Lorraine J. Daston, and Michael Heidelberger, 23–44. MIT Press.

Coleman, James S. 1966. *Equality of educational opportunity.* National Center for Educational Statistics.

Coleman, William. 1987. Experimental physiology and statistical inference: The therapeutic trial in nineteenth-century Germany. In *The probabilistic revolution,* vol. 2, *Ideas in the sciences,* edited by Lorenz Kruger, Gerd Gigerenzer, and Mary S. Morgan, 201–226. MIT Press.

Coletti, Margaret H., and Howard L. Bleich. 2001. Medical Subject Headings used to search the biomedical literature. *Journal of the American Medical Informatics Association* 8 (4): 317–323.

Collier, David. 2011. Understanding process tracing. *PS: Political Science & Politics* 44 (4): 823–830.

Collins, Charles R., Forrest Stuart, and Patrick Janulis. 2022. Policing gentrification or policing displacement? Testing the relationship between order maintenance policing and neighborhood change in Los Angeles. *Urban Studies* 59 (2): 414–433.

Commissioner of Education. 1882. *Report of the Commissioner of Education for the year 1880.* Government Printing Office.

Commissioner of Education. 1887. *Report of the Commissioner of Education for the year 1886/87.* Government Printing Office.

Commission on Medical Education. 1928. *Second Report of Commission on Medical Education.* New Haven: Office of the Director of the Study.

Committee for Economic Development. 1985. *Investing in our children: Business and the public schools; A statement.* Committee for Economic Development.

Commons, John Rogers. 1919. *Industrial goodwill.* McGraw-Hill.

Conant, Eaton H., and Maurice D. Kilbridge. 1965. An interdisciplinary analysis of job enlargement: Technology, costs, and behavioral implications. *ILR Review* 18 (3): 377–395.

Conk, Margo Anderson. 1978. Occupational classification in the United States Census: 1870–1940. *Journal of Interdisciplinary History* 9 (1): 111–130.

Conn, Herbert W. 1888. Bacteriology in our medical schools. *Science* 11 (267): 123–126.

Cook, Katherine M. 1933. The Children's Code. *School Life* 19 (1): 2, 18.

Cooke, Molly, David M. Irby, Bridget C. O'Brien, and Lee S. Shulman. 2010. *Educating physicians: A call for reform of medical school and residency.* Jossey-Bass / Carnegie Foundation for the Advancement of Teaching.

Cooper, Stephanie, Rachel J. Valleley, Jodi Polaha, John Begeny, and Joseph H. Evans. 2006. Running out of time: Physician management of behavioral health concerns in rural pediatric primary care. *Pediatrics* 118 (1): e132–e138.

Council of Economic Advisers. 1997. *Annual Report of the Council of Economic Advisers.* US Government Printing Office.

Council on Community Pediatrics. 2009. The role of preschool home-visiting programs in improving children's developmental and health outcomes. *Pediatrics* 123 (2): 598–603.

Council on Community Pediatrics. 2013. Community pediatrics: Navigating the intersection of medicine, public health, and social determinants of children's health. *Pediatrics* 131 (3): 623–628.

Council on Foods and Nutrition. 1970. Malnutrition and hunger in the United States: Report of the Council on Foods and Nutrition to the AMA Board of Trustees. *JAMA* 213 (2): 272–275.

Coyle, Diane. 2025. *The measure of progress: Counting what really matters.* Princeton University Press.

Crawford, Serena. 2023. *Bringing culinary medicine to Yale's new teaching kitchen.* Yale School of Medicine, June. https://medicine.yale.edu/news-article/bringing-culinary-medicine-to-yales-new-teaching-kitchen/.

Cremin, Lawrence A. 1955. The revolution in American secondary education, 1893–1918. *Teachers College Record* 56 (6): 1–12.

Crenshaw, Kimberlé Williams, Priscilla Ocen, and Jyoti Nanda. 2015. *Black girls matter: Pushed out, overpoliced and underprotected.* New York.

Cronin, Herbert J. 1916. The value of health examinations. *Journal of the American Medical Association* 66 (18): 1374–1376.

Crumley, Frank E. 1990. Substance abuse and adolescent suicidal behavior. *JAMA* 263 (22): 3051–3056.

Cubberley, Ellwood P. 1909. *Changing conceptions of education.* Houghton Mifflin.

Cubberley, Ellwood P. 1919. *Public education in the United States: A study and interpretation of American educational history; an introductory textbook dealing with the larger problems of present-day education in the light of their historical development.* Houghton Mifflin.

Cummings, Homer S. 1933. *The campaign against crime.* November 22, 1933, Columbia Broadcasting Company. https://www.justice.gov/sites/default /files/ag/legacy/2011/09/16/11-22-1933.pdf.

Cummings, Homer S. 1937. We can prevent crime. *Legal Chatter* 1: 32.

Cushing, Harvey. 1933. Medicine at the crossroads. *Journal of the American Medical Association* 100 (20): 1567–1575.

Czerniawski, Amanda M. 2007. From average to ideal: The evolution of the height and weight table in the United States, 1836–1943. *Social Science History* 31 (2): 273–296.

Dalton, Robert Hunter. 1893. A glance at the American medical profession since the beginning of the present century. *Journal of the American Medical Association* 21 (26): 953–955.

Dammery, David. 2016. A historical account of the doctor's bag. *Australian Family Physician* 45 (9): 636–638.

Danielson, Charlotte. 2013. *The framework for teaching evaluation instrument.* Danielson Group.

Daston, Lorraine J. 1987. The domestication of risk: Mathematical probability and insurance, 1650–1830. In *The probabilistic revolution,* vol. 1, *Ideas in history,* edited by Lorenz Kruger, Lorraine J. Daston, and Michael Heidelberger, 237–260. MIT Press.

Davis, Allison. 1939. The socialization of the American Negro child and adolescent. *Journal of Negro Education* 8 (3): 264–274.

Davis, Geo. S. 1895. The Index Medicus. *Journal of the American Medical Association* 24 (24): 944.

Davis, N. S. 1883. Address on the present status and future tendencies of the medical profession in the United States. *Journal of the American Medical Association* 1 (2): 33–42.

Davison, Wilburt C. 1934. *The compleat pediatrician: Practical, diagnostic, therapeutic and preventive pediatrics.* Duke University Press.

Davison, Wilburt C. 1944. *The compleat pediatrician: Practical, diagnostic, therapeutic and preventive pediatrics.* Duke University Press.

Davison, Wilburt C., and Jeana Davison Levinthal. 1957. *The compleat pediatrician: Practical, diagnostic, therapeutic and preventive pediatrics.* Duke University Press.

Dean, Wendy, and Simon Talbot. 2023. *If I betray these words: Moral injury in medicine and why it's so hard for clinicians to put patients first.* Steerforth.

Defund the Police. 2020. Defund the Police: About, June. https://defundthepolice.org/about/.

De Garmo, Charles. 1891. The Herbartian system of pedagogics. *Educational Review* 1:33–45.

Deisher, Robert W., Alfred J. Derby, and Melvin J. Sturman. 1960. The practice of pediatrics: Changing trends in pediatric practice. *Pediatrics* 25 (4): 711–716.

Deming, David J. 2011. Better schools, less crime? *Quarterly Journal of Economics* 126 (4): 2063–2115.

Denney, Matthew G. T. 2021. "To Wage a War": Crime, race, and state making in the age of FDR. *Studies in American Political Development* 35 (1): 16–56.

Desrosières, Alain. 1998. *The politics of large numbers: A history of statistical reasoning.* Harvard University Press.

Detmer, Don E. 1980. "If we're so good, why aren't we better?" Social expectations of medicine in the 1980s. *JAMA* 243 (9): 930–931.

Detsky, Allan S., Stephen R. Gauthier, and Victor R. Fuchs. 2012. Specialization in medicine: How much is appropriate? *JAMA* 307 (5): 463–464.

Dewey, John. 1899. *The school and society: Being three lectures.* University of Chicago Press.

Dewey, John. 1910. *How we think.* D. C. Heath.

DeWitt, Peter. 2018. Are we asking too much of schools? *Education Week* (April 22, 2018).

Dickinson, Elizabeth Evitts. 2016. Coleman Report set the standard for the study of public education. *Johns Hopkins Magazine* 68 (4): 1–11.

Diemer, Hugo, Meyer Bloomfield, Daniel Bloomfield, and E. F. Dahm. 1921. *The foreman and his job: The first work manual of the modern foremanship course.* La Salle Extension University, Chicago.

Dierdorff, Erich C., Donald W. Drewes, and Jennifer J. Norton. 2006. O*NET tools and technology: A synopsis of data development procedures. North Carolina State University. http://www.onetcenter.org/dl_files/T2Development.pdf.

Diliberti, Melissa, Michael Jackson, Samuel Correa, and Zoe Padgett. 2019. Crime, violence, discipline, and safety in US public schools: Findings from the School Survey on Crime and Safety: 2017–18. First look. *National Center for Education Statistics: 2019-061.*

Dilthey, Wilhelm. 1888. Ueber die moglichkeit einer allgemeingültigen pädago-gischen wissenschaft. *Sitzungsberichte der Berliner Akademie der Wissen-schaften*, 807–832.

Dobbin, Frank. 1994. *Forging industrial policy: The United States, Britain, and France in the railway age*. Cambridge University Press.

Dobbin, Frank, John R. Sutton, John W. Meyer, and Richard Scott. 1993. Equal opportunity law and the construction of internal labor markets. *American Journal of Sociology* 99 (2): 396–427.

Dobbin, Frank, and John R Sutton. 1998. The strength of a weak state: The rights revolution and the rise of human resources management divisions. *American Journal of Sociology* 104 (2): 441–476.

Doggett, Lisa. 2023. Doctors have their own diagnosis: "Moral distress" from an inhumane health system. *Public Health Watch, NPR* (August 2, 2023).

Dryfoos, Joy G. 2001. The full-service vision: Responding to critical need. In *The Jossey-Bass reader on school reform*, 233–247. Jossey-Bass.

Dubofsky, Melvyn, and Joseph A. McCartin. 2017. *Labor in America: A history*. John Wiley & Sons.

Duffy, John. 1974. *History of public health in New York City, 1866–1966*. Vol. 2. Rus-sell Sage Foundation.

Duffy, Thomas P. 2011. The Flexner Report—100 years later. *Yale Journal of Biology and Medicine* 84 (3): 269–276.

Dunkelman, Marc J. 2025. *Why nothing works: Who killed progress—and how to bring it back*. Pantheon Books.

Dunphy, J. Englebert. 1964. Responsibility and authority in American surgery. *Bul-letin of the American College of Surgeons* 49: 9–12.

Durkheim, Émile. 1893. *The division of labor in society*. Simon / Schuster.

Dwyer, Rachel E. 2013. The care economy? Gender, economic restructuring, and job polarization in the US labor market. *American Sociological Review* 78 (3): 390–416.

Dwyer, Rachel E. 2025. Job polarization in the US in the twenty-first century: Studying shifts in employment structures using occupations and sectors. In *Global Trends in Job Polarisation and Upgrading: A Comparison of Developed and Developing Economies*, edited by Sergio Torrejón Pérez, Enrique Fernández-Macías, and John Hurley, 83–117. Springer Nature Switzerland.

Eastman, Crystal. 1910. *Work-accidents and the law*. Vol. 2. Charities Publication Committee.

Eckley, W. T. 1888. The germ-theory of disease and antiseptic treatment: Read before the Keokuk County Medical Society, Dec. 6, 1887 and published by special request of the society. *Journal of the American Medical Association* 10 (5): 131–136.

Educational Policies Commission. 1937. *The unique function of education in American democracy.* National Education Association of the United States.

Educational Policies Commission. 1938. *The purposes of education in American democracy.* National Education Association of the United States / the American Association of School Administrators.

Educational Policies Commission. 1939. *American education and the war in Europe.* National Education Association of the United States / the American Association of School Administrators.

Educational Policies Commission. 1942. *A war policy for American schools.* National Education Association of the United States / the American Association of School Administrators.

Educational Policies Commission. 1962. *Education and the disadvantaged American.* National Education Association of the United States.

Edwards, Alba M. 1911. Classification of occupations: The classification of occupations, with special reference to the United States and the proposed new classification for the Thirteenth Census Report on Occupations. *Publications of the American Statistical Association* 12 (94): 618–646.

Elton Mayo Papers. *Business Problems Group, address to,* 1925. Arch GA 54, Box: 5a, Folder: 13. Baker Library Special Collections and Archives, Harvard Business School, Cambridge, MA.

Elton Mayo Papers. *How to obtain maximum efficiency in labor utilization,* 1942. Arch GA 54, Box: 5a, Folder: 45. Baker Library Special Collections and Archives, Harvard Business School, Cambridge, MA.

Elton Mayo Papers. *Interviews, substance analysis, operating branch employees, Western Electric Hawthorne Study,* 1929. Arch GA 54, Box: 4b, Folder: 26. Baker Library Special Collections and Archives, Harvard Business School, Cambridge, MA.

Elton Mayo Papers. *Interviews, substance analysis, operating branch employees, Western Electric Hawthorne Study,* 1929. Arch GA 54, Box: 4c, Folder: 27. Baker Library Special Collections and Archives, Harvard Business School, Cambridge, MA.

Elton Mayo Papers. *Meeting of the Business Problems Group, Rittenhouse Hotel,* February 24, 1925. Arch GA 54, Box: 5a, Folder: 13. Baker Library Special Collections and Archives, Harvard Business School, Cambridge, MA.

Elton Mayo Papers. *New Castle Conference,* 1940. Arch GA 54, Carton: 6, Folder: 18. Baker Library Special Collections and Archives, Harvard Business School, Cambridge, MA.

Elton Mayo Papers. *New Castle Field Notes,* 1940., Arch GA 54, Carton: 6, Folder: 19. Baker Library Special Collections and Archives, Harvard Business School, Cambridge, MA.

Elton Mayo Papers. *New Castle Interviews,* 1940. Arch GA 54, Carton: 6, Folder: 20–32. Baker Library Special Collections and Archives, Harvard Business School, Cambridge, MA.

Emerson, Harrington. 1922. *The twelve principles of efficiency.* Engineering Magazine.

Emerson, Haven. 1923. Periodic medical examinations of apparently healthy persons. *Journal of the American Medical Association* 80 (19): 1376–1381.

Engel, George L. 1960. A unified concept of health and disease. *Perspectives in Biology and Medicine* 3 (4): 459–485.

Engel, George L. 1977. The need for a new medical model: A challenge for biomedicine. *Science* 196 (4286): 129–136.

Engel, George L. 1979. The biopsychosocial model and the education of health professionals. *General Hospital Psychiatry* 1 (2): 156–165.

Enzmann, Dirk. 2015. DIVCAT: Stata module to calculate five measures of diversity for multiple categories. https://econpapers.repec.org/software/bocbocode/s457956.htm.

Erikson, Emily, and Hirokazu Shirado. 2021. Networks, property, and the division of labor. *American Sociological Review* 86 (4): 759–786.

Espeland, Wendy Nelson, and Michael Sauder. 2016. *Engines of anxiety: Academic rankings, reputation, and accountability.* Russell Sage Foundation.

Eurofound. 2021. *Understanding the gender pay gap: What role do sector and occupation play?* European Jobs Monitor series, Publications Office of the European Union, Luxembourg.

Executive Order No. 14177. 2025. President's Council of Advisors on Science and Technology. FR Doc. 2025-02121.

Executive Order No. 14212. 2025. Improving Education Outcomes by Empowering Parents, States, and Communities. FR Doc. 2025-05213.

Executive Order No. 14217. 2025. Commencing the Reduction of the Federal Bureaucracy. FR Doc. 2025-03133.

Farber, Henry S., Daniel Herbst, Ilyana Kuziemko, and Suresh Naidu. 2021. Unions and inequality over the twentieth century: New evidence from survey data. *Quarterly Journal of Economics* 136 (3): 1325–1385.

Finello, Karen Moran, Araksi Terteryan, and Robert J Riewerts. 2016. Home visiting programs: What the primary care clinician should know. *Current Problems in Pediatric and Adolescent Health Care* 46 (4): 101–125.

Firpo, Sergio, Nicole M. Fortin, and Thomas Lemieux. 2011. Occupational tasks and changes in the wage structure. IZA Discussion Paper 5542. http://dx.doi.org /10.2139/ssrn.1778886.

Fishbein, Morris. 1942. Cultural education of a physician. *Journal of the American Medical Association* 119 (16): 1239–1245.

Fisk, Eugene Lyman. 1922. Fatigue in industry. *American Journal of Public Health* 12 (3): 212–217.

Fitch, Charles H. 1882. *Report on the manufacture of firearms and ammunition.* US Government Printing Office.

Fitzsimmons, K. Ross. 1973. Implications of the National Environmental Policy Act of 1969. *Food, Drug, Cosmetic Law Journal* 28 (1): 51–59.

Flexner, Abraham. 1910. *Medical education in the United States and Canada: A report to the Carnegie Foundation for the Advancement of Teaching.* The Carnegie Foundation for the Advancement of Teaching.

Flint, Austin. 1884. Remarks on medicinal and non-medicinal therapeutics: An address delivered at the first annual meeting of the New York State Medical Association, November 20, 1884. *New York Medical Journal* 40: 597–604.

Fogelson, Robert M. 1977. *Big-city police.* Harvard University Press.

Fort, S. J. 1924. Federalization of health activities. *Journal of the American Medical Association* 83 (17): 1354–1355.

Fourcade, Marion, and Kieran Healy. 2024. *The ordinal society.* Harvard University Press.

Frank, David John, and John W. Meyer. 2002. The profusion of individual roles and identities in the postwar period. *Sociological Theory* 20 (1): 86–105.

Frederick Winslow Taylor Collection. *Correspondence between Frederick Winslow Taylor and Bethlehem Steel Company,* 1898. Box: 75, Folder: 4. Stevens Institute of Technology, Samuel C. Williams Library, Hoboken, NJ.

Frederick Winslow Taylor Collection. *Functional plan of organization of the Bethlehem Steel Company,* 1897. Box: 75, Folder: 2. Stevens Institute of Technology, Samuel C. Williams Library, Hoboken, NJ.

REFERENCES

Frederick Winslow Taylor Collection. *How to obtain maximum efficiency in labor utilization,* 1942. Box: 75, Folder: 4. Stevens Institute of Technology, Samuel C. Williams Library, Hoboken, NJ.

Frederick Winslow Taylor Collection. *Memo A3T: Bonus to be paid to gang bosses, tool room attendants, etc.,* December 23, 1913. Box: 130, Folder: 7. Stevens Institute of Technology, Samuel C. Williams Library, Hoboken, NJ.

Frederick Winslow Taylor Collection. *Memo DM1A: Duties of the gang boss,* August 25, 1919. Box: 130, Folder: 1. Stevens Institute of Technology, Samuel C. Williams Library, Hoboken, NJ.

Frederick Winslow Taylor Collection. *Recommendation no. 11, from Frederick W. Taylor to Robert P. Linderman,* October 5, 1899. Box: 75, Folder: 5. Stevens Institute of Technology, Samuel C. Williams Library, Hoboken, NJ.

Frederick Winslow Taylor Collection. *Standing order for a speed boss,* November 24, 1918. Box: 130, Folder: 1. Stevens Institute of Technology, Samuel C. Williams Library, Hoboken, NJ.

Frederick Winslow Taylor Collection. *Standing order for maintenance department,* March 30, 1916. Box: 130, Folder: 3. Stevens Institute of Technology, Samuel C. Williams Library, Hoboken, NJ.

Frederick Winslow Taylor Collection. *Standing order on supervision and duties of the general shop: Preparation, methods, & inspection supervisors,* May 1, 1924. Box: 92, Folder: 9. Stevens Institute of Technology, Samuel C. Williams Library, Hoboken, NJ.

Freeman, Richard B. 1998. Spurts in union growth: Defining moments and social processes. In *The defining moment: The Great Depression and the American economy in the twentieth century,* edited by Michael D. Bordo, Claudia Goldin, and Eugene N. White, 265–296. University of Chicago Press.

French, Will. 1955. The changed role of the American high school. *Teachers College Record* 56 (7): 1–8.

Friedman, Milton. 2002. *Capitalism and freedom.* 40th anniversary ed. University of Chicago Press.

Fritz J. Roethlisberger Papers. *Installation administrator's references, Western Electric Company,* circa 1936. Arch GA 76, Carton: 10, Folder: 4. Baker Library Special Collections and Archives, Harvard Business School, Cambridge, MA.

Fulton, John S. 1905. American hygiene: Chairman's address before the Section on Hygiene and Sanitary Science at the Fifty-Sixth Annual Session of the American Medical Association, Portland, Oregon, July 11–14, 1905. *Journal of the American Medical Association* 45 (17): 1231–1238.

Furnas, Alexander C., Timothy M. LaPira, and Dashun Wang. 2025. Partisan disparities in the use of science in policy. *Science* 388 (6745): 362–367.

Furuta, Jared. 2017. Rationalization and student/school personhood in US college admissions: The rise of test-optional policies, 1987 to 2015. *Sociology of Education* 90 (3): 236–254.

Furuta, Jared, Gili Drori, and John W. Meyer. 2024. The rise of the social state as a global model: A comparative and historical study, 1870–2000. *European Journal of Cultural and Political Sociology* 11 (1): 13–43.

Gallman, Robert E. 1960. Commodity output, 1839–1899. In *Trends in the American economy in the nineteenth century*, edited by the Conference on Research in Income and Wealth, 13–72. Princeton University Press.

Gee, Helen Hofer. 1960. Learning the physician-patient relationship. *JAMA* 173 (12): 1301–1304.

Geiger, H. Jack. 2016. The first community health center in Mississippi: Communities empowering themselves. *American Journal of Public Health* 106 (10): 1738–1740.

Gellhorn, Walter. 1956. *Individual freedom and governmental restraints.* Louisiana State University Press.

General Motors. 2025. *What's it like to work at GM?* https://search-careers.gm.com /en/how-we-hire/faq/. Accessed April 2025.

Giddings, Franklin H. 1924. *The scientific study of human society.* University of North Carolina Press.

Gideonse, Harry D. 1942. The function of higher education in the present war crisis. *Journal of Negro Education* 11 (3): 247–256.

Gigerenzer, Gerd, Zeno Swijtink, Theodore Porter, Lorraine Daston, and Lorenz Kruger. 1990. *The empire of chance: How probability changed science and everyday life.* Cambridge University Press.

Gilbreth, Frank Bunker. 1911. *Motion study: A method for increasing the efficiency of the workman.* D. Van Nostrand.

Gilbreth, Frank Bunker, and Lillian Moller Gilbreth. 1919. *Fatigue study: The elimination of humanity's greatest unnecessary waste, a first step in motion study.* Macmillan.

Gilbreth, Frank Bunker, and Lillian Moller Gilbreth. 1924. The efficiency engineer and the industrial psychologist. *Journal of the National Institute of Industrial Psychology* 2: 40–45.

Gil-Hernández, Carlos J., Guillem Vidal, and Sergio Torrejón Perez. 2023. Technological change, tasks and class inequality in Europe. *Work, Employment and Society* 38 (3): 826–851.

Glaser, Robert J. 1958. Evaluation of the applicant for medical education. *Academic Medicine*, 33 (3): 272–283.

Gleit, Rebecca D. 2022. Cops on campus: The racial patterning of police in schools. *Socius* 8: 23780231221108037. https://doi.org/10.1177/23780231221108037.

Gleit, Rebecca D. 2023. Brokers and boundary managers: School expulsions amid the nonpunitive turn. *Social Problems*, 1–20.

Glueck, Sheldon. 1934. The place of proper police and prosecution in a crime reduction program. In *The Attorney General's Conference on Crime: Constitution Hall and Memorial Continental Hall, December 10 to December 13, 1934, Washington, DC; Addresses and program*. Attorney General.

Go, Julian. 2020. The imperial origins of American policing: Militarization and imperial feedback in the early 20th century. *American Journal of Sociology* 125 (5): 1193–1254.

Goff, Regina M. 1950. Problems and emotional difficulties of Negro children due to race. *Journal of Negro Education* 19 (2): 152–158.

Goffman, Alice. 2014. *On the run*. University of Chicago Press.

Goldin, Claudia, and Lawrence F. Katz. 2009. *The race between education and technology*. Harvard University Press.

Goldmark, Josephine. 1912. *Fatigue and efficiency: A study in industry*. Russell Sage Foundation.

Goldstein, Herman. 1977. *Policing a free society*. Ballinger.

Goldthorpe, John H. 2001. Causation, statistics, and sociology. *European Sociological Review* 17 (1): 1–20.

Goldthorpe, John H. 2016. *Sociology as a population science*. Cambridge University Press.

González, Elizabeth Rasche. 1980. Learning disabilities: Lagging field in medicine. *JAMA* 243 (19): 1883–1892.

Goolsbee, Austan, and Chad Syverson. 2023. The strange and awful path of productivity in the US construction sector. National Bureau of Economic Research, Paper 39845.

Goos, Maarten, Alan Manning, and Anna Salomons. 2014. Explaining job polarization: Routine-biased technological change and offshoring. *American Economic Review* 104 (8): 2509–2526.

Graeber, David. 2019. *Bullshit jobs: The rise of pointless work, and what we can do about it*. Penguin Books.

Gray, George William. 1941. *The advancing front of medicine*. McGraw-Hill.

Green, Emma. 2013. Are we asking too much of schools? *The Atlantic* (July 24, 2013).

Green, Morris. 1994. *Bright futures: Guidelines for health supervision of infants, children, and adolescents*. ERIC.

Greenberg, Stephen J., and Patricia E. Gallagher. 2009. The great contribution: Index Medicus, Index-Catalogue, and IndexCat. *Journal of the Medical Library Association* 97 (2): 108.

Greenley, T. B. 1889. The management of infants under a year old, hygienic, dietetic and medicinal. *Journal of the American Medical Association* 13 (15): 507–512.

Greenthal, Eva, Jenny Jia, Ana Poblacion, and Thea James. 2019. Patient experiences and provider perspectives on a hospital-based food pantry: A mixed methods evaluation study. *Public Health Nutrition* 22 (17): 3261–3269.

Grose, Jessica. 2022. School is for care. *New York Times* (September 1, 2022).

Gruen, Russell L., Eric G. Campbell, and David Blumenthal. 2006. Public roles of US physicians: Community participation, political involvement, and collective advocacy. *JAMA* 296 (20): 2467–2475.

Guessoum, Sélim Benjamin, Laelia Benoit, Sevan Minassian, Jasmina Mallet, and Marie Rose Moro. 2021. Clinical lycanthropy, neurobiology, culture: A systematic review. *Frontiers in Psychiatry*, 12: 718101.

Hacking, Ian. 1990. *The taming of chance*. Cambridge University Press.

Hackman, J. Richard, and Edward E. Lawler III. 1971. Employee reactions to job characteristics. *Journal of Applied Psychology* 55 (3): 259–286.

Hagedorn, Jenn, Claudia Alexandra Paras, Howard Greenwich, and Amy Hagopian. 2016. The role of labor unions in creating working conditions that promote public health. *American Journal of Public Health* 106 (6): 989–995.

Haggerty, Robert J. 1968. Community pediatrics. *New England Journal of Medicine* 278 (1): 15–21.

Haggerty, Robert J. 1974. The changing role of the pediatrician in child health care. *American Journal of Diseases of Children* 127 (4): 545–549.

Haggerty, Robert J., and C. Andrew Aligne. 2005. Community pediatrics: The Rochester story. *Pediatrics* 115 (Supplement 3): 1136–1138.

Haggerty, Robert J., Klaus J. Roghmann, and Ivan Barry Pless. 1975. *Child health and the community*. Transaction.

Hagglund, George. 1981. Approaches to safety and health hazard abatement. *Labor Studies Journal* 6: 7–15.

Haines, Helen R., Gary M. Feinman, and Linda M. Nicholas. 2004. Household economic specialization and social differentiation: The stone-tool assemblage at El Palmillo, Oaxaca. *Ancient Mesoamerica* 15 (2): 251–266.

Haller, Mark H. 1976. Historical roots of police behavior: Chicago, 1890–1925. *Law & Society Review* 10 (2): 303–323.

Halpern, Sydney Ann. 1988. *American pediatrics: The social dynamics of professionalism, 1880–1980.* University of California Press.

Halpern, Sydney Ann. 1990. Medicalization as professional process: Postwar trends in pediatrics. *Journal of Health and Social Behavior* 31 (1): 28–42.

Hambley, Laura, and Madeline Springle. 2023. The rise of the irate customer: Postpandemic rudeness, and the importance of rediscovering patience. *The Conversation* (March 13, 2023).

Hamblin, Robert Lee, and John H. Kunkel. 1977. *Behavioral theory in sociology: Essays in honor of George C. Homans.* Transaction.

Hamilton, S. M. 1887. The profession and practice of medicine: In some of its relations to human society. *Journal of the American Medical Association* 8 (3): 63–67.

Han, Paul K. J. 1997. Historical changes in the objectives of the periodic health examination. *Annals of Internal Medicine* 127 (10): 910–917.

Hannaford, Earle S. 1976. *Supervisors guide to human relations.* National Safety Council.

Hanushek, Eric A. 1986. The economics of schooling: Production and efficiency in public schools. *Journal of Economic Literature* 24 (3): 1141–1177.

Hard, William. 1907. Making steel and killing men. *Everybody's Magazine* 17:579–591.

Harding, D. W. 1931. A note on the subdivision of assembly work. *Journal of the National Institute of Industrial Psychology* 5: 261–264.

Harrell, Erika, and Elizabeth Davis. 2020. *Contacts between police and the public, 2018—statistical tables.* Bureau of Justice Statistics, 255730.

Harris, William T. 1891. Fruitful lines of investigation in psychology. *Educational Review* 1: 8–14.

Harris, William Torrey, Andrew Sloan Draper, and Horace Sumner Tarbell. 1895. *Report of the Committee of Fifteen.* New England Publishing.

Hart, Joseph K. 1941. The general educational implications of the present international crisis. *Journal of Negro Education* 10 (3): 612–616.

Hartmann, Jillian. 2024. New Castle Area School District adds its own police force. WPXI-TV (May 6, 2024).

Hastie, Trevor J. 2017. Generalized additive models. In *Statistical models in S,* edited by John M. Chambers and Trevor J. Hastie, 249–307. Taylor / Francis Group.

Helmholz, Henry F. 1924. Preventive medicine and the future of medical practice. *Journal of the American Medical Association* 83 (7): 485–486.

Henry, Nelson Bollinger. 1955. *Mental health in modern education.* Edited by National Society for the Study of Education. University of Chicago Press.

Henry, Nelson Bollinger. 1960. *The dynamics of instructional groups.* Edited by National Society for the Study of Education. University of Chicago Press.

Hercules, Costas, Evan Charney, Donald Frank, James MacWhinney, Neal McNabb, Albert Scheiner, and Edwin Sumpter. 1969. Availability and attentiveness: Are these compatible in pediatric practice? *Clinical Pediatrics* 8 (7): 381–388.

Herring, Chris. 2019. Complaint-oriented policing: Regulating homelessness in public space. *American Sociological Review* 84 (5): 769–800.

Hertzberg, Hazel Whitman. 1981. *Social Studies Reform 1880–1980.* Social Science Education Consortium.

Hessel, Samuel J., and Robert J. Haggerty. 1968. General pediatrics: A study of practice in the mid-1960's. *Journal of Pediatrics* 73 (2): 271–279.

Hidalgo, César A. 2021. Economic complexity theory and applications. *Nature Reviews Physics* 3 (2): 92–113.

Hill, Heather C. 2017. The Coleman Report, 50 years on: What do we know about the role of schools in academic inequality? *The ANNALS of the American Academy of Political and Social Science* 674 (1): 9–26.

Hill, Joe. 2025. *Everythingism: An essay. The pathology holding back the state.* Reform. https://reform.uk/wp-content/uploads/2025/03/Everythingism -an-essay-published.pdf.

Hill, Joshua P. 2021. So today I learned the NYPD has a bee keeping division. They also have that video game truck now. And a few submarines. And robot dogs. Maybe, just maybe, they have too much money. Twitter (July 6, 2021). https:// x.com/JPHilllllll/status/1412554269094469640. Accessed on April 1, 2025.

Hinton, Elizabeth. 2015. Creating crime: The rise and impact of national juvenile delinquency programs in Black urban neighborhoods. *Journal of Urban History* 41 (5): 808–824.

Hinton, Elizabeth. 2017. *From the war on poverty to the war on crime.* Harvard University Press.

Hinton, Elizabeth. 2021. *America on fire: The untold history of police violence and Black rebellion since the 1960s.* Liveright.

Hoekelman, Robert A. 1983. Well-child visits revisited. *American Journal of Diseases of Children* 137 (1): 17–20.

Hoekelman, Robert A. 1998. Commentary on *A program to increase health care for children: The pediatric nurse practitioner program,* by Henry K. Silver, MD, Loretta C. Ford, EdD, and Susan G. Stearly, MS, Pediatrics, 1967; 39: 756–760. *Pediatrics* 102 (Supplement 1): 245–247.

Hoffman, Charles W. 1934. Modern youth and crime. In *The Attorney General's Conference on Crime: Constitution Hall and Memorial Continental Hall, December 10 to December 13, 1934, Washington, DC; Addresses and program.* Attorney General.

Hoover, J. Edgar. 1934. Detection and apprehension. In *The Attorney General's Conference on Crime: Constitution Hall and Memorial Continental Hall, December 10 to December 13, 1934, Washington, DC; Addresses and program.* Attorney General.

Hopkins, L. Thomas. 1944. Atmosphere for learning. *Teachers College Record* 46 (2): 99–105.

Hughes, Everett Cherrington. 1958. *Men and their work.* Free Press.

Hulin, Charles L., and Milton R. Blood. 1968. Job enlargement, individual differences, and worker responses. *Psychological Bulletin* 69 (1): 41–55.

Hunt, Gavin Raymond. 2000. Human-like, population-level specialization in the manufacture of pandanus tools by New Caledonian crows *Corvus moneduloides. Proceedings of the Royal Society of London. Series B: Biological Sciences* 267 (1441): 403–413.

Hunt, Jennifer, and Ryan Nunn. 2022. Has US employment really polarized? A critical reappraisal. *Labour Economics* 75: 102117.

Institute of Medicine. 2001. *Crossing the quality chasm: A new health system for the 21st century.* National Academies Press.

International City Managers' Association. 1919. *City manager yearbook.* International City Managers' Association.

International City Managers' Association. 1920. *City manager yearbook.* International City Managers' Association.

International City Managers' Association. 1935. *Municipal year book*. International City Managers' Association.

International City Managers' Association. 1938. *Municipal year book*. International City Managers' Association.

International City Managers' Association. 1939. *Municipal year book*. International City Managers' Association.

International City Managers' Association. 1940. *Municipal year book*. International City Managers' Association.

International City Managers' Association. 1941. *Municipal year book*. International City Managers' Association.

International City Managers' Association. 1943. *Municipal year book*. International City Managers' Association.

International City Managers' Association. 1944. *Municipal year book*. International City Managers' Association.

International City Managers' Association. 1945. *Municipal year book*. International City Managers' Association.

International City Managers' Association. 1946. *Municipal year book*. International City Managers' Association.

International City Managers' Association. 1947. *Municipal year book*. International City Managers' Association.

International City Managers' Association. 1948. *Municipal year book*. International City Managers' Association.

International City Managers' Association. 1949. *Municipal year book*. International City Managers' Association.

International City Managers' Association. 1950. *Municipal year book*. International City Managers' Association.

International City Managers' Association. 1953. *Municipal year book*. International City Managers' Association.

International City Managers' Association. 1954. *Municipal year book*. International City Managers' Association.

International City Managers' Association. 1955. *Municipal year book*. International City Managers' Association.

International City Managers' Association. 1958. *Municipal year book*. International City Managers' Association.

International City Managers' Association. 1966. *Municipal year book*. International City Managers' Association.

International City Managers' Association. 1967. *Municipal year book*. International City Managers' Association.

International City Managers' Association. 1969. *Municipal year book*. International City Managers' Association.

International City Managers' Association. 1970. *Municipal year book*. International City Managers' Association.

IPUMS USA. 2024. *Occupation and industry codes and documentation*. IPUMS USA.

Jackman, Tom. 2020. Trump's policing commission, found to violate law, can release report but with disclaimer written by judge. *Washington Post* (November 3, 2020).

Jackson, Michelle. 2020. *Manifesto for a dream: Inequality, constraint, and radical reform*. Stanford University Press.

Jackson, Michelle. 2025. The division of rationalized labor. OSF directory. https://osf.io/am6jz.

Jacobs, Jerry A. 2014. *In defense of disciplines: Interdisciplinarity and specialization in the research university*. University of Chicago Press.

Jacobziner, Harold, Herbert Rich, Nina Bleiberg, and Roland Merchant. 1963. How well are well children? *American Journal of Public Health and the Nations Health* 53 (12): 1937–1952.

JAMA Editor. 1883a. Epidemic cholera. *Journal of the American Medical Association* 1 (3): 90–90.

JAMA Editor. 1883b. Specialties, and their ethical relations. *Journal of the American Medical Association* 1 (17): 511–512.

JAMA Editor. 1883c. Yellow fever. *Journal of the American Medical Association* 1 (4): 122.

JAMA Editor. 1890a. For the good name of medicine. *Journal of the American Medical Association* 14 (24): 869–870.

JAMA Editor. 1890b. Unity the sequence of progress. *Journal of the American Medical Association* 14 (10): 347–349.

JAMA Editor. 1900. The relation between pathology and therapeutics. *Journal of the American Medical Association* 35 (2): 96–97.

JAMA Editor. 1905a. Physical condition of school children. *Journal of the American Medical Association* 45 (14): 1005.

JAMA Editor. 1905b. The social training of the physician. *Journal of the American Medical Association* 44 (24): 1933.

JAMA Editor. 1906. The Index Medicus. *Journal of the American Medical Association* 47 (18): 1494.

JAMA Editor. 1924. Medicine and the community of scientific thought. *Journal of the American Medical Association* 82 (12): 968.

JAMA Editor. 1960. The nurse and the doctor. *Journal of the American Medical Association* 173 (6): 685–686.

James, Paul A., Suzanne Oparil, Barry L. Carter, William C. Cushman, Cheryl Dennison-Himmelfarb, Joel Handler, Daniel T. Lackland, Michael L. LeFevre, Thomas D. MacKenzie, Olugbenga Ogedegbe, et al. 2014. 2014 Evidence-based guideline for the management of high blood pressure in adults: Report from the panel members appointed to the Eighth Joint National Committee (JNC 8). *JAMA* 311 (5): 507–520.

Janeway, Megan, Spencer Wilson, Sabrina E. Sanchez, Tania K. Arora, and Tracey Dechert. 2022. Citizenship and social responsibility in surgery: A review. *JAMA Surgery* 157 (6): 532–539.

Jehl, Jeanne, and Michael W. Kirst. 1993. Getting ready to provide school-linked services: What schools must do. *Education and Urban Society* 25 (2): 153–165.

Jenkins, Daniel Thomas. 1949. *The doctor's profession.* SCM Press.

Jensen, Arthur R. 1967. *How much can we boost IQ and scholastic achievement?* ERIC.

Jeste, Dilip V. 2000. Geriatric psychiatry may be the mainstream psychiatry of the future. *American Journal of Psychiatry* 157 (12): 1912–1914.

Johnson, Lyndon B. 1965. Special message to the Congress: "Toward full educational opportunity," January 12, 1965.

Johnson-Frey, Scott H. 2004. The neural bases of complex tool use in humans. *Trends in Cognitive Sciences* 8 (2): 71–78.

Johonnot, James. 1898. *Principles and practice of teaching* (Revised by Sarah Evans Johonnot). D. Appleton.

Jones, Carolyn, and Mikhail Zinshteyn. 2025. California, other states sue to halt massive layoffs at US Department of Education. *CalMatters* (March 13, 2025). https://calmatters.org/education/2025/03/education-department/.

Kalberg, Stephen. 1980. Max Weber's types of rationality: Cornerstones for the analysis of rationalization processes in history. *American Journal of Sociology* 85 (5): 1145–1179.

Kalleberg, Arne L. 2003. Flexible firms and labor market segmentation: Effects of workplace restructuring on jobs and workers. *Work and Occupations* 30 (2): 154–175.

Kalleberg, Arne L. 2011. *Good jobs, bad jobs: The rise of polarized and precarious employment systems in the United States, 1970s–2000s.* American Sociological Association's Rose Series. Russell Sage Foundation.

Kalleberg, Arne L., David Knoke, Peter V. Marsden, and Joe L. Spaeth. 1996. *Organizations in America: Analyzing their structures and human resource practices.* Sage.

Kalleberg, Arne L., Michael Wallace, and Robert P. Althauser. 1981. Economic segmentation, worker power, and income inequality. *American Journal of Sociology* 87 (3): 651–683.

Kantor, Elizabeth D., Colin D. Rehm, Jennifer S. Haas, Andrew T. Chan, and Edward L. Giovannucci. 2015. Trends in prescription drug use among adults in the United States from 1999–2012. *JAMA* 314 (17): 1818–1830.

Kaplan, Robert M., Jason M. Satterfield, and Raynard S. Kington. 2012. Building a better physician—the case for the new MCAT. *New England Journal of Medicine* 366 (14): 1265.

Kaurov, Alexander A., Viktoria Cologna, Charlie Tyson, and Naomi Oreskes. 2022. Trends in American scientists' political donations and implications for trust in science. *Humanities and Social Sciences Communications* 9 (1): 1–8.

Kennedy, Brian, and Alec Tyson. 2023. Americans' trust in scientists, positive views of science continue to decline. Pew Research Center (November).

Kennedy, John. 1878. *The school and the family: The ethics of school relations.* Harper & Brothers.

Kenney, John P., and Dan G. Pursuit. 1954. *Police work with juveniles.* Thomas.

Kent, Stephen A. 1983. Weber, Goethe, and the Nietzschean allusion: Capturing the source of the "iron cage" metaphor. *Sociological Analysis* 44 (4): 297–319.

Kerner, Otto. 1968. *Report of the National Advisory Commission on Civil Disorders.* US Government Printing Office.

Keynes, John Maynard. 1930. Economic possibilities for our grandchildren. In *Essays in persuasion,* 321–332. Springer.

Kilbridge, Maurice D. 1960. Reduced costs through job enlargement: A case. *Journal of Business* 33 (4): 357–362.

Kilpatrick, William H. 1921. The demands of the times upon our schools. *Teachers College Record* 22 (2): 127–136.

Kim, Jungmyung. 2024. Police resistance to institutional changes through complexity: A study of occupational identity maintenance. Draft paper.

Kimball, Dexter Simpson. 1925. *Principles of industrial organization.* McGraw-Hill Book.

King, Lester S. 1970. Humanism and the medical past. *JAMA* 213 (4): 580–584.

Kirby, James B., Amy J. Davidoff, and Jayasree Basu. 2016. The ACA's zero cost-sharing mandate and trends in out-of-pocket expenditures on well-child and screening mammography visits. *Medical Care* 54 (12): 1056–1062.

Klein, Ezra. 2023. The story construction tells about America's economy is disturbing. *New York Times* (February 5, 2023).

Klein, Ezra, and Derek Thompson. 2025. *Abundance.* Avid Reader Press.

Kliebard, Herbert M. 2004. *The struggle for the American curriculum, 1893–1958.* Third ed. Routledge.

Koblenz, Lawrence. 2013. *From sin to science: The cancer revolution of the nineteenth century.* Columbia University.

Kocher, Robert, Ezekiel J. Emanuel, and Nancy-Ann M. DeParle. 2010. The Affordable Care Act and the future of clinical medicine: The opportunities and challenges. *Annals of Internal Medicine* 153 (8): 536–539.

Koepke, Charles A. 1934. A job analysis of manufacturing plants in Minnesota. *Bulletin of the Employment Stabilization Research Institute, University of Minnesota* 2: 271–316.

Kohn, Lucile. 1934. Schools for workers. *School Life* 19 (9): 190–191.

Kotchen, Theodore A. 2014. Developing hypertension guidelines: An evolving process. *American Journal of Hypertension* 27 (6): 765–772.

Kotlowitz, Alex. 2012. Are we asking too much from our teachers? *New York Times* (September 14, 2012).

Kruger, Lorenz, Lorraine J. Daston, and Michael Heidelberger, eds. 1987. *The probabilistic revolution.* Vol. 1, *Ideas in history.* MIT Press.

Krugman, Paul. 2010. Fiscal fantasies. *New York Times* (April 8, 2010).

Krugman, Paul. 2023. Regulation, productivity and the meaning of life. *New York Times* (February 7, 2023).

Kuehn, Bridget M. 2019. Hospitals turn to housing to help homeless patients. *JAMA* 321 (9): 822–824.

Labaree, David. 1992. Power, knowledge, and the rationalization of teaching: A genealogy of the movement to professionalize teaching. *Harvard Educational Review* 62 (2): 123–155.

Labaree, David. 1997. Public goods, private goods: The American struggle over educational goals. *American Educational Research Journal* 34 (1): 39–81.

Lamb, D. S. 1891. The hygiene of school studies. Read before the Medical Society of the District of Columbia, November 19, 1890. *Journal of the American Medical Association* 16 (1): 4–9.

Lara-Millán, Armando. 2014. Public emergency room overcrowding in the era of mass imprisonment. *American Sociological Review* 79 (5): 866–887.

Larder, William. 1882. *Thirty years at the cutting-board: Being a work designed to assist the student to acquire knowledge in the art of cutting. Containing a series of diagrams laid down to measure.* New York.

Laub, John H. 2004. The life course of criminology in the United States: The American Society of Criminology 2003 Presidential Address. *Criminology* 42 (1): 1–26.

Laurie, Simon Somerville. 1892. *Institutes of education, comprising an introduction to rational psychology: Designed (partly) as a text-book for universities and colleges.* Macmillan.

Lawler, Edward E., III. 1969. 3. Job design and employee motivation. *Personnel Psychology* 22 (4): 426–435.

Lawler, Edward E., III, J. Richard Hackman, and Stanley Kaufman. 1973. Effects of job redesign: A field experiment. *Journal of Applied Social Psychology* 3 (1): 49–62.

Lazarsfeld, Paul F., and Anthony R. Oberschall. 1965. Max Weber and empirical social research. *American Sociological Review* 30 (2): 185–199.

Lebergott, Stanley. 1966. Labor force and employment, 1800–1960. In *Output, employment, and productivity in the United States after 1800,* edited by Dorothy S. Brady, 117–204. NBER.

Lee, Charles A. 1933. Education—here it stands. *School Life* 19 (2): 25.

Lei, Ya-Wen, and Rachel Kim. 2024. Automation and augmentation: Artificial intelligence, robots, and work. *Annual Review of Sociology* 50:251–272.

Lekachman, Robert. 1966. The automation report. *Commentary* 41 (5): 65.

Leon, Carol Boyd. 2016. The life of American workers in 1915. *Monthly Labor Review,* February. https://www.bls.gov/opub/mlr/2016/article/the-life-of-american-workers-in-1915.htm.

Levy, Frank, and Richard J. Murnane. 2012. *The new division of labor.* Princeton University Press.

Lewis, Carmen L., Glenda C. Wickstrom, Maria M. Kolar, Thomas C. Keyserling, Bryan A. Bognar, Connie T. DuPre, and Juliana Hayden. 2000. Patient preferences for care by general internists and specialists in the ambulatory setting. *Journal of General Internal Medicine* 15 (2): 75–83.

Lienke, Roger I. 1970. The family practice model in health education. *JAMA* 212 (12): 2097–2101.

Lincoln, D. F. 1891. The construction of school buildings. *Journal of the American Medical Association* 17 (11): 415–416.

Link, Bruce G., and Jo Phelan. 1995. Social conditions as fundamental causes of disease. *Journal of Health and Social Behavior,* Extra Issue: 80–94.

Lipscomb, Carolyn E. 2000. Medical Subject Headings (MeSH). *Bulletin of the Medical Library Association* 88 (3): 265–266.

Lipsky, Michael. 2010. *Street-level bureaucracy: Dilemmas of the individual in public service.* 30th anniversary ed. Russell Sage Foundation.

Liston, Dan, Jennie Whitcomb, and Hilda Borko. 2007. NCLB and scientifically-based research: Opportunities lost and found. *Journal of Teacher Education* 58 (2): 99–107.

Little, Joseph W. 1981. The workload of the United States Supreme Court: Ruling the pen with the tongue. *Journal of the Legal Profession* 6: 51–73.

Liu, Yujia, and David B. Grusky. 2013. The payoff to skill in the Third Industrial Revolution. *American Journal of Sociology* 118 (5): 1330–1374.

London Jr, Arthur H. 1937. The composition of an average pediatric practice. *The Journal of Pediatrics* 10 (6): 762–771.

Long, Heather. 2022. Why manufacturing workers are voluntarily leaving jobs at rates never seen before. *Washington Post* (January 9, 2022).

Los Angeles Police Department. 1912. *Annual report of police department of the City of Los Angeles, California for the year ending June 30, 1912.* Los Angeles Police Department.

Los Angeles Police Department. 1915. *Annual report of police department of the City of Los Angeles, California.* Los Angeles Police Department.

Los Angeles Police Department. 1916. *Annual report of police department of the City of Los Angeles, California.* Los Angeles Police Department.

Los Angeles Police Department. 1922. *Annual report of police department of the City of Los Angeles, California.* Los Angeles Police Department.

Los Angeles Police Department. 1937. *Annual report of police department of the City of Los Angeles, California.* Los Angeles Police Department.

Los Angeles Police Department. 1938. *Annual report of police department of the City of Los Angeles, California.* Los Angeles Police Department.

Los Angeles Police Department. 1939. *Annual report of police department of the City of Los Angeles, California.* Los Angeles Police Department.

Los Angeles Police Department. 1944. *Annual report of police department of the City of Los Angeles, California.* Los Angeles Police Department.

Los Angeles Police Department. 1968. *Annual report of police department of the City of Los Angeles, California.* Los Angeles Police Department.

Los Angeles Police Department. 1969. *Annual report of police department of the City of Los Angeles, California.* Los Angeles Police Department.

Los Angeles Police Department. 1972. *Annual report of police department of the City of Los Angeles, California.* Los Angeles Police Department.

Los Angeles Police Department. 1973. *Annual report of police department of the City of Los Angeles, California.* Los Angeles Police Department.

Los Angeles Police Department. 1974. *Annual report of police department of the City of Los Angeles, California.* Los Angeles Police Department.

Los Angeles Police Department. 2021. *Strategic plan, 2021–2023, LAPD 2021 & beyond.* Los Angeles Police Department.

Lucas, Samuel R. 2016. First- and second-order methodological developments from the Coleman Report. *RSF: The Russell Sage Foundation Journal of the Social Sciences* 2 (5): 117–140.

Luhmann, Niklas. 2013. *Theory of society.* Vols. 1–2. Stanford University Press.

Luskin, Jack, John Wooding, and Charles Levenstein. 1988. Worker training and education. *Journal of Public Health Policy* 9 (3): 342–345.

Lykes, Richard Wayne. 1975. *Higher education and the United States Office of Education, 1867–1953.* Bureau of Postsecondary Education, United States Office of Education.

Lyman, J. L. 1964. The Metropolitan Police Act of 1829: An analysis of certain events influencing the passage and character of the Metropolitan Police Act in England. *Journal of Criminal Law, Criminology, and Police Science* 55 (1): 141–154.

Lynch, Henry T., Gabriel M. Mulcahy, and Anne J. Krush. 1970. Genetic counseling and the physician. *JAMA* 211 (4): 647–651.

Macpherson, Cheryl C., and Jonathon Hill. 2017. Are physicians obliged to lead environmental sustainability efforts in health care organizations? *AMA Journal of Ethics* 19 (12): 1164–1173.

Mahoney, James. 2012. The logic of process tracing tests in the social sciences. *Sociological Methods & Research* 41 (4): 570–597.

Malinowski, Beth, Meredith Minkler, and Laura Stock. 2015. Labor unions: A public health institution. *American Journal of Public Health* 105 (2): 261–271.

Martin-Caughey, Ananda. 2021. What's in an occupation? Investigating within-occupation variation and gender segregation using job titles and task descriptions. *American Sociological Review* 86 (5): 960–999.

Mauri, Michele, Tommaso Elli, Giorgio Caviglia, Giorgio Uboldi, and Matteo Azzi. 2017. RAW-Graphs: A visualisation platform to create open outputs. In *Proceedings of the 12th Biannual Conference on Italian SIGCHI Chapter*, 28:1–28:5. CHItaly '17. Cagliari, Italy: ACM.

Marx, Karl. 1867. *Capital*. Vol. 1. Verlag von Otto Meisner.

Mayo, Elton. 1927. The scientific approach to industrial relations. In *Proceedings of YMCA conference on human relations in industry*, 19–23.

Mayo, Elton. 1930. Changing methods in industry. *Personnel Journal*, no. 8: 326–332.

Mayo, Elton. 1935. The blind spot in scientific management. In *Sixth International Management Congress: Reports and proceedings*. PS King London.

Mayo, Elton. 1945a. Group Tensions in Industry. A paper prepared for *Approaches to National Unity*, the fifth symposium of the Conference on Science, Philosophy and Religion in Their Relation to the Democratic Way of Life, Inc. Edited by Lyman Bryson, Louis Finkelstein, and Robert M. Maciver. Harper & Brothers.

Mayo, Elton. 1945b. *The social problems of an industrial civilization*. Andover.

Mayo, Elton. 2014. *The human problems of an industrial civilization*. Routledge.

McAfee, Ward M. 1998. *Religion, race, and reconstruction: The public school in the politics of the 1870s*. SUNY Press.

McCauley, Erin J., Katherine LeMasters, Michael F. Behne, and Lauren Brinkley-Rubinstein. 2023. A call to action to public health institutions and teaching to incorporate mass incarceration as a sociostructural determinant of health. *Public Health Reports* 138 (5): 711–714.

McGaghie, William C. 2002. Assessing readiness for medical education: Evolution of the Medical College Admission Test. *JAMA* 288 (9): 1085–1090.

McInerny, Thomas K., Klaus J. Roghmann, and Sydney A. Sutherland. 1978. Primary pediatric care in one community. *Pediatrics* 61 (3): 389–397.

McLeroy, Kenneth R., Daniel Bibeau, Allan Steckler, and Karen Glanz. 1988. An ecological perspective on health promotion programs. *Health Education Quarterly* 15 (4): 351–377.

Melinek, Judy. 2018. Do you have any idea how many bullets I pull out of corpses weekly? This isn't just my lane. It's my fucking highway. Twitter (November 9, 2018). https://x.com/drjudymelinek/status/1060912988532629504.

Merkle, Judith A. 1980. *Management and ideology: The legacy of the international scientific management movement.* University of California Press.

Michaels, David. 2008. *Doubt is their product: How industry's assault on science threatens your health.* Oxford University Press.

Michaels, David, and Jordan Barab. 2020. The Occupational Safety and Health Administration at 50: Protecting workers in a changing economy. *American Journal of Public Health* 110 (5): 631–635.

Minnesota Statutes: Barber Schools; Requirements. 2022. Minnesota Statute 154.07 § 1.

Mirel, Jeffrey, and David Angus. 1985. Youth, work, and schooling in the Great Depression. *Journal of Early Adolescence* 5 (4): 489–504.

Mitchell, Karen, Richard S. Lewis, Jason Satterfield, and Barry A. Hong. 2016. The new Medical College Admission Test: Implications for teaching psychology. *American Psychologist* 71 (2): 125.

Mitchell, Pamela, Matthew Wynia, Robyn Golden, Bob McNellis, Sally Okun, C. Edwin Webb, Valerie Rohrbach, and Isabelle Von Kohorn. 2012. Core principles & values of effective team-based health care. Discussion paper, Institute of Medicine, Washington, DC.

Monk, David H. 1992. Education productivity research: An update and assessment of its role in education finance reform. *Educational Evaluation and Policy Analysis* 14 (4): 307–332.

Monsell, Stephen. 2003. Task switching. *Trends in Cognitive Sciences* 7 (3): 134–140.

Montgomery, David. 1979. *Workers' control in America: Studies in the history of work, technology, and labor struggles.* Cambridge University Press.

Moore, Harry Hascall. 1923. *Public health in the United States: An outline with statistical data.* Harper & Brothers.

Moore, Texa L. 1921. The teaching of citizenship in the grades. *Teachers College Record* 22 (3): 1–4.

Morabia, Alfredo. 2016. Unveiling the Black Panther Party legacy to public health. *American Journal of Public Health* 106 (10): 1732–1733.

Morris, Stephen. 1971. A labour of love. *Journal of the Royal College of General Practitioners* 21 (103): 118–122.

Mouw, Ted, and Arne L. Kalleberg. 2010. Occupations and the structure of wage inequality in the United States, 1980s to 2000s. *American Sociological Review* 75 (3): 402–431.

Mueller, Benjamin. 2025. Trump administration has begun a war on science, researchers say. *New York Times* (March 31, 2025).

Murdoch, J. B. 1885. Nature versus art in the cure of disease. *Journal of the American Medical Association* 4 (13): 337–342.

Murtagh, John, Jill Rosenblatt, Justin Coleman, and Clare Murtagh. 2018. *Murtagh's general practice.* 7th ed. McGraw Hill.

National Advisory Committee for Juvenile Justice and Delinquency Prevention. 1980. *Standards for the administration of juvenile justice: Report of the National Advisory Committee for Juvenile Justice and Delinquency Prevention.* US Government Printing Office.

National Center for Education Statistics. 2002. *Highlights from the 2000 Program for International Student Assessment (PISA).* ERIC.

National Center for Health Statistics. 2025. *2023 National Ambulatory Medical Care Survey Health Center (NAMCS HC) component public use data file documentation.* Hyattsville, Maryland.

National Commission on Excellence in Education. 1983. *A nation at risk: The imperative for educational reform.* Government Printing Office.

National Commission on Technology, Automation, and Economic Progress. 1966. *Technology and the American economy.* US Government Printing Office.

National Education Association of the United States. Commission on the Reorganization of Secondary Education. 1921. *Cardinal principles of secondary education.* US Government Printing Office.

National Institute for Occupational Safety and Health. 1973. *The industrial environment; its evaluation & control.* US Government Printing Office.

National Library of Medicine. 1960. *Medical Subject Headings: Main headings, sub-headings and cross references used in the Index Medicus and the National Library of Medicine Catalog.* US Department of Health, Education & Welfare, Public Health Service.

National Library of Medicine. 2004. Index Medicus to cease as print publication. *NLM Technical Bulletin,* May-Jun (338): e2.

National Library of Medicine. 2021. Medline history. US National Library of Medicine. https://www.nlm.nih.gov/medline/medline_history.html.

National Library of Medicine. 2022. Medline overview. US National Library of Medicine. https://www.nlm.nih.gov/medline/medline_overview.html.

National Metal Trades Association. 1938. Job rating. *Management Review* 27: 123–124.

National Rifle Association. 2018. Someone should tell self-important anti-gun doctors to stay in their lane. Half of the articles in Annals of Internal Medicine are pushing for gun control. Most upsetting, however, the medical community seems to have consulted no one but themselves. Twitter (November 7, 2018). https://x.com/NRA/status/1060256567914909702.

National Safety Council. 1912. *Proceedings of the First Co-operative Safety Congress: Held under the auspices of Ass'n of Iron and Steel Electrical Engineers.* National Safety Council.

National Safety Council. 1914. *Proceedings of the Third Co-operative Safety Congress: Held under the auspices of Ass'n of Iron and Steel Electrical Engineers.* National Safety Council.

National Safety Council. 1956. *Supervisors safety manual: Better production without injury and waste from accidents.* National Safety Council.

National Safety Council. 1973. *Supervisors safety manual: Better production without injury and waste from accidents.* 4th ed. National Safety Council.

National Society for the Study of Education. Committee on Guidance. 1938. *Guidance in educational institutions.* Vol. 37. Public School Publishing.

Nelson, Alondra. 2011. *Body and soul: The Black Panther Party and the fight against medical discrimination.* University of Minnesota Press.

Nelson, Alondra. 2016. The longue durée of Black Lives Matter. *American Journal of Public Health* 106 (10): 1734–1737.

Nelson, Daniel. 1974. Scientific management, systematic management, and labor, 1880–1915. *Business History Review* 48 (4): 479–500.

Nelson, Daniel. 1980. *Taylor and the rise of scientific management.* Wisconsin.

Nelson, Dylan, Nathan Wilmers, and Letian Zhang. 2024. *Work organization and high-paying jobs.* Working paper. http://dx.doi.org/10.2139/ssrn.4765009.

New Castle High School. 1913. *Ne-Ca-Hi 1913.* New Castle High School.

New Castle High School. 1915. *Ne-Ca-Hi 1915.* New Castle High School.

New Castle High School. 1918. *Ne-Ca-Hi 1918.* New Castle High School.

New Castle High School. 1919. *Ne-Ca-Hi 1919.* New Castle High School.

New Castle High School. 1921. *Ne-Ca-Hi 1921.* New Castle High School.

New Castle High School. 1922. *Ne-Ca-Hi 1922.* New Castle High School.

New Castle High School. 1942. *Ne-Ca-Hi 1942; June.* New Castle High School.

New Castle High School. 1955. *Ne-Ca-Hi 1955.* New Castle High School.

New Castle High School. 1961. *Ne-Ca-Hi 1961.* New Castle High School.

New Castle High School. 1965. *The Pergodian 1965.* New Castle High School.

New Castle High School. 1967. *The Pergodian 1967.* New Castle High School.

New Castle High School. 1968. *The Pergodian 1968.* New Castle High School.

New Castle High School. 1972. *The Pergodian 1972.* New Castle High School.

New Castle High School. 1985. *The Pergodian 1985.* New Castle High School.

New Castle High School. 1995. *The Pergodian 1995.* New Castle High School.

New Castle High School. 2012. *The Pergodian 2012.* New Castle High School.

New Castle High School. 2024. *New Castle Junior/Senior High School course description book, 2023–24.* New Castle High School.

Newhart, Horace. 1926. Diagnostic school clinic in the public schools as factor in conservation of hearing. *Journal of the American Medical Association* 87 (23): 1882–1885.

Newman, George. 1932. *The rise of preventive medicine.* Humphrey Milford.

Newmayer, Solomon Weir. 1913. *Medical and sanitary inspection of schools, for the health officer, the physician, the nurse and the teacher.* Lea & Febiger.

Newsholme, Arthur. 1927. *Evolution of preventive medicine.* Routledge.

Noble, Charles. 1986. *Liberalism at work: The rise and fall of OSHA.* Temple University Press.

Noble, David F. 1977. *America by design: Science, technology, and the rise of corporate capitalism.* Knopf.

Noble, David F. 1984. *Forces of production: A social history of industrial automation.* Knopf.

Norlin, Chuck, Morgan A. Crawford, Christopher T. Bell, Xiaoming Sheng, and Martin T. Stein. 2011. Delivery of well-child care: A look inside the door. *Academic Pediatrics* 11 (1): 18–26.

Norton, John K. 1944. The number one job of educational administration. *Teachers College Record* 46 (2): 1–3.

NYC Health+Hospitals Press Office. 2018. NYC Health+Hospitals joins with CAMBA Housing Ventures and CAMBA in celebrating the opening of supportive housing on the NYC Health+Hospitals/Kings County Campus, (April 24, 2018). https://www.nychealthandhospitals.org/pressrelease/new-affordable-and-supportive-housing-units-in-central-brooklyn/.

O*NET. 2021. *Tasks: Some important questions about the tasks of the occupation.* OMB 1205-0421.

O*NET. 2024. O*NET 29 database at O*NET resource center. https://www.onetcenter.org/db_releases.html.

Oesch, Daniel, and Giorgio Piccitto. 2019. The polarization myth: Occupational upgrading in Germany, Spain, Sweden, and the UK, 1992–2015. *Work and Occupations* 46 (4): 441–469.

Office of Education. 1969. *History of Title I ESEA.* ERIC.

Office of National Drug Control Policy. 1989. *National drug control strategy.* Superintendent of Documents.

Office of the Federal Register. 2010. *United States government manual.* US Government Printing Office.

Olishifski, Julian B., and Frank E. McElroy, eds. 1970. *Fundamentals of industrial hygiene.* National Safety Council.

Oreskes, Naomi, and Erik M. Conway. 2022. From anti-government to anti-science: Why conservatives have turned against science. *Daedalus* 151 (4): 98–123.

Osborne, Oliver T. 1905. The therapeutic art. *Journal of the American Medical Association* 44 (19): 1493–1496.

OSHA. 1977. *Investigating accidents in the workplace. A manual for compliance safety and health officers.* OSHA.

Ostheimer, Maurice. 1905. The prevention of summer diarrhea. *Journal of the American Medical Association* 45 (9): 594–597.

Page, Arthur Wilson. 1941. *The Bell telephone system.* Harper & Brothers.

Page, David Perkins. 1885. *Theory and practice of teaching: Or, the motives and methods of good school-keeping.* A. S. Barnes.

Pan, Richard. 1990. Social responsibility: Do physicians have special obligations? *JAMA* 263 (1): 139.

Pandiani, John A. 1982. The Crime Control Corps: An invisible New Deal program. *British Journal of Sociology* 33 (3): 348–358.

Parker, William H. 1954. The police challenge in our great cities. *The ANNALS of the American Academy of Political and Social Science* 291 (1): 5–13.

Parkin, Frank. 1979. *Marxism and class theory: A bourgeois critique.* Tavistock.

Parsons, Graham. 2025. West Point is supposed to educate, not indoctrinate. *New York Times* (May 8, 2025).

Patel, Vimal. 2024. Republicans target social sciences to curb ideas they don't like. *New York Times* (November 21, 2024).

Patterson, Thomas L., and Dilip V. Jeste. 1999. The potential impact of the baby-boom generation on substance abuse among elderly persons. *Psychiatric Services* 50 (9): 1184–1188.

Patton, James R., Jr., and E. Bruce Butler. 1972. The Consumer Product Safety Act—its impact on manufacturers and on the relationship between seller and consumer. *Business Lawyer* 28: 725–740.

Pawluch, Dorothy. 1983. Transitions in pediatrics: A segmental analysis. *Social Problems* 30 (4): 449–465.

Pawluch, Dorothy. 2017. *The new pediatrics: A profession in transition.* Routledge.

Peabody, Andrew Preston. 1870. *What the physician should be: An address delivered at the Commencement of the Medical School of Harvard University; March 9, 1870.* Cambridge, MA.

Pearson, Karl. 1892. *The grammar of science.* Walter Scott.

Peaucelle, Jean-Louis, and Cameron Guthrie. 2011. How Adam Smith found inspiration in French texts on pin making in the eighteenth century. *History of Economic Ideas,* 19 (3): 41–68.

Pennsylvania Department of Education. 2021. *Framework for evaluation: Classroom teacher.* Pennsylvania Department of Education.

Peoples, Whitney A., Paul J. Fleming, and Melissa S. Creary. 2023. Working toward health equity requires antiracist teaching. *American Journal of Preventive Medicine* 64 (4): 604–608.

Perrin, Robert G. 1995. Émile Durkheim's "Division of Labor" and the shadow of Herbert Spencer. *Sociological Quarterly* 36 (4): 791–808.

Peters, Hannah, and William L. Madden. 1950. The cervical smear in office practice. *Journal of the American Medical Association* 142 (9): 624–626.

Pew Health Professions Commission. 1995. *Critical challenges: Revitalizing the health professions for the twenty-first century, the third report of the Pew Health Professions Commission.* Pew Health Professions Commission, Center for the Health Professions.

Pezzuto, Lugene. 2017. Remembering former schools: Growth spurts, consolidations mark history of New Castle district. *New Castle News* (May 29, 2017).

Phelps, Michelle S. 2024. *The Minneapolis reckoning: Race, violence, and the politics of policing in America.* Princeton University Press.

Phelps, Michelle S., Christopher E. Robertson, and Amber Joy Powell. 2021. "We're still dying quicker than we can effect change": #BlackLivesMatter and the limits of 21st-century policing reform. *American Journal of Sociology* 127 (3): 867–903.

Phelps, Michelle S., Anneliese Ward, and Dwjuan Frazier. 2021. From police reform to police abolition? How Minneapolis activists fought to make Black Lives Matter. *Mobilization: An International Quarterly* 26 (4): 421–441.

Pillsbury, E. S. 1904. Pathology and its relation to therapeutics. *California State Journal of Medicine* 2 (7): 216–220.

Piore, Michael J., and Charles F. Sabel. 1984. *The second industrial divide: Possibilities for prosperity.* Basic Books.

Pratten, Clifford F. 1980. The manufacture of pins. *Journal of Economic Literature* 18 (1): 93–96.

President's Advisory 1776 Commission. 2021. *The 1776 report.* White House.

President's Commission on Higher Education. 1947. *Higher education for American democracy: A report of the President's Commission on Higher Education.* US Government Printing Office.

President's Commission on Law Enforcement and Administration of Justice. 1967a. *The challenge of crime in a free society: A report.* US Government Printing Office.

President's Commission on Law Enforcement and Administration of Justice. 1967b. *Task force report: The police.* US Government Printing Office.

President's Commission on Law Enforcement and Administration of Justice. 2020. *Final report.* US Government Printing Office.

President's Committee on Juvenile Delinquency and Youth Crime. 1962. *Report to the President*. President's Committee on Juvenile Delinquency and Youth Crime.

President's Committee on Juvenile Delinquency and Youth Crime. 1964. *Counter-attack on delinquency: The program of the federal government to stimulate communities to develop rational answers to a growing crisis*. US Government Printing Office.

President's Task Force on 21st Century Policing. 2015. *Report of the President's Task Force on 21st Century Policing*. Office of Community Oriented Policing Services.

Price, Derek J. de Solla. 1963. *Little science, big science*. Columbia University Press.

Price, W. Nicholson, II, Sara Gerke, and I. Glenn Cohen. 2019. Potential liability for physicians using artificial intelligence. *JAMA* 322 (18): 1765–1766.

Pugh, Allison J. 2024. *The last human job: The work of connecting in a disconnected world*. Princeton University Press.

Pulliam, John D. 1991. *History of education in America*. 5th ed. Merrill.

Rector, Kevin. 2021a. LAPD after George Floyd: Fewer officers, fewer arrests but hardly defunded. *Los Angeles Times* (May 30, 2021).

Rector, Kevin. 2021b. Push and pull over Los Angeles policing hits roadways and transit. *Los Angeles Times* (February 18, 2021).

Reed, R. Harvey. 1889. The heating and ventilation of the Mansfield schools and churches: A lecture delivered before the Mansfield Lyceum, February 13, 1889. *Journal of the American Medical Association* 12 (14): 469–478.

Reed, R. Harvey. 1891. Original investigations on the heating and ventilation of school buildings. *Journal of the American Medical Association* 17 (11): 389–396.

Reitell, Charles. 1924. Machinery and its effect upon the workers in the automotive industry. *The ANNALS of the American Academy of Political and Social Science* 116 (1): 37–43.

Republican Party. 2016. *Republican Party platform*. Republican Party.

Rice, Joseph Mayer. 1913. *Scientific management in education*. Hinds, Noble / Eldredge.

Richards, Derek. 2006. Medline at thirty-five. *Evidence-Based Dentistry* 7 (4): 89.

Rios, Victor M. 2011. *Punished: Policing the lives of Black and Latino boys*. NYU Press.

Rivkin, David, and Denise E. Craven. 2021. Procedures for O*NET Job Zone assignment: Updated to include procedures for developing preliminary Job Zones for new O*NET-SOC occupations. *National Center for O*NET Development*. https://www.onetcenter.org/dl_files/JobZoneProcedureUpdate.pdf.

Roberts, E. B. 1935. Position analysis and classification: Westinghouse Electric and Manufacturing Company. *Management Review* 24: 195–210.

Roethlisberger, Fritz J., and William J. Dickson. 1934. *Management and the worker.* Harvard University Press.

Rogers, Fred B. 1964. Extending the horizons of preventive medicine. *JAMA* 190 (9): 837–839.

Roosevelt, Franklin D. 1934. Address of the President. In *The Attorney General's Conference on Crime: Constitution Hall and Memorial Continental Hall, December 10 to December 13, 1934, Washington, DC; Addresses and program.* Attorney General.

Rosenfeld, Jake. 2014. *What unions no longer do.* Harvard University Press.

Rosenthal, Marguerite G. 1986. The Children's Bureau and the Juvenile Court: Delinquency policy, 1912–1940. *Social Service Review* 60 (2): 303–318.

Rosenthal, Marguerite G. 1987. Reforming the juvenile correctional institution: Efforts of the US Children's Bureau in the 1930s. *Journal of Sociology & Social Welfare* 14: 47–73.

Rosner, David, and Gerald Markowitz. 2020. A short history of occupational safety and health in the United States. *American Journal of Public Health* 110 (5): 622–628.

Rotch, Thomas Morgan. 1903. The study of pediatrics in its relation to medical education. *Journal of the American Medical Association* 40 (15): 949–953.

Rothstein, William G. 2003. Public health and the risk factor: A history of an uneven medical revolution. Boydell & Brewer.

Rousseve, Ronald J. 1963. Teachers of culturally disadvantaged American youth. *Journal of Negro Education* 32 (2): 114–121.

Rowe, Donald E. 1922. Job analysis as an aid to cost reduction. *Industrial Management* 63: 341–346.

Royce, Josiah. 1891a. Is there a science of education? Part I. *Educational Review* 1 (1): 23–24.

Royce, Josiah. 1891b. Is there a science of education? Part III. *Educational Review* 1 (2): 121–132.

Ruby, Allen, and Joel Morganroth. 1970. The need for a medical ideology. *JAMA* 212 (12): 2096–2097.

Rueffler, Claus, Joachim Hermisson, and Günter P. Wagner. 2012. Evolution of functional specialization and division of labor. *Proceedings of the National Academy of Sciences* 109 (6): E326–E335.

Rueschemeyer, Dietrich. 1982. On Durkheim's explanation of division of labor. *American Journal of Sociology* 88 (3): 579–589.

Rugg, Harold. 1934. After three decades of scientific method in education. *Teachers College Record* 36 (2): 111–122.

Ruggles, Steven, Sarah Flood, Matthew Sobek, Daniel Backman, Annie Chen, Grace Cooper, Stephanie Richards, Renae Rogers, and Megan Schouweiler. 2024. IPUMS USA: Version 15.0 [dataset]. Minneapolis, MN: IPUMS, 2024. https://doi.org/10.18128/D010.V15.0.

Ruhstaller, Thomas, Helen Roe, Beat Thürlimann, and Jonathan J. Nicoll. 2006. The multidisciplinary meeting: An indispensable aid to communication between different specialities. *European Journal of Cancer* 42 (15): 2459–2462.

Ruis, Andrew R. 2017. *Eating to learn, learning to eat: The origins of school lunch in the United States.* Rutgers University Press.

Russell, James E. 1900. The function of the university in the training of teachers. *Teachers College Record* 1 (1): 1–5.

Russell, James E. 1917. Scouting education. *Teachers College Record* 18 (1): 1–6.

Ruttenberg, Harold J. 1939. The big morgue. *Survey Graphic* 28 (4): 266–269.

Sabel, Charles F. 1982. *Work and politics: The division of labor in industry.* Cambridge University Press.

Sandor, Andrew A. 1957. The history of professional liability suits in the United States. *Journal of the American Medical Association* 163 (6): 459–466.

Sato, Mia. 2020. Social workers are rejecting calls for them to replace police. *The Appeal* (August 20, 2010).

Schenthal, Joseph E. 1960. Multiphasic screening of the well patient: Twelve-year experience of the Tulane University Cancer Detection Clinic. *Journal of the American Medical Association* 172 (1): 1–4.

Schwartzstein, Richard M., Gary C. Rosenfeld, Robert Hilborn, Saundra Herndon Oyewole, and Karen Mitchell. 2013. Redesigning the MCAT exam: Balancing multiple perspectives. *Academic Medicine* 88 (5): 560–567.

Scudder, Kenyon J. 1934. Social aspects of crime prevention. In *The Attorney General's Conference on Crime: Constitution Hall and Memorial Continental Hall, December 10 to December 13, 1934, Washington, DC; Addresses and program.* Attorney General.

Shafer, Paul R., Alex Hoagland, and Heather E. Hsu. 2021. Trends in well-child visits with out-of-pocket costs in the US before and after the Affordable Care Act. *JAMA Network Open* 4 (3): e211248.

Sharkey, Patrick, Gerard Torrats-Espinosa, and Delaram Takyar. 2017. Community and the crime decline: The causal effect of local nonprofits on violent crime. *American Sociological Review* 82 (6): 1214–1240.

Shaw-Taylor, Leigh. 2009. The occupational structure of England and Wales, c.1750–1911. https://www.campop.geog.cam.ac.uk/research/projects/interna tionaloccupations/inchos2009/england.pdf.

Shaywitz, Sally E., Bennett A. Shaywitz, Jack M. Fletcher, and Michael D. Escobar. 1990. Prevalence of reading disability in boys and girls: Results of the Connecticut Longitudinal Study. *JAMA* 264 (8): 998–1002.

Shenhav, Yehouda A. 2002. *Manufacturing rationality: The engineering foundations of the managerial revolution.* Oxford University Press, USA.

Silver, Henry K., Loretta C. Ford, and Lewis R. Day. 1968. The pediatric nurse-practitioner program: Expanding the role of the nurse to provide increased health care for children. *JAMA* 204 (4): 298–302.

Silver, Henry K., Loretta C. Ford, and Susan G. Stearly. 1967. A program to increase health care for children: The pediatric nurse practitioner program. *Pediatrics* 39 (5): 756–760.

Slora, Eric J., Kathleen A. Thoma, Richard C. Wasserman, Steven E. Pedlow, and Alison B. Bocian. 2006. Patient visits to a national practice-based research network: Comparing pediatric research in office settings with the National Ambulatory Medical Care Survey. *Pediatrics* 118 (2): e228–e234.

Smetana, Gerald W., Bruce E. Landon, Andrew B. Bindman, Helen Burstin, Roger B. Davis, Jennifer Tjia, and Eugene C. Rich. 2007. A comparison of outcomes resulting from generalist vs specialist care for a single discrete medical condition: A systematic review and methodologic critique. *Archives of Internal Medicine* 167 (1): 10–20.

Smiley, Dean Franklin, and Adrian Gordon Gould. 1941. *Personal and community hygiene.* Macmillan.

Smith, Adam. 1776. *An inquiry into the nature and causes of the wealth of nations.* W. Strahan / T. Cadell, in the Strand.

Smith, Alice M. 1905. A plea for national and local boards of school hygiene. *Journal of the American Medical Association* 45 (14): 978–982.

Smith, Hubert Winston. 1941. Legal responsibility for medical malpractice: V. Further information about duty and dereliction. *Journal of the American Medical Association* 116 (25): 2755–2768.

Smith, Kent A. 2022. Free MEDLINE access worldwide. *Information Services & Use* 42 (2): 161–170.

Smith, Leonard Glenn. 1967. A history of the United States Office of Education, 1867–1967. University of Oklahoma.

Smith, Marshall S., and Brett Scoll. 1995. The Clinton human capital agenda. *Teachers College Record* 96 (3): 1–16.

Smith, Robert Stewart. 1979. The impact of OSHA inspections on manufacturing injury rates. *Journal of Human Resources* 14 (2): 145–170.

Snedden, David. 1923. Sociology, a basic science to education. *Teachers College Record* 24 (2): 1–10.

Snyder, Thomas D. 1993. *120 years of American education: A statistical portrait.* US Department of Education, Office of Educational Research and Improvement.

Song, Ji Seon. 2021. Policing the emergency room. *Harvard Law Review* 134 (8): 2646–2720.

South, Eugenia, Atheendar Venkataramani, and George Dalembert. 2022. Building Black wealth—the role of health systems in closing the gap. *New England Journal of Medicine* 387 (9): 844–849.

Spaeth, Reynold Albrecht. 1920. The problem of fatigue. *Journal of Industrial Hygiene* 1: 22–53.

Spaulding, Francis Trow. 1939. *High school and life.* McGraw-Hill.

Spencer, Herbert. 1916. *The principles of sociology.* D. Appleton.

Stalnaker, John M. 1950. Medical College Admission Test. *Academic Medicine* 25 (6): 428–434.

Starr, Paul. 2017. *The social transformation of American medicine: The rise of a sovereign profession and the making of a vast industry.* Basic Books.

Steiker, Carol S. 1997. The limits of the preventive state. *Journal of Criminal Law & Criminology* 88 (3): 771–808.

Stern, Alexandra Minna, Mary Beth Reilly, Martin S. Cetron, and Howard Markel. 2010. "Better off in school": School medical inspection as a public health strategy during the 1918–1919 influenza pandemic in the United States. *Public Health Reports* 125 (Supplement 3): 63–70.

Stieber, Jack. 1959. *The steel industry wage structure: A study of the joint union-management job evaluation program in the basic steel industry.* Harvard University Press.

Stigler, Stephen M. 1986. *The history of statistics: The measurement of uncertainty before 1900.* Harvard University Press.

Stimson, Philip Moen. 1921. School health supervision. *Teachers College Record* 22 (3): 234–247.

Stout, N. A., and H. I. Linn. 2002. Occupational injury prevention research: Progress and priorities. *Injury Prevention* 8 (Supplement 4): 9–14.

Strand, Michael, and Omar Lizardo. 2022. Chance, orientation, and interpretation: Max Weber's neglected probabilism and the future of social theory. *Sociological Theory* 40 (2): 124–150.

Stretch, John J. 1970. The rights of children emerge: Historical notes on the first White House Conference on Children. *Child Welfare* 49 (7): 365–372.

Stuart, Forrest. 2016. *Down, out, and under arrest: Policing and everyday life in Skid Row.* University of Chicago Press.

Sutton, John R., Frank Dobbin, John W. Meyer, and W. Richard Scott. 1994. The legalization of the workplace. *American Journal of Sociology* 99 (4): 944–971.

Swayne, Jeremy. 2012. The problem with science—the context and process of care: An excerpt from Remodelling Medicine. *Global Advances in Health and Medicine* 1 (1): 78–87.

Swidler, Ann. 1973. The concept of rationality in the work of Max Weber. *Sociological Inquiry* 43 (1): 35–42.

Taylor, Frederick Winslow. 1911. *The principles of scientific management.* Harper & Brothers.

Terris, Milton. 1975. Evolution of public health and preventive medicine in the United States. *American Journal of Public Health* 65 (2): 161–169.

Terry, E. B. 1920. The duty of the physician to the child. *Journal of the National Medical Association* 12 (2): 12–16.

Thoma, Mark. 2013. Who first said the US is "An insurance company with an army?" *Economist's View* (January 17, 2013).

Thompson, Charles H. 1932. Editorial comment: Why a journal of Negro education? *Journal of Negro Education* 1 (1): 1–4.

Thompson, Frank Victor. 1920. *Schooling of the immigrant.* Harper.

Thompson, Mary Harris. 1886. Why diseases of children should be made a special study. *Journal of the American Medical Association* 7 (15): 399–402.

Thompson, Sanford E. 1928. Smoothing the wrinkles from management: Time study the tool. *The ANNALS of the American Academy of Political and Social Science* 137 (1): 89–106.

Thorndike, Edward Lee. 1913. *Educational psychology*. Teachers College, Columbia University.

Timmons, Edward J., and Robert J. Thornton. 2010. The licensing of barbers in the USA. *British Journal of Industrial Relations* 48 (4): 740–757.

Tobey, Scott, and John Revitte. 1981. Building worker competence. *Labor Studies Journal* 6: 41–52.

Tönnies, Ferdinand. 1887. *Gesellschaft und Gemeinschaft*. Fues's Verlag.

Towne, Henry R. 1886. *The engineer as an economist*. Academy of Management.

Tsoucalas, Gregory, Antonis A. Kousoulis, Ioannis Tsoucalas, and George Androutsos. 2011. The earliest mention of a black bag. *Scandinavian Journal of Primary Health Care* 29 (4): 196–197.

Tyack, David B., and Larry Cuban. 1997. *Tinkering toward Utopia: A century of public school reform*. Harvard University Press.

Tyack, David B., Robert Lowe, and Elisabeth Hansot. 1984. *Public schools in hard times: The Great Depression and recent years*. Harvard University Press.

Ufer, Christian. 1894. *Introduction to the pedagogy of Herbart*. Translated by J. C. Zinser. DC Heath.

Uhrbrock, Richard S. 1922. Job analysis as a factor in cost reduction: Qualifications of the analyst and methods of approach. *Industrial Management* 63: 100–102.

Ulrich, C. F. 1900. Hygiene of public schools. *Journal of the American Medical Association* 34 (10): 602–604.

United Nations. 2021. *United Nations Standard Products and Services Code*. United Nations.

US Bureau of Labor Statistics. 2023. *Occupational employment and wage statistics 2023*. US Bureau of Labor Statistics.

US Bureau of Labor Statistics. 2024. *Labor force characteristics by race and ethnicity, 2023*. Technical report. US Bureau of Labor Statistics.

US Census Bureau. 1975. *Historical statistics of the United States, colonial times to 1970*. US Department of Commerce, Bureau of the Census.

US Census Bureau. 2020. American Community Survey and Puerto Rico Community Survey. 2020 subject definitions. https://www2.census.gov/programs -surveys/acs/tech_docs/subject_definitions/2020_ACSSubjectDefinitions.pdf.

US Congress. 1912. *Special Committee to Investigate the Taylor and Other Systems of Shop Management*. Hearings Before Special Committee of the House of

Representatives to Investigate the Taylor and Other Systems of Shop Management Under Authority of H. Res. 90.

US Congress. 1970. *Occupational Safety and Health Act of 1970.* Public Law 91-596. 84 Stat. 1590, December.

US Congress, Committee on the Judiciary, Subcommittee on Crime, Terrorism, and Homeland Security. 2005. *Implementation of the USA PATRIOT Act: Effect of sections 203(b) and (d) on information sharing.* Hearing before the Subcommittee on Crime, Terrorism, and Homeland Security; Serial No. 109–15.

US Department of Education. 1996. *Pursuing excellence: A study of US eighth-grade mathematics and science teaching, learning, curriculum, and achievement in international context.* US Government Printing Office.

US Department of Education. 2025. US Department of Education initiates reduction in force, (March 11, 2025). https://www.ed.gov/about/news/press-release/us-department-of-education-initiates-reduction-force.

US Department of Justice. 2016. Law Enforcement Management and Administrative Statistics (LEMAS) codebook, 2016. United States Department of Justice. Office of Justice Programs. Bureau of Justice Statistics.

US Office of Education. 1917. *Community leaflet: Lessons in community and national life.* US Government Printing Office.

US Office of Management and Budget. 2023. *Historical tables.* US Office of Management and Budget.

US Preventive Services Task Force. 2014. *The guide to clinical preventive services 2014.* Agency for Healthcare Research and Quality (AHRQ).

Uva, Jane L. 1990. Urban violence: A health care issue. *JAMA* 263 (1): 135–139.

VanHeuvelen, Tom, and David Brady. 2022. Labor unions and American poverty. *ILR Review* 75 (4): 891–917.

Van Iddekinge, Chad, Suzanne Tsacoumis, and Jamie Donsbach. 2002. *A preliminary analysis of occupational task statements from the O*NET data collection program.* National Center for O*NET Development.

Veblen, Thorstein. 1921. *The engineers and the price system.* Vol. 31. Transaction.

Vermeer, Michael J. D., Dulani Woods, and Brian A. Jackson. 2020. Would law enforcement leaders support defunding the police? Probably—if communities ask police to solve fewer problems, (August 20, 2020). RAND.

Vernon, Horace Middleton. 1921. *Industrial fatigue and efficiency.* George Routledge & Sons.

Viscusi, W. Kip. 1979. The impact of occupational safety and health regulation. *Bell Journal of Economics* 10 (1): 117–140.

Viscusi, W. Kip. 1986. The impact of occupational safety and health regulation, 1973–1983. *RAND Journal of Economics* 17 (4): 567–580.

Vitale, Alex S. 2021. *The end of policing.* Verso Books.

Voigt, Rob, Nicholas P. Camp, Vinodkumar Prabhakaran, William L. Hamilton, Rebecca C. Hetey, Camilla M. Griffiths, David Jurgens, Dan Jurafsky, and Jennifer L. Eberhardt. 2017. Language from police body camera footage shows racial disparities in officer respect. *Proceedings of the National Academy of Sciences* 114 (25): 6521–6526.

Vollmer, August. 1933. Police progress in the past twenty-five years. *American Institute of Criminal Law & Criminology* 24: 161–175.

Vorhaus, Louis J., and Arthur R. Weihe. 1951. What belongs in the physician's bag? *Illinois Medical Journal* 99 (2): 81–85.

Vosburgh, W. L. 1912. Standardization of arithmetical work. *Mathematics Teacher* 4 (3): 104–117.

Wald, Lillian D. 1905. Medical inspection of public schools. *The ANNALS of the American Academy of Political and Social Science* 25 (2): 88–96.

Walshe, Walter Hayle. 1846. *The nature and treatment of cancer.* Taylor / Walton.

Warner, John Harley. 1986. *The therapeutic perspective: Medical practice, knowledge, and identity in America, 1820–1885.* Princeton University Press.

Warner, John Harley. 1991. Ideals of science and their discontents in late nineteenth-century American medicine. *Isis* 82 (3): 454–478.

Watson, Goodwin. 1956. Education and intergroup relations. *Teachers College Record* 57 (5): 1–4.

Watson, Nelson A., and Robert N. Walker. 1965. *Training police for work with juveniles.* ERIC.

Weatherall, Mark W. 1996. Making medicine scientific: Empiricism, rationality, and quackery in mid-Victorian Britain. *Social History of Medicine* 9 (2): 175–194.

Weaver, Warren. 1948. Science and complexity. *American Scientist* 36 (4): 536–544.

Weber, Max. 1905. *The Protestant ethic and the spirit of capitalism.* Routledge.

Weber, Max. 1978. *Economy and society: An outline of interpretive sociology.* University of California Press.

Weeden, Kim A. 2002. Why do some occupations pay more than others? Social closure and earnings inequality in the United States. *American Journal of Sociology* 108 (1): 55–101.

Weeden, Kim A., Young-Mi Kim, Matthew Di Carlo, and David B. Grusky. 2007. Social class and earnings inequality. *American Behavioral Scientist* 50 (5): 702–736.

Wegman, David H., Leslie Boden, and Charles Levenstein. 1975. Health hazard surveillance by industrial workers. *American Journal of Public Health* 65 (1): 26–30.

Weil, Julie Zauzmer. 2022. The public library is the latest place to pick up a coronavirus test. Librarians are overwhelmed. *Washington Post* (January 18, 2022).

Weinberg, Meyer. 1977. *A chance to learn: The history of race and education in the United States.* Cambridge University Press.

Weisz, George. 2006. *Divide and conquer: A comparative history of medical specialization.* Oxford University Press, USA.

Welch, S. W. 1922. Training in sociology and public health an essential in medical education. *Journal of the American Medical Association* 79 (5): 342–343.

Welch, Wm. H. 1889. Considerations concerning some external sources of infection in their bearing on preventive medicine. *Journal of the American Medical Association* 13 (3): 73–83.

Weller, Gerald M. 1939. The Coordinating Council movement. *Phi Delta Kappan* 21 (6): 247–254.

Werth, S. Rose. 2024. Social Disharmony and Racial Injustice: W.E.B. Du Bois's Theories on Crime. *Social Problems* 71 (1): 18–35.

Western, Bruce, and Jake Rosenfeld. 2011. Unions, norms, and the rise in US wage inequality. *American Sociological Review* 76 (4): 513–537.

Whipple, Guy Montrose. 1938. *The scientific movement in education.* Public School Publishing.

Whitehead, Fred. 1980. The physician as biomedical scientist. *JAMA* 244 (8): 770.

Whitmore, B. T. 1900. From saddlebags to pocketbooks. *Journal of the American Medical Association* 34 (1): 25–26.

Wickersham, George Woodward. 1931a. *National Commission on Law Observance and Enforcement: Report on police.* US Government Printing Office.

Wickersham, George Woodward. 1931b. *National Commission on Law Observance and Enforcement: Report on the causes of crime.* US Government Printing Office.

Williams, Jesse F. 1935. The educational function of specialists. *Teachers College Record* 37 (3): 203–209.

Williams, William Roger. 1908. *The natural history of cancer: With special reference to its causation and prevention.* W. Heinemann.

Wilmers, Nathan. 2020. Job turf or variety: Task structure as a source of organizational inequality. *Administrative Science Quarterly* 65 (4): 1018–1057.

Wilson, Howard E. 1945. Postwar education for international understanding. *Teachers College Record* 46 (9): 246–266.

Wilson, James Q. 1989. *Bureaucracy: What government agencies do and why they do it.* Basic Books.

Wilson, Mark A. 2014. A history of job analysis. In *Historical perspectives in industrial and organizational psychology,* edited by Laura L. Koppes, 249–272. Psychology Press.

Wilson, Orlando W. 1951. Progress in police administration. *Journal of Criminal Law, Criminology, and Police Science* 42 (2): 141–154.

Wise, M. Norton. 1987. How do sums count? On the cultural origins of statistical causality. In *The probabilistic revolution,* vol. 1, *Ideas in history,* edited by Lorenz Kruger, Lorraine J. Daston, and Michael Heidelberger, 395–426. MIT Press.

Wolcott, David B. 2001. "The cop will get you": The police and discretionary juvenile justice, 1890–1940. *Journal of Social History* 35 (2): 349–371.

Wolcott, David B. 2005. *Cops and kids: Policing juvenile delinquency in urban America, 1890–1940.* Ohio State University Press.

Wood, Frank M. 1924. Current criticisms of medical education. *Journal of the American Medical Association* 83 (11): 861–862.

Woodward, Calvin Milton. 1887. *The manual training school: Comprising a full statement of its aims, methods, and results, with figured drawings of shop exercises in woods and metals.* D. C. Heath.

Woodward, Calvin Milton. 1890. *Manual training in education.* Walter Scott.

Woolley, John, and Gerhard Peters. 2024. *The American Presidency Project.* Accessed July 1, 2024. https://www.presidency.ucsb.edu/.

Wotipka, Christine Min, Joseph Svec, Lisa Yiu, and Francisco O. Ramirez. 2023. The status and agency of children in school textbooks, 1970–2012: A cross-national analysis. *Compare: A Journal of Comparative and International Education* 53 (6): 949–966.

Wright, Carroll Davidson. 1884. *Report on the factory system of the United States.* Government Printing Office.

Wright, Carroll Davidson. 1900. *The history and growth of the United States Census: Prepared for the Senate Committee on the Census.* Government Printing Office.

Wright, Erik Olin, and Rachel E. Dwyer. 2003. The patterns of job expansions in the USA: A comparison of the 1960s and 1990s. *Socio-Economic Review* 1 (3): 289–325.

Xie, Yu. 2013. Population heterogeneity and causal inference. *Proceedings of the National Academy of Sciences* 110 (16): 6262–6268.

Young, Richard, Sandra Burge, Kaparaboyna Kumar, Jocelyn Wilson, and Daniela Ortiz. 2018. A time-motion study of primary care physicians' work in the electronic health record era. *Family Medicine* 50 (2): 91–99.

Zedner, Lucia, and Andrew Ashworth. 2019. The rise and restraint of the preventive state. *Annual Review of Criminology* 2: 429–450.

Zerga, Joseph E. 1943. Job analysis: A résumé and bibliography. *Journal of Applied Psychology* 27 (3): 249–267.

Zhang, Ellen. 2022. My Father Wilts. *JAMA* 328 (4): 400.

Zheng, Peng, Ashkan Afshin, Stan Biryukov, Catherine Bisignano, Michael Brauer, Dana Bryazka, Katrin Burkart, Kelly M. Cercy, Leslie Cornaby, Xiaochen Dai, et al. 2022. The Burden of Proof studies: Assessing the evidence of risk. *Nature Medicine* 28:2038–2044.

Zook, George F. 1942. The role of higher education in post-war reconstruction. *Journal of Negro Education* 11 (3): 274–278.

Acknowledgments

I do not remember the first time I realized that the world was too complicated. It would have been long before I started work on this project, and long before I became a sociologist. But writing this book was a stark reminder. I am therefore immensely grateful to all of those people who offered their support and helped to bring the project to fruition.

The faculty, staff, and students at Stanford University's Department of Sociology have always been enthusiastic and supportive. I was lucky to work with several undergraduate and graduate students over the course of this project, and I thank Elana Begay, Blyss Cleveland, Britiny Cook, Shae Dolan, Alysson Farris, Rebecca Gleit, Sophia Hunt, Julia Kwak, Victoria Ren, Kassandra Roeser, and Emma Williams-Baron. Discussions with many colleagues and students were helpful in thinking through the ideas in the book, and I am grateful to be part of such a vibrant academic community. At Stanford, I was also fortunate to spend a year at the Center for Advanced Study in the Behavioral Sciences (CASBS), where the initial ideas for the book were developed.

The academic community also helped to develop the ideas in the book. Florencia Torche was immensely supportive and offered incisive comments on draft chapters. Barbara Kiviat provided a thoughtful critique of draft chapters, and I enjoyed our conversations about insurance and rationalization. Conversations with Martín Sánchez-Jankowski and Mitchell Stevens were helpful in developing and testing the ideas in the book. Jeremy Freese provided enthusiasm and encouragement, and Shelley Correll and Aliya Saperstein were full of good cheer. My late and much-missed friend David Cox was eager to discuss this project as it was being developed, and I am thankful for his contributions to the work. Comments and questions from participants in presentations at the University of Iceland, UW–Madison (ITP), Princeton University, Stanford University (Inequality Workshop), University of Turku, and the Sociological Science conference were also much appreciated.

I received detailed feedback from participants at a book conference, supported by Stanford's Department of Sociology. Four people whose work I very much admire were—to my great surprise—willing to read my work carefully and spend the best part of a day locked in discussion helping to improve it. Thank you to Frank Dobbin, Arne Kalleberg, Shamus Khan, and Florencia Torche for their generosity and for their rigorous approach to testing the arguments of the book. Later, I received more generous, detailed, and thoughtful feedback from the book's reviewers. It is time-consuming to review a book, and I thank the reviewers for their willingness to take on this task and for their close engagement with the book's argument and evidence.

One benefit of working on this project was that I had the opportunity to read a great deal of scientific research from the past century. It would have been hard to complete that reading without feeling a sense of awe for what science has achieved over this period. At a time when science and scientists are increasingly the focus of attacks, I am grateful to all of those who contributed to the collective project that science represents.

Some of my most enjoyable time while writing this book was spent in libraries and archives. I would particularly like to thank Leah Loscutoff at the Archives and Special Collections in the Samuel C. Williams Library, Stevens Institute of Technology, and Melissa Murphy and staff at the Baker Library Special Collections and Archives, Harvard Business School. John Ulrich diligently searched for difficult-to-find materials, and I am grateful to him for his efforts.

I was fortunate to work with Harvard University Press on this manuscript. I initially worked with Andrew Kinney, whose enthusiasm for the project was important as I drafted the early chapters. As I was completing the first draft, Joseph Pomp took over as editor, and he provided fresh ideas and fresh enthusiasm at a moment when the project felt anything but fresh. I thank Joseph, Sana Mohtadi, and the other HUP staff for improving the manuscript and turning it into the published book.

Finally, I thank my family and friends for their love and support. I am so grateful to my mother and late father, Susan and William Jackson, and my two sisters, Catherine Rose and Alexandra Wall. My wonderful pup, Bellatrix, is always by my side. And my husband, David, has been a constant support over the years spent working on this project. He has been both a cheerleader and a critic, and in both of these roles he has shaped the book. Our wedding featured a reading from *The Division of Labor in Society,* and it therefore feels fitting that I am now able to dedicate this book to him.

Index

Page numbers followed by *f* indicate a figure, by *t* indicate a table.